Also by Corban Addison

A Walk Across the Sun
The Garden of Burning Sand
The Tears of Dark Water
A Harvest of Thorns

WASTELANDS

WASTELANDS

THE TRUE STORY
OF FARM COUNTRY ON TRIAL

Corban Addison

Alfred A. Knopf   *New York*   *2022*

Library of Congress Cataloging-in-Publication Data
Names: Addison, Corban, 1979– author.
Title: Wastelands : the true story of farm country on trial / Corban Addison.
Description: New York : Alfred A. Knopf, [2022] | Includes index.
Identifiers: LCCN 2021048239 (print) | LCCN 2021048240 (ebook) |
ISBN 9780593320822 (hardcover) | ISBN 9780593320839 (ebook)
Subjects: LCSH: Smithfield Foods, Inc.—Trials, litigation, etc. | Pork industry and trade—
Law and legislation—North Carolina. | Animal waste—Law and legislation—
North Carolina. | Public nuisances—North Carolina.
Classification: LCC KF229.S65 A33 2022 (print) | LCC KF229.S65 (ebook) |
DDC 346.7303/8—dc23/eng/20211220
LC record available at https://lccn.loc.gov/2021048239
LC ebook record available at https://lccn.loc.gov/2021048240

Front-of-jacket photographs (details): barns © Emery Dalesio / AP Images;
sky © J Shepherd / Photodisc / Getty Images
Jacket design by Linda Huang

Manufactured in the United States of America

First Edition

For the neighbors,
who taught me what it means
to love one patch of earth and sky
more than the world entire.

And for the lawyers,
who showed me the place
where justice and mercy meet,
and who, with passion and patience,
brought about a miracle.

There are no wastelands in our landscape quite like
those we've created ourselves.
—TIM WINTON, AUTHOR OF *Island Home*

I joke that, for the first part of my life, we killed people with
nicotine, and for the second part, we're killing people with pathogens,
odors, and polluted groundwater.
—TOM BUTLER, NORTH CAROLINA HOG FARMER

Contents

Part Three: Sabotage

Part Four: Confrontation

Part Five: The Reckoning

Foreword

BY JOHN GRISHAM

I've sold a lot of books working David's corner, and I'm continually troll-ing for the next one-sided fight to send him into, the next Goliath begging for his comeuppance. There will never be a shortage of uneven conflicts, and they often make for great theater. Who doesn't love another version of the classic Bible story? It is so ingrained in the American psyche that we instinctively pull for the underdog, often with warts and all.

In another career, I was a lawyer in a small office in a small town. My clients were working people who couldn't pay fees but wanted me to fix their legal problems anyway. On the other side of the street were corporations with plenty of money. Each day was another adventure as David and I squared off against the Philistines. Together, we sued insur-ance companies, banks, utilities, hospitals, manufacturers, railroads, pharmaceutical companies, property developers, and incompetent doc-tors. Winning was always difficult, but we got enough verdicts to stay in business.

I cut my teeth punching up, and so I was naturally drawn to stories of other lawyers who took on the Goliaths. The first one I remember was *A Civil Action*, Jonathan Harr's classic nonfiction account of environ-mental pollution and litigation near Boston. Published in 1995, the book found a wide audience, won awards, and was adapted into a fine movie starring John Travolta and Robert Duvall. I've read it several times and obviously admire it, but it has one huge problem: Goliath wins.

Wastelands is even better. It is the uplifting, round-by-round true story of a bunch of rural plaintiffs with no money and seemingly little hope, and the lawyers who smelled injustice and went to war on their behalf. In terms of pure storytelling, this book has all of the crucial elements that writers of fiction constantly struggle to find:

First, there is the tort, the wrongdoing, the pollution. There is the unregulated, wholesale destruction of property values and quality of life by two thousand commercial hog farms in eastern North Carolina.

Second, there are the sympathetic victims, the five hundred or so small landowners unlucky enough to have their lives ruined by massive hog farms next door.

Third, there are delightfully evil bad guys. It is difficult to utter the phrase "Big Pork" without conjuring up all manner of images, none of them good. But Big Pork is king in hog country, and its advocates and apologists get their just rewards in this story. Goliath has never looked so bad.

Fourth, there are the warriors who step into the ring and battle against heavy odds. For thirty years, Mona Lisa Wallace and her partner, Bill Graham, have fought to protect the poor, the injured, the mistreated. They have won big verdicts and even bigger settlements.

Nothing, though, prepared them for their epic battle against Big Pork.

Never in my most creative moments could I have assembled such a colorful and memorable cast of characters, and then blessed them with so riveting a set of facts, and then guided them through the ins and outs and uncertainties of high-stakes litigation.

Beautifully written, impeccably researched, and told with the air of suspense that few writers can handle, *Wastelands* is a story I wish I had written.

March 3, 2021

Author's Note

This book is based on hundreds of hours of in-depth conversations with over sixty people connected in one way or another to the nuisance lawsuits against Smithfield Foods. Most of my sources make appearances in the story (all under their real names), but a few agreed only to speak on background, and a handful of others I consulted on technical points of law and science.

Along with immersing myself in the lives of the main players, I spent months on the road, traveling the byways of eastern North Carolina, visiting people in their homes, sitting on porches, touring hog farms, and learning the rural landscape. I went hiking in the wilderness and up in the air in small planes. I familiarized myself with the North Carolina General Assembly and witnessed key parts of the last federal trial in Raleigh. I traveled to Richmond, Virginia, and attended the appellate hearing before the Fourth Circuit Court of Appeals. As time marched on, the people who animate this story became more than research subjects. They became friends. Yet they never asked more than this: Tell the truth. Let the world see what we saw.

In addition to my original research, I leaned heavily on the voluminous public record in fleshing out the narrative—the court record from the state and federal cases, the legislative record from the North Carolina House and Senate and the U.S. Congress, and the media record, including countless articles in print and online, television interviews and event footage, documentaries, and books. I have included a record of essential sources in the endnotes. Beyond that, I relied on my years of experience as a litigation attorney—and before that as a law clerk in the federal courts—to interpret the legal nuances of the cases and the reactions of the individuals involved.

All quotations in the story are derived from the memories of people who participated in, or witnessed, the relevant conversations, from prior media accounts in which the speaker is quoted, from video or audio recordings of the speaker in the public domain, and from transcripts of legal proceedings. Because most of us speak in a way that sounds better in person than it looks on the page, I applied a light editorial brush to spoken words for the benefit of concision and clarity. Also, in the courtroom scenes, I often condensed lengthy and labyrinthine exchanges between lawyers, witnesses, and judges to maintain narrative pacing and minimize legalese. I included as much dialogue in the story as I could, but I invented none of it.

Six months before the book was scheduled for publication, I reached out to Smithfield for an interview. I also approached two of its lawyers by email, both of whom make appearances in the story. One of the lawyers sent me a prompt and courteous reply, saying he had passed my message along and requested permission to speak with me. From his silence—and that of the company itself—I assume that permission was never granted. Thankfully, it wasn't difficult to tell Smithfield's side of the story. I relied upon the company's many press releases, the court testimony of its representatives, and the public statements of its allies.

Although I wrote this book in the style of a novel, everything you are about to read is true. Some stories really are wilder than the fancies of the imagination.

This is one of them.

WASTELANDS

PROLOGUE

Veredictum

> . . . Come, my friends,
> 'tis not too late to seek a newer world.
> —*Alfred, Lord Tennyson, "Ulysses"*

U.S. District Court, Raleigh, North Carolina August 3, 2018, 8:58 a.m. At first, word of it passes like the whisper of a surprise, from one ear to the next in private quarters on the seventh floor of the United States courthouse in Raleigh, North Carolina. The jury foreman tells it to the bailiff, and the bailiff informs the law clerks, who advise Judge Britt. The judge then sends out emissaries to the legal teams assembled in conference rooms down the hall. The lawyers don't understand the significance of the summons until they assemble in the courtroom. After the judge speaks, it's quiet enough in the vaulted space to hear a heartbeat. It's only nine in the morning. The deliberations have barely begun. Yet the foreman has spoken.

The jury has reached a verdict.

The word spreads like sparks from a brushfire. Smartphones emerge from pockets and handbags, thumbs fly across screens, and messages are cast upon the digital wind, lighting up other phones with chimes and beeps miles away. The lawyers, paralegals, and ancillary staff who chose to stay away this morning, expecting that the jury would dicker for days as its counterparts did in the first two trials, fumble for their keys and race to their cars, praying that the traffic gods will grant them swift passage into downtown Raleigh.

None of them will make it in time.

Inside the courthouse, the parties and the curious alike converge on the wood-paneled courtroom. They file in through double doors, a pair of U.S. marshals in their trademark navy blazers standing astride the entrance like an ancient palace guard. The crowd is rapt, the voices hushed. To one of the attorneys on the plaintiffs' side, a deeply intuitive woman whose decades of success have earned her a place on the A-list of the American trial bar, the implications of the moment are plain—and also painful.

A lightning deliberation almost always means a defense verdict.

She makes her way across the aisle and extends a hand to the lead trial counsel for the defendant, Smithfield Foods, the largest pork producer in the world. "I'm guessing this one is yours," she says. "Congratulations." The man, whose fastidious demeanor cuts a sharp contrast with his bulldog physique, replies with a courtly nod and a word of thanks.

He is nearly alone in the courtroom. Most of the benches on Smithfield's side of the aisle are empty. The company's representatives, the people from the North Carolina Pork Council and other industry-aligned groups, the contract hog growers (or, as the industry likes to call them, "family farmers"), and most of the pork producer's vastly capable and enormously expensive defense team are either working off site or across town at the State Fairgrounds.

It is there that a rally of sorts is taking place.

The event, dubbed the National Ag Roundtable, has drawn the attendance of a host of luminaries from the universe of Big Agriculture—the junior U.S. senator from North Carolina and two U.S. congressmen, a passel of state elected officials, and at least a dozen leaders from national agriculture groups and the academic community. It has also attracted a flock of journalists and something like a thousand spectators, many of them from the eastern part of the state where pork is king. Although billed by its sponsor, the North Carolina Farm Bureau, as a colloquy on the future of agriculture, it is, in reality, a transparent show of force by the mandarins of agribusiness and their handmaidens in government (almost all of them well-fed white men of a certain age) who have controlled the supply of animal protein in the United States for more than a generation. The real purpose of the rally is to protest the proceedings taking place in Judge Britt's courtroom five miles away.

For those in the roundtable's audience, there can be no doubt who the politicos and Big Ag honchos have in their sights. Two of the plaintiffs' attorneys are called out by name, as if to brand them public enemies—Mona Lisa Wallace and her partner, Bill Graham. The doomsaying from the dais is so dire and the emotions in the auditorium run so hot that, in fleeting moments, the crowd's restiveness takes on the character of a mob.

"We have a crisis brewing in eastern North Carolina," says one of the congressmen. "It is a threat not only to North Carolina agriculture, but a threat to agriculture nationwide."

"I would describe what's going on as a blight," declares the state ag commissioner, his pallid visage seeming to darken with every word. "If we don't do something about this right now, there's not a farm in the country that's going to be safe."

The most august of the dignitaries, the junior U.S. senator, spins a daydream of throwing the "trial lawyers" out of the state, despite the fact that Mona Wallace and Bill Graham both hail from North Carolina and have never left. "We've got to do everything we can to put pressure on these people who are coming to our state trying to destroy it. We've got to do everything we can legally to make it difficult for them. Ultimately, I hope we can put these people out of a job."

One of the state legislators compares the lawyers to serial larcenists. "Everybody's heard of Willie Sutton, who was a bank robber. When asked why he robbed banks, he said, 'That's where the money is.' If he were alive today, he'd go to law school."

Eventually, the pork industry's fairest friend, a cantankerous state legislator with florid jowls and an ivory duckbill bouffant, raises a finger. "Smithfield Foods says that they will not settle. Thank God that Smithfield Foods has got the backbone to stand up to these lawsuits."

Unbeknownst to him—indeed to anyone at the roundtable—a young intern from the law firm of Wallace & Graham is in the room, observing the conversation. Her smartphone is one of the many around Raleigh that light up when Judge Britt announces that the jury has reached a verdict. She is sitting on the fringes of the crowd, her nerves on edge, marveling at the symmetry of the moment and wondering if anyone else at the rally is in on the secret.

Apparently not, for the speeches and grandstanding continue without interruption.

Across town in the courtroom, the quiet takes on a preternatural quality when everyone is situated. In contrast to Smithfield's largely empty gallery, the plaintiffs' side is mostly full, the faces waiting in expectation as diverse as the color wheel of the South. The plaintiffs from Piney Woods Road—all of them Black and most of them related—occupy the first few rows. Among them are the lawyers and paralegals, interns and support staff from Wallace & Graham and the Kaeske Law Firm, whose founder, Michael Kaeske (pronounced "Kesky"), is the plaintiffs' chief advocate before the jury. Seated behind them is an informal delegation of community activists (in Smithfield's parlance, "environmental extremists"), who have fought the industry since the nineties. One of them, a garrulous man with a talent for story and song, is a former hog farmer himself. He is slowly dying. But today his heart is alive, and he wouldn't miss this for anything.

For the plaintiffs and their attorneys, the trial in this case and the two that preceded it are the culmination of a five-year journey unlike anything in their experience. Some of the plaintiffs have received threats from irate members of the public and a few of the lawyers and their staff have been defamed as pimps and rapists by an elected official—the same jowly man now reassuring the multitude at the State Fairgrounds that Smithfield will never settle. They have faced disinformation campaigns from the industry's allies and a juggernaut of political power-brokering in the state General Assembly that came within a pair of votes of gutting the cases before they could reach trial.

For the residents of Piney Woods Road—and the nearly five hundred other plaintiffs whose suits are pending in the U.S. District Court for the Eastern District of North Carolina—however, the struggles of the litigation pale in comparison to the suffering they have endured for more than a generation. Some of them have been waiting twenty-five years for the opportunity to tell their stories to people who would not call them liars, for the chance to speak of the befouled air, the poisoned water, and the degraded soil that is their heritage, and to demand a measure of justice from the company whose factory farms have transformed the once-idyllic rural geography around their homes into a farrago of forested wastelands.

The hands of the neighbors and lawyers and activists are entwined at the level of the benches on which they are sitting. They are black hands and white, old hands and young, and they are bound to each other as much by kindred affection as by devotion to the cause. If there is such a thing as the chain of destiny, it is made of links like these.

Judge Britt, a charming octogenarian with the oracular eyes of a barn owl, peers over his glasses at the lawyers, then motions to the bailiff to bring in the jury. The pulses in the gallery quicken as the jurors shuffle toward their seats. It is an unconventional panel, skewed both in age and gender—four of the jurors are college students; ten of the twelve are women. It is also almost entirely white. Only two of the dozen citizens initially seated in the jury box were Black, and Smithfield's lawyers struck one of them with a preemptory challenge.

After the jury sits and silence descends, all thought of the bustling world beyond the walls of the courtroom dissolves into a single horizon—the verdict. For the neighbors and their attorneys (and for Smithfield's counsel, too), this moment is a tangled braid of hope and dread. Both of the previous trials—each involving a different neighborhood—yielded substantial awards for the plaintiffs. A third consecutive victory, a Triple Crown of sorts, could be decisive in the litigation. It could force a multibillion-dollar global industry to admit the inevitability of change. By contrast, a defense verdict—a "not guilty," as it were—could help entrench that same industry's polluting practices for another generation.

"Mr. Baker," the judge intones, "has the jury arrived at its verdict?"

"Yes, Your Honor, we have," replies the foreman.

The judge waves his translucent fingers. "You may hand the envelope to the clerk."

As the envelope makes its short trip to the bench, the plaintiffs in the gallery take a breath and hold it. The pain and sorrow of memory, together with the labor of years and dreams of days yet to come, are on the altar before them. Contrary to the tale of greed and opportunism being spun by the politicians and poohbahs across town, they aren't thinking about a million-dollar payday as they wait for the judgment to be delivered. Instead, they are whispering a simple prayer, the prayer of verdict day, of *veredictum*.

Please, Lord, let them believe us. Let them believe that we told the truth.

PART ONE

THE KINGDOM

Heaven cannot brook two suns,
Nor earth two masters.
—*Alexander the Great*

CHAPTER 1

HOMEPLACE

What is money when I have all the earth?
—*George Washington Carver*

**River Road,
Wallace,
North Carolina
Summer 1958**

On a five-acre plot of sandy loam soil at the hem of a stand of pines lies a house built by hand a few years after the armistice that ended the First World War. The house is painted white, like a bridal veil, though in time the lady of the house, Beulah Stallings Herring, will paint it green and then pink, unlike any in the vicinity—perhaps in all of Duplin County. Not the flamboyant pink of lipstick or roses, nor the translucent pink of skin, but the spring pink of a dogwood flower.

It is a modest dwelling, yet it was constructed to weather the years. Its siding is German Dutch and its bones are likely pine, though precise memory of the framing will soon perish with the builders. The focal point of the house is the porch. It encompasses the structure's entire front face, including the door. To the visitor it signals a welcome, an invitation to sit and stay awhile, to breathe the sweet country air and trace the shape of the clouds.

Though it is solitary, the house is almost never alone. It is the birthplace of fifteen children, all born to Beulah Herring across a quarter of a century. Her first child was old enough to vote by the time the baby, Elsie, came along. Elsie is ten years old now, and though she is the youngest, she is a precocious child, strong-willed and opinionated.

One Sunday afternoon in July, she walks through the kitchen, the living room, and out the front door of the house as if she knows that one day it will be her own.

"Come on, Beef, let's go," she says, taking the hand of her brother Jesse and tugging him through the knot of adults sitting on the porch, enjoying the shade and the breeze.

Her father is in one of the rocking chairs, as is her Uncle Perl, and a neighbor from down the road. They are talking about the tobacco market and the harvest yet to come. They pay Elsie no mind. The afternoon meal is still a ways off, and they trust her to bring Jesse back in time.

Down the steps and out into the yard Elsie strolls, Jesse at her heels. While Jesse is older than Elsie by two years, he is smaller than most twelve-year-olds, his growth attenuated by Down syndrome. On account of their birth order and Jesse's special needs, they have been close for as long as Elsie can remember. To her, he's "Beef," and to him, she's "Elt." Only one person in the world inspires greater affection in Jesse than Elsie does—their mama.

At this moment, Beulah is straightening clothes on the line. Even at the age of fifty-six, she is still a remarkably youthful woman, her gentle demeanor balanced by penetrating wisdom and unflappable resolve. She is Elsie's favorite person, too. It is Beulah's spirit more than any other that gives shape to their family. Her smile means Elsie is home.

"Where y'all headed?" she asks, as if already knowing the answer.

"Just going for a walk," Elsie replies with a grin.

A couple of Elsie's siblings are lounging on chairs in the yard beneath a sprawling tree whose canopy is wide enough to swallow the Carolina sun. Elsie catches the eye of her sixteen-year-old sister, Thelma, and tosses her a languid wave. Thelma's twin brother, Delma, is beside her, sipping Coca-Cola and chatting with a friend. After Thelma waves back, Elsie leads Jesse around to the side of the house and back toward the smokehouse and the gardens beyond it.

The land opens up before her in the hues of emerald and henna, as does the sky in celestial blue. It is her mother's land, all eighty acres of it, just as it was her granddaddy's until he passed on to his reward shortly before Beulah gave birth to her first baby. Elsie knows her granddaddy, Immanuel, through the stories her mother has told her. Those stories are

Elsie's inheritance, too, and Jesse's and Thelma and Delma's. Like the land itself, they are a memorial to their family's place in the world.

Immanuel Stallings was born into slavery, though his father was always free. Marshall Stallings was not a Black man; he was white, a landowner of modest prominence in Duplin County. Immanuel had no memory of his real mother. When he was old enough to inquire of her, he heard that she had died. In his later years, however, he came to believe something darker—that she had been sold by the Stallings family sometime before the Civil War upended the antebellum order and brought emancipation to the enslaved.

By virtue of the genetic lottery, Immanuel was pale enough to stand on the white side of the color line, but the laws of Jim Crow forbade him to claim any sort of standing. While Lincoln might have declared him free, his white neighbors would never consider him their equal. He was Black because his mother was Black. Such were the arbitrary diktats of apartheid.

He grew up in the care of his father's sister, Emily Stallings Teachey. "Miss Emily," as everyone in the family called her, was a kind and generous woman, who loved Immanuel like a son. It was Miss Emily who sold him the first fifteen-acre tract of land in 1891—the very land on which Beulah's house now stands. And it was Miss Emily who, before she died six years later, sold him three more tracts of land, bringing his total acreage to eighty. She wanted to give him an anchor in the world, a piece of God's dirt that no one could take away. She wanted that not only for Immanuel but for his children, and his children's children.

For Beulah. For Elsie.

Elsie's feet are bare and her eyes are bright as she skips across the long-bladed grass, her skin prickling with sweat. She hears the squeak of hogs in the family's pen some distance away, and the sound of Jesse huffing behind her as they pass the peach and apple trees and the chicken coop, with its clucking hens. Her brother doesn't need to ask where they are going, for on a Sunday afternoon in July, with the house too warm for comfort and all the chairs on the porch and in the yard occupied by their elders, there is only one place they would rather be.

The grape arbor.

There are two vines in the garden plot, striking both in their similar-

ity and difference: One produces white grapes and the other black. There
are patches of shade beneath the vines, offering relief from the heat. Jesse
plops himself down, his upper body rocking slightly on the hinge of his
hips, like a metronome in motion. Elsie, meanwhile, examines the fruit.
Some of the clusters are still ripening, but others are plump with juice.

She selects a large bunch of black grapes and scampers back to Jesse,
holding it out to him. Then she picks a cluster of white grapes and sits
down beside him. Her brother is already chewing, murmuring with pleasure, his round face illumined as if by an internal lamp. She removes a
grape from its stem and places it between her teeth, smiling instinctively
at the sudden burst of flavor. She looks at Jesse and sees his own smile
blossom, even as droplets of juice dribble down his chin. She giggles at
him and wipes away the excess before it drips onto his clothes. Then she
gives him a grape from her own stem, and he returns the favor. The black
grape isn't quite as sweet to Elsie's tongue, but its flavor is more complex.

As soon as Elsie polishes off her last grape, she begins to hunt for
more, prizing apart the leaves to find the hidden gems. After picking several bunches, enough to share with the family, she returns to her brother's side. She lies back against the grass and stares at the diamonds of sky
peeking through the leaves of the vine above her. She feels the humid
caress of the breeze, hears the singsong chorus of the birds in the trees
and Thelma's laughter echoing across the yard. Her joy at this moment
isn't a thought or a feeling. It is a way of being. It is everything.

As a child, she has little consciousness of the hardships her family
has faced. She has felt the roughness of her father's hands, seen the lines
worn deep into his forehead from long days of labor under the relentless
sun. But she knows nothing of the stress of sharecropping tobacco, none
of the travails of a Black farmer trying to make an honest living in a
world built to keep the Black man down. She understands the structure
of segregation from the water fountains and public toilets in Wallace and
the way the schoolhouses separate white children from Black. She has
experienced the sting of being snubbed by white friends when they see
each other in town. But out here among the fruit trees and grapevines,
on this fertile land that her granddaddy handed down to her mama and
that, one day, her mama will hand down to her, all of that ugliness is just
a faint shadow lurking behind an otherwise luminous world.

This is Beulah Herring's land. And, like the Beulah Land in the hymn that Elsie has sung at church, it is a land of bounty and delight. If the world will do her wrong, it will happen someplace else. Here, there is shelter. There is plenty. There is family.

To ten-year-old Elsie, that is all that matters.

Hallsville Road, Beulaville, North Carolina
Summer 1958

On that same day, or a day much like it, on a rural plot of land fifteen miles northeast of Wallace, a boy about Elsie's age named Woodell McGowan ventures out into the sun, his eyes fixed on the dark silhouette of forest to the north. His mother, Delores, calls out to him to be home by sundown, then returns to her Sunday chores. She is not the woman who brought him into the world, but she has raised him since the day, seven years ago now, that his birth mother died. As far as Woodell is concerned, Delores and her husband, George McGowan, are his parents. He remembers at the age of three waking up between them in their little house off Hallsville Road. The fact that they are not his blood means nothing to him. They are his family. And this is their land. Hall land. All one hundred acres of it.

The land goes back generations in Delores's line. Woodell knows it like he knows his own home, every crease and fold of it, every patch of field and thicket—hardwood and pine—all the way back to Limestone Creek. The deeds at the courthouse in Kenansville contain a record of the boundaries, but lines drawn on paper mean as much to Woodell as they do to the squirrels and the jays and the crickets that watch over him on his adventures. There are surely places he has yet to see, treasures he has yet to discover, but whatever is out there will not keep its secrets long. He is determined to explore all of it, to map its furthest reaches in his mind, until he can find his way blindfolded. For then, in a way, the land will be his, too.

The big field comes first. Woodell scampers across it in the unhindered manner of youth, half walking, half running, heedless of the motions transporting him. His hands are free, and he is carrying nothing on his back. Where he's going, he has all he needs. Past the field is the big house, where his mother, Delores, and her four siblings were raised. In the family, it's called the "old homeplace." Both of Delores's

parents are gone now. Her father, John Richard Hall, died before Woodell was born, and her mother, Mary Jane Hall, passed more recently.

Like Elsie Herring's grandfather, Immanuel Stallings, John Richard
Hall was born in the waning days of the Old South, before the curtain
closed on slavery. As the story goes, he was young enough that he sat at
the foot of his father's bed and didn't have to work in the fields with the
other slaves. Then came the war and emancipation and Reconstruction.
As soon as he could manage it, John Richard Hall's father—Delores's
grandfather—began acquiring the land that became the one hundred
acres. Now that John Richard and Mary Jane are gone, Delores holds
title to the land together with her oldest sister, Lillie Belle Hall, and her
brother, Raymond.

Beyond the big house, the forest rises up, its branches touching the
sky. Woodell races toward the line of shade, then slows when the afternoon sun retreats behind the crown of trees. He enters the woods at a
leisurely pace, hopping roots in the speckled light, his feet falling softly
on the carpet of leaves and pine needles. As usual, his destination is the
creek. But first, he heads toward the camp. He sees the meadow before
long, wild grass surrounded by pines, and the tent he fashioned with his
own hands, burlap threads spread out over a latticework of branches. If
any place in the world is Woodell McGowan's, this is it.

He lies down in the shade of the tent. There is just enough room for
him to stretch his legs, but that is all the space he needs. He listens to the
calls of the birds and the whisper of the wind moving through the pine
boughs. He watches the hawks pirouetting in the sky and the cloud sails
floating high above them. While he is alone, he is not lonely. Indeed, he
is never happier than when he is by himself in these woods, with nobody
but God for company.

In time, he rises again and sets out for Limestone Creek, a quiet
tributary of the Northeast Cape Fear River that meanders for miles in an
arc around the town of Beulaville. There is a pool he frequents on days
like this, when even shelter is not enough to break the heat. The pool is
too shallow to swim in. But it is clear and cool on his skin and covered
by deep shade, and once in a while he sees fish darting among the rocks.

At the pool, he takes off his shoes and steps into the gently flowing
water. It splashes on his ankles and tickles him enough to make him
laugh. He moves his feet deeper, until the water laps around his calves.

It is a blissful feeling, but the rest of him is still coated in sweat. On impulse, he sits down in the water and reclines his body, immersing himself in the stream.

As the water washes over him, cleansing his pores and cooling his skin, he looks up through the branches at the same gem-cut sky that has captured Elsie Herring's fancy fifteen miles away. He doesn't think about the life pulsing through him or where the years ahead will take him. He wastes precious little thought on the future. But even if he pondered it like Aristotle, his mind could not conceive how time will change the land he loves—the forests turned into fields, and the fields converted into industrial farms; the hog barns laid out row upon row, thousands of pigs packed into them like sardines; the great pits hewn into mud and clay to store the waste of a small city; and that waste sprayed out into the air and onto the soil until the ground can hold no more of it, until a breath smells of effluent and the streams run with poison.

Ideas such as these are as foreign to young Woodell as the towers of New York City and the turrets of the Taj Mahal. Nor can Woodell imagine that his path, in the coming decades, will converge with Elsie's and hundreds of other people like them, and that their collective memories of the land, and their passion for its dignity, will fuel a titanic battle for the soul of this place, and, more broadly, of eastern North Carolina.

Lying in the stream, Woodell is marvelously oblivious to all of this. Just as he should be. He is a boy in summer. His belly is full, and his heart is light. His family is close by.

He is home.

Piney Woods Road, Willard, North Carolina
Summer 1970s

Some years after Elsie and Woodell's ten-year-old summer, on a spoke-straight stretch of rural road across the border in Pender County, a teenage girl named Joyce Messick is preparing herself for a horseback ride. Her brothers' quarter horse, christened "Bugshot," is munching on a clump of grass in a pasture nearby, his sable coat and mane shimmering in the sunlight. He is the third horse that their family has owned, all of them brought home by their father for the benefit of his children, but mostly for his boys, James—who goes by "Red"—and Willie. Before

Bugshot, they had Shetland ponies. Joyce didn't like them as much. Her preference is the quarter horse.

Unlike her brothers, Joyce has little confidence in her equestrian skills. She has never ridden alone in the saddle, nor does she aspire to become a horsewoman. But if Red, her oldest sibling, is heading out on a ride, she is happy to ride along. Wherever Red goes, Joyce wants to be. Although they are only separated in age by two years, Red has always treated Joyce with a paternal touch. When she was old enough to swim in the Sand Hole down the road, it was Red who made certain she didn't drown. Fishing, too, is a skill that Red bequeathed her. They catch crappies, mostly, and some perch. He also taught her the art of throwing daggers. When Red puts up a target in their backyard, she can hit it squarely. Horses are another thing. But if Red is in the saddle with her, she feels safe.

"You coming?" Red asks from the yard, his arms full of riding gear. Willie is with him, carrying the saddle and pad and looking a bit forlorn. He tried to borrow a horse from their cousin down the road, but the cousin was already out in the woods. He will get a turn on Bugshot later on—Red is good about sharing—but for now, he is just the stable boy.

"Yeah," Joyce says, and follows her brothers to the pasture.

Red greets Bugshot with affection and a carrot from his pocket. Then he hands Joyce the brush and watches to make sure she gets all the loose hair off the horse's coat. Bugshot eyes her warily, shifting his weight between hooves, but with coaxing from Red, the horse submits to her ministrations. After she finishes, Willie puts the pad in place and the saddle on top. Red gestures for Joyce to secure the straps and then tests them for tightness, letting out a satisfied grunt when he finds the saddle snug. Red offers Joyce the chance to put on the bridle, but she declines. He shrugs and tosses her a sly grin, then slips the bridle over Bugshot's nose and ears. "Like that," he says, as if the next time she will surely be ready to do it herself.

With a steady hand from her older brother, Joyce places a toe in the stirrup and mounts the horse, gripping the pommel for balance. Red hands her the reins and swings onto Bugshot's rump with ease, holding the back of the saddle, his feet dangling behind the stirrups.

"Ready?" he says with a lilt, for nothing gives him more delight than a ride.

Joyce takes a breath and nods. Lifting the reins, she kicks Bugshot into a trot.

They make their way out of the pasture and onto the grassy shoulder of Piney Woods Road, heading east down the corridor of trees. The road is aptly named, for the woods here are dominated by conifers. On their right is a stand of longleaf pines with slender trunks and vaulted crowns, and on their left are loblollies with proud branches and clump-like needle clusters.

They have only a few neighbors in the vicinity, all of them kin in one way or another. Their family has lived on Piney Woods Road since the 1940s, and in the area much longer than that. There is a Messick Road somewhere back in the woods where their father's people come from. Neither of their parents has told them much about the past. But for Black families like theirs, history has a similar shape. Two or, at most, three generations ago, their forebears were held in hereditary bondage by the ancestors of their white neighbors. In the century since then, their people have lived off the land, struggling to make a life for themselves despite the invisible chains of prejudice and discrimination. What they have gained, they have fought to keep—especially the earth beneath their feet. So it is with the Messicks. Their father's land was owned by his parents before him. Other than family, nothing is more valuable in all the world.

"Easy now," says Red out of habit, though he knows Joyce won't urge Bugshot to go too fast. Speed is not in her nature. She has always been a cautious girl, soft-spoken and shy. She doesn't like to be out front. She is a helper, a caretaker, a giver, content to allow others to take whatever stage happens to be nearby and to cheer for them from the wings.

Soon, they reach the trail that heads northeast into the sun-dappled heart of pine forest. She has never seen the end of the road, but Red and Willie have ventured far beyond it, riding for miles up in the woods and bringing back stories that give Joyce the shivers. The snakes trouble her more than anything. She hates those stories the most.

As Bugshot carries them beneath the needled canopy, his hooves clopping on soft soil, Red works with Joyce on her horsemanship. "Steady now," he says, his breath tickling the back of her neck. "Don't pull back on him, or he'll rear up." She follows his direction, holding the reins loosely and allowing Bugshot to navigate from memory. Although she trusts Red with her life, something about the horse feels dangerous to her, fraught with unquantifiable risk. Her unease, however, is not potent enough to spoil her sunny mood. The day is brilliant, suffused with sunshine, and the sultry air is cooler beneath the pine needles.

"You got it now, right?" Red says, a trace of excitement creeping into his voice.

"Yeah," she replies.

He repeats the question a second time, with greater emphasis.

If she weren't afraid of losing the reins, she would turn and stare at him. But the horse's bulk and her responsibilities hold her back. "Yeah," she assures him.

What happens next shocks her.

Without warning, Red launches himself off of Bugshot's hindquarters and slaps his rump so hard that the horse bolts like a thoroughbred at Belmont. Joyce lets out a scream and clamps down on the reins, holding on with all her strength. The quarter horse races down the trail at a gallop, his pounding hooves filling the air with thunder. As the seconds melt into one another, Joyce feels something come over her, something she has never felt before. There is terror, real and encompassing, but there is also a thrill. She is still in the saddle. Bugshot hasn't thrown her. The wind is alive on her cheeks, her body is moving in cadence with the horse, and the sun and sky are dancing in the branches overhead.

Suddenly, and irrevocably, the terror gives way to joy. A smile dawns on her lips, then spreads across her entire face. As fleeting as the moment is, it is precious and durable. Decades later, the memory will still make her laugh, even as the thought of Red pierces her with sorrow.

After serving in the army, he will fight to keep a roof over his head and die too young. Willie, too, will struggle and return to live with her after his own stint in the army. His passion for horses will never leave him. But his explorations will be constrained by the hog farms that men from other places will build on the land a short distance down the road. Whole swaths of forest will become off-limits to him, for fear of the stench that sometimes blows on the wind.

Joyce will become the anchor of her family. The home she builds on her parents' land will be the home that brings her relatives together and grounds them in their common history. Over the years, she will see more than her share of tragedy. But she will labor through the pain, assuaging the suffering of those around her, both in her family and in the community, as a hospice nurse. Among her siblings, she will be the one who keeps the light on for the rest of them, for that is her nature. That is her way.

At this moment, however, on a galloping Bugshot, young Joyce is weightless in her freedom. She rides the quarter horse farther down the trail than she ever meant to go, then reins him in slowly and turns him around. She gives him a gentle kick and he adopts a comfortable trot. For the first time ever on horseback, she is in command. Her chest swells with pride. It is a glorious feeling. She almost wishes she could spur Bugshot into another gallop. But she sees Red running toward her, a grin splitting his face.

"I knew it!" he hollers, holding his arms wide. "I knew you could do it!"

She draws Bugshot to a halt in front of him, probing his dark eyes for the truth. More than anyone, she craves her older brother's affection.

To her enduring delight, she sees only love.

CHAPTER 2

THE CHAMPION

The door that nobody else will go in at, seems always
to swing open widely for me.
—*Clara Barton*

**North Main Street,
Salisbury,
North Carolina
March 2013**

From the cruising altitude of a hawk on the wing, one can see the whole sweep of Salisbury. To the north is the crenellated tower that sits astride the entrance to Catawba College, and to the south the rolling meadows of the National Cemetery, where thousands of Union and Confederate soldiers lie interred. On the east end of town are the industrial yards of the old Isenhour Brick and Tile plant, under new ownership after a century-long run. And off to the west is the pinnacle of Salisbury's fame—the headquarters of Food Lion, a grocery chain with the distinction of having turned a $28 investment in 1957 into $1 million by 1988, leaving Salisbury awash in mom-and-pop millionaires.

The streets of the town's historical center are laid out like a checkerboard, with the stately, red-brick commercial district filling out the blocks around the hilltop intersection of Innes and Main. Many of the homes dotting Jackson and Fulton Streets date back to the first half of the nineteenth century. The town itself is older still, its roots twisting deep into the soil of pre-revolutionary America. In 1753, the British provincial government made it the seat of the westernmost Crown court in the colonies.

While the people of Salisbury take pride in their heritage, they are not hidebound to the past, nor have they consigned the town's core to the fading decline of time. While not quite as thriving as other communities in the economic halo of Charlotte, Salisbury is justly described as a "new, old city." Its downtown has been largely revitalized and its infrastructure restored, thanks to a spirit of civic investment among its long-time residents and the miracle of Food Lion stock. Along with a bevy of boutiques, it has a well-stocked wine shop, a vibrant indie bookstore, and an art scene, and its restaurants bustle with patrons. The discerning foodie can get Cuban fusion at Mambo, café Greek at Mykonos, rustic Italian at La Cava, and bistro French at Carpe Vinum 121.

Salisbury also boasts a coffee shop hip enough to rival its big city cousins—Koco Java. From the vantage point of the hawk, carving its gyres over North Main Street, the squat building with the nondescript rooftop looks like nothing much. The old Greek Revival courthouse with its imposing Ionic columns and the original Spanish Mission–style train depot are more likely to catch the eye. But the coffee shop is busier than any place around it, with half a dozen cars in the drive-through line and customers entering and exiting on foot. One of these customers stands out from the others, both on account of her height—she is six feet tall in her work heels—and the way her long blonde hair shines in the light of the sun, like a field of wheat at harvest time.

Her name is Linda Wike, and she is a veteran paralegal at the law firm of Wallace & Graham just up the street. Really, though, the term "paralegal" is too anodyne to describe her. If the firm is an engine and the lawyers in the civil litigation department are its pistons, Linda is the flywheel, absorbing their energy and delivering it smoothly and evenly to their clients and the world. She is faithful, loyal, and indispensable.

On this bright morning on the cusp of spring, she is at Koco Java on a mission for her boss, John Hughes, who keeps his bloodstream thrumming with caffeine from sunup to sundown. Most of the time, he drinks the pedestrian swill in the office pot, but once in a while, Linda brings him the good stuff from up the street. Despite the line in the shop, she is in and out in five minutes and back at the office in ten, a cup in each hand—black coffee for him and a caramel macchiato for her. She enters the firm's lobby, her heels clacking on the floor, strolls past the conference rooms, with their paned-glass French doors, past the front desk where Teresa, the firm's beloved receptionist, is on the phone, and makes her way back to John's office in the windowless innards of the firm.

He is pecking away at the keyboard, working on a brief. His reading glasses are perched on the bridge of his aquiline nose, his wispy graying hair shoved back over his ears like an afterthought. When John is writing—and he is almost always writing—everything else is an afterthought. The son of a celebrated professor who taught at Duke and chaired the accounting department at UCLA, he might have followed his Mensa-level intellect and passion for poetry into the cloister of academia, but he pursued law instead because, like the lawyer-poet Wallace Stevens, he wanted to be out in the world. He still composes verse in his free time, but his most prodigious output is legal prose.

"Thanks, Linda," he says distractedly, taking the coffee from her.

Linda smiles knowingly. She's worked with John for almost a decade. His moods are like the climate in Newfoundland—variable, with equal chances of sun and fog, and always the possibility of rain. When he is in the writing tunnel, she gives him a spacious berth. She walks to her own office, which shares a wall with his. But before she can sit down, her phone rings.

"Linda, can you come in here, please?" The upbeat voice, subtly inflected with Carolina twang, belongs to Mona Lisa Wallace—John's boss and the masthead founder of the firm.

Her macchiato still untouched, Linda wends her way through the honeycomb of offices, past award trophies and framed newspaper articles from years gone by, to the smaller of Mona's two workspaces—the nook she shares with her assistant, Jennifer Cox. Like John, Mona is typing, but when Linda appears, she loses interest in the computer. Her blue eyes are aglow, her face radiating the full wattage of her Dolly Parton smile.

"I'm thinking about Brandon Taylor," she says. "There's more to it than worker's comp. There's a civil case. It never should have happened."

Linda nods, listening while Mona talks. The next few minutes are a ride on the Mona Lisa Wallace express train. When the wheels in her mind start turning, there is no telling where they will end up. Especially when a case is so fraught, so resonant with wrong, as the death of a young husband and father at the hands of corporate malfeasance.

The Taylor case has been eating at Mona for weeks. Brandon Taylor was only twenty-six years old when he lost consciousness, in the middle of the night, atop a tanker truck at the Smithfield packing plant, a hog slaughterhouse down east in Clinton. He died before anyone could revive him, leaving behind a pregnant wife and a two-year-old autistic son. The cause of death: toxic fumes, especially hydrogen sulfide, emitted by the slurry of hog waste emptying into his tanker from an overhead storage unit. He was not wearing a mask, despite the fact that hydrogen sulfide is known to be deadly, despite the fact that other workers had been severely injured by gases coming out of a tanker's hatch, despite the fact that potentially fatal levels of the gas had been documented just a few weeks before. Mona has evidence that both Smithfield and Taylor's employer, McGill Environmental Systems, were aware of the dangers, including the peril of handling the transfer at night. Yet they allowed the practice to continue. And Brandon Taylor died because of it, devastating his young family. It's the kind of case that gets Mona up in the morning—Linda, too, and John down the hall.

When Mona takes a breath, Linda starts to reply, but the ringtone of Mona's mobile phone preempts her. "Hold that thought," Mona says. "I need to take this."

Linda glides out of the room, as Mona presses the phone to her ear. The caller is a colleague on the board of Catawba College, what Mona's friends affectionately refer to as her second job after running the firm. She listens briefly yet actively, offers a morsel of advice, including the name of someone who can help, then agrees to arrange the contact. It doesn't bother her that she is always being summoned to fix things. On the contrary, she takes delight in it. No day in her life is quite complete without a problem that someone brings her to solve.

If one had to describe Mona in a word, it would be "champion." But in the Middle English sense, before the modern age turned its meaning inward, allowing a champion to seek glory alone. Mona has never met an underdog she didn't cheer for, never encountered a charity that didn't evoke her sympathy and, perhaps, inspire a gift. She has spent the vast bulk of her fifty-eight years—and most of her legal career—fighting for the little people, the forgotten ones, whether mesothelioma patients poisoned by asbestos, blue-collar retirees stiffed out of medical benefits, car buyers scammed by unscrupulous dealers, or victims of payday lending fraud. She is undaunted by corporate giants, with their multi-million-dollar legal gristmills and delay-and-deny strategies designed to drive plaintiffs and their lawyers into bankruptcy before they ever get to trial. The case that finally gave Mona her big break back in the 1990s, that paved the way for everything else, was against Duke Energy, one of the largest energy behemoths in the United States. Duke stalled for a decade, nearly rendering her insolvent. But she persisted tenaciously, keeping the lights on by working every case that came in the door, no matter how menial, and holding up the mirror of the law to the company's executives until, at last, weary of the siege, they acceded, and agreed to compensate their injured workers.

When Mona puts her mind to it, she can bend gravity—or make it look that way.

But her secret is not perseverance. That is consequence, not cause. It is drive, mojo, energy, restless and relentless. Those who know her best marvel at it. Her older daughter, Whitney, puts it memorably: "Mona has enough energy for all of us." She is not ageless. But the years have yet to slow her. After six decades of life, she still walks the earth as if it is mostly frictionless. That is one of the reasons why people are drawn to her, that and her kindness. Mona loves people, and people love her back.

Scrolling through her contact list of notable friends—the governors and senators and legal celebrities from coast to coast who know her by first name—it would be easy to imagine that Mona was born into a prominent family, surrounded by the accoutrements of wealth and power. Nothing could be further from the truth. She comes from the working-class side of the tracks, from the town of East Spencer, a mile past the Isenhour brickyards. Her father was a mechanic, a jack-of-all-trades, and her mother a polio survivor who struggled with the lingering effects of the disease. Although Mona and her two siblings—her older sister, Susie, and younger brother, Spencer—never lacked their basic needs, the world around them was defined by want. It was a hardscrabble world, where the color line was blurred by the proximity of poverty, where the houses were spartan and family incomes modest and unpredictable. It was not a place where a child was taught to expect much from life. Privilege was the inheritance of other people. If success was to be had, it had to be earned.

It was here, on these rough-and-tumble streets, in schoolhouses only recently desegregated, that Mona Lisa Lane—named by her mother after the Nat King Cole song that was playing on the hospital radio—saw the injustice of poverty and prejudice with the unsullied eyes of a child. It was here, also, that she learned how to fight. Not with her fists but with her mind. To be quick on the draw and always ready with a reply. In some ways, the genetic lottery was kind to her. She was born with her father's wit and winsomeness and her mother's good looks and empathy. She was gifted with a knack for leadership, and she exuded a genuineness that endeared her to people. She was strong. She was real. She was a person you could confide in, someone worthy of trust.

In an era fraught with racial tensions—and in a small southern town where men held the reins and women deferred—she ran for student body president of her integrated high school and won with support from Black and white peers alike. At the time, a young woman of her standing was not expected to attend college, let alone enter a profession like the law. Most stayed close to home, found a man, and settled down. But Mona wanted more. She wanted to see where the sun rose and where it set, to find her own place in the world. Not only was she admitted to the University of North Carolina at Chapel Hill, the state's flagship university, but she earned a National Merit Scholarship and graduated in three years, instead of four. She had aspirations to leave North Carolina, to study law and foreign affairs at Georgetown University. But Cupid intervened and kept her close to home.

The young man's name was Lee Wallace. But his birth certificate reads Leo Wallace III. Lee, unlike Mona, did grow up in a mansion—a chateauesque masterpiece modeled after the Biltmore House in the Asheville highlands. Lee's great-grandfather, Victor Wallace, was one of Salisbury's first merchants, and his grandfather and father, Leo I and Leo II, maintained the family business and expanded into real estate. Numerous buildings in downtown Salisbury still bear the Wallace name.

The man Mona met, however, was utterly unpretentious, and he remains that way to this day. It was the spring after her college graduation, and she was working behind the desk at the local Holiday Inn when she came across a young woman crying in the restroom. She listened to the woman's story and offered her consolation. It turned out that the young woman, who was in the middle of a divorce, was Lee's sister and the Holiday Inn was a Wallace property—one of the first Holiday Inns in the United States. When Lee learned of Mona's benevolence, he decided to meet her. The next evening, he asked her on a date. That was in May. By August, they were married. Instead of leaving North Carolina for law school, Mona went to Wake Forest University in nearby Winston-Salem. Lee went with her, but he always meant to come home.

Lee Wallace is the reason Mona planted herself in small-town Salisbury, despite a world that was wide open to her. He is the yin to her yang, the water to her fire. Along with her partner, Bill Graham, he is Mona's steadying hand and one of her closest advisors. He is also, quietly, her most reliable cheerleader. Even as Mona has gone to war with the titans of industry on behalf of the injured, the sick, and the loved ones of those taken too young, Lee has managed the Wallace enterprises with his brother, Victor, and together they have helped preserve the town.

✳

The rest of Mona's morning disappears in the usual flurry of calls, emails, and conversations. While she makes no bones about the firm's for-profit status, she and Bill run it like a family shop, balancing high-octane professionalism with a work environment built to encourage longevity. Outside of her family and Bill, Mona has never trusted anyone as much as she trusts John Hughes and Linda Wike. And Mona employs some of her family, too. Her daughter, Whitney, has an office close to hers, and Lee's nephew, Daniel Wallace, will take the space next door when he graduates from law school in a few months.

Around noon, Mona joins Linda in the dining room for lunch. They talk about the Taylor case and the working conditions at the Smithfield packing plant in Clinton.

At some point, Teresa, the receptionist, politely interrupts their musings. "Mona," she says, "I have Richard Middleton on the line for you. Would you like me to put him through?"

Mona trades a curious glance with Linda. Middleton is an old acquaintance from the trial bar. A Georgia boy from Savannah, he is a former president of ATLA—the Association of Trial Lawyers of America (now the American Association for Justice)—the nation's preeminent association of plaintiffs' attorneys. He is not a person whose call she would ignore.

"I'll take it in my office," she says. "The big one."

A few minutes later, she returns to the dining room, a new fire in her eyes. "You're never going to believe it," she says, answering Linda's unasked question. "He's got a new case. It's against Smithfield, of all people. But it's not about the slaughterhouse. It's about the hog farms."

Mona shares the story in soundbites. At the heart of the case is a place: hog country. In four counties alone—Duplin, Sampson, Bladen, and Pender—there are five million hogs and only two hundred thousand people, many of them poor and Black. All those hogs generate an unfathomable amount of waste, equivalent to a city twice the size of New York. Yet the method of waste disposal that Smithfield uses at all of its company-owned and contract hog farms—close to two thousand across the state—is as antiquated as an outhouse.

Back in the eighties and nineties, the company's hog-producing forebears dug holes in the ground the size of Olympic swimming pools and dumped billions of gallons of feces and urine into them. When the "lagoons" reached capacity, they hooked up pumps to giant spray guns and turned them on the surrounding fields, converting what once was forest and farmland into waste-deposit sites and trusting the soil to act as a sponge, absorbing the nitrogen, ammonia, and pathogens in the waste without allowing it to seep into the groundwater or the neighbors to suffer harm from the runoff.

It was a colossal exercise in magical thinking. Between lagoon spills and flooding from storms and hurricanes, the industry has despoiled waterways across eastern North Carolina and befouled the air and land in dozens of communities. Yet the corporate hog barons—Smithfield chief among them—have never been held to account. Rather, they have raked in profits by the billion.

"What's the claim?" Linda inquires.

"Nuisance," replies Mona.

She explains that environmental groups have taken the industry to task over the water pollution but have struggled to gain traction in the courts. Middleton represents some of the people who live around the hog farms. His goal is to enforce one of the oldest legal claims in the book— the right of a person to enjoy his home without unreasonable interference from his neighbors. Middleton and his trial partner, Charlie Speer, proved the concept in Missouri. They tried a number of cases to verdict and forced one of Smithfield's subsidiaries, Premium Standard Farms, to settle.

"Do they want us to be local counsel?" Linda asks.

Mona nods. The North Carolina bar requires attorneys who aren't licensed in the state to enroll a local partner, partly out of pride and partly to ensure that the out-of-state lawyers don't run roughshod over the ethics rules. It's a subordinate role in any trial team, a mere factotum in some, but Mona Wallace has never been anybody's functionary. Most of her marquee cases have originated inside the firm, and on those occasions when she has brought in trial counsel to run point in the courtroom, she has always seen the arrangement as a partnership. Nevertheless, she's intrigued. In her obsession with the hazards of hog waste at Smithfield's slaughterhouses, she never considered that there might be corollary effects on the production side, in the rural communities where the pigs are raised.

She calls a war council in the dining room, interrupting John Hughes in the middle of his wordsmithing and summoning Bill Graham on speakerphone. Before long, they reach a consensus. The case checks all the boxes of a Wallace & Graham litigation: It's substantial, it's worthy, and it's on the leading edge of law. A series of big nuisance verdicts against the world's largest hog producer could shift the balance of power between Big Agriculture and communities across the country. Moreover, the neighbors are precisely the sort of clients that Mona and Bill have always sought. Their individual claims are not valuable enough to support a multi-year pitched battle with a mega-corporation. But when combined with hundreds of other claims like them, they could fashion a broadsword formidable enough to make the giant blink. Additionally, if Smithfield's indifference to worker safety at its Clinton slaughterhouse is any indication of its corporate philosophy, it just might be the kind of malefactor that juries love to flay.

"Are we missing anything?" Mona asks with a sunniness that betrays her feelings.

"We should do our due diligence," John says. A former big-firm lawyer who nearly forfeited his soul defending the Smithfields of the world before Mona offered him a path to redemption, he is one of the strings that tethers Mona's kite to the earth. "Also, we need to make sure they understand that we're not a rubber stamp. They need to work with us at every step."

"I don't have any reservations," Bill chimes in, "assuming everything checks out."

Mona casts a glance at Linda. The paralegal's expression is Delphic, her hazel eyes impossible to read. In conferences with the lawyers, Linda prefers to stay in the background. But Mona trusts her instincts, the quality of her judgment. Linda delivers it with a subtle nod.

"Okay," Mona says. "I'll call him back."

CHAPTER 3

DOWN EAST

The pain of place is without end.
—*Myronn Hardy, "Jaguaripe"*

**Eastern
North Carolina
Spring and Summer
2013**

If you were to cut a slab of birch wood in the shape of North Carolina, hang it on your wall, and stare at it for an extended moment, preferably with your favorite drink in hand, you might see an old gnarled hog emerge. The long snout and the shelf-like forehead, the prominent hindquarters, the stumpy back legs, and the twisted tail. The only anatomical pieces missing are the pointy ears and forelegs. And North Carolina's "hog country," as it's called, is right where you would expect it: in the intestinal region of that vast derriere.

There are nine million hogs in the state, nearly one per person. If humanity suddenly went vegan, almost every North Carolinian could have a pig for a pet. All but a nominal fraction of those hogs are concentrated in the vast expanse of coastal plain east of Interstate 95. In Duplin County alone—where Elsie Herring and Woodell McGowan have spent most of their lives—there are nearly thirty-five hogs for every human being, a density higher than any other place on earth.

Yet this truth has remained largely hidden.

How many millions of sun worshipers make a pilgrimage to the Outer Banks every year, crowding the beaches and bars and plying the waters of the Pamlico and Albemarle Sounds? How many nature lovers hike the cloud-draped mountains around Asheville? How many busi-nesspeople frequent the Research Triangle? How many hoops fanatics descend upon the leafy college towns of Chapel Hill and Durham to watch the Tar Heels and Blue Devils play? North Carolina is famous for many things, but being home to the pork capital of the world is not one of them. Quite conveniently—for the tourist bureau, at least—the hog kingdom is tucked away in a rural region of the state invisible to outsid-ers and forgotten by most North Carolinians, except when they make the drive down Interstate 40 to the port of Wilmington.

Mona's team at Wallace & Graham is no exception. When the hog cases first come in the door, the only memory most of them can conjure of the countryside down east is the vague recollection of a spot some-where along I-40 where inside their cars their nostrils have curled up. A rumor starts circulating in the litigation department: Was it pig shit we were smelling? But a few memorial whiffs of hog odor—if it *was* hog odor—doesn't satisfy the skeptics, in particular, the firm's resident devil's advocate, John Hughes. For the professor's son, the law is about evidence. Emotion can multiply jury awards, but to justify the massive investment of cash and human capital necessary to bring a corporate Goliath to trial, you need cold, hard, provable facts.

In the days after Mona's call with Richard Middleton, John reads up on the victories that the Savannah lawyer and his partner from Kansas City, Charlie Speer, racked up in Missouri against Premium Standard Farms and its partner, ContiGroup—formerly Continental Grain. In more than a dozen nuisance suits, Middleton and Speer notched over $32 million in verdicts on behalf of some three hundred neighbors living in proximity to the hog farms, including an $11 million verdict in 2010. With the help of the U.S. Environmental Protection Agency (EPA) and the Missouri attorney general, they also negotiated a consent decree—a court-enforced settlement—that imposed tougher waste-management restrictions on the state's pork producers. But jury decisions are ines-capably local. A big plaintiffs' award in one state is a poor predictor of a comparable award in another state. And North Carolina has little in common with Missouri. Though Mona is nobody's skeptic, she shares this conviction with John: Due diligence—and the case development that follows—must be local, too.

For the litigation team at Wallace & Graham, this diligence takes a number of forms and involves a variety of people. All of it, however, is coordinated and choreographed by Mona, who watches over her brood like a mother eagle, even from afar. The first step is the most obvious—to introduce themselves to the clients. Mona appoints her daughter, Whitney, and another young attorney, Mark Doby, to handle the initial meet-and-greets down east.

Whitney—"Whit" to her friends—is a spark plug like her mom. Cheerful and energetic, she has the work ethic of a dynamo and is quick on the draw with an incandescent smile. She is also a classic first child: cautious, conscientious, and careful. After earning a sociology degree from UNC–Chapel Hill, she spread her wings and headed west to Texas, trying her hand at policy work in the state legislature. She wasn't sure how she wanted to spend her life, but she was certain of this: she loved helping people. She considered the possibility of social work, but the law beckoned like an old friend. Having spent her childhood watching her mother fight for the downtrodden, she knew that Mona's brand of lawyering was like social work with a sculptor's chisel. Along with delivering clients the justice they deserve, a great lawyer could reshape the world.

The law—and her family—brought Whit home.

Mark Doby, meanwhile, is the archetype of a Carolina boy. Half the things in his office are cornflower blue: the pennant celebrating the Tar Heels' seven championship basketball teams; the lineup of Coke cans imprinted with the UNC logo; the commemorative basketballs signed by Roy Williams and two of his teams; the Final Four ticket stubs and beer mugs; even a Magic 8 ball. If one were to open up his veins, I suspect they would carry a cerulean tint. Easygoing and affable, Mark is everybody's friend. And Whit's more than most. They and their spouses are tight, their kids close in age. Together, they make an ideal advance team. Whitney carries the standard of the Wallace name, and Mark, alone among the firm's lawyers, has an instinct for the world down east. His mother grew up on a tobacco farm on the edge of hog country, and his father served for five years as Duplin County's superintendent of schools.

The drive from Salisbury to Duplin feels twice as long as any timepiece would account for. It's two hours across the Piedmont to Raleigh, then another hour and a half through the working fields and forests of the coastal plain to the hamlets of Warsaw and Beulaville, Kenansville

and Wallace. To the uninitiated, the land past I-95 appears largely fea-
tureless, a never-ending mural of earth tones framed by blue sky and
cotton-boll clouds. The sprawling farms housing all those millions of
pigs are built back into the folds of the land, shrouded by the veils of
green that surround the countless creeks and tributaries in the Northeast
Cape Fear watershed.

The signs for Warsaw and Kenansville come first. Just off the interstate, the trees give way to a panorama of active agriculture. The horizons are not as spacious as they are in the American heartland. But the
scene is just as bucolic. Nothing is in a hurry here. The rat race never
arrived. The land doesn't greet the eye with spectacle or finery. It takes
time to see its beauty, like the goodness in a sturdy face, or the wisdom
behind wrinkled eyes.

The plaintiffs' communities are scattered across the landscape like
constellations in the night sky. One by one, Whit and Mark begin to
visit them. The homes are often humble, many of them trailers set on
roadside plots, though a few have sturdier construction. On the outside,
they appear faded, as if the years have brought only wear. The driveways
are dirt or ruts in the grass, and the cars are mostly dated. The place
feels lost in time, like a snapshot from the late seventies slump before the
boom of the eighties made so much of the country rich.

This impression remains with Whit and Mark until the neighbors
invite them inside. There, they witness a transformation. The living
areas, while functional, are well-loved and carefully tended. There are
comfortable sofas and chairs, mementos on bookshelves, and family
photos on walls and tables, together with pictures of Barack Obama.

Another detail catches the young lawyers' attention. There are can-
dles burning all around, and the air is redolent of spice and flowers. Yet it
is midday in summer, with the air conditioners in the windows running
at full tilt. It isn't until they hear the gentle spritzing sound of a door-
mounted air freshener and smell the bloom of artificial scent that they
begin to understand. The air outside can be unbearable. The neighbors'
only recourse is to deodorize the air indoors.

Most of the visits are quick, just a handshake and an update. Word
of the lawsuits has been spreading rapidly in the community, and quite
a few folks are eager to learn more. Whit and Mark walk them through
the basics, making no assurances about an outcome, but explaining the

nature of the claims. A few of the older plaintiffs, however, seem eager to talk, to share their lived experiences with these fresh-faced attorneys who have come such a long way to meet them. It is a credit to the neighbors' unhurried way of life. When they were growing up, people stopped by unannounced and stayed for hours. Company was a blessing, not an imposition.

It is in these simple living rooms, with bottles of water in hand and America's forty-fourth president watching over them, that Whit and Mark begin to learn the history of this place—the advent of the hog farm boom in the eighties; the sudden transformation of multigenerational tobacco farms into concentrated animal feeding operations, or CAFOs, with a thousand hogs in a single barn; the first time the tractor-trailers delivered the weaned pigs to the feeder farms, and then, a few months later, carted them away as 250-pound finished hogs; the giant guns that shoot liquified hog waste into the air, leaving it to drift like a cloud on the breeze; the greasy flies that grow fat as bees and swarm the neighbors' yards on bad days; the dead boxes overstuffed with hog carcasses, and the dead trucks that come at all hours of day and night to collect them; and the long-winged buzzards that flock to the rotting flesh, sometimes perching in the trees, sometimes atop the plaintiffs' homes, claws scratching on roof tiles, as they search for another meal.

Like students at freshman orientation, the young lawyers hear names that will soon become familiar to them. There is Don Webb, a larger-than-life hog farmer turned anti-CAFO crusader, who founded the Alliance for a Responsible Swine Industry, or ARSI. There is Rick Dove, an erstwhile military judge and now riverkeeper from the sailing community of New Bern, who plays Dr. Watson to Don Webb's Sherlock Holmes. There's Elsie Herring, the most outspoken of the neighbors, who has told everyone who would listen—reporters, politicians, lawyers, and filmmakers—about the animal pollution that she and her mother and brother have been forced to endure for decades. There is Steve Wing, a pioneering epidemiologist at UNC, who has been studying the health effects of hog waste exposure for fifteen years.

The neighbors, in their gentle way, tell Whitney and Mark about those health effects. They talk about the headaches and brain fog they have experienced, the way the pollution has burned their eyes and noses, troubled their breathing, and even triggered asthma and heart issues.

They tell stories about waking up at night feeling like they are asphyxiating, like the air has turned into poison in their lungs. They have seen guests in their homes vomit from the smell. And there have been times when they too have been overcome.

As time passes and the stories accumulate, the young lawyers learn the names of the organizations, as well, some of them local, some regional and national, that have stepped into the ring with the hog industry and demanded reform. Along with ARSI, they hear about REACH, a grassroots group founded by Devon Hall. They hear about the Concerned Citizens of Tillery, led by Gary Grant, and the North Carolina Environmental Justice Network, helmed by Naeema Muhammad. They hear about the Waterkeeper Alliance, a global association of citizen groups keeping watch over the world's waterways. They also learn about Boss Hog's royal family: Wendell Murphy, the local boy turned godfather of industrial swine; Lois Britt, his omnipresent right hand; and Don Butler, the pork industry's public face.

All the names and acronyms begin to swirl in their heads until Whitney and Mark feel faintly dizzy. The history here is like an underground cave system, and they've barely explored the entrance. But the stories confirm for them that the problems down east are neither invented nor overblown. The hog farms are right there beside the neighbors' homes, like alien ships descended from the sky. For plaintiffs like Elsie Herring, a sprayfield is only steps away from their front porch. For Violet Branch, it's just across the road. Woodell McGowan could lob a stone from his yard and hit the hog farmer's dead box. And Woodell's neighbors, Linnill and Georgia Farland, wake up every morning beside three thousand hogs and a cesspool of waste.

Along with the plaintiffs' stories, Whitney and Mark take home another impression from down east. The land is haunted by a vaguely ominous spirit. It's not just the gleaming roofs of the hog barns that hover over the fields around every country bend. It's the pockets of wealth that form a Kafkaesque contrast to the clients' modest neighborhoods. It's the Duplin airport with its enormous private hangars and the country club with its eighteen-hole golf course across the road. It's the strangely upscale Holiday Inn Express in Wallace, and the ostentatious Mad Boar Restaurant next door, with its pricey menu and the copper-and-granite sculpture of its namesake out front. And it's the manicured lawns,

imposing brick walls, and decorative wrought-iron gates of River Land-
ing, a residential golfing community that looks like a transplant from
Palm Beach. It turns out the Mad Boar is a pet project of Dell Murphy,
Wendell Murphy's son, and River Landing is the brainchild of Wendell's
brother, Pete. The fingerprints of the Murphy clan are everywhere in
Duplin County. It's like that scene in *It's a Wonderful Life,* when George
Bailey gets a glimpse of what the world would look like if Mr. Potter
owned everything.

It's like Duplin is Murphysville.

While Whitney and Mark are visiting clients in hog country, Mona is on
a due diligence mission of her own: to seek advice from the only lawyer
in North Carolina who has succeeded in bringing a hog farm nuisance
case to trial on behalf of a neighboring family. His name is Robert Morgan, and he is something of a folk hero among the state's trial bar.

From 1974 to 1980, he sat in the U.S. Senate.

Morgan is a kind of Mr. Smith figure in the annals of American
political history, a farm boy from rural Harnett County who ascended
to the highest deliberative body in the land with his conscience unsullied. During his tenure as attorney general of North Carolina, he became
known as a quintessential public servant, a man who had learned the
meaning of duty as a radio operator on an aircraft carrier in the Sea of
Japan. In the Senate, too, he held fast to his ideals, defying the partisans
who sought his fealty, including Jesse Helms, the senior senator from
North Carolina. It was his independence that ultimately cost Morgan
his reelection. He viewed U.S. control of the Panama Canal as a "vestige
of colonialism," and voted with President Carter to cede the canal to the
Panamanians. When Carter fell to Reagan in 1980, Morgan lost his seat
to a Helms-backed Republican. He came home to Lillington and revived
his law practice in a quaint 1930s-era residence on Front Street. Around
town, he is known as "the Senator," and beloved for his generosity and
humility. Despite his prominence, he is quick with a smile and a friendly
word. Those who know him best say he has never forgotten where he
came from. Robert Morgan is "the poor man's friend."

He greets Mona and Linda Wike in the entryway to his law office.

The first thing the ladies notice about Morgan is his stature. He is unusually diminutive. Yet what he lacks in physical presence, he makes up for in charm and studied poise. After introducing them to his long-time assistant, Jeannette, he shows them the way to his personal office, a tidy space filled with antiques and decorated with framed photographs of U.S. presidents and scenes from his life.

He motions the ladies toward a sitting area opposite his desk. "Jeannette says you're looking into the hog farm issue. I'm happy to help in any way I can."

"We'd like to hear about the *Parker* case," replies Mona solicitously.

The senator nods, a lopsided smile deepening his spiderweb of wrinkles. "It's been a while. Jeannette's memory is better than mine. I'll let her tell it."

Jeannette accepts the narrative baton as if she is accustomed to it, while the senator chimes in details. The tale they spin takes a familiar shape. The Parkers were a rural family in Johnston County that suffered for years on account of the hog farm next door. The stench they described was like a decaying bedsore, a smell so acrid that it stung their eyes and noses and adhered to their clothing. The rotten air had driven them inside, depriving them of the use of their yard and swimming pool. Their wounds were emotional, too. It was impossible not to see their sadness, their hurt. The senator took the case on a contingency fee because the law of nuisance is unambiguous, the equities were indisputable, and the Parkers were people of limited means. He struggled, however, with the question of who to sue. While the hog farmers, Terry and Rita Barefoot, owned the property along with its barns and waste lagoon, the pigs generating the waste weren't their own. They were raising the animals for one of the corporate integrators under contract. From a moral standpoint, Morgan blamed the integrator far more than he did the farmers. Yet the law of the matter suggested otherwise. In the end, he brought suit against the Barefoots and tried the case to verdict in the summer of 1996.

He knew the jury's decision would turn, in part, on expert testimony—whether he could prove scientifically that the odor was the cause of the Parkers' discomfort. At that time, however, the science of hog odor was rudimentary, like email at the dawn of the Internet. To bolster his case, he sought help from Dr. Susan Schiffman, a professor of medical psychology at Duke, who had been profiled in the *New York*

Times. When the senator first met Dr. Schiffman, she seemed delighted to assist. Her work was groundbreaking—and damning to the hog industry. One of her studies established that people living in the vicinity of industrial swine operations experienced more depression, anger, fatigue, and confusion, and less vigor, than others in their community. To the senator, the prospect of Schiffman's testimony was pure gold.

Until, without warning, it melted away in his hands.

Unbeknownst to Morgan, Dr. Schiffman was bound by invisible cords. She was serving on a state-sponsored odor task force advised, in part, by the hog barons, and she had agreed to conduct a new odor-related study with support from the industry. The conflicts of interest were a minefield in all directions. Morgan considered calling her as a witness anyway, if nothing else to establish the predicate of her prior work. But in the end, he foreswore the risks and tried to find someone to replace her. Unfortunately, Schiffman's study was *sui generis,* alone in the field. The senator tried the case without a scientist, and the jury came back for the hog farmer.

While the defeat was a disappointment, it wasn't a wipeout. The jurors were sympathetic. Had the judge not threatened to bring them back on Saturday if they failed to deliver their verdict on Friday, they might have found for the Parkers. But the experience of taking up arms against the hog industry left more than a mark on Senator Morgan. It left a mess of scars. And those scars are what really animate his tale. As if lifting his shirt to reveal the wound, he shares the truth with Mona and Linda. He doesn't mean to discourage them from taking the case—far from it. He's known about the industry's misdeeds since he sat in the attorney general's chair, and he's convinced that the only path to change leads through the courthouse. His intent is subtler, more personal. He wants them to count the cost before they file the first complaint.

The industry's success in tying up Dr. Schiffman, he explains, is emblematic of a broader bias in the state's academic community. North Carolina State University, the alma mater of pork kingpin Wendell Murphy, is a reliable industry ally, thanks to Murphy's munificence toward the school's endowment and athletics programs. In addition, Murphy is a looming shadow behind the boards of the state's other major universities. His daughter-in-law, Dell Murphy's wife, chairs the board of trustees at UNC Wilmington, and Lois Britt, the former vice president of

Murphy Family Farms, served for years on the UNC board of governors. If Mona and her team find another expert like Susan Schiffman, they need to realize that the hog barons will deploy every weapon in their arsenal to undermine him—or destroy his credibility.

"There's another thing you should know," Senator Morgan says, an ominous note creeping into his voice. "I gave everything I had to that case. I nearly lost my house over it. You need to understand that they won't relent. They'll fight as hard as anybody you've ever seen. I hope you take this case. I really do. The people down east have needed help for a long time. But be careful if you do. They'll bankrupt you in a heart-beat. They will show no mercy."

At this moment, sitting in Senator Morgan's office, neither Mona nor Linda appreciates who "they" are, not in any personal sense. But their education will come swiftly.

"They" are the heirs of the hog kings, the masters of Murphysville.

CHAPTER 4

FORTUNATE SONS

Get big or get out.
—*Earl Butz, U.S. Secretary of Agriculture, 1971–76*

Rose Hill, North Carolina, and Smithfield, Virginia 1938–2008

The American hog kingdom was built by the genius, ruthlessness, and blistering ambition of two men: Wendell H. Murphy and Joseph Luter III. They were visionaries, blessed with the gift of far sight. As public personalities, they were larger than life, near caricatures of the self-made man. In their vigor, their machismo, their boundless Ur-male energy, they were Rooseveltian. In their zeal to expand their dominion and hold it against all rivals and regulators, they recalled the Gilded Age industrialists—the Carnegies, Rockefellers, and Vanderbilts. They walked through the world as if they were born to rule it, and rule it they did, each for a time wearing the curlicued crown of hog king, the largest producer of porcine stock on the face of Planet Earth.

But the throne was not theirs by birthright. They were commoners, small-town boys, their origins as meek as their aspirations were lofty.

Wendell Murphy was the first to come squalling into the world. Born in 1938, in the calm that preceded the conflagration of the Second World War, he came of age in the rural community of Rose Hill, North Carolina, a few miles up the road from Beulah Herring's home. All the men in his life were tobacco-stained, their labor valued and vouchsafed by the regnant crop of the Old South. Murphy was born on his grandfather's farm, and many of his formative memories hail from that place—the bed he slept in until the first grade, despite the fact that by then his parents had a place of their own down the road; driving the mules that pulled the tobacco sleds at harvesttime; managing the laborers and the curing process after his father took a job at the local tobacco warehouse. He was shaped by the land and its rhythms, tutored in the old ways of tilling and planting and tending, all while praying for a bountiful yield. The hardiness he acquired from his father and grandfather, these rough-hewn men of the soil who had survived wars and pandemics and the Great Depression, would define the rest of his life. But their satisfaction with the simple things, their contentment with the known world, their disinterest in rising any higher than their neighbors, felt to young Murphy like a straitjacket.

The known world was not enough.

For Albert Einstein, it was a flash of insight into the limits of the laws of motion that sent him from patent office obscurity to the pinnacle of the scientific pantheon. For Wendell Murphy, the country boy with outsized dreams, it was a feed mill. "I thought my skull was going to burst open," he recounted many years later. "I've never had a feeling like that before or since." The idea was startlingly simple: If the denizens of Rose Hill wanted to process their own corn into feed for their livestock, they had to get it milled in a neighboring town. Wendell envisioned a plug for the hole, a mill in Rose Hill that would save people time and fuel. Every way he looked at the venture, he saw the promise of profit. But he was a high school teacher and his wife an office clerk. They didn't have $10,000 to purchase the equipment. The banks offered to loan him the money, but they wanted security—a mortgage on the Murphy farm. His father balked. He had seen bankers turn into raiders during the Depression. Debt wasn't a benefit. It was misery in waiting. But plucky Wendell didn't concede. He dickered with the bankers until they dropped the farm lien and pestered his father to cosign the note. At last, his father acquiesced.

The feed mill thrived, vastly exceeding expectations. Over time, Murphy would expand it into the largest mill of its kind in the world, nicknamed "The Chief." But the feed mill was only a waypoint on Wendell Murphy's path to glory. It enabled him to invest in a second business—hogs. He kept them in pens on the ground, like generations before him. But instead of buying feed, he fed them from his own mill. It was an early nod to vertical integration, an innovation that would build him a rocket ship to the stars and, decades later, bring it crashing down, thanks to one man.

Joseph Luter III.

※

Luter made his natal entrance a year after Wendell Murphy, in 1939. He was born in the colonial-era village of Smithfield, Virginia, on the banks of the Pagan River, a few crow miles from Hampton Roads. As in Murphy's family, Luter's father, Joseph Luter II, and grandfather, Joseph Luter I, were in business together. But their product wasn't tobacco. It was hogs. In a way, they were destined to it. Since revolutionary times, the town of Smithfield had been famous for its hams. But the Luter men weren't artisanal curers. They were in the rendering trade, the business of blades, blood, and bones. After serving the meatpacker P. D. Gwaltney in various capacities—the elder Luter as a salesman and his son in management—they struck out on their own, founding Luter Packing, which would later become Smithfield Packing, the progenitor of Smithfield Foods.

The youngest Joe Luter spent his summers and holidays working at the family's plant across the river from town. He mastered jobs on the kill floor, the sliced-bacon room, the pig pen, and the loading area. "It was tough, hard work—dirty work," he recounted later. Luter was industrious and diligent, like his father and grandfather. But his ambitions far exceeded theirs. When his father died of a heart attack in 1962, Joe Luter III was about to graduate from Wake Forest. He returned to Smithfield, cobbled together loans from every creditor who would lend to him, and bought 8.5 percent of the company's stock. Together with his father's 42 percent, that gave him a controlling stake. His eyes were on the corner office, but he had the good sense not to claim it right away. He spent four years in sales, learning the business, before installing himself in the president's chair.

He was twenty-six years old.

Despite being callow, arrogant, and untested in the burdens of leadership, Luter found that he had an instinct for command. In a mere three years, he drove the slaughterhouse's throughput from 3,000 hogs a day to 5,000 and nearly doubled the number of the company's employees. In 1969, he received a buyout query from a venture capital firm, backed by a New York investment bank. Smithfield wasn't for sale, he said, but they persisted, telling him to name his price. He said $20 million—three times the company's book value and over twenty times its earnings. He never expected them to pay it. But they surprised him, taking the offer and the helm—and firing him six months later.

Before long, they would drive the company into a shallow grave.

The last year of the sixties was a pivotal one for Wendell Murphy, too. His herd of mud-raised pigs, fattened by feed from his own mill, had swelled in size. As with all livestock, however, the bigger the herd, the higher the likelihood of disease. It was a cholera epidemic that laid waste to his hogs. By order of the U.S. Department of Agriculture (USDA), he had to submit his entire herd to euthanasia and quarantine the dirt. The forced eradication might have felled a lesser businessman, but Murphy saw opportunity in the pattern of misfortune. While his own pens might be fallow, he still had the feed mill. Why not pay farmers with uncontaminated land to raise his hogs using his feed? The poultry industry, led by Tyson Foods, had been outsourcing production to contract farmers since the 1950s. Why couldn't that arrangement be translated into pork? Ever the optimist, Murphy drew up the papers, set the price he would pay, and sought out a few acquaintances to join the experiment.

The day the first Duplin County farmer became a Wendell Murphy grower was the day the modern hog industry was born. The growing agreement radically reshaped the allocation of risk in a commodity market that had always been supplied by independent producers. In the world before, the most successful farms had managed the risk of volatile market prices by diversifying their herds and crops. But not every farmer had the resources or wisdom to create the ideal mix, and some were just unlucky. Wendell's growing contract eliminated the price risk from the equation. His hogs came with the feed and a gold-plated guarantee: $1 per pig, regardless of the going rate at the slaughterhouse. A farmer with room on his land to raise 1,000 Murphy hogs could make $3,000 a year ($20,000 in today's dollars), assuming a four-month turnover, and not lose a dime if the retail market tanked. For a lot of folks in Duplin County, it sounded like a sweetheart deal.

The tobacco market was in the midst of a long, slow decline, and many small farmers were desperate for a way to keep their land viable in a world of rising industrialization and consolidation. Earl Butz, the foul-mouthed vulgarian that Richard Nixon installed atop the USDA in 1971, had delivered the ag world a new creed: "Get big, or get out." Many farmers had neither the means nor the instinct to super-size their operations. But they could join forces with Wendell Murphy, especially if the terms were good. And what better than a risk-free guarantee?

Word about Murphy's contract spread like a brushfire across the coastal plain. Before long, he had so many takers that he had to import feeder pigs from other states and develop a new kind of barn to hold them, one with climate control and a waste disposal system. The CAFOs he deployed in every new Murphy contract farm were both revolutionary and rudimentary. With heaters for the cold months and ventilation for the summer heat, the barns could operate year-round. Managing the waste, however, was a Herculean challenge. The average hog produces between three and ten times the feces and urine of a human being. Yet where we humans use complex chemistry and treatment facilities to process our waste and recycle the water, Murphy wanted to minimize his expenses. So he reached back into bygone times and revived an ancient technology: the cesspool.

When the hogs do their business in their confinement pens, the waste falls through slatted floors into collecting pits beneath the barn. The contents of those pits are then flushed into massive, clay-lined cesspools, euphemistically called "lagoons," that are open to the air. Diluted by rainwater, the waste settles into sedimentary layers and decomposes through a natural process called anaerobic digestion. Lagoons, however, are only so big, and thousands of hogs penned together generate the feces and urine of a small municipality. Without some means of disposing of that waste, the lagoons would overflow. To complete the system, Murphy's scientists connected the lagoons to pumps and spray guns that deposited the liquid on the grower's fields. Since animal waste is a natural fertilizer and productive land is often nutrient-depleted, it was an elegant solution—at least, it seemed that way at the time. Murphy and his burgeoning team of growers ran with it, and the state regulators signed off on it. In eastern North Carolina, agriculture is a way of life. If Murphy could keep it going, everyone from the statehouse to the local store clerks would hail him as a hero.

In such heady times, with so much in flux and the stakes so high, no one stopped to inquire what the neighbors of these new contract farms felt about the changing face of the landscape. Most of the neighbors were poor and Black, the children of sharecroppers with limited education and only modest sophistication. It was all too easy for Murphy and his crowd of fawning admirers to ignore them.

And ignore them Murphy did. For decades, and with virtual impunity.

*

While Wendell Murphy was busy reimagining the business of pork, newly minted rich kid Joe Luter was quite happy to wash his hands of it. He spent the early seventies sowing his wild oats as a ski bum and real estate developer at Bryce Mountain, a four-season resort in northwest Virginia. Again, he performed like Midas, converting residential lots into cash at a brisk pace. He treated Smithfield Packing like it was another life, until word reached him that the family business was on the brink of collapse. Accused of falsifying earnings reports by the Securities and Exchange Commission (SEC), the finance geeks at the company's helm had watched Smithfield's share price plummet and then cannibalized its divisions in a futile attempt to stanch the bleeding.

Luter made his triumphal reentry in 1975. "They lost money in December, which is like a beer company losing money in July," he told the *Richmond Times-Dispatch,* explaining his decision to return. "Once I heard that, I knew that unless they had a management change, the company would not survive." By the end of the decade, he would add another feather to his cap: turnaround magician. When the board and principal creditor installed him as president for the second time, Smithfield was dead in the water, hull down and listing. Luter threw everything overboard that wasn't riveted to the deck, gave every employee still on the payroll a bucket, and kept them bailing until the last bulkhead was dry. Then he sprinkled some of his pixie dust and went on a buying spree.

He acquired packing plants in Norfolk, Virginia, and Kinston, North Carolina, and in 1981 he bought out his longtime rival, P. D. Gwaltney. The Gwaltney merger secured Smithfield's status as the kingpin of East Coast meatpacking. But hard-charging Luter wasn't satisfied. He saw a bargain in Milwaukee—an underutilized plant with expansive capacity—and snapped it up for pennies on the dollar, then repeated the strategy in Baltimore. Unlike Murphy, whose innovations transformed the historical structure of hog farming, Luter took the packing world like an apex predator, devouring his competitors and absorbing their market share, until no one was left to challenge him. As his star rose, he developed a taste for the finer things, marrying a Washington, D.C., socialite and interior designer (his second marriage), filling his garage with flashy cars, and buying a yacht and a posh apartment in New York.

During the eighties boom, the world of pork was wide enough for both Murphy and Luter. Indeed, their ambitions were symbiotic. While Murphy was multiplying his growers from North Carolina to Utah, Luter was ramping up his slaughter capacity. Luter needed Murphy's hogs to keep his plants humming and his grocery customers supplied, and Murphy needed Luter to buy his hogs and finance his expansion. But this synergy, like a radioactive isotope, was inherently unstable. The two men, driven by an insatiable hunger to exceed the limits of the world laid down by their small-minded fathers, were bound to collide. It was the brute force of market economics that set them on that course.

In the mid to late eighties, Wendell Murphy had an epiphany. The more growers to whom he gave his gold-plated guarantee, the more he widened the risk profile of Murphy Family Farms. To some extent, this was acceptable. He had the margin to weather a downturn. But there was a way to reduce that exposure dramatically and drive profit at the same time: He needed a slaughterhouse of his own. It was the logical extension of the insight that had fueled his early production: to feed his hogs from his own mill. If he could acquire the last piece of the supply chain—a packing plant—he could insulate himself against market fluctuations and get better terms for his finished hogs.

In 1989, Murphy went to Luter and floated the idea of a merger. Luter, who already had a production deal in place with Murphy and his three main competitors (Carroll's, Prestage, and Goldsboro—together known as "The Circle"), was open to a more formal union. But Murphy balked when his financial advisors laid out the tax ramifications of a deal. Instead, in 1991, he took a seat on Smithfield's board, following the old adage about keeping your enemies close.

The nineties were a decade of breathtaking success for both men. By late 1997, Murphy was the unqualified champion of pork production, the "Ray Kroc of Pigsties," according to *Forbes*. He had 275,000 birthing sows, double the capacity of the runner-up, and 6 million hogs across his supply chain, from farrow (birth) to finish (slaughter). *Forbes* calculated Murphy's stake at a hefty $1 billion. As for Luter, in 1991, he broke ground on the world's largest slaughterhouse, a 973,000-square-foot facility in Tar Heel, North Carolina, that could process 32,000 hogs a day. That investment made Luter the equal of Murphy on the packing side. The détente between them lasted until 1998, when the bottom fell out of the hog market. It was then that Wendell Murphy found himself exposed to a storm he could not weather.

It was then that Joe Luter got the upper hand.

※

The crash of 1998 was less a consequence of ordinary market volatility than bad government policy mixed with a dash of financial contagion from overseas. It is an irony—uniquely American—that farmers are a reliably conservative voting bloc, yet they benefit from one of the most socialized of all welfare systems: the farm subsidy program. As Christopher Leonard explains in *The Meat Racket,* "By 1994, taxpayers were spending $7.9 billion every year in direct payment to farmers. The money kept the price of food low and helped big farms prosper regardless of market prices for their crops." Those direct payments were not guaranteed, but rather based on farmers' agreement not to produce more than the amount of wheat, corn, and soybeans set by the USDA.

As un-American as this may seem, USDA control was rooted in common sense. Unstable commodity prices had beggared countless farmers during the 1930s. By setting production caps, the government eliminated the central danger of falling market prices—that farmers will produce more of their crops to make up their own shortfall in income. The peril is self-evident. A spike in supply without a matching increase in demand further depresses prices, which leads to yet more overproduction—a vicious cycle. The only way to maintain the balance is to pay farmers *not* to overproduce. Ergo, the farm subsidy system.

When Newt Gingrich and his Republican revolutionaries swept Congress in 1994, they vowed to put an end to this relic of New Deal agriculture. But the Big Ag lobby—and perhaps their own consciences—wouldn't allow them to eviscerate the emergency farm bailout measures that had formed the heart of FDR's reforms. When they tossed out the direct subsidies, they replaced them with a new emergency bailout program. Enacted in 1996, the Freedom to Farm Act created a novel system of "disaster" payments for farmers impacted by unforeseen events.

What the drafters of the bill didn't appreciate, however, is that every year presents a hardship for some corner of the farming community. If it isn't raining too much, it's raining too little. There are locusts and blights and soil issues. There are macroeconomic and geopolitical forces, too: wars and trade deals and Chinese Five-Year Plans. It's a complex and dangerous world, and most farmers aren't sophisticated—or lucky—enough to see their way through the bramble year in and year out. So what did the farmers do when Congress scrapped the old subsidy system? They filed for disaster payments. And the taxpayers bailed them out.

For politicians hell-bent on cutting government waste, Freedom to Farm was an unqualified failure. It cost the government more than the ancien régime—$12.4 billion in 1998 and $21.5 billion in 1999. But that wasn't its worst feature. In withdrawing the direct subsidies, Congress also removed the production caps, leaving farmers to grow as much wheat, corn, and soybeans as they could. With the USDA out of the picture, farmers started overproducing on a scale that the country had not seen in decades. As a result, commodity prices cratered.

This might have been a windfall for hog producers like Wendell Murphy, who had seen the price per hog soar in 1996 and 1997 and had set aggressive production targets for 1998. But then the Asian financial crisis hit, drying up demand in the world's largest pork-consuming region and causing a domino effect across the United States, shuttering a number of packing plants. Suddenly, Murphy and his fellow producers had more hogs to sell than meatpackers who wanted to buy them. Hog prices fell through the floor, right alongside the feed staples. And Wendell Murphy started hemorrhaging cash—more than $1 million a week.

"It was bad," he said in an interview years later. "We lost a lot of money in 1998 and 1999. We were producing more animals than there was slaughter capacity. It's kind of like filling a cup. You put drop in, drop in, drop in, and when you reach the top all of a sudden it runs over." It was the first time Murphy had ever seen the slaughterhouses run out of capacity. It confirmed his instinct a decade ago that the future of the hog business was a marriage between producers and meatpackers, a single, vertically integrated entity that could transcend the vagaries of the market. But by then it was too late for him.

His days as hog king were done.

In 1999, Joe Luter bought Murphy Family Farms and turned it into a new hog production division of Smithfield Foods, Murphy-Brown LLC. (Given the popularity of the TV character with the same name, the marketing folks thought the moniker was cute.) Like the union of the Median and Persian empires, the Murphy-Smithfield merger was Joe Luter's ultimate victory. But it was not his only victory that year. He also bought out Carroll's Foods, the world's second-largest producer, giving him the next best thing to a total hog monopoly—the undisputed throne. On the cover of his 1999 annual report to shareholders, Luter crowed, "We are proud to report that Smithfield Foods is now the largest hog producer and processor in the world."

For the next seven years, until he retired from the corner office in 2006, Joe Luter reigned as king of the hog kings. The multibillion-dollar company he built is still headquartered in Smithfield, Virginia, on the banks of the Pagan River, a short walk from his childhood home. If his father were still alive, he would scarcely believe the heights his son achieved. On its face, Luter's life is an extraordinary American success story, as is Wendell Murphy's.

But their hegemony came at a cost. As magnanimous as they were to their friends, they were just as ruthless toward their enemies. They consolidated power wherever they could find it—in the business world, in the universities, and in politics. They ruled with an iron fist, in the manner of the Caesars, and rarely, if ever, admitted error. Luter fought a decade-long war against the unions to prevent the workers at his Tar Heel slaughterhouse from organizing, and Murphy won himself a seat in the North Carolina legislature and leveraged the perquisites of public office to rig the regulatory system in favor of Big Ag and to tie the hands of his critics. The hog kingdom they built, at first separately and then together, retains this authoritarian character.

It is the fountainhead of power in eastern North Carolina.

Those who dare to question it reap the whirlwind.

CHAPTER 5

DARK ARTS

The supreme art of war is to subdue the enemy
without fighting.
—*Sun Tzu*

**Salisbury
and Raleigh,
North Carolina
Summer 2013**
The words—and warning—of the old barris-
ter Robert Morgan linger with Mona Wallace
long after she and Linda Wike leave Lillington. His empathy for the plight of the neighbors resonates in her like a struck chord, as
does the gravity of his choice to defend them,
and the perils he endured on account of it. The stories that her daughter,
Whitney, and Mark Doby have been telling her of the people down east
turn her stomach and kindle in her a contemplative rage.

Memories of when her children were young come back to her at
random moments: their laughter and play beneath pristine skies, the
scents of meadows and forest around their house, the song of the birds
in the trees. She imagines how different their childhood would have
been if a hog farmer had been spraying waste on the other side of the
fence. The people who have asked for her help in Duplin and its envi-
rons, these mothers and fathers, grandparents and children, deserve
clean air no less than Whitney and her sister, Lane. Yet the hog barons
have snatched it from them, befouling their heritage to make themselves
billionaires.

It is this structural injustice—the boot of the strong on the neck
of the disenfranchised—that has inspired Mona's passion for the law

since the beginning. She will never forget the way one of the Salisbury mothers spoke about her when she was a young girl in the Order of the Eastern Star, the way the woman's elitist attitude made her feel, like a poor urchin from East Spencer, a wretch born on the wrong side of the tracks. She has no doubt that Senator Morgan is right, that this case will demand much of her, that it might, in fact, take her to the edge of herself. But she is unafraid of the corporate titans. She has taken them on before and won.

Armed with this conviction, she plots her opening moves, even as her team works against the clock, conscious of the statute of limitations and the three-year time limit it imposes on filing private nuisance claims. Since the nuisance in this case is ongoing, not a single incident fixed in history, there is no drop-dead date, no prospect of a dismissal for filing late. But the sooner they stop the clock, the further they can look back into the past in telling the story of the harm.

In contrast to many toxic tort cases—chemical dumping cases, for instance, or oil spills—Mona can't file this as a class action with a hand-picked group of lead plaintiffs to represent the rest. The circumstances of each community are sufficiently distinct that a jury award in favor of one would not justify an award in favor of another, let alone for everyone together. If this lawsuit is to be prosecuted, it has to be brought as a mass action, in which an array of cases, each with its own client-specific allegations, is launched like buckshot toward a single target.

The first step in organizing a mass action is to identify the building blocks—the plaintiff groups that offer an ideal mixture of logistical efficiency and recovery potential. Toward that end, Mona tasks a whip-smart young lawyer named Aaron Goss, who is also a computer whiz, with the job of assembling a digital map of every neighborhood and hog farm in their client roster. The result is at once a visual feast and an information goldmine—an interactive mélange of imagery from Google Maps overlaid with searchable data from the firm's client database and the state's master registry of industrial hog operations.

Once Mona and her team have a God's-eye view of the landscape, they observe things that were invisible to them on the ground. They see just how close the industry has positioned its waste lagoons and sprayfields to the waterways that are the ecological lifeblood of the coastal plain. They are also able to calculate the distance between the plaintiffs' homes and the hog farms. With these measurements in hand, the lawsuits take on a logic of their own.

If the mass action is a locomotive and each case is a wheel on the drive shaft, then the hub of each wheel is the hog operation and the spokes are the plaintiffs living within a mile and a half of that operation—the odor-affected zone established by the UNC epidemiologist, Steve Wing, in a classic study on the link between hog waste and human disease. To qualify as a named plaintiff in the suits, a person must not only own or rent a home within this radius, she must be able to articulate a credible complaint, corroborated by others in the vicinity.

While some attorneys prefer a spaghetti approach to mass torts, trusting the discovery process to reveal the likeliest claims, Mona Wallace is fastidious about doing her homework. She won't approve a pleading unless every plaintiff has been vetted. Along with Whitney and Mark Doby, she sends additional lawyers and staff down east to collect facts and nail down histories, to solicit documents from the local Soil & Water office, and to pull land records from the register of deeds. Among them is Rene Davis, a no-nonsense army vet and longtime paralegal who has assisted on many of Mona's headline cases. As a Black woman, Rene is especially sensitive to the injustice at the core of the case. She documents the neighbors' mistreatment with care, as does the rest of the team. Nothing goes out the door bearing the signature of Mona Lisa Wallace unless every allegation is supported by evidence. It is not just the ethics rules that inspire Mona's perfectionism; it is the memory of her mother, who died when she was in law school. If there is an angel on Mona's shoulder, it is Betty Everhardt Lane.

While the lawyers at Wallace & Graham are busy narrowing the field of plaintiffs and preparing the complaints in the case—twenty-six communities will eventually make the cut—there are other individuals, unbeknownst to them, who are plotting in secret to derail the mass action locomotive before it arrives at the courthouse.

The saboteurs are legislators in the state General Assembly, corn-fed men from down east who have made defending "the agricultural way of life" their raison d'être in Raleigh. Some of them are farmers themselves, their livelihoods dependent on keeping the fetters off Big Ag, in both pork and poultry. Others are merely sympathizers wishing to please the people who cast ballots in their districts. In the gaggle of conspirators, two men emerge as ringleaders:

Brent Jackson in the Senate and Jimmy Dixon in the House.

Jackson is a living caricature of a small-town official, an alderman or court clerk, who has managed, through grit and patience and an over-fertilized ego, to climb higher than his station and claim a fatter prize. A fruit-and-vegetable farmer turned food broker, he presents as the kind of civic-minded man of the land that Tocqueville hailed in *Democracy in America*. He has worn enough board hats to outfit an exhibit at the National Hat Museum. And now, as a fiercely conservative state senator representing the top pork-producing counties in the United States, he is an exponent of the "government is not the solution, it's the problem" brand of Republicanism, except when it comes to shielding Big Ag from having to pay the piper for its polluting ways. In that case the government is Davy Crockett, defender of the Alamo.

Dixon, by contrast, is nobody's idea of a village statesman, except perhaps Jimmy Dixon's. Soft and jowly, with a ham-hock complexion, a snow-capped pate, and a stare that says mean, Dixon is a rabble-rouser and political roustabout, a man of the people only when the people are his. Like Jackson, he is a farmer by occupation, but his trade is livestock—hogs and turkeys. He is a right-winger in the mold of Jesse Helms, the legendary conservative battle-ax who represented North Carolina in the U.S. Senate for thirty years. Yet he has the practiced mien of a populist, a man who trades in hoary aphorisms and treats politics like the football he played when he was young, where winners are crowned with glory and losers walk away to jeers.

In a peculiar quirk of fate, Jackson takes up the hog farmers' banner in the legislature the same week that Richard Middleton invites Mona to join the neighbors' cause. In fact, it is the specter of Middleton's multi-million-dollar courtroom victories in Missouri and the settlement he and Charlie Speer exacted from Smithfield that animates the industry and its besuited bedfellows in the state capital to act, and act swiftly. In their minds, it is anathema to the American way that the law would permit a jury to declare a hog farm a nuisance. Hog farms put bacon on our plates. They give us the smell of breakfast. Thus, the law must be wrong.

So they decide to change it, to dig a moat around the pork industry to keep out the marauding lawyers.

This particular moat is called the Right to Farm Act.

Like Wendell Murphy's CAFOs, the first Right to Farm laws were born in the 1970s, when the Big Ag revolution bumped up against rapidly expanding suburban communities where former urbanites were snatching up land and building homes. This collision between city and country values set the stage for a battle royale over land use that continues to this day.

On the face of it, the Right to Farm laws were designed to protect family farmers from the machinations of city slickers who didn't like the sounds and smells of the barnyard invading their shiny new subdivisions. The backbone of Right to Farm was a concept called "coming to the nuisance." First in time was first in right. If the farm was already there when a person bought property, no judge would hear a complaint. But the city slickers didn't relent, and, eventually, the courts intervened. In 1994, the North Carolina Court of Appeals carved out an exception with the potential to upend the rural order. It held that a neighbor could sue a farmer if the nuisance arose from a "fundamental change" to the farm that came after the neighbor's arrival. In other words, if a farm went industrial, or decided to grow hogs instead of turkeys, it could be held liable for disturbing the neighbors.

For nearly two decades, this ruling was more a rumor of danger than an imminent threat to North Carolina agribusiness. That is because hog country is almost exclusively rural. There have never been any cities or suburbs between Interstate 95 and Wilmington. Moreover, the folks living near Wendell Murphy's ever-expanding army of contract growers were mostly low-income people of color. When a few of the more enterprising among them went in search of local lawyers to plead their case, the lawyers turned them away, afraid of being hog-tied and marched out of town. Robert Morgan was the solitary exception, and he came within an inch of ruin.

Then came the Missouri litigation, the jury verdicts, and Smithfield's decision to settle. All of a sudden, the rumor of danger had a face. The prospect of Richard Middleton and Charlie Speer setting up shop in Duplin drove the Pork Council into a tizzy. It was the Pork Council and their friends at the North Carolina Farm Bureau who drafted the Right to Farm amendment that Brent Jackson introduced in the state senate in the last week of March 2013.

※

Word of the industry's plot takes a few weeks to reach Mona in Salisbury. That is partly because Jackson's bill gets ambushed in committee, allowing Jimmy Dixon and his groupies in the House to make the effort their own. In May, Mona is blindsided by House Bill 614. While the bill wouldn't impose an outright ban on nuisance claims, Dixon's version of Right to Farm would establish a presumption that a farming operation *is not* a nuisance, so long as the grower is using standard practices and is in compliance with his permit. This is a monumental departure from precedent. In the past, and under the common law, a farmer was obligated to honor his neighbor's property rights like any other person. This latest bill, however, would explicitly permit the "everybody else is doing it" excuse.

In her thirty years of lawyering, Mona has never seen elected officials take such breathtaking measures to insulate a private industry from exposure in the courts. To her relief, the worst parts of the bill don't survive the gristmill of committee review. But Jackson and Dixon don't relent. Instead, they seek to narrow the pool of possible claimants so that only the longest-standing residents of hog country can file a nuisance claim, those who held title to their land before the hog farms sprouted up at every point of the compass.

People like Elsie Herring, Woodell McGowan, and Joyce Messick.

With the Right to Farm bill sure to pass, Mona focuses her team's attention on finalizing the twenty-six complaints. Like Robert Morgan, she isn't a fan of suing the growers. In truth, she feels sorry for them. They didn't invent the system. Many of them signed on just to keep their farms. The men whose idea it was to dig the cesspools and spray shit into the air around people's homes—the men who built the multibillion-dollar behemoth behind the curtain—they are the ones who should pay. But Morgan's approach has support in the law. It also has the benefit of precedent. Middleton and Speer included the growers as defendants in Missouri. For technical reasons, Mona agrees to use that framework in North Carolina.

She files the first court paperwork in July—a request for pre-suit mediation. Smithfield, however, has no interest in negotiation. According to its lawyers at McGuireWoods, the thousand-attorney global law firm, the hog giant is ready for war.

As soon as Mona sees Smithfield's waiver, she releases her first salvo of complaints. They land in the clerk's office at the Wake County Circuit Court in Raleigh on July 30, twelve days after the Right to Farm bill is signed into law. But their real impact is felt down east in hog country. There, the pleadings read like an indictment of the world itself.

Nearly six hundred neighbors of fifty-nine hog farms across the coastal plain are alleging that Smithfield's hog operations are a menace to their way of life. The neighbors allege that the spray has harmed their breathing, that the heavy truck traffic has woken them up at night, that the hog odor has driven them off the land they love and into the shelter of their homes. Even there, they have to freshen the air to ward off the stench. Instead of holding cookouts and birthday parties and family gatherings like they did when they were young, they have been forced to endure pestilential flies and buzzards. The story they tell has echoes of a biblical plague. And in their prayer for relief, they demand more than recompense. They demand change.

In the face of such condemnation, the hog barons bare their knuckles and hit back hard—not in the courts, but in the public square. On August 4, 2013, the *Sampson Independent* runs a story about the lawsuits and quotes Don Butler, the director of government relations and public affairs at Murphy-Brown. After delivering the usual nostrums about the company's "unwavering commitment to environmental stewardship," Butler paints a grim picture of the economic harm that would result if the industry pulled its billions out of eastern North Carolina. He makes no mention of the communal harm that his company perpetrated to make those billions, or the baleful stories told by the folks who have had to live beside its factory farms.

Three weeks later, the hog industry holds its first summit on the lawsuits at the Agri-Expo Center in Sampson County. Something like two hundred farmers, community members, politicians, and passersby answer the summons. The mood in the auditorium is restive, and the speakers make no attempt to assuage that agitation. Jimmy Dixon is there, wearing a "Don't fuck with me" look. Brent Jackson is with him, sporting a ribbon-cutting grin. Other state politicos are there, too, along with honchos from Smithfield like Don Butler.

Ronnie Jackson, the owner of a tractor supply store and president of the Sampson County Friends of Agriculture, lays out the stakes for the crowd. "I don't need to remind you that the counties of Sampson and Duplin put together—farm income in those counties is close to two billion dollars a year. That's one billion each. Over sixty percent of that income is hogs, and it's a huge thing here." Surveying the faces before him, Jackson makes the nuisance suits personal. "It's not really an attack on Smithfield Foods; it's not really an attack on Murphy-Brown. It's an attack on our whole way of life. You may sell shoes down the street, or you may sell insurance, or you may sell cars. But whatever you do, you have a stake in the hog business."

Like an aria on the lips of Pavarotti, this is sweet music to Don Butler's ears. Jackson has taken the bull's-eye that Mona Wallace and her compatriots have painted on Smithfield's logo and shifted it by a rhetorical sleight-of-hand to the Sampson County Expo Center and all of the good folks sitting in the chairs. A lawsuit against the company is an attack on the community, Jackson is saying. What looks like a piece of laser-guided ordnance is really a carpet bomb.

When Butler takes the stage, he speaks in the voice of a wizened elder, as if reminding the rabble of the king's benevolence. He holds forth about Smithfield's adherence to global standards of environmental management, about new technologies the company has implemented in the past decade, and the internal compliance system that takes every complaint from the community seriously. It's elegant window-dressing, soothing corporate pablum designed to reassure the crowd that Smithfield, even though it is huge and rich, is just as committed a public citizen as they are. In time, however, Butler's speech takes on a sharper edge.

"It's our opinion that these nuisance lawsuits have no basis in fact. In many cases, you have a group of plaintiffs who have been recruited by these out-of-state ambulance chasers. And you have farms on the other side of town that don't even know who the plaintiffs are, don't recognize the names. We see this purely and simply as a money grab."

So much for Mona Wallace's insistence on due diligence, and the fact that she is North Carolina born and raised. And Butler is just getting started. His goal is not just to discredit the plaintiffs' case. Like a knight recruiting villagers to defend the king's castle, his objective is to summon the community to stand in defense of the company.

To serve, in effect, as a human shield.

"We've notified the courts that all of our contract growers, and all of the affected producers, have joined together with us," he says. "And we've notified the courts that we are waiving the mediation process. We're not going there. We've told them, bring it on."

He makes a promise then that will echo down through the years. It is a promise that many a company under fire has made to appease its disgruntled shareholders, and later broken when circumstances changed. On the lips of Don Butler, however, it doesn't sound like grandstanding. It sounds like a solemn vow.

"This is an attack on our way of life, and we will not settle!"

Almost as an aside, Butler mentions something else, a fact that many in the auditorium must find confusing. From Wendell Murphy's earliest days in business, he draped his company in the Stars and Stripes and wedded it to North Carolina pride. That patriotic vision didn't change when Murphy sold out to Smithfield, for Smithfield was a Virginia company with deep roots in North Carolina. It didn't change when Smithfield acquired subsidiaries in Poland, Romania, and Mexico, for the hog giant's headquarters was still just up the road. Now, however, another company has offered to purchase Smithfield Foods. Its name is hard to pronounce and even harder to spell. At the very same moment that Don Butler is strutting the stage in Sampson County and issuing his call for solidarity, his bosses are in the process of completing a multibillion-dollar stock sale to the largest foreign pork producer in the world.

It is called Shuanghui, and it is based in the heartland of China.

CHAPTER 6

THE BUTCHER

The best time to plant a tree was twenty years ago.
But the second best time is today.
—*Chinese proverb*

**Luohe, China;
Smithfield, Virginia;
and Washington, D.C.
March–September
2013**

Ultimately valued at $7.1 billion, the takeover of Smithfield Foods by Shuanghui International Holdings is the largest acquisition of an American company by Chinese buyers in history. It is not an impulse purchase. It has been in the works for seven years, ever since the king of the hog kings, Joe Luter, sat down in his Park Avenue living room with Wan Long, "China's Number One Butcher," and said, with the self-assurance of a man comfortable on the throne: "We ought to do something together." Dominating the pork markets in North America and Europe is not sufficient for Luter. He imagines an empire on which the sun will never set.

In the land of the Red Dragon, however, his bold notion of conquest meets an ancient and mercurial wall—Chinese politics. No friend of foreign control in domestic business, the Communist Party is especially touchy about agriculture. In China, pork is not only a favored source of dietary protein; it is a pillar of the country's food security. Just as the United States maintains a strategic oil reserve to guard against price hikes and fuel the nation in an emergency, China holds a strategic pork reserve to prevent supply shortages and forestall civic unrest.

And Shuanghui is the keeper of that reserve.

Like da Vinci's flying machine, the grandest of Joe Luter's visions finds a more ready home in the world of dreams. Wan, the Chinese magnate, is justly curious about the idea of a planetary joint venture, but he resists the overtures of his brash American suitor until the politics of pork in China merge with the business metrics. It is then that Wan turns Luter's favorite phrase—"capital seeks opportunity"—on its head.

In March of 2013, he makes a play for Smithfield Foods.

✳

Born in 1940, Wan grew up in Henan province, an agricultural region in the Yellow River valley three hundred miles west of Shanghai. For a young man of ambition, it was at once a perilous and propitious time to be alive. The country was in the midst of a vast upheaval. China's civil war was over, the nationalist leaders exiled to Taiwan, and Mao Zedong's Communist revolution was underway. At the age of nineteen, during the Great Leap Forward—Mao's ill-fated quest to rapidly industrialize the hinterlands—Wan joined the Red Army and was dispatched to western China, where he built and repaired railroad tracks.

After soldiering for a number of years, he returned home to the city of Luohe and took an office job at a state-owned slaughterhouse, one of the smallest in the province. Over the course of the next two decades, he impressed his colleagues with his leadership and administrative acumen, and in 1984, they offered him the helm of the enterprise, electing him their manager. Like Wendell Murphy and Joe Luter, who were in the thick of their empire-building during the 1980s, Wan took advantage of relaxed regulations and a fecund economic climate in China to grow the business into a national powerhouse, exporting its products to Russia and Israel. He was the first meatpacker in China to sell pork in the Western manner, using a brand name. That brand was Shuanghui, which means "double gathering"—a kind of auspicious convergence, a meeting blessed with fortune.

The way his friends tell it, Wan never stopped working. He pushed Shuanghui to the frontier of productivity to gain an edge, just as Wendell Murphy did with his feed mill. He was a capitalist, a dealmaker, a new breed of Chinese businessman who welcomed foreign investment and ignored the backlash from domestic critics. Twenty years after he assumed control of Shuanghui, he engineered a buyout of the government's stake with financing from a Chinese private equity firm and Goldman Sachs. As much as he chafed at the shackles imposed by the provincial bureaucracy, he played by the rules of the Communist Party, currying favor with powerful men and harnessing their beneficence to his advantage. In the late 1990s, those provincial elites elected him to serve in China's National People's Congress, a national parliament somewhat like Britain's House of Lords. The election was a peerage of sorts. It meant that Wan Long, the country boy from Henan, was now a baron of the realm.

In 2011, luck smiled on him again. In its twelfth Five-Year Plan, the central government shined a spotlight on food insecurity and encouraged the purchase of farmland overseas. Chinese investors responded by going on a buying spree, increasing China's stake in U.S. farmland by 1,000 percent by the end of 2012, along with acquiring immense acreage around the world. The Five-Year Plan also encouraged investments in biotechnology and allocated huge subsidies to support it. With such a directive from the central government, it was only a matter of time before the world saw a Chinese agricultural company make a record-setting pass at a U.S. competitor.

That milestone arrives in March 2013, the very same month that Mona Wallace takes up the banner on behalf of the neighbors down east.

When the call comes in to Smithfield's headquarters in March, an investment banker from Morgan Stanley is patched through to the C-suite overlooking the placid waters of the Pagan River. Joe Luter, however, is no longer there to pick up the phone. He is enjoying a posh retirement in Palm Beach and Aspen, while still serving as Smithfield's chairman of the board and spiritual Yoda. His longtime CFO and protégé, Larry Pope, is sitting in the spacious chief executive's suite.

A fresh-faced southern boy with a can-do esprit and a mathematical mind, Pope cut his teeth at Smithfield retooling all of Luter's bargain-basement meatpacking acquisitions into viable company assets. Unlike Luter, he is not a trailblazer. He lacks the relentless moxie, the sangfroid, and the impenetrable obstinacy of his predecessor. He is instead a pol-

ished and capable manager, skilled at converting other people's proto-
types into functional products.

For a while now, Pope has been obsessed with Luter's idea of break-
ing into the Chinese export market. China consumes half the world's
pork. Its rising middle class has developed a taste for meat at every meal.
Yet it has only 7 percent of the world's farmland. America, on the other
hand, is a hog producer's heaven, with Big Ag efficiencies and farm acreage to spare. But consumers in Boston and San Francisco have a more
tepid view of the "other white meat" than consumers in Shanghai. While
bacon is almost universally beloved, other products like baby back ribs,
barbecue, and pork belly are mostly regional crowd-pleasers. Even the
choicest cut, the pork tenderloin, all gusseted and garbed by the best
farm-to-table chefs, is less popular than the same cut of beef. In short,
what the U.S. has in supply, China has in demand.

A partnership with Shuanghui could be a bonanza for Smithfield.

And God only knows how much the company needs it. Its share
price has been on a five-year slide, thanks to a punishing run of bad luck.
First, the subprime mortgage crisis sent the economy into a tailspin and
Smithfield's stock into the single digits. Then, only months later, reporters traced a global outbreak of "swine flu" (H1N1) to a Smithfield-allied
hog farm in Vera Cruz, Mexico (though later testing found no evidence
of the virus in the herd). After that came a spike in the price of feed,
as ethanol producers horned in on America's corn stock, converting it
to biofuel. Now, with the company's shares struggling to regain their
pre-recession value, one of Smithfield's mouthiest investors has been agitating to break up the company's production and processing divisions,
effectively unwinding Joe Luter's crowning achievement.

Pope has been in talks with Wan Long about an investment arrangement in which each company would purchase a minority stake in the
other. He knows how connected Wan is to China's brass. One of Shuanghui's investors is the son of China's outgoing premier, and the man who
is about to replace him is the former party secretary of Wan's own Henan
province, a man who helped Wan remove a barrier to Shuanghui's expansion back in 2004. With Wan's influence in Beijing, Smithfield might
finally gain access to the country's consumer market.

Larry Pope is totally unprepared for Wan's counterproposal: a full
buyout of Smithfield.

At first, Pope takes umbrage and says that Smithfield isn't for sale. But the offer, when it comes, is mind-bogglingly generous. Wan has taken the U.S. company's market capitalization of just under $5 billion (the outstanding value of its shares) and raised it by 30 percent. His offer of $7.1 billion is too enticing for Smithfield's shareholders to refuse. Even Joe Luter reluctantly concedes that the merger is the right move. It is the apotheosis of the old hog king's vision of total vertical integration—from feed to fork, on a global scale. It is also a brilliant coup. What he did to Wendell Murphy, Wan Long has done to him.

The only question is whether the U.S. government will approve the union.

✳

The Shuanghui takeover bid raises a host of prominent eyebrows in Washington, D.C. It is not just the inflated offer price that gives economists, intelligence analysts, and politicians pause. It's China's strategy of foreign investment. In industry after industry—steel, paper, glass, auto parts, and solar energy—the Chinese have used a spiral-drill approach to undercut foreign competitors. In the first turn of the bit, they leverage government subsidies and sweetheart loans to acquire intellectual property and technological innovation from countries like the U.S. In the second turn, they combine that imported tech with low-cost Chinese labor to manufacture products at a lower price. Finally, in the third turn, they export those cheaper products back to U.S. consumers, capturing market share from U.S. companies and triggering wage depression and job losses among American workers.

To any sophisticated observer, it's obvious why Wan Long and his compatriots are enamored of Smithfield. The hog giant's genetics and feed technology are light-years beyond those of China's hog producers, many of which are still raising pigs like their ancestors did in small farms on the ground. Moreover, Smithfield's processing machinery is far more efficient than Shuanghui's. Once Wan owns the American tech, he will surely deploy it back home, updating his own slaughterhouses to roll out high-end processed pork products to compete with U.S. companies on the export market.

There's something else, too—a finer point, but no less troubling.

The cost of raising a hog in North Carolina is about half that of raising a comparable hog in China. In part, that is the result of industrialization—Wendell Murphy's CAFO revolution. But it's also due in no small measure to North Carolina's extraordinarily lax waste disposal regulations. Hogs in China urinate and defecate just as much as hogs in America, but the Chinese government doesn't allow its hog farmers to use lagoons and sprayfields. It has invested in treatment facilities for wastewater, digester systems that convert manure into biogas for heating and electricity generation, and biological odor control systems to protect neighbors. When it comes to managing hog waste, China is a paragon of progress, and North Carolina is a backwater of pollution.

As soon as word gets out about the merger, senators on Capitol Hill call for a public hearing. Chuck Grassley, the Iowa Republican, raises the specter of Chinese Communist Party influence in the takeover. Is Shuanghui a puppet of Beijing? Debbie Stabenow, the Democratic chairwoman of the Senate agriculture committee, summons Larry Pope to testify. She also calls three experts to join him—Usha Haley, a professor of business at West Virginia University; Matt Slaughter, a Dartmouth academic and fellow at the Council on Foreign Relations; and Daniel Slane, a security analyst serving on the U.S.-China Economic and Security Review Commission.

The hearing takes place on July 10 in an ornate, wood-paneled room in the Dirksen Senate Office Building. With a menagerie of aides, journalists, and policy geeks looking on, Larry Pope settles into the hot seat. The restive senators give him a grilling. Like a veteran diplomat, the Smithfield CEO ducks and dodges, defending the transaction as a boon to U.S. consumers and not a Chinese food and technology grab. When Sherrod Brown, the Democrat from Ohio, asks him how much he stands to benefit from the transaction, Pope crafts a pair of non-answers that run down the clock on Senator Brown. The answer, as reported by Reuters, is $46.6 million—a number that would not have played well in the hearing room.

Eventually, Senator Pat Roberts of Kansas gets a turn at the microphone. Since Kansas is one of America's largest feed-producing states, Roberts is sympathetic to the merger. He lobs a softball question at Pope, asking why Smithfield voluntarily submitted the transaction to the interagency Committee on Foreign Investment in the United States, which reviews the national security implications of investments from abroad. Pope gives the ball a proper whack. Smithfield did it because it's a good corporate citizen, because it wants the transaction to be transparent.

Roberts then tees up the question he's really wanting to ask: "Did you realize you were the victim of a Chinese Communist plot?"

Pope laughs aloud, as does half the gallery. "Senator," he replies, humor dancing in his eyes, "to this moment I'm not sure I understand that I'm the victim of a Communist plot."

There's just one problem with this exchange: It obscures an unsettling truth. The Chinese government is, indeed, an animating spirit behind the Smithfield buyout. It takes some legwork by the Center for Investigative Reporting to reveal the particulars, but when the light breaks in, all doubts are dispelled. The state-owned Bank of China financed the merger with a $4 billion loan that it approved in a single day. Even more tellingly, while Shuanghui has its headquarters in Hong Kong and its shares are listed on the Hong Kong stock exchange, it does not exercise ultimate authority over its own business decisions. It is obligated to follow the Five-Year Plan.

The journalist who broke the story, Nathan Halverson, received confirmation of this from Wan Long's own son, Robert Wan, in the hushed precincts of the Shuanghui chairman's corner office, seventy-six stories above Victoria Harbour in Hong Kong. In Robert Wan's words:

> The Chinese government acts like a de facto board of directors, even for publicly traded companies like Shuanghui. The Communist Party issues the five-year plan, and Shuanghui is expected to follow that direction. The government can say it wants the Chinese meat industry to employ certain strategies, and all domestic companies are expected to adhere. Yet the day-to-day management of the company, how it chooses to carry out those directives, is left to the company's management.

So when Larry Pope tells the U.S. Senate in July 2013 that "the Chinese government has absolutely no ownership stake or management control in Shuanghui," he is being either naïve or duplicitous. Beijing is the ghost in the machine, an inescapable presence.

When the hearing adjourns, Smithfield's merger plans proceed apace, as if the way ahead is unobstructed. Final clearance authority rests in the hands of the inter-agency committee, with heavy influence from Treasury, but no one really believes the outcome is in question. Americans love mergers, especially those that promise benefits to consumers and job growth, and, in the context of agriculture, there is no recognized limit to the salutary effects of size.

Uncle Sam is sure to give a thumbs-up.

The announcement lands on September 6, two weeks after Don Butler rallies Smithfield's growers at the Sampson County Expo Center and vows to fight the nuisance suits to the bitter end. Three weeks later, on September 26, the historic deal closes, and Shuanghui assumes command of a hog empire that spans the globe.

CHAPTER 7

ACTS OF WAR

As long as you have money to perpetuate the myth,
the war is going to go on and on.
—*Rhonda Perry, Missouri Rural Crisis Center*

Salisbury and Raleigh, North Carolina October 2013– Winter 2014

After the federal government puts its stamp of approval on the Shuanghui acquisition, Smithfield launches a furious assault on the nuisance lawsuits. In a filing with the Raleigh court, Smithfield accuses its old nemeses, Richard Middleton and Charlie Speer, of committing a cardinal sin: ginning up the lawsuits and soliciting plaintiffs to participate, using an ethically suspect contract. For that, the company asks the court to throw the lawyers out of the state.

While there are no allegations of improper conduct against Wallace & Graham (and never will be), the filing hits Mona Wallace like an ambush. There are affidavits attached to the objection, sworn statements from people down east—people Mona's team has never heard of—who say they were solicited by lawyers on their porch, or in a gas station parking lot. The documents are dated weeks earlier and thin on detail. One of them is anonymous. Mona finds the affidavits dubious. But more than that, she knows that Smithfield's caricature of the case is a lie. The stories of suffering that her daughter Whitney and Mark Doby heard were credible and substantiated, as was the history of the neighbors' struggle with the industry, the two decades of grassroots activism and agitation for change. Yet Smithfield's objection isn't really about the substance of the lawsuits. It's a jeremiad against Middleton and Speer.

While John Hughes scrambles to draft a response, the industry takes its screed to the media, seeking a beachhead for its narrative. On September 24, State Senator Brent Jackson publishes a scathing editorial in the *Sampson Independent,* parroting Smithfield's allegations. He rails against "out-of-state trial lawyers seeking to end hog farming by launching baseless lawsuits and accusations against local farmers." And he compares the neighbors' legal team to bandits. "These trial lawyers know that farming is a low margin business and that farmers need to put their money into the farm, not into legal fees. Like they have in other communities, they expect to ride into town, file bogus claims, and ride out with North Carolinians' money." (Apparently, the senator missed the news that Smithfield has retained a legal team to represent the individual growers, *at the company's expense.*) He concludes, as Don Butler did a month before, with a collective call to arms.

> What makes eastern North Carolina special is that our neighbors and our community are our extended family. Our children go to school together; we attend high school football games together; we worship together; we mourn the passing of relatives together; and we protect one another from hardships, both economic and personal. These outside lawyers are threatening our family-owned farms and exploiting members of our community in order to cash in on our most important local industry.

Mona has no precedent for this, no frame to make sense of the rabbit hole into which she and her team have fallen. Never has she witnessed a legislator spewing such venom in the press. Nor can she recall an episode so fraught with willful blindness. Jackson acts as if he is speaking for the community. He behaves as if the lawsuits are an invasion. Yet many of the plaintiffs named in the lawsuits are *his constituents.* In dismissing their pain, in treating them as tools of unscrupulous lawyers, he is unearthing a centuries-old fault line running dagger-straight through the soul of the coastal plain. That fault line is racial prejudice. Nearly all of the plaintiffs are Black. The farmers who so dominate his concern are, with rare exception, white. In calling for the "community" to rise up against the nuisance suits, he is, wittingly or unwittingly, fomenting an internecine war against minority rights.

As the seasons begin to change, Mona fires back her reply to Smithfield's motion. The brief is vintage John Hughes—elegantly crafted yet razor-sharp. He defends Middleton and Speer on every point, knocking down Smithfield's arguments like bowling pins. He lays out the history behind the lawsuits, dissects each of the defendant's affidavits (most of which, upon examination, are groundless or threadbare), and counters them with sworn statements from the plaintiffs, detailing the indignities they have endured over decades, and the lengths to which they have gone to seek relief. In contrast to Brent Jackson's specious fancy, the lawyers from Georgia and Missouri didn't ride into the state like outlaws. They spoke at a conference in New Bern in 2001 and signed up their first clients in 2004. They didn't gear up the present lawsuits until 2012 because they were busy in Missouri. When the Missouri cases settled, they came east, much to the relief of neighbors like Elsie Herring, who had been waiting on them for nearly ten years.

In truth, Smithfield's motion to exclude Middleton and Speer is a heavy lift. Courts rarely prohibit people from choosing their own lawyers, so long as they are in good standing with the bar. Mona and John fully expect Judge Don Stephens—the venerated senior judge assigned to preside over all twenty-six cases—to rule on the briefs and issue a summary order denying the motion. But the judge hands them another surprise: He calls a hearing for the following week.

The scene that unfolds in Judge Stephens's courtroom in Raleigh is downright peculiar. Four sets of attorneys are massed before the bar, like goldfish crammed into a bowl. There to defend the motion on behalf of Smithfield is one of McGuireWoods' premier trial lawyers, Mark Anderson. Mona Wallace and John Hughes are there to oppose the motion. The targets of the motion, Richard Middleton and Charlie Speer, have flown in for the occasion. But instead of allowing Mona and John to make the case for their admission, Middleton and Speer have brought in yet another legal team to attest to their professionalism, the brothers

Wade and Roger Smith from the Raleigh firm of Tharrington Smith. The Smith brothers are legendary denizens of the state bar, and Wade Smith has a knack for showing up in high-profile cases. Indeed, before long, *Super Lawyers* magazine will call him "Our Atticus Finch."

Although the matter is a technical one, the gallery behind them is packed. Legal support staff and people from the hog industry are sitting beside plaintiffs and community activists. Judge Stephens, a clear-eyed jurist with a cap of ivory hair and reading glasses, opens the hearing with humor, roasting himself for nodding off while reading the briefs.

"Eventually, I think I got to the end of it," he says wryly. "And I think I know right much about the contentions on both sides." The wryness disappears. "Although I appear to be treating this lightly, I am not. We all know that this will not be decided on sound and fury. It will be decided on what's right in the law and the nature of the case."

His peregrine eyes scan the lawyers huddled together before him. He gives Mona the floor, but not for long. When she tries to offer personal context, he interjects. He knows her history. He's read all the affidavits. He wants to know if the case is about money or change. She tells him it's about both, about compensating the plaintiffs for past injuries and fixing the industry for the benefit of future generations.

"I believe you," the judge says. "I believe you, North Carolina lawyer. I believe that's why you're here. But I don't know this out-of-state crowd. I don't know why they're here. It might surprise me if they were here to help North Carolina fix its environmental problems."

As John Hughes did in his brief, Mona offers the judge her best defense of Middleton and Speer. She points out the accolades they have received, their familiarity with this area of the law, the verdicts they have won in other states. As she wraps up, she admits the peculiarity of her position. She isn't used to having to vouch for other lawyers. At the same time, she genuinely does believe that Middleton and Speer have the expertise and experience necessary to serve their clients and the people of North Carolina.

When she takes her seat, Judge Stephens motions toward the defense, giving Mark Anderson a chance to lay out Smithfield's reservations. Anderson is a classic big firm ace—square jaw, crew cut on the white side of gray, rimless spectacles, and the confidence of a man who has amassed a trophy collection on par with Vince Lombardi's.

Like a prizefighter, he comes out swinging. He tells a story of a community in uproar, of growers terrified of losing their livelihoods. And he talks at length about the alleged solicitation campaign. He doesn't deny that community groups down east have been working for years to reform the industry. Sure, some of those folks may have knocked on doors and told their friends about the lawsuits. That's not a violation of the ethics rules. That's protected by the First Amendment. But Middleton and Speer are different, he insists. They have no right to practice law in North Carolina. It's a *privilege* to practice law in the state.

The judge listens to Anderson's soliloquy, then responds: "I've heard everything you said. But somewhere back in my mind there's this nagging concern." He shuffles through documents until he finds what he's looking for. "Some of these plaintiffs' affidavits kind of resonate with me. I'm looking at Violet Branch."

The judge launches into a disquisition of his own. "She lives in Warsaw. Lived there all her life. Lives alone. This is where her parents and her family lived. Raised her children and her grandchildren. Hog farm is directly across the street. The ditch runs down the side of the property. Hog calls, bad odors. Got worse and worse over the years as they started spraying the wastewater on the fields. Had to keep her windows closed. Can't hang her clothes outside to dry because of the odor. Smells have gotten worse. Been interviewed by newspapers. Contacted the state and government agencies. Worked with local groups to try to get some kind of relief. Water's contaminated. Her wells have been padlocked so she's got to pay for county water. Wrote the editor explaining how her life has been made worse by the air and the water. No longer clean, no longer healthy. Trucks going past the house carrying dead hogs. Flies, smells, dead hogs fall off. And there's this dead hog box, apparently, that's part of the problem. Newspapers have written stories about me for years and years, and nothing's been done because I was never able to find a lawyer to help me to seek justice in a court until now."

Judge Stephens continues: "She's contacted the Duplin County Health Department, the Department of Environmental Health and Natural Resources in Wilmington, the State Laboratory of Public Health Division in Raleigh, the Environmental Protection Agency Center for Safe Drinking Water in Washington, D.C. She's gone to the REACH

Office, anywhere she could to beg for help. And she's found some law-yers willing to help her. As best I can tell, no North Carolina lawyer has stood up to help her. No North Carolina lawyer has been willing to take her case. And that's consistent with a lot of these folks' affidavits. So, I note with some interest that these problems have been going on for an awfully long time, and this lawsuit is filed today. It appears to be one that was generated primarily by out-of-state lawyers who have finally gotten at least Ms. Wallace and her firm to take notice of them. And that's sort of hanging back, Mr. Anderson, in my mind. Okay? Somehow or another, in the back of my mind that bothers me."

Eventually, the judge calls out the elephant in the room, the target Smithfield has painted on the plaintiffs' legal team. "This is not about the lawyers, frankly," he says. "The lawsuit's not about the lawyers at all. It's about claims that have been made. So, we start out in this case of great consequence fussing about who the lawyers are going to be."

After a bit more badinage, Anderson finally takes his seat. The judge summons Wade Smith to speak. From the familiarity of their opening exchange, it's obvious that he and Judge Stephens go back a long way. Like the judge, Smith is an old lion, with a receding mane of snowy hair, tortoiseshell glasses, and a courtly, avuncular air.

"Your Honor, you are quite correct," he begins. "This should not be about the lawyers. I'll tell you who it's about. It's about Violet Branch. Ms. Branch, could you stand up?" Smith holds out his hand toward a Black woman in the gallery. "This is Violet Branch."

Violet blinks. A homebody by nature, she is soft-spoken even in her own living room, though she is opinionated, too, and proud of her heri-tage. Her mother, a rugged and resourceful woman, raised Violet and her ten older siblings (seven girls and four boys) on the family's hundred-acre tobacco farm, after Violet's father died young. Even as the baby of the brood, Violet grew up pulling her own weight, churning butter and driving the mules on the tobacco truck. In her seventy years, she has never left her homeplace. Her mother gave her a portion of the farm before she died, and Violet has honored the bequest, caring for the land with unflagging tenacity through hurricanes and fires and her decades-long contest with the hog industry.

"Good morning, Ms. Branch," says Judge Stephens, with warmth.

"Good morning," Violet replies. She has a moon-shaped face that is made for smiling, a crown of curly hair, still more pepper than salt, and librarian glasses that perch on her nose.

"This is what this case is about," declares Smith.

"I know that," replies the judge, as Violet sits down. "I know that."

After such a memorable moment, the rest of the hearing might as well be perfunctory. Smith spins his argument eloquently, extolling the many accomplishments of the attorneys Anderson has pilloried. But that isn't really at the core of what the old lawyer wants to say. He wants to say something about the profession to which he has devoted his life, about how the law can, in the right hands, balance the scales of power.

"Nothing is going to be done about this issue—nothing has been done—because the power structure in those communities is not going to allow something to be done about it," Smith opines. "Those farms are going to control the poor people who live across the street from them, and the poor people who live across the street from them have had no relief whatsoever."

In the end, it is Mona's character to which Smith appeals. The industry can take shots at the past conduct of the out-of-state lawyers all day, but Mona Wallace is the bulwark against any future concern. As long as she is there at the helm of this litigation, representing the interests of people who need her, the court need not worry.

Judge Stephens has been on the bench a long time. He knows Wade Smith is telling the truth. He can trust Mona to shepherd this case. Yet still he hesitates. By the way he interrogates the lawyers a final time, it's as if he wishes that he had a looking glass, a way to peer back across the years and see how the case was built, to conjure the ghosts of the people who inspired it, and decide whether these men from distant cities deserve the privilege of representing people like Violet Branch.

The judge retires to his chambers to wrestle with his doubts. Days later, he sides with the plaintiffs and puts his faith in Mona, entering an order that the hog cases may proceed.

But what if he could have seen the past? What if he could have summoned history's ghosts to take the stand and tell him the story of how this war began? So many people could contribute a thread or two, but it would take only three to weave most of the tapestry.

Don Webb. Cindy Watson. And Elsie Herring.

PART TWO

REBELLION

Any people anywhere,
being inclined and having the power,
have the right to rise up.
—*Abraham Lincoln*

CHAPTER 8

THE FOUNTAINHEAD

Open wide your arms to life,
Whirl in the wind of pain and strife,
Face the wall with the dark closed gate,
Beat with bare, brown fists—
And wait.
    —*Langston Hughes, "Song"*

**New York City
and Eastern
North Carolina
1966–1995**

The summer after Elsie Herring graduated from high school, she left home. It was 1966, just two years after Congress enacted the Civil Rights Act, and Jim Crow was still very much the rule—if not the law—in Duplin County. A young Black woman with a head on her shoulders and ambitions to rise beyond the place of her birth had no options for employment in rural North Carolina. So Elsie joined the millions-strong tide of Black people leaving the South and moved northward, looking to make her own place in the world. More than a few of her siblings had already settled in New York City. She joined three of her sisters in Brooklyn.

For the next twenty-nine years, she lived among Gotham's towers. Every weekday, she walked across the Brooklyn Bridge to the financial district. She worked first as a cashier at Dunn & Bradstreet, then as a bookkeeper and treasury administrator at ABM Bank. On the weekends, she tossed her backpack over her shoulder and went exploring. Although she was a Black woman with only a high school education, she rose through the ranks by grit, intellect, and shrewdness.

Elsie Herring got the job done.

As much as she loved the city, however, her heart never really left

Duplin County. She was Beulah Herring's baby, the last of fifteen children and heir to her ancestral land. That world of broad fields and pine
groves and the little pink house with the wide porch that her father
built beckoned to her across hundreds of miles. Eventually, inevitably,
she returned home.

The year was 1992, and Beulah was now in her nineties. She was
still remarkably spry and formidable for her age, but she needed help
tending Elsie's brother Jesse, who had never been able to leave home on
account of his disabilities. After three decades working in finance, Elsie
had amassed enough of a nest egg to fund an early retirement. She left
Brooklyn with many cherished memories and took up residency with
her mother and brother, starting a new chapter in her life. She expected
it would be a time of service, caring for the woman who had raised her
and for her brother with Down syndrome until God saw fit to take them
to glory. She was right, and she was wrong. Although she had no way
of knowing it, Beulah's little house was like a farmstead on the River
Somme in the prelude to the Great War.

Before long, it would be under siege.

The awful truth sprang upon her suddenly. She was out walking
with one of her sisters on Beulah's land when she felt a mist on her skin.
She looked up in surprise, searching for a sign of rain, but the sky was
cloudless, a brilliant blue. She turned to her sister in confusion.

"It's just hog waste," her sister said with a shrug.

Like that, Elsie began to understand.

The land to the west of Beulah's inheritance was Murray land. Elsie
had grown up with the Murray children, Major Murray and his four
sisters. Though they were white and she was Black, they were distant
cousins. Elsie's grandfather, Immanuel, and the Murrays' grandmother,
Nanny, had the same father—Marshall Stallings. On account of their
history and proximity, the families had been friendly during Elsie's
childhood, though the Murrays pretended not to know Beulah and Elsie
when they were about town. During Elsie's sojourn in New York, however, the peace between them had broken. Land that once had been part
of Beulah's inheritance, the Murrays now claimed as their own. Beulah
had the deeds that her father had left to her, but the county courthouse
had no record of them. Whether it was a clerical error or intentional
malfeasance, Elsie would never be able to prove. But the mix-up likely

had happened in 1975 when Beulah hired a white surveyor to clarify the land boundary for purposes of her estate. The surveyor was supposed to file the deeds with the new plat in Kenansville. But some of the papers never made it into the official land records.

The disputed land was to the southwest of Beulah's house, on the far side of a stand of woods. Elsie had walked that land freely as a girl, but in her absence, Major—who she called "Buddy"—had transformed it. In 1985, he had gone into the hog business with Carroll's Foods, building two barns beside the road and a lagoon behind them. Until that day when Elsie was out walking with her sister, she hadn't much cared how Buddy made his living. She had nothing against hogs. Her parents had kept a pig pen and slaughtered the animals for food. She didn't understand that Buddy's operation was nothing like her family's farm.

Then came the mist—and the awakening.

There was a second baptism after the first. It happened on a lazy Saturday in summer, when Elsie was relaxing on the porch with Beulah and Jesse and their nephew from across the street. They heard the heavy diesel sound of a tractor engine coming from the Murrays' property, across a stretch of field. Buddy was in the driver's seat. He pulled the tractor up to the boundary line, opposite the Herrings' porch, and detached what looked like an oversized spray gun with a hose attached. Buddy left the gun on the ground and disappeared for a time. Suddenly, Elsie heard a bursting sound, and the gun sprang to life. The torrent it released wasn't like water from a lawn sprinkler. It had a strange muddy-pink color to it, as if infused with dirt and blood.

The odor enveloped them like a cloud. The smell was unlike anything Elsie had ever experienced. It was what she would later call a "live" odor, as if the spray was a fist driven into her gut. She scrambled to get Beulah and Jesse into the house. But the odor followed close on their heels, intruding through the open windows. Her nephew, meanwhile, tried to take refuge in his house across the street. But the stench trailed him there, too, onto his porch and into his living room. The air was charged with it, like electricity before a thunderstorm.

After battening down his windows, Elsie's nephew returned to Beulah's house. Elsie met him in the yard, enraged by Buddy's callousness. It wasn't long before she saw the hog farmer's truck passing by on the road. She raced across the grass to intercept him.

"That stinking spray is blowing on us," she said, when Buddy pulled to a stop. "I had to take my mother and my brother inside. You've got to turn it off."

Buddy's jaw was set, his face chiseled out of stone. "It's my invest-ment," he replied. "You don't know anything about $150,000."

With that, he drove on down the road, not looking back, as the westerly breeze caught the shit-tinted spray and carried it across the fifty yards to Beulah Herring's home.

When Elsie retreated indoors, she heard it on the roof—the soft pitter-patter of rain.

※

Unlike many of the folks down east who witnessed the advent of the mist, Elsie was not afraid of a fight. She had spent half her life mastering the white man's rules in the biggest city in America. She had no fear of taking her complaint to the authorities. This was 1994, not 1924. The law couldn't possibly allow Buddy Murray to pump hog waste onto her mother's home.

She started making phone calls. She contacted the Duplin County sheriff's office, but the sheriff, George Garner—who also happened to be a hog farmer—didn't want to get involved. He recommended she call the health department. The health department, in turn, directed her to the state Department of Environment and Natural Resources (DENR), and they passed her off to the Division of Water Quality. DWQ sent some people out, but they didn't stop Buddy from spraying.

So Elsie took out her pen. She wrote letters to the Duplin county commissioner, the state attorney general, Mike Easley, and the gover-nor, Jim Hunt, not realizing that Hunt and Wendell Murphy had been friends since their college days at NC State. When the politicians showed little interest, Elsie wrote the Reverend Jesse Jackson and the NAACP for help, but none came. Despite the opposition, she refused to relent. She became such a thorn in Buddy Murray's side that he hired a local attorney to deliver her a cease-and-desist letter. The lawyer accused her of harassment, and threatened her with a lawsuit and a restraining order.

Of all the officials that Elsie Herring contacted, only one took up her cause. Her name was Cindy Watson and she was Elsie's representative in the state House of Representatives. A golden-tongued marketing agent with a personal attachment to the land—she had grown up on a farm and her husband was in the poultry business—Cindy was a dyed-in-the-wool conservative who had ridden the down-ballot wave of the Gingrich revolution to victory in 1994. She was the cliché of a corporate darling. But there was a flaw in her armor, a curse in her genetic code: She had an open heart. She was actually interested in listening to her constituents—*all* of her constituents.

One subject came up like a song on repeat: hog farm pollution. At first, she couldn't understand why this issue seemed to cleave her community in two. Then one day she attended the meeting of a grassroots group that had clearly never market-tested its name—the Alliance for a Responsible Swine Industry, or ARSI. It was as country as a corncob pipe, and as rough around the edges as its founder, Don Webb. But, good Lord, could that man bring the fire. He was one of the most gifted orators Cindy had ever heard. He was a giant of a man with a chest like a whiskey barrel, eyes that went from shining like Jeremiah to twinkling like Old St. Nick, and a basso profundo voice that shook everything in sight, especially his audience. Love him or hate him, you could not help but be mesmerized by him. And Cindy Watson was mesmerized.

Don spoke of the land like a preacher. The earth was the Lord's, and everything in it. And he spoke about eastern North Carolina as if he was its shepherd. His words were simple, unadorned. He said things blunt-nosed, like "I am here to talk the truth." He called hog waste "feces and urine," because if people's stomachs churned a bit, they might start to care about the plight of his people—the poor folks that the hog barons had shat upon in their quest for the Almighty Dollar. He wrote speech notes but never stuck to them. He went off on tangents that would develop almost miraculously into unforgettable points. He told stories like a raconteur. And when he wanted to, he took the roof off the building. So said one of his friends, who saluted him as "perhaps the most effective speaker in the environmental movement today."

But such praise obscured an astonishing fact: Don Webb was once a hog farmer, too.

He had gotten into the business early, back in the eighties, and he had made good money raising 4,000 hogs. Those were the days before industry consolidation, when the integrators—the guys like Wendell

Murphy, who owned the hogs—still paid their growers a living wage. Don never thought twice about the impact of his operation, until one day a neighbor lady approached him at the country store. "Mr. Webb," she said, "the smell from your hog farm is making my life miserable." She told him she couldn't hang her clothes on the line anymore because the smell got into her laundry. She couldn't have family over for cook-outs or spend much time on her porch because the odor made her sick. She asked if there was anything he could do to make it better.

As much as Don Webb could talk, he was just as keen to listen. Like Cindy Watson, he had a compassionate soul. He cared about his neighbors. After a single conversation in the grocery aisle, he vowed to make a change.

He went to the state Soil & Water people and asked them for advice. They told him to put baking soda into his lagoon. He went out on a boat and stirred buckets of the stuff into the wastewater. But the exercise only exacerbated the stench. He went back to the Soil & Water people, and they told him to try carbon. That experiment also failed. Finally, he drove down to Rose Hill and shared his problems with Wendell Murphy. By this point, Murphy was a prince on his way to the throne. He told Don something he surely figured would assuage the hog farmer's concern. For Don, however, it exposed the vast gulf between them.

"Don't bother about that smell," said Wendell Murphy. "It's the smell of money."

Instead of just scrapping that advice, Don Webb subverted it. He shut down his hog farm—absorbing the financial hit without complaint—and then he rounded up some friends and created ARSI to demand that the industry reform its ways. He knew next to nothing about community organizing, but he saw with prophetic certainty that somebody needed to stand up to the hog barons before their devotion to Mammon rent the fabric of eastern North Carolina in two.

Don Webb became that man.

Listening to his barnstormer of a speech, Cindy Watson felt something splitting open inside of her. Don wasn't a "save the whales" hippie from Greenpeace or tree-hugging neo-Malthusian from the Sierra Club. He was a redneck farm boy from North Carolina who spoke—and prayed—about transforming the hog industry like Elijah on Mount

Carmel. When she left the ARSI meeting that day, Cindy didn't suddenly jettison her conservative credentials. She added to them. Later on, she would say, "Just because I wear a conservative hat, does that mean I don't care about God's earth?"

But Don Webb didn't turn Cindy Watson into an activist. She had to see the pain of the wrong in the face of another human being before she would take up arms against the industry. Elsie Herring was the witness who completed her conversion. In the midst of her telephone campaign, Elsie placed a call to Cindy's office. She told her that everyone in the county had been disinterested, impotent, or hostile to her situation, and she invited Cindy out for a visit.

It was a Sunday afternoon when Cindy Watson first drove down Beulah Herring Lane. She parked in front of the little pink house and saw Buddy Murray's spray gun standing in the field to the west. Buddy had been spraying that morning. Elsie met Cindy in the yard and gave her a tour of the property. After a few minutes, a young man sauntered onto Elsie's land, as if he owned the place. It was Buddy's son, Forrest. Cindy knew him on sight—her daughter went to school with him. She also knew he was trouble. He had a history of brawling.

Forrest started yelling before he even reached them. His words were ugly, obscene. Elsie was the focus of his ire. "We didn't have no problems until she moved back from New York!" he said, with hatred in his eyes. "Ain't never had any problems here at all."

"Do you know who I am?" Cindy asked, taken aback, but trying to remain polite.

"I know who you are, Cindy Watson," Forrest shot back, then added what he must have thought was a zinger. "And I want you to know, Representative, that I'm a damn Democrat."

Forrest's brazenness left Cindy speechless. She had seen anger from hog farmers before. But the rage on his face was incandescent.

"How would you like to live with this every day?" Elsie asked, staring Forrest down.

At last, Cindy recovered her tongue. "Miss Herring, I'm sorry."

A minute or two later, Buddy Murray appeared on the far side of the field, walking toward Forrest with his wife, Alice, in tow. The closer they approached, the clearer Cindy could see their agitation. *Oh, dear Lord,* she thought, *what in the world have I got myself into?*

"These are the Murrays," Elsie said. "And that's the man that sprays the waste all over my mama's house."

At this, Forrest started seething again, calling Elsie a "bitch." His parents joined the fray, Buddy hollering at Elsie about all the tribulations she had brought to them, and Alice pleading with Cindy to see things their way.

"Look at us," she said, gesturing at Buddy. "Look at his age. We're old. We don't have any other way to make money."

"I'm not here to take your income," Cindy replied. "I represent both of you. Who do you grow for, Ms. Murray?"

The question seemed to ground the woman. "Carroll's of Warsaw," she answered.

"Carroll's of Warsaw. Now, would you be willing to let me be the go-between and work with Carroll's and Miss Herring and see if we can't find a way to resolve this?"

Alice reluctantly agreed. But Buddy wasn't mollified.

"I just figured you for a Goddamned nigger lover," he spat.

If before Cindy was flummoxed, now she was scandalized. "Miss Herring, I've had about enough of this meeting today. I've never had anybody speak to me like this." She turned to the Murrays. "I'm not going to do anything to harm you. But I represent her as much as I represent you. Everywhere I go, that gun right there has been the problem. It's created animosity between brothers. I've seen neighbors that don't speak to each other. I've never seen more hatred in my life, because of the spray. Somewhere we can find a resolution. I can't do it today, but I'm willing to deal with this issue and try my best to find an answer for both of you."

When Cindy Watson left Beulah Herring Lane that day, she was a changed woman. What Don Webb had given her in passion, Elsie Herring had delivered her in truth. She didn't wish to see the Murray farm shut down. But there was a malevolence in the Murray family that cast the hog problem in a new light. This wasn't just about the waste. It wasn't even just a dispute over land or money, though that was a substantial part of the story. It was about racism—historical, entrenched, pestilential prejudice. If there was a cause worthy of her devotion, this was it.

Her first order of business was to contact the Murrays' integrator, Carroll's Foods. She got in touch with their people, and they passed her along to Don Butler, who at the time was Carroll's real estate manager. Butler agreed to accompany Cindy on a trip to Beulah Herring's property. When they arrived, he walked the boundary line with her, but stood there blank-faced.

"I don't understand what you're saying," he said. "There's a green field down there, and when Mr. Murray sprays, it gets absorbed."

Cindy shook her head. "Sir, there's not one blade of green grass. It's plowed dirt."

And it was. On this property, at least, the industry's whole line about the waste being a boon to the land, fertilizing the crops with excess nitrogen and phosphorous, was a deceit.

Don Butler just stared at her like she had sprouted a second head. If it hadn't dawned on him before, he must have realized at this moment that Cindy Watson was no friend of his employer's. And unlike Elsie Herring and Don Webb, she had clout. She could be a threat. But only if she kept pushing. That was the question no one could answer. Would Cindy Watson take the trail marked out for her by every other elected official in Raleigh, pretending concern while beating a quiet retreat? Or would she take the war drum to the General Assembly?

If she pressed the issue, the industry would have to take her down.

CHAPTER 9

THE FIVE FAMILIES

When justice can be bought there is no justice.
When government can be bought, there is no democracy.
—*Don Webb*

**Raleigh
and Eastern
North Carolina
1995–2012**

The first piece of legislation that Cindy Watson sponsored to rein in the hog industry was about as intrusive as the tea tax imposed by King George III. It was a modest setback requirement, establishing a 1,500-foot buffer between new hog operations and nearby residences. In her mind, the bill was the fruit of ordinary reason, an innovative application of the old aphorism that good fences make good neighbors. But to the folks at Murphy Family Farms, Carroll's Foods, and the other big integrators, Dogwood, Prestage, and Brown's of Carolina—a group Cindy would come to know as the "Five Families of Pork"—it might as well have been the shot heard round the world.

That year, 1995, the hog wars began in earnest. As soon as Cindy filed her setback bill, she ran into a thicket of resistance. Her bill went nowhere. She tried other tactics, brought forward companion bills, all of them rational and limited and readily defensible, but they met the same ignominious end: silence. At one point, she grew so frustrated by the legislature's intransigence that she cornered one of the industry's top lobbyists, Roger Boone, who was also a friend, and demanded an explanation.

"Representative Watson," he said, "there's not one thing wrong with any of your bills. They are probably well needed, and they'll probably pass eventually. But them five families down where you are pay me a lot of money not to get any legislation done."

Cindy thought of Elsie Herring and her confrontation with the Murrays. "Well," she replied, "I have 55,000 good people that sent me up here to find an answer for them."

She was wrong. Not all of those people were good. One evening, she returned home to find a message on her telephone: "Ms. Watson, we know the route you take home, and if you don't back off this hog issue and you don't quit trying to run some legislation on it, you're going to find yourself floating facedown in the Cape Fear River."

Trembling but undaunted, she took the tape out of the machine and drove it to the federal courthouse in Raleigh the next morning. As soon as she walked into the lobby, she confronted one of the marshals: "I want to know if there is an FBI agent around here anywhere."

"I think I can find you one," he replied.

When an agent materialized, Cindy explained, "I'm a state representative. I have a death threat. I've got a tape right here. I don't trust anyone in the General Assembly. I don't trust anybody I'm serving with. I want you to know that if I am killed, if I am drowned, if I am murdered, I have a record right here of a threat made against me."

But informing the FBI was not enough. The following day, Cindy told her colleagues on the floor of the House. "I have a little tape in my hand. Some of my hog farmers aren't real happy with me. They've threatened to kill me, to drown me in the Cape Fear River. I just want you all to know it. I want to make a public record, Mr. Speaker."

No one on the floor moved. No one spoke. But the message got through. The hog farmers left her family alone.

In the midst of this season of ferment, the media mounted a charge of its own. North Carolina's paper of record, the Raleigh *News & Observer*, published a series of exposés that turned the hog industry's shenanigans into kitchen table conversation for hundreds of thousands of people who had never really pondered where their bacon came from. The report-

ers reserved their sharpest scribbling for Wendell Murphy. In their telling, Murphy was a hometown hero turned *maître manipulateur,* who
had leveraged his decade in the General Assembly, first in the House,
then in the Senate, to rig every lever of state power to his advantage,
exempting the materials for hog farm construction from sales tax, banning localities from using zoning laws to regulate the industry, and
trying—though other legislators threw up a roadblock—to shield the
industry from state censure for environmental impact, including waste
spills.

Murphy, unsurprisingly, dismissed the coverage as hogwash. Years
later, Don Butler would call it a "drive-by shooting." But the story was
out, and soon national outlets like ABC News and *60 Minutes* picked it
up, beaming it into millions of households. For their reporting, the *News
& Observer* journalists won a Pulitzer Prize.

In 1995 and 1996, two other fronts opened up in the hog wars—in
county governments and in the courts. Local commissioners and boards
of health, responding to the outcry from advocacy groups like ARSI,
used their own authority to build on Cindy Watson's ideas. In Robeson County, on the fringes of hog country, the commissioners imposed
a half-mile setback requirement for new hog operations. In Bladen
County, the board of health went further still: it debated a proposal
to declare hog farms a public nuisance. This was hardly the first time
that someone had dared to call a factory hog farm a "nuisance." But to
the hog barons whose tax dollars funded the Bladen government, it was
tantamount to a betrayal.

Don Butler, a Bladen County native, read the meddlesome health
officials his version of the riot act, threatening them with a six-figure
lawsuit from Carroll's Foods if they didn't scrap the writ. Cowed, the
health board backed down. Carroll's would air its grievances in the
courts multiple times in the mid-nineties, bringing suit against Scotland
and Robeson Counties for treading on its inalienable corporate rights.
And in both cases, the hog producer would prevail. Also, as Mona Wallace would learn later on, the one time a lawyer had the audacity to
take the industry to court—when Robert Morgan filed suit against the
Barefoots—the hog barons showed the former U.S. senator who really
held the scepter in North Carolina.

Over and over again, the industry met the citizen rebellion with overwhelming force. It sidelined Cindy Watson and Elsie Herring and swatted away Don Webb and his blood brother, Rick Dove, the river-keeper from New Bern. It put down the public health revolt and convinced judge and jury that its bonanza of growth into every riverbend in the coastal plain was a godsend to the economy, the farmers, and the nation. Only the journalists, ensconced in their newsrooms and protected by the Constitution, seemed capable of notching a victory against the Five Families.

Until, that is, the hog expansion imperiled a southern icon: Pinehurst.

In the fall of 1996, word leaked that a hog farmer was planning to break ground on two new CAFOs in Moore County, home to one of the most storied golf courses in America. The about-face performed by the legislators in Raleigh happened with such swiftness that it left Cindy Watson with whiplash. Suddenly, the chummy gents in the Good Ole Boys Club were raising Cain about the possibility that their beloved links might be despoiled by hog waste. The Speaker of the House—the same Speaker who had been holding up her bills—came to her and said, "Representative Watson, I think we can get something done for you."

So Cindy took her case to the Environment Committee. By this point, however, her aspirations had grown wings. No longer was she merely seeking to constrain the worst of the industry's abuses. She wanted something far more substantial: a one-year moratorium on all new hog operations. She wanted to halt the expansion. The speech she delivered to the committee was fierce and impassioned. Wendell Murphy was in the room that day, watching her through glacial blue eyes. When Cindy invoked the moratorium, his knuckles were the color of chalk dust. The bill passed. The committee sent it to the floor.

The next day, Cindy opened *The News & Observer* and read that Governor Jim Hunt, Wendell Murphy's old college pal, had raised the bar and called for a moratorium of two years, not one. She had spoken to the governor about the hog farm issue before. "We've got a problem in Duplin County," she said. "I understand the politics of all this stuff now. But I need your help, and we need to make a change. You don't need to go down as the 'feces and urine governor.'" She had borrowed the colorful moniker from Don Webb.

Apparently, it cut Hunt to the quick. In August of 1997, he signed the two-year moratorium into law.

Like the Five Families of New York, however, the Duplin mafia (as Cindy Watson thought of them) knew how to hold a grudge. It didn't matter that she had won the respect of the governor and gained celebrity across the American heartland as an advocate for environmental stewardship. It only mattered that she had wounded them. The score had to be settled. The debt had to be paid. With ringleading from Don Butler and Lois Britt, Wendell Murphy's majordomo at Murphy Family Farms, the Five Families of Pork set aside their rivalries and pledged to work together toward a common goal: to scare the legislature away from adopting any further regulations, and to unseat Cindy Watson.

Having negotiated the pact, they unleashed a whirlwind.

They called the campaign "Farmers for Fairness" and created a non-profit organization to advance its agenda. In the inner sanctum of the group, they admitted that the odor issue had legs, that neighbors like Elsie Herring and activists like Don Webb were not hallucinating when they bemoaned the spray. Jim Stocker of Murphy Family Farms said in a strategy session with the Pork Council that chemical additives would not be sufficient to relieve the stench. The only viable long-term solution was to construct a mechanical means to cover the lagoons and burn off the trapped gases. In public, however, the group claimed that the industry was already overburdened by regulation and that the only viable solution was to enforce existing rules.

The group then engaged a glossy public affairs firm run by high-flying conservative pollster and political advisor John McLaughlin to debristle the industry's image with a series of hoary radio and television commercials designed to evoke rose-tinted memories of life on the family farm. This was the first time the corporate hog elites had made a concerted effort to use their growers—many of whom were rural families—as an emotional ploy to divert attention from the unsightly reality of their business model. But it would not be the last. The farmers would become the industry's greatest asset in shaping public opinion.

The Farmers for Fairness rebranding campaign succeeded in every way that mattered. The ads penetrated deeply into the North Carolina media market, softening displeasure with industrial hog operations, and instilling in many a citizen's mind the cheerful voices and fresh-faced visages of farming families that anyone would want living next door.

That was phase one. Phase two, which the group debuted a few months later, had a more personal mission: to drive a ten-foot pike through Cindy Watson's reelection prospects, and those of her co-sponsor on the moratorium bill, State Representative Richard Morgan from Moore County, who had raised the clarion call about Pinehurst.

In a foretaste of the dark money campaigns of the future, Farmers for Fairness spent millions of dollars conducting voter surveys and running radio and television advertisements in a pair of rural Republican primaries where the cost of a typical campaign barely exceeds five figures, all while maintaining the façade of a public interest group—which allowed it to conceal its donations. Cindy Watson complained to the state Board of Elections, and Richard Morgan castigated Farmers for Fairness as "a shady, sinister, disreputable group driven by their own pure greed," but they couldn't stop the juggernaut.

On the day of the primary election in 1998, Cindy Watson received calls from employees of Wendell Murphy who said they had to change their party affiliation to Republican so they would be eligible to vote, or they would lose their jobs. She called the attorney general's office about election tampering, but Mike Easley's people just laughed at her.

"Jim Hunt's your governor," they told her.

Richard Morgan, whose district was some distance from hog country, managed to survive. But Cindy's luck had run out. She lost the primary to a hog farmer by twenty votes.

✳

Cindy Watson's fall from grace came as no surprise to Elsie Herring. She had witnessed the hog industry's wrath firsthand. If Buddy Murray could convince a lawyer to threaten her with jail time for telling the truth, it didn't require much imagination to comprehend what Wendell Murphy, Lois Britt, and Don Butler could do when they drew a bull's-eye on someone's back.

Still, as heartbroken as Elsie was to see Cindy defeated, she had come to realize that the state legislature would do nothing to redeem her circumstances. The lawmakers might impose setback requirements on new hog operations, they might even call for a temporary cessation of new farm construction, but they would not force a single existing hog farmer to change his ways. Neither the governor nor the attorney general nor the General Assembly was going to tell Buddy Murray to stop spraying his hog waste in the field beside her mother's front porch.

Beulah and Jesse had moved permanently inside on account of the spray. The land Beulah had walked for more than ninety years felt like it didn't belong to her anymore. The deeds were still in her name, but she had lost the freedom to enjoy it like she wanted to. The rocking chairs, the gentle breezes, the breath of wind in pine boughs, the song of the birds—these were only memories in Beulah Herring's new cloister. Elsie conjured a different image when she thought of her mother. She saw prison walls. In those days, Elsie's hopes distilled to a single point of light: a lawsuit in court.

It was a prospect she had discussed with a few people in the community, including Don Webb and Rick Dove. As a former military judge, Rick had laid out the framework of nuisance law for her. She knew she could make a case and win it with a fair-minded jury. But a lawsuit required a lawyer. And what lawyer in Duplin County had the moral fiber and financial means to sue Wendell Murphy or Carroll's Foods? She raised the idea with some local attorneys, but they were so frightened by it that they showed her right back to the door, as if the mere whisper of such a conversation might jeopardize their careers.

It was Don Webb who finally found a lawyer who showed interest in their case. His name was Charlie Speer, and he was from all the way out in Kansas City. As Don told it, Charlie had experience with nuisance litigation. He and his trial partner, Richard Middleton, were representing neighbors like her against an industry-allied hog CAFO in Missouri, one of the largest hog-producing states in the country. It was still early in the case. They didn't know what a jury would decide. But they were optimistic. Maybe they could break new ground. And if they did, perhaps they could replicate the victory in other states.

Elsie was far too shrewd to pin her hopes on such a diaphanous promise. But Don Webb stayed in touch with Middleton and Speer, as did Rick Dove, and in 2001, the lawyers agreed to speak at a colloquium in New Bern hosted by the Waterkeeper Alliance. Elsie was part of the program, too. She never turned down an opportunity to share her story. That first appearance by Middleton and Speer grew into a second at a prominent Black church in Warsaw, then a third at a meeting of REACH, Duplin County's version of ARSI. The two men were symbiotic. Speer was the cerebral one, the backstage mastermind, and Middleton was the classic flamboyant front man. She liked them both. They knew hog farms and they understood the law.

But only one thing really mattered to Elsie: Would they agree to help her family?

That was where things got complicated. On their third trip to hog country, in 2004, Charlie Speer drove out to Elsie's house and laid out a vision for a nuisance lawsuit in North Carolina. By that point, Elsie had been waiting for relief for ten years. Her mother, Beulah, hadn't lived to see it. She had passed on to her reward in 2001, at the age of ninety-nine. But Jesse was still living with Elsie in the little pink house, and their relatives in the neighborhood were suffering, too. Speer's signal of willingness was a welcome step. Yet it said nothing of when.

Neither, as it happened, did Charlie Speer.

The months piled up and turned into years. Jesse, Elsie's sweet "Beef," died in early 2006, leaving her alone in the house. She got a dog to keep her company, a chihuahua and Jack Russell mix, but someone stole it out of the yard. She replaced it with a more intimidating black Lab named Midnight.

The world continued to turn. The surge in Iraq gave way to the mortgage meltdown, then the financial crisis and the election of Barack Obama. On many occasions, Elsie reached out to Middleton and Speer to inquire about their return. They said they would come as soon as the Missouri lawsuits wrapped up, but they gave no definitive answer. She tried to see things from their perspective. But it was a long time to wait.

She busied herself with REACH and the North Carolina Environmental Justice Network (NCEJN). She helped organize the neighbors in Duplin, Sampson, and Pender Counties, even as Don Webb gathered support up in Stantonsburg and Wilson. If the out-of-state lawyers ever came, they would be ready. She kept telling her story whenever anyone asked. And, as time passed, more and more people asked. Reporters wrote stories about her, authors interviewed her for books, and filmmakers shot footage of her for TV and documentaries. Her little pink house became duly famous. Everyone who stopped by for a visit commented on it. It was Beulah's spirit, Elsie believed. Her mother had loved the land for nearly a hundred years.

At the beginning of the new decade, the Tea Party swept into power and the Arab Spring came and went. Before long, Obama was on the ballot again, squaring off with Mitt Romney. At some point along the way, Buddy Murray got too old to manage the hog farm and sold it. But the transfer of ownership didn't change Elsie's reality. The new hog farmer went right on spraying. Elsie still couldn't sit on her mother's porch without fear of the stench. Sometimes, when the wind was just right, she still heard a faint mist falling like rain on the rooftop.

The call she was hoping for came at last in the fall of 2012, after more than eight years of fighting and praying, agitating and waiting. The Missouri cases had settled. Premium Standard Farms and its parent, Smithfield Foods, had come to terms. Middleton and Speer were on their way to pick up where they had left off. Could she help organize a community meeting?

The silence had lasted so long that the sudden activity didn't quite feel real. Eighteen years had passed since the day Buddy Murray brought out the gun for the first time. Was it really possible that the courts might intervene, that a jury might hear her case and give her justice?

It was a question that only God could answer. But there was something she could do in the meantime. When Elsie Herring hung up the phone, she did what she does best.

She went back to work.

CHAPTER 10

TABULA RASA

Great necessities call out great virtues.
—*Abigail Adams*

**Salisbury
and Raleigh,
North Carolina
January 2014**

Almost as soon as Judge Don Stephens admits Richard Middleton and Charlie Speer to serve as counsel of record in the hog farm cases, he finds reason to doubt his decision. Mona Wallace is asking permission to withdraw from the case. Her motion is antiseptic, bare-bones. She offers no explanation, doesn't even dangle a hint about her reasons. But her request is proper under the ethics rules. All of her clients have consented, and Wade Smith's firm has agreed to step in as local counsel. Ordinarily, such a motion is a formality, granted as a matter of course. But this is not an ordinary case. The prospect of allowing it to proceed without Mona at the helm gives the judge considerable pause. He wants to talk to her before he decides. As he did back in October, he calls the lawyers to a hearing in Raleigh.

The summons from Judge Stephens catches Mona by surprise. Honestly, she isn't happy about it. But then, she isn't happy about the whole situation. Over the past ten months, she and her team have given the case the fullest measure of their devotion. They have invested thousands of hours of labor, made numerous trips down east, had countless conversations with the clients, built a digital map of hog country, and helped draft more than two dozen complaints, all without compensation. That is the way Mona rolls. The clients don't owe her a dime until the defendant pays. When she thinks of Smithfield now, she doesn't just see Brandon Taylor lying beside his tanker truck. She sees Elsie Herring on her porch and Violet Branch in her favorite chair. Much longer and these women would become like family to her. She can't stand the thought of walking away from them. But she has no choice.

Her relationship with Middleton and Speer has broken down.

Her only concern now is the clients' well-being. With a Chinese-owned, multibillion-dollar company on the other side, the neighbors need a legal team who can wield the sling with the facility of David. That is what she told the clients when she asked permission to withdraw. She told them they could trust Wade Smith to see the case through to the end. When she filed the motion to withdraw with client consent, she never expected Judge Stephens to push back.

Now she doesn't know what to think.

She takes John Hughes and Linda Wike with her to Raleigh. They are quiet on the drive, pensive like she is, absorbed in their own private worlds. At the Wake County Courthouse, they find the gallery mostly empty. As before, Mark Anderson is there with his retinue from McGuireWoods, representing Smithfield. The venerable Wade Smith is present with his brother, Roger. He's also brought along Hill Allen, a litigator at his firm. Rounding out the group are Middleton and Speer. Mona greets everyone amicably, as if she's genuinely pleased to see them. Then she takes a seat at the plaintiffs' table with John Hughes.

In time, Judge Stephens ascends to the bench, looking uncharacteristically grave. He cuts to the chase. "I normally sign these pro forma, but I ordered this matter before the court because one of the primary reasons that I allowed the out-of-state attorneys to join the case was that Mona Lisa Wallace and her firm were in it."

The judge casts a glance at Mona over his glasses. "Your firm is one of the few firms in this state that I thought could prosecute this case, the enormity of it, the complexity of it, the expense of it, and serve the plaintiffs well. So, if I allow the motion for Mona Lisa Wallace and John Hughes to get out of the case, then I'll have to reevaluate the original decision I made allowing the out-of-state attorneys to participate."

Mark Anderson has kept his knives sharp since the last hearing. Sensing an opening, he's the first into the fray. He renews Smithfield's objection to Middleton and Speer.

Judge Stephens interrupts him. He doesn't need to hear Smithfield's position again. He wants to hear from Mona.

Mona chooses her words with care. "I want you to know that we believe in these cases. Nothing has changed. We just filed a death case for a young man who breathed hydrogen sulfide at one of Smithfield's plants and died. We are going to continue to do everything we can, as we've always done, for the citizens of North Carolina. We want to do what is right."

She takes a breath, then offers the sketch of an explanation. It is the only statement she will ever make about the matter, even years later. "After the hearing, some circumstances arose that caused me to be unable to work with co-counsel. I'm simply not comfortable being with co-counsel. And by withdrawing, I certainly would never forgive myself if anything I did would be detrimental to the clients, because we believe in the clients. We love the clients. We had six to eight lawyers on the case. We had a staff. We worked tirelessly. But I simply can't work with co-counsel."

The judge regards her thoughtfully, pondering, no doubt, the unspoken remainder. But he doesn't press her for more. "All right. Mr. Smith, do you have some role here?"

Wade Smith rises to his feet, looking slightly pained. It's an awkward moment for him. But he is an old pro. He does the rhetorical two-step with panache, affirming his belief that the out-of-state lawyers are the most qualified in the country to handle this kind of litigation.

Judge Stephens doesn't buy it. Cases of this magnitude are unique, and he isn't convinced that Hill Allen has enough experience to manage it.

The judge turns his bespectacled gaze on Middleton and Speer, who have been sitting quietly while others debate their future. "You want to be heard?" he asks.

Charlie Speer decides to ride the bull. He pleads his résumé, all the good he did for the people of Missouri, the consent decree he and Middleton obtained from the court, the settlement they negotiated for their 285 clients. "These are the only cases I do," he explains. "I don't do med mal. I don't sue doctors. I don't do car wrecks. I feel very passionate about this from a private property rights standpoint. I think that's near and dear to everybody in America—conservative and liberal. Frankly, the country was founded on those principles, and juries get it."

"I understand," Judge Stephens replies. "Well, it's kind of a dilemma for me. But not really. If Mona Lisa Wallace can't work with you, I can't work with you. It's as simple as that. I'm going to vacate my order allowing out-of-state counsel to join the case."

The silence in the courtroom is deafening. Mona is thunderstruck, as are John Hughes and Linda Wike. None of them has ever heard a judge say something like that from the bench.

"Ms. Wallace," says Judge Stephens, "are you prepared to represent the plaintiffs now?"

The judge is staring at Mona expectantly, his eyes at once buoyant and grave. He has offered her a tabula rasa, a blank slate. But this gift is freighted with burden, the commission commensurate with the cost. A mass action of this magnitude against a corporation with parachutes for pockets and the Chinese government for a benefactor could take five years or more to resolve. The expenses alone will run into the millions, and the attorney time could approach one hundred thousand hours. She isn't worried about her team. They are equal to the task. And the price tag, while hefty, isn't too steep. That's one of the blessings of her success—the freedom it has given her to take big risks, to follow her heart into the breach, to take on causes that others have thought lost. She's inclined to say yes, but she isn't the only one at the table. If she accepts the charge, there are others who must come along with her.

"Your Honor," she says, "I'd like to talk to my law partner, Bill Graham, and I'd like to talk to the lawyers who are committed. . . . But, yes, sir, we'd be willing to consider that."

"Well," says the judge, "right now, you are counsel of record in this case. I'm going to give you thirty days to consider your motion to withdraw as counsel."

Mona nods compliantly, thinking that she doesn't just have to talk to Bill. She has to talk to her husband. She has to talk to her daughters. Her career has always been a family affair, and a case like this will test them all. Companies like Smithfield don't just try to defeat their opponents.

They try to destroy them.

The days that follow are consumed by conversation. Bill Graham isn't difficult to convince. He's a buccaneer at heart, a smooth-talking, hard-charging man of the people who even made a Cinderella run for the governor's mansion back in 2008. Mona's family, on the other hand, is less sanguine. Whitney shares her mother's passion for the cause, but she's candid about the downside. What if a jury agrees that the pork barons have screwed over the neighbors for twenty years but can't decide how to value the wrong? When a person dies on the highway, it's easy to calculate his lost earnings. The concept of pain and suffering is a bit of a conjurer's trick, yet juries figure it out. But a nuisance claim? For hog shit sprayed in the air? The harm is disgusting but unquantifiable. It's a Hail Mary claim. If the jury fumbles on the numbers, they could succeed on the moral question, but lose on damages. How much is Mona willing to spend if she could win verdicts in all twenty-six cases and still walk away with nothing?

Mona takes the point, but she can't get the plaintiffs out of her head. Their stories are a part of her now. What is the price of clean air? What is the value of uncontaminated water? What is the dollar equivalent of human dignity, of a woman's claim to the land her great-grandfather acquired after toiling on it as a slave? Some things are worth the fight no matter the reward.

Her husband Lee's objection, however, nearly derails her. He remembers the toll that an eleven-year war with Duke Energy took on them. He has never forgotten how close they came to wiping out, how she had to crawl around on her hands and knees in the land records office doing title work just to keep the lights on at the firm. They are a long way from those days now, but she's almost sixty years old, and he's a decade older. He's not worried that Smithfield will break the bank or her spirit. He keeps the Wallace balance sheet and knows the fortress in her soul. He's concerned that the hog company will steal time from them, years they will never get back.

When Mona and Lee argue, it's a kind of dance, a pas de deux that they have perfected over thirty years. But their trust in each other is total. When one has a word to say, the other listens. So it is with the hog farm cases, with Judge Stephens's extraordinary entreaty.

"He really said you're the only one who could do it?" Lee asks in his gravelly sotto voce.

Mona nods but doesn't reply. Instead, she watches as he ruminates. "Hmm." He's quiet for a moment longer. "You really want this?"

"These people need our help," she says with feeling. "They don't have anybody else."

At last, his resistance crumbles, and he smiles gently. "Okay."

CHAPTER 11

APPEALING TO CAESAR

There is one human institution that makes a pauper the equal
of a Rockefeller, the stupid man the equal of an Einstein,
and the ignorant man the equal of any college president.
That institution, gentlemen, is a court.
—*Atticus Finch,* To Kill a Mockingbird

Sometimes the soundest refuge from the spirit
of the law is its letter. When Judge Stephens
enters his order four days after the hearing, he
doesn't banish Richard Middleton and Charlie Speer from practicing law in North Carolina, not explicitly, at least. He merely relieves
them of their duties in the hog farm suits pending in Wake County. The
out-of-state lawyers interpret his censure literally, and turn their eyes
eastward in search of a more solicitous forum to sue. In short order, they
initiate a new lawsuit in Duplin County.

A kind of déjà vu ensues. Mark Anderson lodges an impassioned
objection, and the judge in Duplin, Doug Parsons, calls the lawyers to
yet another parley, this time in the county seat of Kenansville. Since
Wallace & Graham has no interest in the case, Mona would prefer to
ignore this most recent spat between the Capulets and the Montagues.
But there's a hitch: the new filing includes plaintiffs that her firm represents. To give them a voice, she has to make an appearance. She rounds
up John and Linda and her nephew, Daniel, for the long trip down east,
sure the effort will be a glorious waste of time. It turns out to be quite the
opposite. It gives her a looking glass into the future.

The Duplin County courthouse is a relic of a bygone era, an imposing Greek Revival edifice with towering Ionian columns and a crowning cupola that could double as a belfry. Given the faded luster of the town, the building has the aura of boomtown hubris, like a temple erected in a frontier village when men still believed there was gold in the hills. The people inside are a throwback, too, like a scene in *Mississippi Burning*, the South unreformed by civil rights.

There's a crowd milling in the back of Judge Parsons's courtroom when Mona and her team make their entrance, all white men of middle age with hard eyes and solemn stares and postures wound tight as a spring. They are Smithfield people, clearly, growers and perhaps a few employees. There's an air of menace about them, as if this is their turf, their patch of earth, and no fancy-talking out-of-town lawyers are welcome. Unless, of course, they're with the industry.

The judge takes one look at the audience and calls the lawyers into chambers. It's a peculiar move, cutting out the public before a word is spoken. But he's a pragmatic man, and he knows Duplin County. He has a few things to say. The first is a potential conflict of interest: The lawyer Smithfield hired to represent the growers is an old friend. As one, the attorneys on both sides waive their objections. The second is more substantive. He is well aware of the politically charged nature of the lawsuit, and the unique challenges posed by the venue. This is, of course, an oblique reference to the stone-faced observers in the gallery, the long shadow cast by Boss Hog. He doesn't feel the need to expound on the point, but he wants it out in the open.

When they repair to the courtroom for argument, John Hughes is still mulling over Judge Parsons's words. Last year, when he and Mona were debating where to file the cases, they looked at all the legal options and landed on Wake County, because it's an urban area and light-years more progressive than Duplin, where elementary school kids were still segregated into mono-racial classrooms as late as 1992. But Raleigh was always a tenuous pick. The headquarters of Murphy-Brown LLC—Smithfield's hog production subsidiary—is in Duplin, and all the hog farms are down east. Murphy-Brown's only connection to Raleigh is the mailbox company that receives its court filings and, in addition, some of its legal and lobbying contacts. If Smithfield's lawyers were to move for a change of venue—a likely eventuality—the plaintiffs would have only one meaningful counterargument: community bias.

How could they hope to get an impartial jury in Duplin County?

Mona Wallace is having similar thoughts. She can feel the loathing of the industry men behind her like a tickle on the nape of her neck. She tries to imagine what a trial would be like in this courthouse, when so many county jobs are tied to the fortunes of the hog barons, when church plates on Sunday brim with the tithes of growers, when just about everybody knows or is an employee of Smithfield. The industry's influence is like a fog in the air, an oppression so tangible that Mona can almost reach out and touch it.

She thinks of Violet Branch, remembers sitting in the woman's living room last fall beneath a vintage photograph of her father, the tobacco farmer. Violet is seventy now. She lives by herself just down the road from the hog farmer whose stink she has endured for decades. How many malicious glances would be directed her way if she sat in this gallery day after day? How many vile words or not-so-veiled threats would she overhear in the hallway? Would she even feel secure in her own home? Although the night riders have long since hung up their hoods, white supremacy is still alive in North Carolina. It would take only one closet racist to slash her tires or toss a brick through her window.

Mona scarcely notices when Judge Parsons delivers his ruling from the bench, barring the door to Middleton and Speer, as Judge Stephens did in Raleigh. She is too distracted by her own musings. With each minute that passes, she feels more certain that none of her Black clients would have a chance at an honest verdict in this county, or anywhere else in hog country. The color line is a hurdle they could never clear. The spell of history's prejudice is too strong.

Mona's reflections about racism and John's about venue are like freight trains on converging tracks, until they leave the courthouse and head home. The conversation is fraught. If the cases end up in Duplin County, they will die. The only way to keep them alive is to wrest them out of the state system and refile them in federal court.

This is not a new idea. Mona and John have discussed it many times. But being in Judge Parsons's courtroom instilled it with fresh urgency.

There's only one problem: The law won't allow the switch.

In a complex mass action like this, federal court is often desirable. The filing system is electronic. The clerks are all competent. The judges are sharp, and some of them are legitimately brilliant. They have a staff of bright young law clerks. The dockets are not as backlogged as their state counterparts, which means faster hearing dates and trials. But the doors of the federal system are not open to everyone. A cause of action has to be rooted in the U.S. Constitution or federal law. Or the dispute has to involve parties from different states. Nuisance, however, is a creature of state law. And while Smithfield Foods—the corporate parent—is a Virginia company, the hog growers and their integrator, Murphy-Brown LLC, are domiciled in North Carolina.

From every angle, Mona and John rehash the issue, but neither can see a workaround. "Let's do the research again," Mona says. "There has to be something we're not seeing."

Her optimism is partly aspirational—an outgrowth of her never-say-die personality—but it's also grounded in information. Not long ago, she had an epiphany about Murphy-Brown. It came to her at the strangest moment from the unlikeliest source.

But that's why she remembers it so well.

It was evening in the Wallace household, and Mona was watching college basketball in the family room with Lee. It was tournament time, March Madness, and Carolina was on the floor. Lee was sitting pensively in his leather chair, eyes glued to the screen, following every shot attempt by Marcus Paige, Brice Johnson, and Isaiah Hicks. On any other day, Mona would have been in the chair beside him, focused on the action on the court. In her family of Tar Heel alumni, every UNC tournament game was an event. This evening, however, she was preoccupied with an arcane question: How did the two rival hog kings, Wendell Murphy and Joe Luter, structure their merger deal back in 1999?

That merger was the birthplace of Murphy-Brown LLC and Murphy-Brown was the entity that now held all the contracts with Smithfield's growers. Those contracts gave Murphy-Brown, not the Smithfield parent, control over the growers' operations. And that control made Murphy-Brown the only necessary defendant in the cases. If anyone should be held liable for the fallout of the lagoon and sprayfield system, it was the company that invented the system and made it de rigueur all over the state—the company built by Wendell Murphy.

Except that Murphy's company was now Smithfield. And it was Smithfield's logo, not Murphy-Brown's, that graced the signs hanging outside every farm. It was Smithfield's logo that adorned all the hog trucks. Which made Murphy-Brown look like a shell, a liability shield for Smithfield Foods. That was why Mona was interested in the details of the buyout. If the two companies emerged from the deal as separate enterprises—albeit with one as a wholly owned subsidiary of the other—then she had no choice but to sue Murphy-Brown, a North Carolina company, in state court. But if Murphy-Brown was just a front and Smithfield, a Virginia company, was calling the shots, then they might be within striking distance of federal court.

Unfortunately, the merger documents were never released to the public. But Mona found a substitute, a keyhole into Wendell Murphy's mind. After the deal closed, the IRS alleged that Murphy and members of his family had dodged taxes on roughly $90 million in capital gains arising from the transaction, using a labyrinthine accounting mechanism dreamed up by the wunderkinds at Ernst & Young. Murphy filed suit against the government, disputing the tax assessment, and the case ended up going to trial, which Murphy ultimately lost. Not long ago, someone from Mona's team stumbled across the trial transcripts, and she brought them home as evening reading.

Tuning out the basketball game, she began to wade through them. The transcripts were a legal haystack, hundreds of pages long. The first thing that came to her was an observation about Wendell Murphy. His protestations of ignorance about the tax-avoidance scheme were not credible. He was too savvy a businessman to have misunderstood what his accountants were doing and why. He had declined to pursue an earlier merger with Smithfield because he didn't like the tax ramifications. But he was arrogant. He believed Ernst & Young had picked the lock of the Internal Revenue Code—until the IRS called the whole thing a sham.

Something else nagged at her, too, something in the background of Murphy's testimony. It took a while before she saw it. But then, suddenly, the idea resolved like a three-dimensional image inside a stereo-gram. When Joe Luter took Murphy's throne, he didn't just acquire the old hog king's stock and leave his organizational chart untouched—a kind of "one country, two systems" approach that Shuanghui took in buying Smithfield. Rather, Luter integrated Murphy's entire hog pro-duction company into his own. He consummated the union.

"They're the *same company*," Mona exulted, first to herself, then to her befuddled husband. Lee just stared at her, enjoying the light in her eyes. She tried to explain her thinking, but gave up quickly. She called John Hughes instead.

John listened to her carefully, dropping an occasional "Okay" along the way so she knew he was there. At last, when she fell silent, he donned his devil's advocate hat. While the two companies might functionally be the same, the technicalities were still an obstacle. Murphy-Brown was an LLC whose sole member was John Morrell & Co. And Morrell's office was on Highway 24 in Warsaw, North Carolina, just like Murphy-Brown's. The only way to pin this case on the Smithfield parent would be to convince a judge to pierce the corporate veil not just of Murphy, but also of Morrell. A motion like that was a moonshot.

Mona, however, wasn't deterred. She felt certain she was on the cusp of a breakthrough. Now, driving home from Judge Parsons's courthouse, she feels the same conviction. The wall separating Smithfield from Murphy-Brown is a legal fiction.

As it turns out, she is right. But she won't have proof of it for a little longer, not until the folks at John Morrell & Co. submit the company's annual report to the North Carolina secretary of state.

It is John Hughes who sees the new record first. He is still digesting the trip down east, the time warp of the hearing in Kenansville. He pulls up the secretary of state's website to double-check the new corporate filings for Murphy-Brown and John Morrell. It's just a "t" to cross off on his to-do list. Why would anything have changed since last year?

When he sees the notation, he brushes his hair back, incredulous. He calls out to Linda and asks her to run the search from her computer. She makes the same discovery. John picks up the phone and calls Daniel

Wallace on the other side of the building. Daniel confirms it. John Morrell's principal office is no longer listed in Warsaw, North Carolina.

It's on Commerce Street in Smithfield, Virginia.

John scrambles to find Mona and gives it to her straight: Morrell just changed its status with the state. Its office is now Smithfield's corporate headquarters in Virginia. He hasn't a clue why they did it, but the door is open to them. They can refile the cases in federal court.

Mona's eyes dance with delight. She gets him to lay it out for her, the whole argument for federal jurisdiction. A grin spreads across her face. In law and logic, their position is unassailable. Yet still it feels flimsy, as if the scrivener who gave the gift could just as easily take it away again. Upon learning of their plans, Smithfield's lawyers could change Murphy-Brown's membership structure or reconstitute the LLC as a C-corporation. But these changes would have legal and economic ripple effects. Would Smithfield really take such a significant action just to keep the nuisance suits in state court?

Trusting that the bridge will hold them long enough to reach the steps of the federal courthouse, Mona tosses the state court complaints in the dustbin and asks John to rewrite them from scratch, reframing the case around the themes of social and environmental justice. The plaintiffs' stories will remain their lodestar. But they will situate those stories within the context of an industry run amok. They will tell the tale of hog farming's industrial revolution, from Wendell Murphy to Wan Long. They will show how Murphy and the Five Families used high-powered lobbyists, slick public relations campaigns, and hardball litigation to stifle dissent and reap untold riches. In addition, they will ground the case in the science. They will bring together the literature from public health and epidemiology to establish the linkage between hog odor and disorders of the body and mind. From their first federal pleading to their last, they will make the argument that this isn't just a nuisance dispute between hog farms and their neighbors. This is about civil rights and the sanctity of God's green earth.

The assignment unlocks something so elemental in John Hughes that he won't recognize its significance until years later. It turns his work into an extension of his poetry, investing it with newfound meaning. He pours himself into the drafting with a tirelessness that defies his age. The pages multiply, and the narrative takes seamless shape. There is a virtuosity about it, a clarity of register that can only arise from an undefiled source—like love, for instance, or hatred, moral indignation or religious zeal. In John Hughes, there is a little bit of all of that.

He is righteously and royally pissed off.

The document that emerges is more indictment than complaint. In numbered paragraphs, it is an impassioned critique of an entire system, like Luther's Ninety-Five Theses, a litany of the wounds inflicted on ordinary souls by men who pretend to be their betters. Yet it also carries a whiff of the scholastic. He devotes three pages to the academic research supporting the plaintiffs' claims and another page and a half to the China connection—the plenitude of links between Wan Long and the Chinese Communist Party, and the effect that the exploding demand for pork in the Chinese market may have on North Carolina production. Had the federal rules given John the option of nailing the complaint to the door at Murphy-Brown's headquarters, he would likely have taken it, if nothing else for the poetic symmetry of the protest.

But a protest is not sufficient in a courtroom. The law requires proof. And proof, to be convincing to a jury, must be corroborated. Behind the brutal show business of a trial, there is an order that proof must take, pieces that when assembled together are sturdy enough to absorb the defendant's counterblows and persuasive enough to carry a verdict.

In this case, many of those pieces are obvious. There are the plaintiffs who can explain how they have been forced to live, and witnesses who can back up those claims from their own experience. There are photos and video footage of spray guns in action, cesspools festering like sores in the dirt, and hog barns as big as aircraft hangars teeming with porcine multitudes. There are executives from the hog company's payroll who will either admit that Smithfield knew what it was doing or make fools of themselves trying to deny it. And there are experts from the academy, commerce, and medicine to clarify how everything works and works together—from the movement of bioaerosols through the air to the health effects of hog odor.

But in a fight like this, the plaintiffs need something more. They need a witness or two who can speak with a kind of prophetic authority. After a year on the case, Mona and John have a sense about who these people are—or should be. One of them is only a hypothesis, a unicorn. They need an inside man, a hog farmer with the conscience of Don

Webb who still has a contract to grow pigs. At this point, however, they have no idea if such a hog farmer exists, and if he does, where they might find him.

Thankfully, the other person they have in mind is within reach. He's an epidemiologist over in Chapel Hill who has written the scientific bible on hogs and community health.

His name is Dr. Steve Wing.

CHAPTER 12

A MAN FOR ALL SEASONS

If honor were profitable, everybody would be honorable.
—*Sir Thomas More*

In the prelude to the federal case, all roads seem to lead to Steve Wing. Elsie Herring is one of the first signposts. She and Wing go back a long way, to the founding of REACH. "You should talk to Steve," she tells Mona and John. "He knows the whole story." Don Webb is another supporter of the UNC professor. "Have you talked to Steve?" he asks, his eyes aglow with that inimitable light. "You've gotta talk to Steve." Others pose the question as a straightforward litmus test: "Does Steve Wing support your case?"

The reverence for Wing among the Black community down east is astonishing to Mona and her team. They speak of him not just as an ally but as a patron saint within their movement. They trust him. They believe in him. Perhaps they even love him.

And the reverse appears to be true too: He loves them back.

In late May, a couple of weeks after the hearing in Judge Parsons's courtroom, Mona plucks John out of his writing cave and whisks him away on a day trip to Chapel Hill. They meet Wing at a place of the professor's choosing—the Open Eye Café in Carrboro, west of the university. It is a propitious spot, one of John's hometown favorites. The coffee shop wasn't around when he was growing up, but in the early years of his practice, before Mona rescued him from the ball and chain of Big Law, he used to make the drive over from Raleigh and hole up at one of the tables like an undergrad. The Open Eye Café was where he shed his cynical skin and mingled with the muse, where he wrote his poetry.

Swaddled in their business suits, Mona and John look like creatures from another dimension as they stroll in. The décor of the place is industrial chic, all exposed brick and unpolished metal with a network of steel-gray air ducts hanging from the rafters like an old biplane at an air and space museum. These days, it's a student hangout, littered with MacBooks and smartphones. But it has a retro vibe, almost neo-hippie, as if at any moment Allen Ginsberg might walk out of the restroom and hold court in a smoke-filled corner.

Steve Wing looks like he would have been right there with them—in another life. He's a handsome man, in a whimsical, unaffected way. His wavy hair, streaked with silver, is longer than it needs to be, and it's slightly mussed, as if the only grooming it gets is by the comb of his fingers. His smile is guileless, even gentle, as is his manner of speech. He presents as a man at home within himself, whose waters run deep but whose surface is no less real.

When they order coffee, he gets himself a tea and shows them to a table, his sandals clapping on the concrete floor. He is skeptical of them, of their motives. He isn't unkind about it, but he wears his doubt openly. More than anything, he wants to know why: Why did Wallace & Graham take the cases? He's done his research. He's seen the glossy online photos, the big law firm staff, the impressive accolades. They don't look like public interest lawyers. They look like they're in it for the money, the prestige of victory, not to clean up the environment.

Eventually, he comes out and says it: "How do I know if your heart is in the right place?"

Mona responds with her most winsome charm. She makes it personal, tells him about her daughters, about Whitney's passion for the clients and Lane's budding environmentalism. She lays out her own curriculum vitae like a boxer, listing the corporate malefactors she's taken down and the industries she's helped reform.

At some point, John speaks up in a way that gets Wing's attention. "My dad is a professor like you. I could have gone that route. I could have spent my life writing research articles. I went into the law because I wanted my work to have an effect on the world. That's Mona's gift. She knows how to get things done. She's comfortable in the circles of power. She knows the right people. She has the resources to make this case work. And I can say with certainty that she's not just in it for the money. She's in it for the impact."

Something shifts in Wing's expression. He's tracking. He tells them a little about his scholarship on the topic, gives them an overview of his role in the hog wars.

He was a naïf, a wet-eared babe in the woods, when he answered the call of Gary Grant at the Concerned Citizens of Tillery to translate into the argot of science what activists across the state had witnessed anecdotally: the fact that new hog farms were overwhelmingly being located in low-income communities of color. Wing gathered the locations of all 2,514 industrial hog operations in North Carolina and juxtaposed them with the demographic and economic data. His findings were as striking as they were politically explosive. He needed only three maps to make the point. The first revealed the concentration of hog CAFOs in the coastal plain. The second showed the distribution of poverty in the same region. And the third displayed the spread of the nonwhite population. Put simply, people who were poor and Black, Hispanic, or Native American were far more likely to live in close proximity to a hog farm.

Of course, showing such a correlation wasn't the same as proving causation. The data offered no insight into the mind of Wendell Murphy or the purposes of the Five Families. Were they intentionally planting their pollution factories near low-income minority communities, or were they simply converting rural land where it was cheapest and easiest to find? Regardless, Wing found the correlation troubling enough that he denounced it as environmental injustice. In the years to come, he would take his opprobrium a step further.

He would call it environmental racism.

In the spring of 1999, a year before Wing and Grant formally published their study, Wing accepted an invitation to present his findings at a national public health forum. He had no idea what was in store for him when he approached the podium. As soon as the media picked up the story, word of his findings made the transit down east, and the hog barons sensed a tremor in the earth. They issued a tentative rebuke, conscious of the letters behind Wing's name and the reputation of his university. The industry's boosters started calling him on the phone, offering friendly yet condescending lessons in animal husbandry, as if he were nothing but a misguided academic wandering the halls of his ivory tower. One of these boosters, he found out later, was a member of the UNC Board of Governors.

Despite this backlash, Wing persisted, presenting his study to the agriculture committee in the North Carolina House of Representatives with testimony from Gary Grant. This was an offense that the industry could not abide. They had suffered enough losses during Cindy Watson's tenure, and only this year, after ousting Cindy, had they reestablished their blockade. One of the industry's lobbyists confronted Wing after the hearing and threatened to sue him if he didn't furnish a copy of his report immediately. The man's hostility took Wing aback. He was accustomed to the gentlemen's club of the academy, the starchy dialogue and staid diplomacy. The lobbyist's posture was more like a barroom brawler.

It would only be a month before Wing met his first hog country haymaker.

In May of 1999, the state Department of Health published the results of a groundbreaking survey that Wing had conducted on the health effects of hog odor. With outreach from grassroots groups, he and his team had interviewed 155 people, almost all of them Black, from three communities in eastern North Carolina—one proximate to a hog CAFO, another close to a dairy farm, and a third rural neighborhood devoid of any livestock. The results were just as damning as his environmental justice study. People living near the hog farm reported more respiratory and digestive disorders than residents of the other two communities. The data set was the first of its kind in the country, and the hog barons reacted as if Wing had set fire to the hills.

The same day that the survey results went public, lawyers from the North Carolina Pork Council sent Wing and his co-author a blistering letter demanding all of their personal notes, memoranda, and research, including—critically—the names of all of the people who participated in the survey. From a strategic standpoint, it was a masterstroke. UNC was a publicly funded institution, which meant that Wing could claim no exemption from a public records request. As a matter of law, at least, his study was an open book. Yet the ethics of public health mandated that he keep his participant data confidential, and he had made that promise to all the people he interviewed, to protect them from reprisal.

The university's attorney showed no concern for Wing's dilemma. On the contrary, he pressed Wing to divulge his entire file. Wing appealed to the administration. The response among UNC's mandarins varied from anemic to antagonistic. One official told him that if he refused to follow the attorney's advice, the university would contact the State Bureau of Investigation and have Wing arrested for stealing state property. Like Thomas More faced with the wrath of Henry VIII, Wing refused to sacrifice his oath. He knew that the Black community down east would see any concession as a betrayal and never forgive him for it. It didn't matter if the law demanded disclosure. The law had been against them for centuries.

At last, at Wing's insistence, the university's attorney allowed him to scrub his files of all identifying information before turning them over to the Pork Council. The industry complained loudly and threatened to file suit, but ultimately it caved.

Later that summer, Wing delivered a lecture on his community health survey at NC State in Raleigh, the alma mater of Wendell Murphy. The pork producers showed up en masse, challenging Wing aggressively during the Q&A session. Afterward, an assistant professor at another state university took Wing aside and confided that he, too, had been studying hog CAFOs before he heard about Wing's tussle with the Pork Council. "I'm dropping my research," he said. "I'm afraid that if I have to deal with legal problems like yours, I'll never get tenure."

Wing, by contrast, took the intimidation in stride. Instead of retreating, he expanded his footprint in hog country, recruiting Black community organizers like Devon Hall at REACH and Naeema Muhammad at NCEJN to join him in future studies. He conducted a survey that pegged the industry with harming the respiratory health of North Carolina schoolchildren, and a study that documented disruptive amounts of swine odor up to 1.5 miles from hog CAFOs. He joined in a number of studies that established the long-term damage that hog odor causes to community life and health, and he updated his prior investigation of the discriminatory impact of industrial hog operations on communities of color using new census data. For fifteen years now, Wing has taken a wrecking ball to the claim that hog farms make good neighbors. Every one of his studies has proven exactly the opposite.

Now, in the Open Eye Café, Wing wraps up his story like a Zen master, evincing no pride in his own accomplishments. He regards Mona and John sagely, allowing the silence to extend. "So how exactly can I help you?" he finally asks.

It is John who gives the answer. "We're about to refile the cases in federal court. We want to lead with the science, to construct a public record of the industry's abuses. We'd love for you to do an affidavit, put all your research in it. It can be as long as you like. I guarantee it'll get Smithfield's attention. And the media will be able to see it, too. It'll be in the record forever."

Wing's smile dawns slowly, his eyes free of his earlier skepticism.

With this encouragement, John goes for the close. "Assuming we survive the motion to dismiss, we'll also be able to get access to the hog farms. We can put a team of experts in them, get data you've never seen before. We can use the case to advance the science."

Wing absorbs this, looking from John to Mona and back again. "I'll do it," he says.

❋

It's late August, summer's end, when Mona files the first federal complaints in Raleigh. Mark Anderson does her the courtesy of accepting service on behalf of Murphy-Brown, and, just like that, the timekeepers start their clocks, and the lawyers begin their march toward the opening skirmish in what promises to be a protracted war.

Before that happens, however, they need a judge.

In the federal system, judicial assignments are like an old-fashioned carousel. There are horses of all sizes, some attractive, others less so. While all the steeds are moving in the same direction, a handful are galloping, and a few are stuck to the floor. In the federal courts, however, the rider doesn't pick the horse. The union is prearranged.

It's a fateful moment when a lawyer learns the name of her judge. In the hands of a careful and sympathetic jurist, the law can be the midwife of justice. In the courtroom of a hostile judge, on the other hand, a case can fly apart like clay on a potter's wheel. With the hog farm lawsuits, the lottery system treats each case separately at first, assigning an array of judges. Then, on a Friday in September, a great rearrangement takes place. John and Linda and a couple of others are gathered around Linda's computer as the email updates come in from the court.

The outcome is singular: Their judge is William Earl Britt.

The lawyers pull up his background. An octogenarian Carter appointee with a name as homespun as shrimp and grits, he's a native of McDonald, North Carolina, a tumbleweed town in the southern part of the state. Like Mona and John, he got his law degree at Wake Forest, then did two years in the army and a clerkship at the state Supreme Court before spending twenty years in private practice. He's been on the bench since Reagan was governor of California, and he's been on senior status since 1997, when the Smashing Pumpkins were one of the biggest names in music. The man is an antique, a throwback to a bygone era.

Mona's team digs into his past decisions, searching for a looking glass, but they find no indication of favoritism, no hint of ideological persuasion. Only one case rises above the pile. Back in the nineties, he presided over a big toxic tort suit in which the residents of a trailer park sued the petroleum giant Conoco for contaminating their well water. Judge Britt allowed the case to proceed to trial over Conoco's objections, and it resulted in a sizeable plaintiffs' verdict and a $36 million settlement. With federal judges, however, it's perilous to prognosticate. They are appointed for life, which makes them almost impervious to criticism, and they are a proud lot. The rule of law is like a religion to them. While the public may brand them as partisans, most take pains to remain impartial. At the same time, bias is a feature of human nature. Some judges display a subtle deference to behemoth companies and their glitzy big firm lawyers, as if they consider it an honor to host such august personages in their courtroom. Earl Britt doesn't read like that kind of judge. He looks like a man with an even hand.

That assessment turns out to be accurate. Over the next five years, through countless hearings and a quintet of month-long jury trials, the lawyers at Wallace & Graham will come to revere Judge Britt for his wit and magnanimity, his decency, and his near-fanatical devotion to fairness. He is not a plaintiff's judge or a defendant's; his decisions are neither conservative nor liberal. He is a faithful custodian of the scales, a devotee of Pericles and Augustus, of James Madison and John Marshall. His only creed is equal justice under law.

When Smithfield opens with a thunderous broadside, attacking the neighbors' damage claims as specious and the complaints as scandalous for spotlighting the company's Chinese owners and the ties of its chairman, Wan Long, to the Chinese Communist Party, Judge Britt waits for the billowing smoke to waft away and then quietly takes the defendant's motions under advisement. He doesn't even call the lawyers to a hearing. He dusts off the law books, examines the wisdom of precedent, and issues rulings that are astonishing in their brevity.

Unlike many federal judges, he makes no attempt to write for the history books. He limits his audience to the courtroom. He allows the neighbors' claims to proceed, holding that the law may very well allow them to seek recovery for discomfort, annoyance, and decreased quality of life as well as for concrete losses like the diminished value of their land. In a nod to humility, however, he leaves the door open for Smithfield to revive the issue later on, once the comb of discovery has clarified the factual landscape. Little does he know that two years from now the hog giant's friends in the General Assembly will sneak through this door like thieves in the night, hoping to snatch the gavel from his hands and force a decision in favor of Smithfield.

As for the China allegations, Judge Britt agrees with Mark Anderson that Mona and John went a little too far. In their amended complaint—a more embellished version of John's original polemic—they devoted roughly twenty pages to the Chinese takeover of Smithfield in 2013. Along with laying out Wan Long's ties to the Communist Party and his service in the People's Liberation Army and the National People's Congress, they raised questions about the influence of China's Five-Year Plan on Smithfield's pork production, highlighting the Bank of China loan that funded the merger and citing the opinion of the experts who testified before Congress that Shuanghui—now called WH Group— operates under the aegis of the Chinese government.

Britt finds many of these allegations to be inflammatory and only obliquely relevant to the neighbors' nuisance claims. Like an English professor, he takes out a red pen and strikes them from the complaints. But he allows Wallace & Graham to talk about Smithfield's foreign ownership, the company's exports to China, and the $597 million bonus taken by Wan Long and another Shuanghui director as a reward for the Smithfield buyout. In the judge's view, these allegations offer meaningful context to the case and are material to the plaintiffs' claims.

With these guardrails in place, John Hughes decamps to his writing cave and knocks out a third draft of his Lutheresque indictment. Weighing in at sixty pages, it is the longest of all of them, nearly double the size of the first. It is intimate—embroidered with the plaintiffs' stories. It is erudite—a bullet-point tour de force of the hog industry's abuses, denials, and coverups. And it is unflinching. As a piece of persuasive rhetoric, its effect on the reader is irresistible: If Mona and her team can actually prove all of this, they might just accomplish the impossible.

They could bring this billion-dollar company to heel.

CHAPTER 13

THE CLOUD AND THE FLAME

I hear, I know. I see, I remember. I do, I understand.
—*Confucius*

**Eastern
North Carolina
Summer 2014**

It's one thing to listen to a story. It's another thing to live it. Empathy can offer a simulation of human experience. But it can't give you the feel of falling when you dive off a waterfall or the flicker of butterfly wings in your stomach when you fall in love. It can't reproduce the music of your child's first cry or the rush that comes from winning a race. Neither can it conjure in your nose the peerless putrescence of hog shit wafting through the air.

That distance—at once psychological and empirical—is one of the occupational hazards of being an advocate. Only a few rare lawyers have ever walked a mile in their clients' shoes. Everyone else is left to reach across the gap like Michelangelo's Adam. It is an act of faith to take on someone else's story, a feat of trust to stake one's reputation on a stranger's veracity. It is especially trying for those who, like the biblical Thomas, prefer to see before they believe.

Daniel Wallace is that kind of lawyer. He is young and careful, methodical by default, and still testing the ropes. The hog farm cases are his first assignment after passing the bar exam. He's followed Mona's legal career from the catbird seat, as the son of Victor Wallace, Lee Wallace's brother. Mona is like a second mother to him. Her daughters, Whitney and Lane, are like his sisters. But this wasn't the job he expected to take after law school. He had an offer lined up in Charlotte. Mona, however, was insistent. She called him up shortly after graduation and told him about the hog cases. She needed his help. Would he come home?

What the heck, he thought. *I always figured I'd end up there eventually.*

At the beginning, the litigation is an enigma to him. He's never been down east except on the interstate. He knows Smithfield as the bacon guys. He's never thought about where the pork comes from. In his mind, hog waste is a concept—cringeworthy perhaps, but not a cause.

His illumination comes in waves. He takes a trip to Kenansville with John Hughes to haunt the archives of *The Duplin Times,* searching for tales from history's crypt, evidence of the industry's misdeeds. The stories are legion. He reads about the lagoon breach at Vestal Farms in 1995, the 1.5 million gallons of wastewater that spilled into the Northeast Cape Fear River, and Wendell Murphy's hackneyed excuse: vandalism by environmentalists. He unearths photos of the damage after Hurricane Floyd in 1999, the hog farms submerged beneath the floodwaters, drowned pigs floating in filth. He even uncovers an article about the investigation undertaken by the U.S. Department of Education into Warsaw Elementary School. The government found that the administrators at the majority Black school had grouped all the white students in their own classrooms to appease the parents. Daniel stares at the date in shock. That happened in the early nineties. He starts to see the shape of the wrong, but it's still indistinct, an outline in the fog.

He attends the hearing in Judge Parsons's courtroom, sees the industry men crowd into the gallery like Tony Soprano's gangsters. He senses the power dynamics, the twisted gravity of the place. Still, he doesn't quite get it. How bad can the odor be? It's an agricultural community. People have been raising hogs on the coastal plain since colonial times. No pig pen smells like a rose garden. What if Smithfield has a point? What if the plaintiffs really are just disgruntled neighbors making trouble for the hardworking farm families growing the world's food?

Early in the summer, Daniel takes a drive down to Beulaville. He's all by himself, following the GPS on his old Sprint phone. He's looking for the Joey Carter farm on Hallsville Road. The community around it is his assignment—Woodell McGowan, Linnill and Georgia Farland,

Elvis and Vonnie Williams, and all the rest. He's memorized their names, but they're just letters in his head. He's never met any of them before.

The landscape is a blur of fields and trees crisscrossed by tarmac. The GPS connection is spotty. The directions aren't making sense. He pulls into a driveway to fiddle with his phone. The address isn't coming up. He looks through the windshield and realizes that he's at the entrance to a hog farm. He can see the rooftops of barns in the distance, the integrator's sign hanging by the roadway. He doesn't realize that a man is watching him, that his sudden appearance has set off an alarm.

He turns around and heads toward the town of Wallace, hoping for better cell service. At some point, he glances in his rearview mirror and sees a truck not far behind. He doesn't pay the driver any mind until the man starts mimicking his turns. His suspicions are confirmed when he pulls into the lot at Bojangles. The man takes the spot next to him but doesn't climb out.

He wants me to see him, Daniel thinks. *To know I'm being watched.*

As soon as Daniel's signal clears, he leaves Bojangles behind, figuring the truck will follow him. But the driver stays put, his point made. This isn't the only time that Daniel will pick up a tail in Murphysville. Indeed, before long, everyone on Mona's team will have a similar story to share.

It takes Daniel twenty minutes to reach Hallsville Road. Thankfully, the GPS connection doesn't drop this time. He cases the McGowan neighborhood at a slow clip, taking in the squat houses made of brick and clapboard, the well-kept yards, the quaint mailboxes, and the signpost at the entrance to Joey Carter's farm.

The hog operation is split in two, like the wings of an airplane, with Hallsville Road as the fuselage. The north operation, a newer site with four barns and one lagoon, backs up against the wetlands around Limestone Creek. The south operation, consisting of three barns and another lagoon, is thirty years old. Carter's sprayfields extend outward from the barns, surrounding the McGowan neighborhood on three of four compass points.

Daniel turns down Howards Farm Road, which makes a loop around the south operation. There are homes scattered among the towering pines, and most are closer to the swine facilities than the residences on the main road. One home, in fact, shares a fenceline with a sprayfield.

It is the home of Linnill and Georgia Farland.

When the young lawyer pulls into the Farlands' driveway, he is shocked to see no buffer standing between their property and the hog farm. A handful of stately pine trees are growing in the yard, but their needles offer no protection. The barns are right there, a few hundred feet away. If Daniel had a rock, he could almost hit one of them.

He is not prepared for the smell that greets him when he steps out of the car. It's like a cloud in the air, at once vile and violent. *Good God,* he thinks. *Joey Carter isn't even spraying.* In an instant, all of his doubts about the case fly away. The odor invades his nostrils, assaults his senses, makes him wish he didn't have to breathe. Part of him wants to jump back in the driver's seat and get away from this place. But he can't.

The Farlands are waiting for him.

The family meets him on the porch. The old patriarch, Linnill, examines him from behind his reading glasses, his limpid eyes cradling a lifetime of sorrow. The newsboy cap perched on his balding head hearkens back to a simpler time. His wife, Georgia, manages a dignified smile, despite the rot in the air. Their daughter, Lendora, is with them. She's a carbon copy of her mother, except for her height, which, it seems, she inherited from her father.

Lendora dominates the conversation. She's affable and humorous and a natural storyteller, which is useful because she has been a witness to the whole drama, since way back in 1985 when Joey Carter started coming around the neighborhood, looking to build a hog farm.

She was fourteen when she first heard the man's name. The land to the south was then a dense stand of woods that abutted a field where a neighbor grew tobacco, corn, and cucumbers. Her father built their family house with his own hands, having bought the land in 1970, the year before she was born. It was a tightly knit community. People cared for each other. And some of the neighbors were kin, branches on the Hall family tree, whose roots reached back more than a hundred years. The stories of Lillie Belle and Delores Hall and their brother, Raymond, aren't Lendora's, but she has learned them from Woodell McGowan.

When Lendora was growing up, the neighbor kids all ran in a pack. The Farland house was their gathering place, in no small measure because Georgia was a gifted cook. The kids threw balls in the middle of the lane and rode bikes around the loop road. They explored the woods and found the secret places where the wild berries grew. They had egg hunts on Easter and community cookouts in the yard. Linnill was the neighborhood barber. He built a little shop beside the house where he cut people's hair. Everyone called him Brother Farland.

So it was that when Joey Carter showed up with plans to construct an industrial hog farm just over the fence, it fell to Linnill to intervene. He had no aversion to pigs. Like many of his neighbors, he kept a few hogs in his own pen. He slaughtered them for food, cured the meat and smoked it. It was his family's Sunday dinner and breakfast bacon. But a few *thousand* hogs? Linnill didn't like that idea at all.

He put together a petition and all but one of his neighbors signed it. Lendora and her sister helped Linnill with the drafting. Lendora formed the letters with care, so that all the folks up in Kenansville would know beyond doubt why they didn't want Joey Carter—or anyone else— converting their community into a hog factory. Linnill had the paper notarized, then filed it at the courthouse. The petition promptly disappeared. Over the years, he made many attempts to recover it, including a written appeal to the local judge. But no one ever saw the petition again.

This opposition from the neighbors didn't stop Joey Carter. He went right on building. He finished his first barn in 1985 and added two more in 1992, all adjacent to the Farlands' property. A couple of years later, he built the north operation, more than doubling his herd. The Farlands watched this construction with a dismay that bordered on despair. The kids stopped coming over, and the neighborhood cookouts ceased. When Georgia hung her laundry on the line, the smell got into their clothes. Lendora and her siblings endured ridicule on the school bus. Eventually, Georgia took the clothes down for the last time. It happened the day she found little brown specks on the fabric. She thought they were ants until she looked closer.

They were flecks of dried feces from Joey Carter's spray.

There were occasions in the early days when the neighbors complained to the authorities. But nothing ever changed. Joey Carter's father was a prominent real estate investor in the area, and Joey himself was a man on the make. Hog farming was a side business. His day job was law enforcement. He was an officer with the Beulaville police and a deputy with the sheriff's office. He had the power of arrest everywhere within the four corners of Duplin County. His badges made him a man that Black folks like the Farlands didn't wish to cross.

Especially when the town of Beulaville made him chief of police.

As Daniel listens to Lendora's story, he can't get the stench of hog shit out of his nose. The odor is milder inside the Farlands' home, but it's still lingering on the fringes of the room, hanging in the air like a cloud. Or maybe it's just his memory playing tricks on him. Smell can be like that, a burr clinging to the mind, a brand that won't let you forget.

In time, Lendora escorts him back outside and shows him her father's barber shop. It's an adorable wood structure about the size of a tractor shed, with a pair of paned windows on either side of the door, and a porch to catch the breeze. Lendora tells him that her father used to cut the hair of the neighbor kids, the ones who couldn't afford a cut in town. That kindness was yet one more casualty of Joey Carter's casual cruelty. Her godmother once stopped Joey on the road as he was driving by. She asked him why he was spraying when the family had clothes on the line. He just nodded his head, like the explanation was obvious, then took off.

"He didn't stop spraying," Lendora says, "and we never saw him again."

Eventually, Daniel takes his leave, explaining that he has appointments with the other plaintiffs. When he climbs back in his car, he can feel the fire igniting inside of him. The injury these people have suffered isn't some far-off thing, a gauzy remnant of the distant past. It is as clear and present as the diseased air filling his lungs.

That's the thought in his head as he drives up the road toward Woodell McGowan's house, his mind full of questions. He won't get much out of Woodell in that first visit—or for some time to come. The Woodell McGowan he meets at the door to his little white house is the antithesis of Lendora Farland, a quiet man in his mid-sixties, made even more taciturn by the years. The stories of his boyhood adventures in the forest are locked inside of him like boxes in an attic, the weight of time layered on thick, so much weariness and loss and suffering. His mother, Delores, and her siblings are gone now. He is the curator of the Hall family history. No one else in the community knows all the stories of the old homeplace and the lineage of the land. But he doesn't really want to share them. Not even with his lawyers. Someday he will, but not yet.

Joey Carter, on the other hand, Woodell is happy to talk about. He tells Daniel about the dead box that used to sit within spitting distance of his porch, all those carcasses heaped upon one another, bloating and decaying in the open air. He recounts the way the sprayfield smells when the wind blows just right. He put up a hammock for his late wife, Wanda, but she didn't get much use out of it on account of the odor. He doesn't know Joey well, but he once talked to him about the dead box. The hog farmer refused to move it. So Woodell took pictures of it and filed a complaint with the county. Finally, Joey relocated the box.

When the conversation wanes, Daniel bids Woodell farewell and moves on to another house. He makes a few more stops before getting back on the road. By the time he drives away, the flames of conviction have grown so hot that they sear the memory of the odor into his brain.

These people shouldn't have to live like this, he thinks to himself.

No one should have to live like this.

CHAPTER 14

HUNTING THE UNICORN

He who allows oppression shares the crime.
—*Desiderius Erasmus*

**Salisbury
and Lillington,
North Carolina
Winter 2015**

With Dr. Steve Wing onboard as an expert witness, Mona has half of her prophetic contingent. His scientific research is second to none, and he has that *je ne sais quoi* element, that priestly charism that makes people want to believe. But his testimony alone won't be sufficient to claim the mantle of righteousness before the jury. Mona still needs to find her unicorn—a grower who will speak the truth against his own interest, who will blow the whistle on the hog kingdom's abuses. A man unafraid to be called a traitor to his kind.

She understands the improbability of her own hypothesis. She knows how unlikely it is that such a person exists, let alone that she might find him—at least not without the benefit of blind luck. Even if she could dredge up the phone numbers of every hog farmer down east, there's a good chance that all of them would hang up on her. The industry has them by the short hairs. She needs a divining rod, somebody who knows the landscape, perhaps a grower who has already left the fold, but not too long ago, who can quietly spread the word that she's looking.

John Hughes has an idea: What about a grower who has filed suit against Smithfield? He searches the Lexis database and unearths a bankruptcy case dating back to 2009. The hog farm was allied with Premium Standard Farms before Smithfield acquired the company. The grower brought a claim against Murphy-Brown in bankruptcy, alleging that the company cancelled his contract without cause. John wades through the court record and finds the contract. It's the first grower agreement he has ever seen. He reads it with fascination. He knew the relationship was lopsided, but the full extent of the imbalance blows his mind.

Murphy-Brown owns the hogs. It sets the schedules for the delivery trucks, feed trucks, and dead trucks. It establishes the procedures that the growers have to abide by if they wish to keep pigs in their barns. The grower, by contrast, holds all of the risk. He pays the operating costs of the farm. He employs the workers and maintains the facilities and equipment. He keeps the property insured. When a hog dies in his care, he takes the loss. The grower, moreover, is required to dispose of the hog waste in accordance with state and federal law. When it rains, he cleans up after the floods and spills. He services the hundreds of thousands of dollars of debt that he took on to build the place, and any other debt that he has incurred to improve it.

If Murphy-Brown isn't satisfied with the grower's yield—the number of suckling pigs born per sow, for instance, or the death rate of finished hogs—the company can demand that the grower upgrade his facilities, install new technology, or hire new employees, all at the grower's expense. If the grower fails to make these improvements—or can't afford them—the company can terminate the contract and depopulate the farm. The relationship is purely provisional. The grower must live with the constant risk of total loss, all to earn a subsistence income of a few dollars per marketable hog. Murphy-Brown, meanwhile, collects the fully grown hogs from its farms, slaughters them at its slaughterhouses, packages the meat for sale—or exports it to China or elsewhere overseas—and rakes in around a billion dollars a year in profit.

The growers, in effect, are modern-day sharecroppers.

That's essentially the complaint that the grower in the bankruptcy case made—that Smithfield demanded improvements to his farm that he couldn't afford, and that it yanked its hogs when he failed to comply, ruining him financially. But he couldn't prove the case in court. Smithfield made a credible argument that his operation was outdated and filthy and that the cancellation was justified. From the documents, John has no quarrel with the court's findings, but he wants to hear the grower's story. Perhaps the man might be willing to help them.

John reaches out to the grower's lawyer, and before long he has the man on the phone. It's been five years since he shut down his farm, but he's still angry about it. He despises Smithfield. So do the majority of growers, he says. It's an abusive relationship. But they need Smithfield's money to keep their lights on, to hold on to their family farms.

As the grower tells it, Smithfield inflated his sins so they could pull his contract. But Mona's team isn't sure. The nuances are hard to discern. What's obvious is that in his last few years of operation, he was bleeding cash. The cost of the farm pushed him to the edge of a cliff. And the Murphy men showed no mercy. They gave him a shove and watched him fall. Then they joined his other creditors in feasting on the carcass.

It's a sympathetic tale. The man has a family. He invested fifteen years in the venture, only to be bullied into insolvency by a mega-corporation that had every means to help him, yet elected not to do so. But he isn't a witness that Mona can offer to the jury. Smithfield's lawyers could use the bankruptcy to hang him on the stand.

They probe him for a reference, another grower who might be willing to talk, but they come away empty. Nobody wants to bite the hand that feeds them. And even those growers who wouldn't mind seeing the hog barons take a punch or two don't want to talk to Mona Lisa Wallace.

They think she's coming after them, and they hate her just as much.

Months pass without a unicorn sighting. The growers' defensive line doesn't break. It doesn't even budge. But Mona's faith doesn't waver. She knows what she needs to offer the jury, the voice of an unsullied insider, whose character and motives can't be impeached. She moves ahead as if that person exists and instructs her team to keep looking.

It's Mark Doby who finally sees a crack in the human shield.

He's at the law firm on an unseasonably warm day in January 2015 when he happens across an article in *National Geographic* magazine with an evocative title "What to Do About Pig Poop? North Carolina Fights a Rising Tide." He scans it quickly, finding little enlightening. Most of the contributors he knows—Elsie Herring, Steve Wing, Rick Dove. Then he sees a new name: Tom Butler. The more Mark reads, the more his eyebrows arch. Butler is a hog farmer. He has a 7,500-head contract operation down in Harnett County. He admits that odor is a problem. He covered his own lagoons to trap the smell. He installed a digester to turn his wastewater into methane and a generator to convert the methane into electricity. And he did all that on his own, at a cost of over a million dollars, funding most of it with grant money, but paying a quarter of it out of his own pocket. This is not a story that Mark has heard before.

It has the makings of a revelation.

Mark looks up Butler Farms and leaves the grower a voicemail. Butler sends him a different number over LinkedIn. Mark shoots the *National Geographic* piece over to Daniel Wallace, saying, "Let's call him." Right away, they sense he's the genuine article, a salt-of-the-earth man of the soil whose pride in his own innovation is matched by an equal and opposite humility. Yet on the phone he's reticent, as if not quite sure he should be talking to them. That's when they bring in Mona. Before long, Tom drops his guard halfway and invites her out to the farm for a visit.

Mona doesn't hesitate. She's on the road the next day. Daniel and Mark Doby are with her, along with her daughter, Lane. The timing is serendipitous: In her coursework at Duke, Lane was just studying the process of converting methane from animal waste into energy.

While Harnett County is rustic, it's not quite the same as Duplin. It's in hog country's outer ring, west of the I-95 corridor. It's a pastoral landscape of soft hues and feathered hills, the kind of tableau that the nineteenth-century artist and environmentalist Thomas Cole might have painted when all the roads were cart paths and the farmhouses fresh built. Half a mile from Butler's farm, they roll down the windows, letting in the sky. This is their maiden trip to a hog operation. More than seeing the place, they want to smell it, to imprint the memory on their olfactory glands so they can't forget.

They turn at the sign and meander up the drive. The wind is down and the odor is faint, mingled with the scent of grass and hayseed, nothing like the stench Daniel experienced at the home of Lendora Farland. Around a bend, the barns appear suddenly, standing on the crest of the hill. They're as large as grain silos lying on their side, their exhaust fans turning like the engines of a jumbo jet. Above them the clouds are clotted, the ceiling low and threatening.

Tom Butler is waiting for them behind the barns. He's getting along in years. His hair is white and his skin is lined like vellum. He's nervous. They can tell it from the stiffness in his frame, the halting manner of his welcome. But they are nervous, too—even Mona, though she hides it with a smile. This is a portentous moment. In the flock of growers, Butler is a rare bird. His contract is with Prestage, one of the Five Families that never sold out to Joe Luter. While his financial interests are aligned with those of the industry, he's not beholden to Smithfield.

Mona handles the introductions with a warmth that belies the wintry scene. She's dressed down for the occasion, though she still looks like a lawyer in her sweater, slacks, and city boots. She emphasizes the familial connections, that Lane is her daughter and studying environmental science at Duke, and that Daniel is her nephew. Only Mark isn't a member of the Wallace clan, but he's like Andy Griffith. He puts people at ease without trying.

They stumble a bit early in the conversation, as if crossing unfamiliar terrain. It's Lane who bridges the gap with her interest in Tom's novel technology. She's not as effervescent as her sister, Whitney, but her friendliness is just as sincere, and, on this subject, she knows more than the lawyers. To an inventor like Tom Butler, her curiosity is pure joy.

With Lane asking questions and hanging on his every word, Tom delivers a soliloquy about his laboratory approach to hog farming, while showing them his facility: the ten barns side by side, the two lagoons covered by high-density plastic, the labyrinth of machinery converting biogas into power. Before long, Mona and her team realize that the grower's homespun accent and mannerisms are a veil obscuring a revolutionary intelligence. He is as much a visionary as Wendell Murphy ever was. What he is plotting is the wholesale redemption of his industry.

The more time he spends with them, the more he leavens the science with storytelling. Before the advent of CAFOs, this was his family's farm. It reaches back generations to the days of his great-grandfather, when tobacco was king. Tom grew up on this land, swimming in the pond with his siblings, and helping with the animals—the cows and pigs they raised for food, and the mules that aided them with the labor.

Like so many others, he got into industrial pork production in the nineties, when the sky was rose-tinted, business was booming, and farm credit was a river as wide as the Mississippi. When he signed his first promissory note, he was flush with optimism and entrepreneurial zeal. He held the industry's guarantee like a totem in his heart, the nest egg he would build for his family as soon as he paid back his lenders. He never gave thought to the perils of hog waste, never considered what it would mean to be responsible for disposing of effluent equal to a town of 30,000 people without the benefit of a modern treatment facility.

His epiphany came through the intervention of a neighbor. It was a member of his extended family, a born iconoclast and boat-rocker, who called Tom one day in 2000 and told him that his beautiful new living room, the one he had just finished building, smelled like hog shit. Before this, Tom had heard only whispers of disenchantment through the grapevine. These were rural people, hardy, gracious, and self-reliant. They weren't the kind to complain.

Tom responded with plainspoken candor. He said he had poured almost a million dollars into the farm, most of it on credit. The only way he could eliminate the odor was to shutter the operation and decommission the lagoons. But that would require giving up the deed to a property that had been in his family for more than a century. To keep the farm, he had to keep the hogs. But he intended to find a solution.

That was the beginning of his transformation, the day the industry's golden promise turned to dross in his hands. If there was a way forward, he had to chart it himself.

The lagoon covers came to him like a gift from Minerva. He was at a conference out west when he crossed paths with the CEO of an environmental company that was working to cover dairy lagoons. The company wanted to expand to the East Coast and to test its covers on a swine operation. Tom volunteered his farm for the project. The covers, once installed, cut his lagoon odor to zero and reduced the frequency of his spraying by keeping out the rain. But they weren't a panacea. His barns and sprayfields still stank, and now he had a new problem. The covers trapped natural gas that would otherwise have dispersed into the atmosphere. The easiest solution was to digest and burn it, but that was both toxic and wasteful. Eventually, he cobbled together enough grant money to install a generator that could feed his local electrical cooperative.

By now, he was way off the edge of the map. Among the community of growers, he was a gadfly. To the hog barons, he was a dewy-eyed dreamer. They didn't yet see him as a threat, but that day would come soon enough. Because Tom Butler wasn't satisfied with tinkering at the fringes of the problem. His experiments with odor control had given birth to a grander vision. The solution he needed—no, the solution the entire industry needed—was a technology that could treat the waste in real time while recovering the water and the nutrients.

In short, he needed a way to ditch the cesspools and the spray.

Thankfully, Smithfield was already looking for one—or so they said. Around the time of Tom's conversion in 2000, the company had entered into an accord with Mike Easley, the state's attorney general, that would become known as the "Smithfield Agreement." Having suffered the humiliation of defeat in its battles with Cindy Watson over the hog farm moratorium and with Mother Nature in the form of Hurricane Floyd two years later, the industry had come to the bargaining table. The result was a ceasefire with the government. Smithfield would get a reprieve from state pressure—in effect, ten years of peace—in exchange for funding new research into waste management techniques that could, ultimately, replace the lagoon and sprayfield system.

The Smithfield Agreement was managed by a consortium of scientists at NC State. The objective was to find a technology that would be operationally efficient, protect the environment, and not push the industry into bankruptcy. For years, Tom Butler looked on as the researchers spent Smithfield's cash on a smorgasbord of potential solutions. The reports they published in 2004 and 2005 struck a hopeful tone. There were a handful of promising technologies, especially something called Super Soils (later renamed Terra Blue), which involved separating the waste stream into solids and liquids, processing the solids for sale as fertilizer, and treating the liquids to be reused in flushing out the barns. But a report from 2006—the first one that addressed the economic feasibility question—soured Tom's impression of the enterprise. According to NC State, all the innovations were too expensive. The five representatives from the industry who sat on the economic subcommittee took it a step further. They argued that for the new tech to be affordable, it had to be cost-neutral. They didn't want to shell out a penny more to clean up the mess.

Thus hobbled, the NC State researchers lumbered on, testing a second generation of Super Soils in 2007 and reporting a 25 percent reduction in operational cost. To Tom Butler, this news was a looking glass into the future. With Super Soils, the hog barons could bring an end to the nightmare. With a few strokes of their platinum-tipped pens, they could eliminate the lagoon spills and fish kills and overfertilization of the land. They could mothball the big guns and the center-pivot systems polluting the air, the water, and the ground. They could usher the pork business into the twenty-first century. And the cost? In the long term, it wasn't prohibitive. A few more generations of experimentation on test farms and the efficiency gains would turn the system into a workable investment for a multibillion-dollar industry. Growers like Tom couldn't afford it. But Smithfield could.

Smithfield, however, rejected it out of hand.

That's when Tom Butler started to see things differently. That's when he felt betrayed. The Smithfield Agreement wasn't a collaborative effort to reform the industry. It was a bribe. For the trifling sum of $15 million and change, the behemoth company created by Joe Luter and Wendell Murphy had managed to put the attorney general's office to sleep, pacify the activists, and throw the media off the chase. But Tom Butler saw through it. The industry was lying.

The promise of change was a fraud.

This is why he answered the call from Mona Lisa Wallace. He's heard horror stories about her from his grower friends and other industry allies. But when he meets her in the flesh, he senses the authenticity of her interest. He answers Lane's queries with relish and tells them about the past, even takes the time to explain how his grower contract works, the nature of his expenses and his (pathetic) profit margin. He wants them to understand what the industry has done to him, the shiny nugget of fool's gold they sold him in the beginning, the way they preyed on the American Dream. He doesn't know what he's going to do after Mona leaves. He's afraid that Prestage might retaliate, that it might pull his contract and put him out of business just for talking to her. But the truth is important enough to justify the risk.

He tells them as much. He puts his fear on the table. Mona listens with sympathy. She knows how valuable he could be to her case. She can imagine Tom on the witness stand, his aging hands folded in his lap, the country sparkle in his eyes, the apotheosis of silver-haired dignity. His story would drive a ten-foot pike through Smithfield's armor. His covered lagoons and cutting-edge biogas system—all of it self-funded— would put the giant corporation to shame. The jury would trust him implicitly. This sweet, generous, brilliant man is the grower she's been looking for. He is the unicorn. But she won't do anything to hurt him. Whatever he decides, he needs to reach the conclusion on his own.

That's the way they leave it at the end of the visit—the most important things left unspoken. But the seeds have been planted. Tom Butler knows what the lawyers are up against. He knows that the industry will not reform itself.

Only brute force will bring about change.

CHAPTER 15

OUTSIDE MAN

One must still have chaos in oneself to be able
to give birth to a dancing star.
—*Friedrich Nietzsche*

**Utah,
North Carolina,
and New York City
Autumn 2015**

Michael Kaeske is a creature of wind and sky, of green rivers and snow-capped mountains, of red rock and glacial ice and pillow-soft western powder. If he has a shrine, it is the Utah desert—Moab, Cedar Mesa, the Valley of the Gods. He's sought adventure all over the world, but this is the place he feels most alive.

When he isn't in the courtroom, that is.

Mike Kaeske is a trial lawyer. It's what he does for a living, but also who he is on a cellular level. It's in his veins, his guts. He's a connoisseur of the great cross-examination, a Sun Tzu–level master of adversarial psychology, a method actor whose highest role is playing himself before the jury, of making a case that even he would believe.

His roots are in the working class, in the Green Bay of the seventies and eighties. He's the son of a social worker and a nurse, people who instilled in him the meaning of sacrifice and service. When he was a boy, he had a fantasy that one day he would own a car fancier than his house. It was the stuff of adolescent daydreams, but the law would make it come true. After studying philosophy and international relations at Syracuse, he found his calling at the University of Texas School of Law, where he discovered an appetite and aptitude for legal combat. He spent less time in class than he did in moot court. He wasn't a ladder-climber. He didn't care about landing a prestigious judicial clerkship or a job at an elite law firm. He wanted to live in the trenches, to try cases to verdict.

He was lucky. Two lions of the Texas trial bar were looking for a protégé: Fred Baron and his wife and partner, Lisa Blue Baron, of the law firm Baron & Budd. They met Mike when he was still a fresh-faced kid with a ponytail. They saw what he was made of, the dazzle in his wit and the flint in his soul, that rare breeding of charisma and adamantine will. They took him under their wing and honed his native instincts. He became a weapon in their hands, a buzz saw with a scalpel's precision. He tried cases by the dozen and won them all.

But that was just the beginning.

Mike Kaeske came into his own when he went off on his own. He became the quintessential outside man, the one with the special set of skills, the ghost nobody has ever heard of, except the few people who needed to know—his friends, his girlfriend, Haven, his two kids, and the clients who have watched him put a blade into giant corporations and bring home multi-million-dollar awards.

In the early fall of 2015, he's at the end of one of his five-year cycles, the seasons by which he structures his life. The past five years have been an express train of nonstop litigation. Most of it he's wrapped up now. He's sitting pretty in the saddle and in a playful mood. He's thinking of unplugging for a while, meeting some friends way off the grid, then taking Haven to Cabo and on to California where they met. He's not envisioning another disappearing act. The cycle before this one he devoted entirely to bicycling—training for road races, traveling, racing, and then training some more. He's in his mid-forties now and his body, as fit as it is, can't take that kind of punishment anymore. Besides, he's grown a bit weary of his youthful obsessions. He's thinking that some quiet would be nice. Some time with his loved ones under an open sky.

When the call comes from Texas, he takes it because it's Lisa Blue, his mentor in the law and, for years now, one of his best friends. He listens to her because he trusts her. These days, she's like a sister to him. She has a case he might be interested in, a litigation in North Carolina against Smithfield Foods, the world's largest producer of pork. It's about hog farms and odor. He's skeptical at first, doesn't quite get the rub.

He has no idea that this case will lay claim to the next five years of his life.

※

Mona Wallace and Lisa Blue go way back. They fought together in the asbestos wars of the nineties and early aughts, when every lawyer with a shingle, it seemed, was suing companies like Amchem and Owens Corning over the epidemic of mesothelioma and other cancers triggered by their asbestos-laden ceiling tiles, adhesives, textiles, and cement. That was before Fred Baron, one of the generals in the asbestos litigation, received his own cancer diagnosis and he and Lisa sold the firm. These days, Mona thinks of Lisa not as a trial lawyer but as a psychologist and jury consultant, a mind reader that America's premier plaintiffs' attorneys call upon to help them select a panel of jurors that will deliver their clients justice—with six to nine zeroes attached.

As Lisa sees it, however, she never really left the practice of law. She's still the woman who has tried over 230 cases to verdict. She just took a hiatus when Fred was sick. She's a trained psychologist as well as an attorney. She is happiest wearing both hats, combining jury consulting and mindfulness training for lawyers and judges with occasional trial work. Now that she has children, though, she's extremely careful about the cases she takes. Trials are a meat grinder. To leave her daughters for weeks or months at a time, the work has to be truly compelling.

When Mona calls in early October, Lisa hears her out as a friend. Her first impression is that the hog farm cases are unusual, her second that they're unwieldy. Twenty-six cases and hundreds of rural plaintiffs, few of them highly educated, with a core claim of odor nuisance, and a Chinese-owned multinational conglomerate on the other side of the "v." She's never heard of such a thing. How would they even value the damages? Mona is in the market for a litigation partner, someone with experience and resources who will enter the case as joint counsel and share the expenses and the commission. It's common practice in mass actions. The cost of trying a series of big cases to verdict can run into the tens of millions of dollars. Even the most successful plaintiffs' attorneys seldom go it alone.

The longer they talk about Smithfield, however, the more the conversation tilts in Lisa's mind.

"Have you decided who's going to try the case?" she asks.

Lisa doesn't mean any offense by it, and Mona takes none. Mona is no stranger to high-stakes jury trials. She's tried countless cases and settled many more. But she's spent much of the last decade building her firm and managing her stable of lawyers. A case as monumental as this needs to be tried by a specialist, someone tough enough to take the most brutal blows and sharp enough to maintain an impossible edge. Mona has the toughness in spades. She's damn near unbreakable. But sharpness is an acquired trait, lost far more easily than it is gained. Fifteen years ago, Mona could have done it all herself. Now, maybe not.

Mona speaks a couple of names aloud, trial lawyers she trusts. Lisa listens for a moment, then makes a suggestion. She knows someone else, a lawyer she whelped in her days at Baron & Budd. He's not a fan of the spotlight. But his trial skills are second to none.

His name is Mike Kaeske.

Mona agrees to a telephone introduction and then to a meet-and-greet in person. The plans come together swiftly. She figures that the best way to educate Mike about the case is to show it to him. She calls in a few favors and arranges a baptism on land and in the air.

The immersion will take place down east.

The Duplin County airport is like a big-top circus tent in the middle of the Dust Bowl. It's the kind of place that makes you wonder why it's there. And who's behind it. In this case, the answers are easy to discern. It's there because the hog barons like to fly private. The public terminal is compact and functional, with a small lounge and restrooms to accommodate day-trippers stopping in to refuel. But the private hangars are cavernous, large enough to house a trio of business jets. At least one of them—hell, maybe all of them—might as well have "Wendell H. Murphy" emblazoned over the rolling doors.

It's a glorious autumn day in early November 2015 when John Hughes and Daniel Wallace meet Rick Dove in the airport's lounge. Rick is a stalwart bear of a man with the iron posture and crew cut of a jarhead, the stern face and resonant voice of a jurist, and the pocket-heavy wardrobe of someone who spends his life outdoors. In short, he looks like what he is—an ex-Marine, former military lawyer and judge, and now manager of the Waterkeeper Alliance's outpost in New Bern, at the mouth of the Neuse River. When he isn't plying the waters in his boat, he's up in the sky in a light aircraft, photographing every hog factory for hundreds of miles. Over the past decade, he and his pilot buddies in the Neuse River Air Force—their half-joking call sign—have documented every bend and fold of the landscape from an altitude of one thousand feet. Their archive is a treasure trove of law-breaking by the industry—sludge accumulation, spraying after rainfall, breached lagoon walls, storm-surge flooding. Rick knows the regulations by heart, and every farm by name. He's been in the game since the early nineties, since he met Don Webb and Don opened his eyes to the truth.

Rick greets John and Daniel with a handshake, and they chat for a bit as they stare out the windows at the tarmac, waiting for a plane to arrive. Lisa Blue and Mike Kaeske are flying in from Dallas. According to the FlightAware app, Lisa's Hawker 800 is due any minute now.

The building around them is mostly empty, just an airport attendant behind the desk and a pair of men standing in the corner by the entrance. At first, John and Daniel pay no attention to the men, but Rick notices them. He can spot company men a mile away.

It isn't long before the men are joined by a second pair. They saunter through the doors and stand together awkwardly, trying but failing to look like they belong. Their voices are too low, their eyes linger too long on the group from out of town. They have smartphones in hand, and one of them is holding a compact video camera. Out of the corner of his eye, Rick catches them taking surreptitious photographs. If he had to guess, they're recording audio, too.

"See those guys?" he says softly. "They're with the industry."

Daniel frowns, nonplussed. "What are you talking about?"

Rick tilts his head. "Those guys that just walked in are with the industry."

John follows the gesture with his eyes. The men remind him of the ones that crowded into the back of Judge Parsons's courtroom. Lily-white, middle-class, corporate types with too-inquisitive gazes and spring-stiff frames. The slightest whiff of menace about them. He wonders how they knew to be here. It isn't until later that Rick tells him the airport is a surveillance post for Murphy-Brown, the staff on the lookout for unwanted guests—activists, scientists, lawyers. As soon as inbound flight plans hit the air traffic control system, calls go out and welcome parties get dispatched. The company men never try to hide. Their goal is intimidation.

The Hawker comes in from the southwest, opposite the light wind, and touches down gracefully. It's a beautiful plane, rakishly lined, with half a dozen windows on each side.

John and Daniel lead the way out onto the tarmac, with Rick trailing a step behind. He casts a glance at the Murphy men and his lips curl into a smirk. *Yeah, it's big, isn't it?* he thinks, as they stare at the jet in astonishment. It might even be bigger than Wendell Murphy's.

When the airplane door opens, three people emerge from it, not two. Lisa Blue is in her sixties, but she carries herself like a younger woman, her eyes and lipstick bright, and her wavy chestnut hair curled at the tips. She's dressed casually, as if for a jaunt to the supermarket. You might never guess that she's a friend of U.S. presidents.

Mike Kaeske is trim, fit, and handsome, though he wears his aesthetic gifts lightly. His close-cropped hair is starting to silver. He has a boyish grin that he flashes like a lucky coin, day-old stubble on dimpled cheeks, and an aura of carefree imperturbability. In his dark T-shirt and jeans, he has the air of an everyman headed to see his favorite indie band play at Lollapalooza.

With them is another woman about Mike's age, with bone-straight blonde hair, azure eyes, and a sweet Donna Reed smile. Her name is Lynn Bradshaw. If Lisa Blue doubles as Mike's sister-mother, Lynn is his consigliere and conscience. They were an item once—for a while, actually. He thinks of her kids as his. He helped raised them, and he still works closely with Lynn. She's a whip-smart attorney and her sense of balance helps him keep his own.

For all three of them, this is their inaugural trip down east. Mike's not even sure he's been to North Carolina before. Their first impression is an unforgettable one—the flies. The air is dancing with them. It's not quite a swarm, but there are far too many for an autumn day, even in the South. The flies find their way into the plane, buzzing around the cabin.

Mike and Lisa shoo them away as they descend the steps with Lynn. They have the same thought:

Are these things coming from the hog farms?

Their second impression is just as memorable. The Murphy men are on the tarmac now, cameras out in the open, shutters snapping like the paparazzi. Mike and Lisa ignore the attention. But they interpret the signal as clearly as John and Daniel did in the terminal. America might be a free country, but they're on foreign soil now. Wherever they go, whatever they do, someone from the company will be watching.

After the obligatory introductions, Rick Dove outlines the plan. He brought a Cessna over from New Bern. It's all fueled up and ready to fly. It won't take long to show them from the air what the industry has camouflaged on the ground. After that, they'll take a trip down the road to REACH, where they'll meet the neighbors who have been fighting this war from the beginning.

The thing is, only Mike and Lisa feel the urge to brave the single-engine plane. Rick shrugs, as if it's everyone else's loss, and beckons them to follow him down the flight line. Meanwhile, John, Lynn, and Daniel find seats at the edge of the tarmac, away from the meddling eyes and ears of the Murphy men, who are still lurking in a gaggle by the terminal.

The wheels of the feather-light Cessna leave the earth almost as soon as Rick throttles up. With the wings overhead, the cockpit is a glassed-in panopticon affording a God's-eye view of the ground. At a few hundred feet, Rick banks the plane to the east and points a finger.

"Take a look," he says over the headset.

The horizon opens up into geometrical fields bordered by dense stands of forest that surround the riverine wetlands. On the fringes of the fields are clusters of shimmering white barns, and beside them are ponds of pink liquid, like giant swimming pools laced with Pepto-Bismol. As they climb higher and loop to the west, the hog farms multiply until, somewhere in the vicinity of the town of Magnolia, they dominate the landscape in every direction. Like a tour guide, Rick identifies the biggest operations and ticks off the list of their code violations.

For Mike and Lisa, the view from above is an existential portal, as affecting as it is revealing. It's that way for everyone who sees it. A pilot buddy of Rick's even wrote a poem about it. In "Looking Down," Bob

Epting speaks of the land in its virginal state, of the oceans that preceded the sandy fields and boggy ground, of a coastal paradise teeming with life, walked by men at peace with nature. He limns the story of the ruin that followed, the centuries-long exploitation of the poor by the rich, the plow enforced by the lash, the buying and selling of souls, and the conversion of the soil into gold, first planted crop, then hogs by the million, crammed into cages, their eyes never seeing the sun until the day they're taken away. The hogs are hidden, kept out of sight. Better for people not to know how the bacon is made. Except that up in the air, there's no concealing the waste. It's everywhere, billions of gallons of it, as far as the eye can see.

Mike and Lisa talk about it when they're back on the ground and driving to REACH, the Murphy men tailing them in a black Suburban. They talk about it with Don Webb and Devon Hall and Elsie Herring. They keep talking about it on the flight home to Texas, that and the plague of flies.

At the same time, they are pragmatic about the choice before them. This is a lawsuit they are discussing. The target is a flagship American corporation underwritten by the Chinese government. They could make it all the way to the finish line, having invested millions of dollars to get there, and receive nothing from a jury but pennies and a pat on the back. It's too hard, they think, too risky.

Lynn Bradshaw encourages them to reconsider. She's a farm girl from Kansas. She knows what it's like to love a place like it's a child. She's also fitted with a moral compass that barely wavers. Like John Hughes, she's an idealist in a realist's skin.

She poses a quiet question: "What if it's the right thing to do?"

✳

Mike and Lisa agree to meet up again the following week, this time with Mona Wallace and John Hughes in New York City. It's a celebration of sorts, Mona's sixty-first birthday. Along with doing business, they're going to have a little fun. There's a new musical on Broadway that everybody's raving about. They have tickets to see *Hamilton*.

They stay at a hotel in Midtown and grab a pre-show dinner at a

seafood place where fresh fish and crustaceans are set out in crates of
ice—Fagri, Lethrini, Dorado Royale, and on and on. John Hughes is
out of his depth. He asks Mike to order something for him. Kaeske isn't
a person that the professor's son would normally trust. John has always
been dubious of the cool kids of the world. They have never understood
him, and sometimes they have abused him. But Mike has this disarm-
ing way about him, this guilelessness beneath the surface polish, as if he
has never lost his boyhood heart.

He's got a good core, John decides. *I think I can work with him.*

When it comes to Lisa, John is fascinated. She's as brassy as a political operative, and she's a walking Rolodex of Who's Who among the
trial bar. Yet her relationship with Kaeske is almost filial, as if she knows
all his secrets. She's also got a depth to her, an unexpected spiritual side.
She's Jewish by birth, but she's a straight-up practicing Buddhist. She's
into mindfulness and meditation, and she's a health nut. If there's any
pretense about her, John can't see it.

Over dinner, they keep the conversation spirited, a procession of
banter and stories from the past. On the walk back to the hotel, however,
with the lights of the city twinkling around them, Mike cracks the door
a bit and offers John a glimpse of his thoughts about the case, along with
the rules he lives by.

"I do only one case at a time," Mike says. "I do that so I can focus.
When I take on a case, I'm the captain. I talk through every decision
with my team, but I can't have multiple people speaking to the other
side. You should know up front that I can be hard to deal with. By the
end of this, I'll probably drive all of you crazy. Honestly, though, I'm still
on the fence about it. Just doing one case at a time, it has to be the right
case. Something that's big enough for you might not be big enough for
me. How many cases does your firm have?"

John raises an eyebrow. "You mean including the worker's comp and
PI stuff?" When Mike nods, Johns answers: "It must be hundreds."

"Right. And how many lawyers?"

"Ten, and about sixty staff," replies John.

"For me, I've got this core group of four or five people, and that's
my team."

As John mulls over the arithmetic, he toys with doubt. For a lawyer doing only one case at a time, a speculative litigation like this would be a monumental gamble. But the angel in his head whispers a different word: *Kaeske's going to do it.*

Mike, however, is still wrestling with the cost. He can't shake what he saw down east, and he can't get Lynn's appraisal out of his head. She lobbied hard after they got back to Texas. She told him he could do it, and that if he didn't do it, it might not get done. He doesn't disagree with her. The case is worthy. It's necessary. And it's winnable.

But the practicalities still matter. He can't pay his people with sentiment. There's something he has to do before he can commit.

He needs to convene a focus group—a mock jury—in Raleigh.

✳

Mike throws himself into the preparation like a madman, though madness isn't how he would describe it. He's a laser beam. This is the way it goes when he gets turned on. He pesters Daniel Wallace and Mark Doby for documents and contracts, everything they've got in their files, and he devours them, absorbing the details, putting connections together, building the narrative in his head until he knows it like it's his own story. In just a few weeks, he learns the case so well that he can not only present the plaintiffs' side but argue Smithfield's, too.

That's one of his core strategies, the question he always asks before he says yes to a new case. How is he most likely to lose? He needs to figure out the nature of the poison before he can fashion an antidote.

It's vintage Sun Tzu: Know your enemy. And know yourself.

They run the focus group in December, in the festive slow-walk before the holidays. Everything about the event is secretive, buttoned-up. No last names or firm names are disclosed to the participants. It's Mike and Lisa's show, but Mona brings a contingent over from Salisbury to observe. Daniel Wallace and Mark Doby are there, as is John Hughes.

They watch behind the two-way mirror as Lisa offers an overview of the format and a précis of the case. She's pleasant, endearing, looking people in the eye, emphasizing the importance of their mission. She needs them to be candid with her even if it's uncomfortable, to speak their minds and decide what award, if any, the neighbors should receive in compensation for their injuries. That is their sole duty, the opinion they're being paid to offer. Then she trades places with Mike.

Kaeske's locked in, an actor in character, his attention nowhere but the stage. The whimsical, wisecracking man on the street is stowed away back at the hotel, though the good humor is still there, the glitter in his eyes. First impressions are everything. He wants the panel—the first of two he will address today—to like him instinctively, more than that, to find him trustworthy. He's dressed like a lawyer for the occasion, his suit a shade of dark blue, his freshly pressed shirt light blue, and his shoes hand-crafted in Germany, though in a nod to his laid-back personality, he's wearing his collar open, saving the tie for the courtroom.

He dives into his presentation with gusto, distilling the plaintiffs' case into a quarter of an hour. He presents as a man who's been living with the case for years, not weeks, his command of the material a credit to his indefatigable preparation. That's his signature in the courtroom, his edge over the global defense firms with their massive budgets and legal rosters. They can have him outnumbered and outgunned, but they will *never* know the case better than he does. When they stumble in the weeds, that's when he takes them down.

In the focus group context, however, he plays the bad guys, too. He performs the about-face with relish, putting a cudgel in Smithfield's hands, as if *trying* to turn the panel against the neighbors. He and Lisa want to put a peg in the board on the worst-case end of the spectrum. For this reason, they skewed the jury to the right. The folks he's talking to are white conservatives. They have little native sympathy for trial lawyers and a soft spot for big business. Also, as *southern* white conservatives, they aren't necessarily sympathetic to all the goals of civil rights. If he's lucky, he might have even bagged himself a racist.

When he wraps up the mini-openings, Lisa hands out a feedback form and gives everyone a few minutes to fill it out. Then she collects them and has a conversation with the group, a debriefing of sorts. "Would you find for the plaintiff or the defendant?" she inquires, going around the room. Over and over again, the mock jurors say the same thing: "I'd find for the plaintiffs . . . the plaintiffs . . . the plaintiffs."

"And how much would you award?" says Lisa. The numbers aren't inspiring, but they are orders of magnitude above zero. With a few follow-up questions, Lisa probes the edges of the panel's collective conscience. She wants to know how the case struck them and how they figured their awards. It turns out that these white conservatives are disgusted by what the neighbors have been forced to endure. They calibrated their awards to give the neighbors the option to move, to leave the hog farms behind.

After lunch, the lawyers bring in a new panel. This one is racially and demographically mixed, much closer to the jury they would expect in Judge Britt's courtroom. Again, Lisa and Mike do their dance, as Mona and her team watch behind the mirror. As before, the focus group is unequivocal. The plaintiffs win, they say. The plaintiffs win.

When Lisa makes her inquiry about numbers, Mike and Mona and their companions in the observation room take a collective breath. For Mike, the panel's answer will inform his calculation of risk, whether it makes sense for him to take the case. For Mona, on the other hand, the focus group is an early reckoning. She has already devoted nearly two years to this litigation. She's signed pleadings. She's sat in people's living rooms and made promises from the heart, promises to go the distance and bring these cases to trial. There is no turning back now.

As the panel members begin to speak, every face in the observation room brightens, as if reflecting the glow of some distant sun. *Holy shit,* thinks Daniel Wallace, as he trades a glance with Mark Doby. The numbers conjured by the panel are not just higher than the first group's. They are higher by a factor of ten. These people want to see Smithfield pay.

So do Mike and Lisa Blue. With Mona, they're all in.

CHAPTER 16

A VISION ON THE MOUNTAIN

If you are free, you need to free somebody else.
If you have power, your job is to empower somebody else.
—*Toni Morrison*

**Park City,
Utah
January 2016**

Shortly after the New Year, Mona Wallace sends an advance team from her firm—John Hughes, Daniel Wallace, and Mark Doby—out west to the snow-draped mountains of Utah to spend some quality time with Mike Kaeske. Their goal is to select the bellwether cases, the handful of trial balloons they will float first in front of the jury.

The choice of bellwethers is pivotal in a mass action, like choosing the glass for a crystal ball. The success or failure of the initial cases will prefigure the future of the litigation. If the bellwether verdicts come back for the plaintiffs, they will likely set the stage for a global settlement involving all the cases and neighborhoods. If one or two bellwether juries find for Smithfield, they will probably foreshadow a long conflict, a slog through the trenches en route to an uncertain armistice. In the doomsday case, a series of defense verdicts in the bellwethers could portend a wipeout for the plaintiffs, an outcome that would leave the neighbors without recourse and their lawyers financially gutted.

Mike Kaeske, however, isn't just interested in strategizing with the advance team. He wants to learn the mettle of the men from Mona's firm and to bond with them, to earn their trust.

He invites them into his world and shows them his winter playground, takes them to his favorite restaurants and treats them to a get-away on the slopes. His home sits on a mountaintop two thousand feet above the town of Park City. It's more ski chalet than house, with acres of polished cherry wood and rustic stone, an indoor swimming pool and gym, mammoth windows that look out over the aspen forest, and a ski run a stone's throw from his terrace door. It's easy to get spoiled here, to fall into Mike's spirited rhythms (a few bullet trips down the black diamonds before cracking open a computer) and to feel pampered by Haven's hospitality (her banana bread is legendary). The two of them are generous hosts. They spare no expense for their friends. But Kaeske's life is not just a joyride. He's one of the hardest workers they have ever seen. He's a nuclear reactor in human flesh. When he turns the lights on, he doesn't turn them off again—for years.

After diverting themselves, the four men set up a mobile office in Mike's game room. Around them are wood-trimmed tables for pool and craps, an original Pac-Man arcade station, an array of high-end pinball machines, and a fully stocked walk-up bar. They sit in the circular booth beside the bar, computers at the ready and a couple of TV monitors mounted nearby. Their focus is the master digital map of the hog farms and the plaintiffs' communities.

They examine the cases one by one, with Daniel and Mark chiming in with details about the clients, and John contributing an occasional dash of legal commentary. They consider the clients' history and ancestry, their roots on the land. They calculate the distances to odor points: the barns, lagoons, and sprayfields. They scrutinize the map for any contaminating factors—a nearby poultry operation, for instance, or a hog farm not affiliated with Smithfield that Mark Anderson could finger as the "real" culprit. Their evaluation is coldly analytical, devoid of personal feeling.

Their first pick is *McKiver* in Bladen County. The adjacent hog operation, Kinlaw Farms, is a sprawling enterprise, with twelve barns, a trio of lagoons, and 15,000 hogs. In addition, the clients down the road have an unshakable claim to the land. Joyce McKiver, the eighty-year-old matriarch, has lived on her property for half a century. She raised her children there; a number of them are also plaintiffs. Her husband, who bought the land in 1951, died there. The driveway to Kinlaw Farms is ten yards from her lawn. Other neighbors in the *McKiver* group have been on the land even longer, going back to the 1920s. They watched Billy

Kinlaw build the farm. They objected to it at the time and have been objecting ever since. It's a classic weathervane case, with durable historical claims and an ideal sampling of core facts.

Kaeske puts a pin in it. When he and Mark Anderson lock horns over the trial schedule, he's going to push hardest for this one. And one way or another, he's going to get his way. Ultimately, *McKiver* will be the bellwether of the bellwethers, the first case to go to trial.

There are other client groups with equally convincing claims to the land. Daniel tells them about his visit to the Farlands' house outside Beulaville and the story Lendora recounted about Joey Carter. He tells them about meeting Woodell McGowan and learning that his mother's family has been on that land for over a century. They pull up a map of Hallsville Road and sift through the details. On its own, the Farlands' claim is golden. Any jurors in their right mind would sympathize. But when Mike Kaeske hears that the hog farmer is the retired chief of police, a deputy sheriff, and a volunteer firefighter, he hesitates. Smithfield's going to want this one, he says. They'll parade Joey Carter around as the poster child of a righteous grower.

His instinct is spot on. *McGowan* will be Mark Anderson's grand cru selection. The hog barons will adopt Joey as their mascot and throw all of their weight behind his case.

The four of them talk about the legacy claims, the neighbor activists who have fought the Five Families for decades—Elsie Herring, Violet Branch, Rene Miller, and Don Webb. All of them have compelling stories to tell. All of them have developed a certain comfort with the media and the spotlight. Yet their public profile could be a disadvantage in the courtroom. Cases that have been tried in the press often backfire in litigation. On cross-examination, prior statements shorn of context can be retooled into weapons of impeachment, and even the most morally justified of grievances can look like a self-righteous vendetta.

Much better to start with a blank slate before the jury.

When they get to the *Anderson* case, they see the resemblance to *McKiver*. The group is big, with twelve neighbors, and the mother of the lead plaintiff, Eunice Anderson, lived on the land from the Great Depression until her death in 2010. The other plaintiffs have all owned their properties since the seventies and eighties, well before the advent of the CAFO revolution. Two Smithfield operations are in the vicinity, with a total of 5,700 hogs between them. And the Crooked Run facility has a sordid history of violation notices from the state. On paper, at least, the growers look like slumlords. Kaeske flags *Anderson,* too.

And on it goes, just like this, for the better part of a week. After breakfast and a workout, Mike and Daniel hit the slopes for a couple of hours—the powder is feet thick—and then circle up with Mark and John in the game room. They aren't sure how many bellwether cases Judge Britt will allow in the initial discovery pool—the cases green-lighted for discovery and placed on the trial docket—or how ornery Smithfield will be in the negotiations. They wrestle through the map data like bunkmates at basic training, the business talk seasoned by fraternal banter between Mark and Daniel, windy musings by John Hughes, and doses of Mike's sardonic humor.

They rank the *Artis* group in Pender County as another possible Smithfield candidate. The twenty-one plaintiffs are sprinkled along an extended stretch of Piney Woods Road, and neighbors like Eddie and Lenora Nicholson and Joyce and Willie Messick are a mile away from the nearest hog house and two-thirds of a mile from the nearest sprayfield. That's well within the 1.5-mile radius established by Steve Wing's research, but on the outer edge of distances in the litigation. Mike Kaeske can almost hear the McGuireWoods lawyers grilling Willie Messick on the stand: "You're telling this jury that odor from the hog farms a mile down the road—*a mile through trees and forest*—has interfered with your enjoyment of the land? Really?"

Amid the badinage, the lawyers boil down one of the key weaknesses of their case, the fact that smell is the least reproducible of the five senses and the hardest to communicate to others. An unfamiliar odor can't be captured in a photograph or memorialized in a recording. It can't be placed in a bottle and passed around the jury box like O.J.'s leather glove. Odor is episodic and unpredictable, and its intensity and unpleasantness are subjective. The same scent can fall on one person's nose like a gentle hand, on another's like a swung fist.

There's a partial solution to this: a scientist who can educate the jury about the "fate and transport" of chemicals, the way the molecules that present as odor travel through the air. But that's abstract art compared to a crime-scene photograph or a live-action reproduction of an accident scene. It also happens that the institutions where such scientists work—university ag departments and private labs—are largely beholden to the hog barons for their research dollars, or afraid to cross swords with Smithfield. Mona and John have been talking to experts from coast to coast. Many have politely declined. A few have said "hell no." One of the outliers, Dr. Shane Rogers at Clarkson University, has shown promise. He did CAFO research at the EPA. He's worked on hog farms in North Carolina. Still, even if he signs up, he won't be able to hand the jurors a vial of pink lagoon water and say, "This is what it smells like." Because that's *not* what it smells like. The odor is in the air, and reproducing the air for the jury is like conjuring the spirits of the dead. There's a reason there are no seances in the courtroom.

Kaeske has one other item on his to-do list. Since 20 percent of the cases involve hog farms owned and operated by Murphy-Brown, they need a company-owned farm as a bellwether. After shuffling through the files, they land on *Gillis*. The Sholar Farm in Sampson County, near the birthplace of Wendell Murphy, is one of the first hog king's original properties. It's a 6,120-head feeder-to-finish farm at the end of a cul-de-sac with neighbors who can trace their ancestry on the land back to Reconstruction. Some of the plaintiffs—all Black—are almost as close to the facility as the Farlands are to Joey Carter's operation. The larger of Sholar's two lagoons, a colossal puddle of shit, might as well be in the backyard of the closest neighbor—Mary Tatum. Among the company-owned farms, Sholar is best in show.

By the end of the exercise, they have *McKiver, Anderson,* and *Gillis* as top picks. There are other cases that they highlight, too, but none will survive Kaeske's negotiations with Mark Anderson. The two lawyers will agree in principle on four bellwether cases, but they will fight like Dobermans over which four. Mike will concede the Joey Carter case—*McGowan*—to Smithfield on account of Daniel's confidence in the plaintiffs. But Anderson will shoot down every quartet Kaeske proffers, and vice versa, until, at last, worn and weary, Mike will throw in *Artis* if Smithfield agrees to *McKiver, Anderson,* and *Gillis*. That olive branch will seal the deal and lock in the five discovery pool cases—though, in a cosmic irony, the *Artis* case won't turn out as either of them anticipates. *Artis* will be the Joker card.

All of this, however, is still in the future when Mike and Haven bid farewell to the advance team. Although the mountaintop is suddenly quiet, Kaeske's brain is a hive of constant motion. In a case as big as this, the planning operates in eleven dimensions, like string theory. There are countless hypotheticals to be considered, contingencies to prepare for, moves and countermoves to plot. He's consumed by it at all hours, not just when he's on the phone with Mona's team or working at his desk, but also when he's eating Pad Ga Prow at Bangkok Thai and snowshoeing through the alpine forest with Haven and their goldendoodle, Tük. At this point, however, the case is still at a distance. He's thrown his energy into it, but the reverse is not quite true, not yet. The case hasn't taken root in his heart.

It's a feature film that performs the alchemy.

Kaeske has been a patron of the Sundance Film Festival for fifteen years, mostly for the benefit of his parents, who live at the base of the mountain and go to forty or fifty shows every year. He and Haven always accompany them to the big premieres. This year, the headliner is *The Birth of a Nation,* an historical epic about Nat Turner's slave rebellion.

The four of them make the trip to the Eccles Theater on opening night. They take seats in the front row, as the lights dim and the movie opens with a quote from Thomas Jefferson: "Indeed, I tremble for my country when I reflect that God is just; that his justice cannot sleep forever." At the outset, Mike is his skeptical self, walls up around his emotional core. He's hoping to be entertained, not transported. He's certainly not expecting an awakening.

The story of Nat Turner opens Mike Kaeske's eyes.

It's not the history of slavery that moves him so profoundly. It's the way that history is depicted, the way it's *personalized*. The characters come alive for him—young Nat, the child of prophecy, who will one day be a leader of his people; Nat's father, who is forced to leave his family and flee after being caught stealing food; Nat's mother, who fears the wrath of her mistress when the woman learns that Nat can read; Cherry, the pretty girl Nat rescues from the auction block and later marries, only to have her raped by slave catchers and left for dead. The drama is encompassing, the cinematography exquisite, and the script inspired.

Mike thinks of his clients in eastern North Carolina, most of them Black, many of them the grandchildren and great-grandchildren of slaves. One hundred and fifty years ago, it was a crime for people like them to read. White men treated them as beasts of burden, dispensable and disposable. Although the institution of slavery is gone, the exploitation of poor Black people by rich, patronizing white people is still with us. He has seen the filth with his own eyes.

When he walks out of the Eccles Theater into the cold January night, Mike Kaeske is ready to go to war for Elsie Herring and the Farland family, Woodell McGowan and Joyce Messick, and the five hundred others who have entrusted their claims to Mona Wallace. Their stories are a part of him now, bound to him by some mysterious cord. His eyes take on a resonant glow. This case is bigger than the law, bigger than the courts, bigger than the verdicts to come. Maybe the hog barons will have a come-to-Jesus experience and clean up their industry. Most likely they won't. But dammit, they will change their behavior *for these people*.

It doesn't matter how many years it takes or how much it costs him. He's going to force those fuckers at Smithfield to make it right.

PART THREE

SABOTAGE

The coward's weapon, poison
—John Fletcher

CHAPTER 17

HOG SUMMER

What gives one human being the right to
blow animal waste on another human being?
—*Elsie Herring*

Eastern
North Carolina
June–August 2016

After three years of constant preparation, of
due diligence and trips down east, of pleadings
and motions practice and preliminary discovery, the plaintiffs and Murphy-Brown take
their banners onto the field. At last, the battle
lines are drawn, the parleys are concluded, and
the archers are at their stations, arrows notched and bows bent.

In late May and early June 2016, the arrows fly.

The action happens everywhere and all at once. In Salisbury, the
first salvo of Smithfield documents hits Mona's servers—over 11,000
pages of electronic discovery. Some of the documents are relevant; many
are useless; few are organized. Another 5,000 pages land a week later,
another 8,000 pages a week after that. Then on the last day of June, the
granddaddy of document deliveries takes place—52,000 pages.

At the same time that Smithfield unloads its virtual dump trucks
on Wallace & Graham, the defense team demands that all eighty-
eight plaintiffs in the five discovery pool cases turn over their medical records—including pharmacy receipts—for the past ten years. On
its face, the request looks wildly overbroad. Nowhere in the twenty-six
complaints is a single health-related claim. Sure, there are passing references to the physiological effects of odor exposure—nausea, headaches,

burning and watery eyes, and stress. But all of this is just color in the story of the nuisance, not a legal claim requiring medical experts to kick-box over the question of causation.

The omission was strategic. Mona and John Hughes wanted to avoid precisely this fight and focus the jury's attention on the more straightfor-ward nuisance claims. But Mark Anderson's team isn't satisfied. And the discovery rules are written so broadly that the court, if pressed, would likely give it to them. It takes Wallace & Graham's fifteen-member med-ical unit weeks to gather the relevant documents—between 50,000 and 100,000 pages—and assemble them for disclosure. Mona and Bill even hire an outside vendor to assist. What they don't know is that they are hamsters on a wheel, running full tilt but getting nowhere.

Smithfield will end up using almost none of it at trial.

In the midst of the document crossfire, Daniel Wallace is tasked with assembling the pieces of a revelation. The information isn't entirely novel to the plaintiffs' team. They obtained it through an exhaustive review of the state's hog farm archive, which dates back decades. But it's new to Mike Kaeske. So Daniel assembles the material in a slide deck for Mike. Despite the success of the Murphy men in knocking down Cindy Watson's reformist agenda in the nineties, one hog farm dispute slipped through the blockade and forced something of a local reckoning.

The Mitchell Norris farm was a Murphy-allied facility built in 1994 on a parcel of farmland in Bladen County. It was a six-barn feeder-to-finish operation, meaning Norris got his pigs after they left the nursery and raised them to a market weight of 250 pounds. With one of its two-acre lagoons a mere hundred yards from the nearest neighbor, the Norris farm was the subject of countless complaints, and a prime target for Don Webb's citizen activist corps at ARSI. Wendell Murphy, however, did his typical straight man schtick, as did Mitchell Norris, the grower, and the regulators at DENR busied themselves with other things.

Until 2001. That was the year Bladen County finished construction of a new high school for 800 students just up the road from Norris's 7,300 hogs. As the crow flies, it was less than half a mile from the near-est cesspool to the parking lots. When the winds blew out of the west, the odor plume had a habit of camping out over the football field. Some days, the stench was so pervasive that it seeped into the classrooms, the hallways, the lunchroom, and the gymnasium.

The parents, predictably, blew a gasket. Suddenly, the folks at DENR were bursting with ideas about how to make the air around the Norris farm less grotesque. The state required Norris to install a bioreactor to increase the digestive efficiency of his lagoons and a treatment system to control the odor inside his barns. He had to plant a stand of cypress trees to serve as a windbreak. And when it came to spraying, he had to dispense with the big guns and deploy an AerWay tractor system to pump wastewater down onto the soil instead of up into the atmosphere. There was also the matter of the air permit. The Division of Air Quality at DENR required the hog farmer to maintain a stringent air quality permit for eight years. It was the only permit of its kind ever issued in the state of North Carolina.

Mitchell Norris didn't handle the regulators alone. His integrator, Murphy-Brown, stood beside him at every stage of the process and aided him in negotiating a resolution. When the hog farmer submitted his proposed odor management plan to the state, he got assistance from Kraig Westerbeek, then a technical specialist at the company and now its vice president of environment and support operations. Westerbeek's name is all over the state's correspondence file.

To the team at Wallace & Graham, the Mitchell Norris farm is the long-sought missing link. It's proof that the Murphy men don't just know about the odor problem.

They know exactly how to fix it.

In early June, the depositions commence in earnest. Over the languid months of summer, Smithfield's lawyers depose every plaintiff in the bellwether cases at a nondescript office building in Wilmington. The depositions, all recorded by video, grind on for hours. Some last the better part of a day. This is not unusual in such a consequential case. Any defense firm worth its weight in U.S. scrip will take the liberty to poke, prod, and plunge its fingers into the guts of the plaintiffs' stories. The questions don't have to be admissible at trial, just "reasonably calculated to lead to the discovery of admissible evidence," which gives a lawyer wide latitude to explore the fringes of relevance for useful impeachment material. To the plaintiffs, however, the defense team's queries seem plodding, gratuitous, and sometimes gruesome. Most of the folks from down east have never sat for a deposition before. Some have never been inside a courtroom. And none has ever been subjected to a verbal body cavity search by a big firm attorney dressed in a bespoke suit and trained at a top-flight law school.

For the plaintiffs' lawyers sitting beside them at the table, the ordeal has a different feel, but it is no less indelible. While Mona and Mike make occasional appearances, they delegate the bulk of duty to Daniel Wallace and Mark Doby. The young lawyers spend the summer living out of a rental house in Wrightsville Beach just down the road from the deposition site. To put the neighbors at ease, they never dress above business casual. They prep each witness carefully, showing them the landmines and fortifying them against the coming humiliation, the pain of being questioned about the worst things that ever happened to them, all for the benefit of the same billion-dollar corporation pumping hog shit into their neighborhoods. If not for the clients, who are always winsome and willing, the depositions would be a nonstop dental drill for Daniel and Mark. As it is, they take solace in keeping the defense lawyers on a leash, and then, when the blaze of afternoon gives way to the softer light of evening, they decamp to Tower 7, their favorite surfside watering hole, for fish tacos, margaritas, and the blessed catharsis of humor.

When every day feels like a scene from *Groundhog Day,* Tower 7 is a grace.

As the discovery phase progresses, Smithfield trots out an old pony—the glossy public relations campaign—and dresses it up in the new century's finery. Just as they used "Farmers for Fairness" to defeat Cindy Watson in the late nineties, they form a nonprofit called "NC Farm Families," hire an attractive girl from down east to be their public face, and blitz the airwaves, television, and social media channels with their version of the story—family farmers under siege by hog-hating environmentalists and greedy out-of-state lawyers.

On the surface, NC Farm Families looks like an independent group. The documents produced in the litigation, however, show otherwise. The organization is a Smithfield plant, formed with company dollars and support from the hog giant's favorite local ally, the NC Pork Council.

One document in particular sparkles like an uncut gem. It's an email exchange between four top Smithfield executives in the prelude to Christmas 2015. The subject: the formation of NC Farm Families and the potential for a novel advertising campaign. The participants in the exchange include Ken Sullivan, Smithfield's president; Gregg Schmidt, president of Murphy-Brown, the hog production division; Keira Lombardo, Smithfield's senior vice president of corporate affairs; and the venerable old swine hand, Don Butler.

In an opening missive to Sullivan, the big boss, Lombardo sketches out the design of the nine-ad campaign and offers a morsel of background about the organization. The ads are being crafted to reach key demographics—people under thirty, women with children, Black people, and residents of eastern North Carolina. In other words, people like the plaintiffs and folks in their communities. Of the $4 million proposed budget, the Pork Council has offered to contribute $1 million; the National Pork Producers Council (which Don Butler used to run) will contribute $200,000; and "the integrators" (the remaining Five Families) will contribute a "major" sum. Lombardo asks Sullivan for a $1 million donation from Smithfield, in addition to the funding the company already allocated to the Farm Families launch.

Ken Sullivan doesn't reply right away. He's just returned from China. Gregg Schmidt chimes in first. In a few words, he rips the bodice off the whole enterprise. "I would only add that NC Farm Families is the vehicle that was created out of concern for the nuisance suits we are battling and is the forum to focus the growers in the fight."

The first Farm Families ads start running in January 2016. A second round runs in February, and a third in April. By the time the summer comes around and Daniel and Mark are mixing it up with McGuire-Woods in Wilmington, NC Farm Families has become a household name down east. Its girl-next-door spokeswoman, Maggie Linton, has become the industry's genie, recasting the factory-like aura of a modern hog operation in the sepia-hued light of the ye olde family farm. The Murphy men might as well have dressed her up in a hoop skirt and

bonnet when they gave her the script for "Struggle," the Farm Families'
inaugural ad:

> Weeks of rain undo months of a farmer's work. Animal disease
> knocks another farm flat on its back. A farmer works six days a
> week because farming gets in his blood. Then he goes to church
> to give thanks. My family's farm is a century old. There's no bet-
> ter place to raise a family than a farm. Hog farmers in North
> Carolina feed 20 million Americans.

Linton's homespun fable—and the entire Farm Families
campaign—is a propagandistic venture, at once a rallying cry for the
growers and a spoonful of sugar to distract the public from the gall-
laced memory of twenty years of bad press. Those objectives are, in fact,
two sides of the same coin. The growers are essential to Smithfield's
legal defense. Without Rockwellian visions of the farm family to soften
its image, the company would look like what it is: a multibillion-dollar
Chinese-owned conglomerate saturating some of the poorest neighborhoods in the state with hog waste to satisfy the world's craving for bacon.
Yet to maintain the hoary illusion, Smithfield has to keep the growers
in line. Farm Families marries both of these ends. It gives the growers a
tantalizing taste of community power while casting a mesmerizing spell
on the public. After years of tinkering and tweaking, the hog barons
finally have their human shield.

Like all magic, however, it has its limits. It can't survive a sustained
confrontation with the truth. But even truth, to land effectively, must be
packaged and displayed.

It requires a production to bring out the shine.

To bring the neighbors' truth to life, Mona Wallace hires Corey Robinson, a *National Geographic* videographer who has shot film on seven
continents for a bevy of television channels and famous brands. Along
with being an artist and an adventurer, Corey is a conservationist. His
passion is telling stories that matter from every corner of the globe.

The hog cases suit him perfectly, though this is the first time he's worked on a litigation. In the autumn months, when Mike and Mona get the court's permission to visit the hog farms, Corey will have to calibrate his shots with minders breathing down his neck, inventing ways to obstruct him. For now, in the sultry heat of summer, Corey divides his time between capturing every angle of the neighborhoods and playing spy games with Smithfield.

Like everyone who has spent much time around the neighbors, Corey finds much to admire in their long-suffering dignity and kindness. He's a suburban kid from upstate New York who makes his living by the lens. He's seen the farthest reaches of the earth and made a home for himself out west in the land of white-toothed mountains and bluebird skies. He can't imagine how these people have endured the buzzards and the flies and the dead trucks and the shit-tinted spray for so many years without being soured by it, without losing their sense of decency and their faith in humanity. He doesn't think he has that kind of grace.

It's the grace that he aims to reproduce in pixels of light and color, standing on porches and out in the neighbors' yards. Many of his shots are magazine-worthy; a few are divinely inspired. There is one in particular that Mona's team will return to throughout the trials. It's a shot of Linnill Farland, now age seventy-seven, sitting in a chair outside his barber shop, wearing his trademark newsboy cap. There are branches behind him, and the trunk of a tree—one of the great pines that tower over the house he built with his own two hands. Behind that tree, in the fading distance but still obscenely close, are the roofs and water tanks of Joey Carter's hog barns. A thousand words would fail to do justice to the sorrow song in Linnill's half-smile. A whole life is mirrored in that look—a look that says, "It shouldn't be this way. But it is."

Then there is the espionage. To document the facts of life in Smithfield's kingdom, Corey has to chase the truth, track it down, and stake it out. With neighbors feeding him tips, he spends countless hours casing hog country's back roads in pursuit of a dead box with buzzards pecking at hog corpses or a spray gun flinging excrement into the sky.

The real excitement, however, doesn't happen in the daylight. It comes when most of the world is asleep. If the Murphy men had any concern at all for the neighbors, they would run their dead trucks and delivery trucks between dawn and dusk. But they don't. With thousands of hog farms to service, they work the clock like the bridge of a warship, day and night. Indeed, when the highways are empty, the trucks are most efficient. If these mechanical monsters were quiet in their passage, the neighbors might not have complained. But they are not quiet. They are loud enough to call forth the souls of the dead. When the trucks visit in the night, it's like an alarm clock of heavy air brakes and snarling pistons going off at 1:58 a.m. or 3:12 a.m.

There are only two ways that Corey can capture this phenomenon for the jury. Either he is there in the flesh when the hog trucks round the bend, their high beams piercing the dark like a grave robber's lamp, or a motion-sensitive deer camera snags the footage in his absence.

On his surveillance missions, Corey takes a partner along. Her name is Maryclaire Farrington—M.C. to her friends. She's the wispy, sunny, cute-as-a-buttercup daughter of two of Mona Wallace's dearest friends in Salisbury. And she's been working with Mona on the hog cases since she was in high school. She's now a rising sophomore at Carolina with the dream—thanks to Mona—of one day going to law school. Although she's grown up among the country club set, she's not remotely preten- tious. She's happy riding the rural byways with Corey and crawling around the mud and tick-ridden underbrush to set up a deer camera.

One midnight stakeout really marks itself in their collective mem- ory. It happens in the *Artis* community in August, a mile down Piney Woods Road from the home of Joyce and Willie Messick. Over the long summer months, M.C. has gotten to know the neighbors quite well. They didn't know what to think of her at first. They had to check her bona fides with Mark Doby. But now they adore her. She's like every- body's little sister. They've even given her a nickname—"Little Bit." She was in the neighborhood on her twentieth birthday when the commu- nity's gardener, Jimmy Jacobs—a man of few words and legendary col- lard greens—surprised her with a dozen eggs. The neighbors have often done that for Mona's team. The produce of the land is their way of say- ing thanks. M.C. loves the clients just as much. She would do anything for them, including waiting around in the dark of night for a hog truck.

She and Corey conduct a stakeout in Jimmy Jacobs's yard, which abuts the entrance to Greenwood Finishing 2, the second of a pair of hog farms separated by a sprayfield. Greenwood 1 is a third of a mile west along Piney Woods Road, closer to the Messicks. The Greenwood hog operations used to be owned by a guy named Paul Stanley, but he sold them off a couple years ago. The new owner is a young real estate whiz from Elizabethtown named Dean Hilton.

Like the Farland family and Mary Tatum, Jimmy Jacobs couldn't get away from the hogs if he tried. Every truck that services Greenwood 2, he can't help but see, hear, and smell. The dust clouds choke his garden. The stench seeps into his house. The brake and engine noises make his placid property sound like a truck stop. He can't remember how many times he's been startled out of sleep by all the clanging, chugging, revving, and screeching. He's more than happy to let Corey and Maryclaire erect deer cams on his boundary line and haunt his driveway. He wants to catch Smithfield in the act. He wants the jury to see.

The night is eerily quiet, just the crickets and nocturnal birds to keep them company. It's warm in Maryclaire's little white Kia, even in the early morning. But they can't keep the air conditioning on without the engine, and they don't want to idle for hours at a time. They have no idea when the hog truck is coming. They could roll down the windows and get some fresh air, but then they'd have to fend off the bugs, and they couldn't play their music. So they keep the windows up and the engine off, but the ignition stays on to power the stereo.

As the stars trace out their arcs above them, they while away the night singing "Connect the Dots" by Misterwives and "Green Light" by Lorde. The adrenaline rush is more effective than caffeine. Maryclaire feels like a secret agent. Every so often, they turn off the music and allow the silence to envelop them, their ears alert for the telltale growl of an engine. Corey wants to capture the hog truck in high definition. One of his cameras is standing on a tripod in the yard. All he has to do is get there in time to switch it on and focus the lens.

At last, at a quarter till five, a hog truck trundles down Piney Woods Road and slows with a hiss outside Greenwood 2. Corey and Maryclaire throw open the car doors and race to their positions—Corey behind his camera and M.C. with her iPhone, immortalizing the scene in shards of grainy light. For a handful of seconds, everything is cacophony and commotion. And then, just like that, the hog truck disappears behind the trees and stillness returns.

"Did you get it?" Maryclaire asks, breathless from the excitement.

"I got it," Corey replies, as elated as she is.

They take a selfie in the car, wide awake despite the weight of their exhaustion. Later, M.C. adds a caption to the photograph: "4:47AM. Mission Accomplished."

✳

The stakeout is a vision of hog summer, and a piece of the evidentiary brick and mortar that Mike Kaeske will assemble in Judge Britt's courtroom. But for all the memories that will later define this season in the eyes of Mona's team, one scene stands above the rest. It's a scene of bravery as profound as a soldier running into the guns.

It's Steve Wing's *de bene esse* deposition.

The beloved epidemiologist is dying of cancer. He received the diagnosis in 2015, much to the shock of everyone in his community. His condition deteriorates in the spring of 2016, and he spends time in the hospital, undergoing surgery. The treatment buys him a few more months. His condition is terminal.

In the face of such a prognosis, most people would clear their calendars and fill their remaining days with the ones they love the most. For Steve Wing, that would be his wife and daughters, his students at UNC, his forested spread outside Chapel Hill, and his music. He devotes himself to all these things. But he doesn't walk away from the hog farm cases. Instead, after clearing it with his doctor, he notifies Judge Britt that he can sit for a deposition. And not just any deposition. The deposition he has in mind is one that can be used in lieu of live testimony. It will allow him to speak to the jury from beyond the grave.

In the last week of August, he sits before the cameras for two days straight, patiently fielding every question put to him by Mike Kaeske and Mark Anderson. Despite his natural affability and passion for the cause, the experience is exhausting. He is gaunt and frail, a shadow of his vigorous former self, but the light in his eyes is undimmed.

He takes the lawyers on a guided tour of his research and the blowback he received after he challenged the hog industry's orthodoxy in 1999. Then he offers an assessment of each case, each neighborhood, and compares them to the communities he researched. When Kaeske shows him a chart of the distances in the *McGowan* case—how close the Farlands are to Joey Carter's hog facilities—Wing's eyes narrow, and his face tightens. He's never seen people living so close to hog barns and sprayfields. He leans forward and folds his hands on the table.

"You can imagine," he says, "living just a block away or a few blocks away from a gigantic pit of feces and urine. If you lived in a neighborhood where there was a giant pit of feces and urine and that material was then sprayed out near your home—" He interrupts himself. "I mean, the distances here—this is less than a tenth of a mile from people's homes. It doesn't take a stretch of the imagination to appreciate that this amount of animal waste that's decomposing, where the gases and particles are being emitted from the confinements and from the cesspools and the sprayfields, could have a severe impact on people."

It is a bravura performance made all the more stirring by the admission he concedes about his cancer. He will never have the chance to see the effect of his words in the courtroom, the way the jurors will come to hang on his every pronouncement. In early November, less than two and a half months after his deposition, he will pass away at home, surrounded by family and friends. But over these two days in August, his voice is strong, his mind is clear, and he speaks with the self-assurance that Mona and John witnessed when they met him two years ago at the Open Eye Café. He speaks like a man for all seasons, like Thomas More.

A man who knows before God that he is right.

CHAPTER 18

THE MURPHY MEN

The highest reach of injustice
is to be deemed just when you are not.
—*Plato*

There's a certain pseudo-swagger that marks a company man, a gleam in the eye like a borrowed ray of sunshine, a swell to the chest that compensates for a subordinated ego, and a smirk at the ready to conceal the pucker of one who's kissed the ring. The Murphy men are no exception, especially the satraps and prefects who now run the kingdom built by Wendell Murphy and Joe Luter. Men like Don Butler, John Sargent, and Kraig Westerbeek.

All of these men Mike Kaeske summons in the fall of 2016 to answer his questions about the world they have made, to swear a solemn oath and explain how they can justify a system that exploits everyone but themselves. It would be more gratifying, of course, if Kaeske could depose the old hog kings. But the law only allows the plaintiffs to look back three years from the date the lawsuit was filed, and both Murphy and Luter vacated the throne long before 2010. So Kaeske subjects their underbosses to his version of the Inquisition.

John Sargent, the vice president of hog operations at Murphy-Brown, has the distinction of being the first Smithfield man in the spotlight. With his close-cropped hair, receding widow's peak, and knuckled nose that looks like it's seen a few blows in its time, he has the unobtrusive, melt-into-the-background appearance of a high school athletics director.

In deposing Sargent, Kaeske is really only interested in soliciting one thing: a portrait of serfdom in the kingdom, the scripted life of a Smithfield contract grower. As commissions go, it should be a breeze. The feudal relationship is spelled out in black and white in the company's grower contracts. Still, Sargent struggles to admit the obvious. When Kaeske presses him about the touchy concept of "control," Sargent does a cockatoo dance around it.

"We do not control the growers," he says. "They have specific guidelines in the contract that they're responsible for, and we have guidelines that we're responsible for."

It's an artful dodge, but Kaeske is ready for it. "Murphy-Brown controls the requirements of the grower's facilities through the standard operating procedures, correct?"

After a turgid chuckle, Sargent replies, "Again, we don't control . . . We control . . . Actually, I want to say it right. We have a specification of the facilities they are supposed to have. If we find a better way to do it, we can change those requirements."

As if prompted, Kaeske turns to the contract itself. In a series of short queries, he outlines the shape of the growers' servitude. "You get to mow the grass if you don't like the way the grass is being mowed, right? . . . You get to spray for weeds if you don't like the way the weeds are being sprayed, right? . . . Murphy-Brown gets to decide when the hogs are ready to leave the grower's facility, correct? . . . Murphy-Brown controls the feed brought to the facility, right? . . . And Murphy-Brown controls when the dead hogs are picked up, right?"

All of this Sargent admits, albeit reluctantly.

Next, Kaeske illuminates the way the growers are paid. It's a take-it-or-leave-it offer. It's not a living wage. It's not adjusted for inflation. It's nonnegotiable. The growers receive a flat day rate for each hog in their custody, along with a small performance bonus. But they don't get to choose how many hogs they take, or how long those hogs stay in their barns, or when the barns get replenished after the hogs are taken to market. In addition, Sargent can't recall the last time the growers got a raise. He doesn't know if there's been any increase in the past ten years.

Toward the end, Kaeske zeroes in on the hog waste. He gets Sargent to admit that, even with all the control the company exercises over the growers, it has never attempted to monitor the odor level or manage waste disposal at any of the farms in the discovery pool.

The portrait that emerges from Sargent's deposition turns the parable of the Prodigal Son on its head. Instead of treating its growers like favorite sons, the hog barons rule them with an iron fist, pay them with pig scraps, and let them clean up the shit.

※

The next Smithfield executive to tangle with Kaeske is the vice president of environment and support operations, Kraig Westerbeek. In contrast to Sargent, Westerbeek has the stolid face and glowering eyes of a rodeo bull. And he takes a decidedly bovine approach to his testimony, trying repeatedly, if vainly, to throw the trial lawyer off his back.

The documents Kaeske shows him are not grower contracts but news articles and scientific studies that Mona's team uncovered in Murphy-Brown's own archives. Back when Wendell Murphy was at the helm, the company kept an exhaustive record of negative media coverage. As a consequence, Kaeske doesn't have to browbeat Westerbeek about whether Smithfield knew about the health studies and neighbor complaints and award-winning exposés. The Bates stamps on the documents from McGuireWoods are as good as fingerprints.

Westerbeek, however, insists that all the scientists and journalists were wrong. He takes issue with a Yale study and a Johns Hopkins study and University of Iowa study and a host of other peer-reviewed research on the adverse health effects of industrial agriculture. He disagrees with Steve Wing's work on hog CAFOs. It's as if he thinks that all the scientists are living in a hermetically sealed bubble and have no clue what they're talking about. Westerbeek doesn't see the trap Mike Kaeske has laid for him until the jaws snap shut.

"Sir," says Kaeske, "can you name me a single scientific study published in the world's literature that says there are *no* human health effects from industrial hog operations?"

"I don't think studies like that are necessary," Westerbeek replies.

Kaeske asks the question again, but Westerbeek dissimulates. "I think what we see in these studies is people trying to prove that something exists that I think folks that live in these communities know doesn't exist."

Asked the same question yet again, Westerbeek pivots and offers the vague hypothesis that the "National Pork Board" has conducted such a study, but he's not prepared to identify it.

Eventually, Kaeske reframes the inquiry in the guise of common sense. Westerbeek isn't really trying to deny that hog waste sprayed into the air around a residential neighborhood has an unpleasant odor, is he? Surely, Westerbeek isn't saying that shit doesn't stink.

Westerbeek blinks. "In specific situations, that would be possible." Then he backtracks quickly. "I didn't say there would be *bad* odor. I said in certain situations there could be odor."

Westerbeek doesn't seem to realize how ridiculous this farce is going to look to a panel of jurors. In spouting nonsense in front of the camera, he has placed his own neck in the noose.

He has given the jury carte blanche to kick over the stool.

※

Don Butler doesn't help, though he gives it the old college try. He is a classic company front man, well practiced in corporate statecraft and double-speak, and firmly in control of his manners. With an implacable stare that almost never wavers, he looks a bit like an Easter Island head. And his messaging is equally unyielding. After decades spent flogging for Carroll's Foods and then Murphy-Brown, he has recently been promoted to run public affairs for the entire Smithfield empire. He can recite the company line in his sleep. He wrote the book on it.

But he has never had to tangle with the likes of Mike Kaeske.

As with Sargent and Westerbeek, the trial lawyer is clear-eyed about his goal with Butler. He wants to dismantle the human shield that the PR man has erected to ward off public censure and invite public sympathy—the illusion of the Smithfield family farmer. He knows Butler isn't going to swing the wrecking ball willingly. He's going to have to force the man's hand.

Kaeske puts the seminal question to Butler bluntly. "You use this term 'family farmer' a lot. What does the term 'family farmer' mean?"

"It means a family that's engaged in agriculture," replies Butler.

"I've seen you say many times—you, Don Butler, on behalf of Smithfield—that 80 percent of all the hog operations in North Carolina are owned by family farmers. Correct?"

Butler affirms the statistic, then clarifies that, in his view, a hog farmer doesn't have to live at his operation—or even near it—for his farm to be considered a "family farm." Indeed, the farmer's family doesn't have to work at the operation. The farmer doesn't have to get most of his income from the operation. The farmer doesn't even have to own the hogs. "A family farm is just a farm owned by a family that's engaged in agriculture," he explains.

Kaeske presses him on this.

"So, basically, the requirement is that there be a human who owns an operation and he have a family. Is that what's required to be a family farmer?"

"A family farmer is a person who owns a farm," replies Butler.

"A *person* who owns a farm?"

"Or a family," Butler adds.

Kaeske gives him a hypothetical. Robbie Montgomery is one of three investors in Bandit 3 LLC, which owns the Crooked Run hog operation in the *Anderson* case. Montgomery is a Smithfield employee. Neither he nor his brother or father (the three members of Bandit 3) manages Crooked Run on a daily basis. They bought it as an investment. Indeed, Montgomery's only link to the hog operation is the stake he holds in the LLC that owns the facility.

"Is he a family farmer?" Kaeske asks.

Butler's composure splinters. "That farm would be a contract operation," he says, with a trace of irritation, "and would fall under my definition of a family farm."

Kaeske raises the Farm Families advertising campaign. "In your public relations efforts on behalf of the hog industry, you do not tell the people of North Carolina that many of the hog farms that you're referring to as 'family farms' are really investments bought by people with no background in agriculture, correct?"

Butler doesn't bite. If a hog farm isn't company-owned, he says, it's a family farm in his book. Full stop. Indeed, he takes offense. "I've been involved in recruiting many of these people who are today contract growers, and they are in every sense of the word 'family farmers.'"

It's an effective parry, but Kaeske doesn't relent. "So if Exxon, for example, owned fifteen hog operations, you would call them a family farmer, correct?"

Butler stares into the middle distance. "No," he finally admits. "Family farmers are people who invest in agricultural operations, including livestock production."

Mike Kaeske continues to spar with him, but no amount of verbal jiujitsu can force Don Butler to give ground. What the PR man's deposition *does* reveal, however, is that the Big Ag revolution has so transformed the economics of agriculture that a contract farmer in 2016 bears almost no resemblance to the Old MacDonald that generations of American children have sung about in their nursery rhymes. This iconic figure in our national landscape, a man whose wealth and virtue are grounded in the land, this independent patriot that Thomas Jefferson lauded as our "most valuable citizen," has been reduced to a scabrous shadow of his former self. His farm has been turned into a machine, his animals into cogs and pistons. The modern contract farmer is a servant to his lenders and a pawn in the hands of global corporations that siphon off his labor and leave him diminished and dependent.

The hog kingdom isn't just a dystopia for the neighbors. It's a dystopia for the farmers, too, though men like Don Butler have conditioned the farmers not to see it.

That's where Mike Kaeske and the team from Wallace & Graham travel next, after all the company men have been deposed. With permission from Judge Britt, they go down east into the heart of hog country to see the CAFOs for themselves.

CHAPTER 19

FATE AND TRANSPORT

Nothing is hidden that will not be revealed.
—*Jesus of Nazareth*

**Eastern
North Carolina
October–December
2016**

It is an unfortunate fact of historical nomenclature that the term "malaria"—Italian for "bad air"—was invented by classical physicians to identify an illness caused by a mosquito-borne parasite, not the noxious off-gassing of the Roman swamps, as the ancients believed. Were the word not already in the lexicon, it would be an ideal moniker for the maladies that have afflicted the neighbors of hog farms since the CAFO revolution. Almost everything they have suffered can be linked to despoiled air—the atmospheric mix of nitrogen, oxygen, and other elements befouled by hydrogen sulfide, ammonia, and airborne pathogens that breed in pig waste. As it is, these swine-induced maladies have been called by other, more common names, and have been ignored and dismissed by those for whom the bad air means good money.

Steve Wing was a pioneer in proving the link, but his work on community health was mostly anecdotal, a correlation between physical proximity and weather phenomena on the one hand, and the stories of headaches, nausea, breathing problems, and other ailments on the other. To make his opinions stick for the jury, and to corroborate the lived experience of the plaintiffs, Mona Wallace and Mike Kaeske need a scientist who can go onto the hog farms and into the neighborhoods and split the sky into component parts like a prism divides the sunlight, who can point to the otherwise invisible pollutants in the air and show the way they rise in columns and move upon the prevailing winds before invading the homes and lungs of the neighbors. They need a "fate and transport" guy, in other words. They get him in Shane Rogers.

Rogers is a professor of environmental engineering at Clarkson University in Potsdam, New York, a postage-stamp college town closer to Montreal than to any major American city. Like every engineer, he sees the world as a matrix of variables organized by equations that describe the way those variables interact. He loves giving long-winded disquisitions in the polysyllabic nerd-speak of biochemistry. But he has an equally ambitious right brain. He's a musician by night. He plays keyboard for the Bee Children, an eclectic indie rock band that has two studio albums to its credit. And he's highly creative in his pedagogy, using the allure of paranormal mystery to engage his students. He's even garnered a bit of local fame as a "ghostbuster" for hypothesizing—and attempting to establish by air quality testing—that some perceived "ghosts" in so-called "haunted houses" may actually be a kind of hallucinogenic effect of toxic mold exposure in aging structures.

His roots, however, are in agriculture. He hails from the breadbasket of Iowa and he completed his academic work at Iowa State, one of the preeminent animal science universities in the country. After earning his PhD, he secured a research post at the EPA, where he conducted studies of air and water pollution around industrial livestock operations, including swine CAFOs. He has continued that work since he came to Clarkson a decade ago. When Mona Wallace and John Hughes contacted him about Smithfield, he wasn't surprised. Since his days at the EPA, he's had a sense that his work might become the subject of a lawsuit. He's told his students as much, encouraging them to draft their papers with the public in mind. Yet, somehow, the lawyers have stayed away. This is his first rodeo as an expert witness. He's ready for it. Or so he thinks. In truth, he has no idea what's coming.

His contribution to the discovery phase of the litigation takes place in stages. The first stage is a study of the neighborhoods. In the fall and early winter, he and others from Mona's team pay random visits to select homes in the discovery pool communities to test the air quality and collect surface samples from walls and porches. A hog farm with thousands of pigs crammed into sunless sheds, a multi-million-gallon waste lagoon, and acres of sprayfields generates a rank potpourri of volatile organic compounds, or VOCs, and bioaerosols attached to airborne particulates and hog dust. The most common ingredients are gaseous hydrogen sulfide and ammonia, which assault the nose like a mixture of rotten eggs and disinfectant. The witch's brew of trace components, however, may be more dangerous—endotoxins from decomposing bacteria, antibiotic remnants from swine feed, fecal fragments, allergens, and microorganisms like *Salmonella, Staphylococcus aureus* (aka MRSA), *Listeria,* and *E. coli.* It's a cauldron of unpleasantness, and a vector for disease.

Like any good scientist, Shane Rogers is interested in every dimension of the stew. But perhaps more than anything he's interested in a certain DNA marker that is unique to hog feces. Originating in bacteria that only live in the porcine gut, it is tantamount to a chemical signature. If you can find the DNA marker in the air or on a surface, you can be sure that hog feces are there, too. And if the feces are there, then there must have been odor, since, as Kraig Westerbeek confessed in his deposition, the world has yet to witness the phenomenon of stink-free shit.

The name of the signature marker is Pig2Bac.

Shane has worked with DNA markers in fecal bacteria before, including Pig2Bac, but he's never tested for it on exposed surfaces like brick, wood, and paint. He knows from the start that it's a speculative enterprise, with the chance of spectacular failure. Fecal bacteria don't survive very long outside the salubrious guts of their host animals. The decay rate is alarmingly fast. Even if the fecal material is still present on the microscopic level, the bacterium—and its DNA markers—may have disintegrated to the point of being untraceable. As a result, time is of the essence. The DNA material must be captured, sealed, and shipped off to the lab within hours, or, at most, a few days after the wind deposits it on the wall of a neighbor's house.

Using swab kits and air-sampling equipment, Shane tests for Pig-2Bac at seventeen homes, including the residences of Linnill Farland and Woodell McGowan in the *McGowan* case, Mary Tatum in the *Gillis* case, and Jimmy Jacobs in the *Artis* case. Much to his delight, fourteen of the tests come back positive. The trio of negative results confirm the reliability of the positives, and the farthest positive is three-quarters of a mile from the hog operation. Given the volatility of the DNA marker, it's likely that the hog feces—its fellow traveler—spread much farther.

Also, the Pig2Bac isn't just on the outside of the plaintiffs' homes. It's in Mary Tatum's kitchen, on her stove and refrigerator.

This is nothing short of an evidentiary breakthrough. Smithfield will no doubt throw a tantrum about its admissibility. But the simplicity is beguiling. If you close your eyes, you can almost see the tiny fecal particles rising from the barns, wafting through the air, and alighting on Linnill Farland's barber shop or Jimmy Jacobs's collard greens—or coming to rest beside a loaf of bread on Mary Tatum's countertop.

It's enough to turn any juror's stomach.

✳

The second stage of Shane Rogers's research takes him onto Smithfield's turf. As the leaves of the forest turn and the holidays approach, he joins a group of scientists from Johns Hopkins, a smattering of lawyers from Mona's team—usually Mike Kaeske, Mark Doby, and Daniel Wallace, and, at least once, John Hughes—and Corey Robinson, the videographer from *National Geographic,* to inspect the hog operations named in the discovery pool cases.

The fact that they are allowed to do much more than step foot on the growers' dirt is a victory. Smithfield's defense team fought a protracted battle to put the plaintiffs' scientists in a straitjacket on-site. Once the court established guidelines for the visits, the hog company dispatched a team of minders to assist its lawyers with enforcement. Ostensibly, Smithfield's concern is biosecurity—the health and safety of the hogs. But that explanation only goes so far. Its hog farms are tucked away in the folds of the land, far from prying eyes, for good reason. It has no interest in allowing the team from Wallace & Graham to inspect anything beyond the explicit remit granted by Judge Britt.

Mona's team uses the rental house in Wrightsville Beach as a base of operations. They crowd into the bedrooms, throw their equipment on any free patch of floor space, spill out onto the deck that overlooks the backyard, and shoot hoops in the driveway or play pool in the rec room when they aren't prepping for or debriefing from a CAFO tour.

Mona and Mike rent an RV to serve as a mobile command post in the field. Shane Rogers and his cadre of scientists pack the vehicle with their testing gear, and Corey Robinson adds his cameras and video equipment to the stash. By the time they trundle up the dirt track to the first hog houses on November 21—the now-defunct Paul Stanley 7 site off Piney Woods Road—they are functioning as a crew, with bailiwicks established and tasks assigned.

By order of the court, they are permitted on-site for no more than eight hours between sunup and sundown. They hit Paul Stanley 7 and Willow Creek—a depopulated farm in the *Anderson* community—on the same day. The barns have stood empty a long time. The lagoons are stagnant, the sprayfields overgrown. The Smithfield folks don't waste much breath objecting to their work because there isn't much to see. Shane and his helpers use the experience as a dry run to calibrate their equipment for their first live farm, also in the *Artis* group: Greenwood 1, just down the road from the home of Joyce and Willie Messick.

The Greenwood inspection is a baptism of fire and filth. As soon as they pull up behind the hog sheds, one of the growers' attorneys— not from McGuireWoods but from a separate Raleigh firm—gets up in Mike Kaeske's grill. "You can't go into the barns if you've already been out in the fields," he argues. Kaeske, true to form, refuses to yield. The court laid out the ground rules, and that stricture isn't in them.

When the sparks die down, others ignite. A woman clad in a fresh-off-the-rack safari getup complete with a curved-brim bush hat walks up to Shane Rogers and peppers him with questions. Mike Kaeske has no idea who the woman is. The defense lawyers gave him no advance notice of the people they were sending. But he doesn't like her tone.

"Hi, I'm Mike," he says, summoning his trademark boyish grin. "Who are you?"

"I'm Jennifer," she replies, without elaboration.

Kaeske raises an eyebrow. "Uh-huh, and you are?"

"Google me," she says, in a voice laced with contempt.

Right, Kaeske thinks, staring her down. *We're going to get along fine.*

Her name, he finds out later, is Dr. Jennifer Clancy and she's a microbiology consultant from Vermont who has recently discovered the value of parlaying her knowledge into expert gigs in the courtroom.

Smithfield's lawyers hired her to shadow Shane Rogers during the site visits, and then to submit a report refuting his findings.

In contrast to Shane, she will conduct no observable science. Instead, she will stick to Shane like a burr, forcing him to do his research with her breath on his neck. She will question him about the samples he takes, demanding that he split each one with her, and then she will destroy the samples he offers her because what's in them doesn't matter. The only thing that matters is undermining him.

It's a gambit straight out of the playbook of the elite defense firms. In the courtroom, the plaintiffs bear the burden of proof. If Clancy can poke holes in Shane's methodology, if she can make his approach look like junk science, the jury might discard his testimony.

Shane has never conducted research in the presence of an adversary before. It's a surreal experience for him. But he's comfortable in his own skin and blessed with Spock-like sangfroid. He handles Clancy by pretending she's not there.

The Greenwood 1 facility is the textbook definition of a shithole. The stagnant lagoon is a quarter full of rock-hard sludge; the dead boxes are stuffed with forlorn corpses; and the fattened hogs in the barns are caked in their own shit. Indeed, their flesh-colored hides are so dark that they look as if they have had a pigment transplant. As for the barns, they haven't seen the business end of a hose or a broom in months, perhaps years. There is dust on every surface, cobwebs in corners and rafters, and cockroaches crawling around like they own the place. Pipes are rusting, boards are broken, and in many of the stalls, the floor slats are no longer visible beneath an inch-thick layer of clumpy brown waste.

As horrid as the place looks and smells—and the smell is god-awful— Corey Robinson captures all of it from a thousand different angles: up close in still shots and videos, and high above the ground, using a state-of-the-art drone. The most shocking images are also the saddest: the captive hogs snorting through their shit-covered snouts, wallowing in flats of their own filth, only the whites of their eyes still clean. They look rueful, even ashamed.

And perhaps they are. Pigs are surprisingly intelligent creatures, smarter even than many dogs. They are capable of multi-stage reasoning, and, like apes and dolphins, they have the capacity for self-awareness.

They can recognize themselves in the mirror. Along with raising hogs for food, some people have kept them as pets, like Wilbur in *Charlotte's Web*. Yet here they are, cooped up by the thousand in cages of misery and debasement. It's enough to make an animal lover shed tears. It's also enough to inflame the conscience of the most calloused juror.

Then there are the skeletons. The plaintiffs' team doesn't find them in the barns that day or on their tour of Greenwood 2 in December. They discover them in the reports of Murphy-Brown's auditors who have, on multiple occasions, happened across hog bones, hides, and carcasses in Dean Hilton's buildings. There is only one way that hog bones end up in a working barn. As intelligent as pigs can be, they are not above eating their own dead—if the carcasses are left in the pen to rot.

The other hog farms they visit are not as grotesque. But it's obvious that Smithfield and its growers have taken prophylactic measures. When Joey Carter greets Mike Kaeske and the site visit team on the morning of December 12, he has the bleary-eyed look of a man who has been awake all night mucking out his barns. The retired police chief is a scarecrow of a man with a ruddy complexion and squinty eyes, as if he's spent too long staring at the sun. He is cordial to the visitors, but his expression is anything but kind. From the freshly scrubbed appearance of his farm, it's like he's auditioning to be the industry's spokesperson.

He's a Murphy man, no less than Don Butler.

It's a gray and soggy day, the sky close and pregnant with rain. On this trip, John Hughes is tagging along, as is Viney Aneja, an environmental science professor at NC State. Aneja was on the research team that implemented the Smithfield Agreement. He spent years testing the new waste-management tech, and he's convinced that Super Soils could have revolutionized the industry and possibly even prevented these lawsuits. The third generation of Super Soils, renamed Terra Blue, was half the price of the second-generation system. Terra Blue was not only vastly superior to cesspools and sprayfields from an environmental standpoint, it was affordable, especially after the Chinese poured their billions into Smithfield in 2013. In Viney Aneja's telling, by rejecting Terra Blue, Smithfield brought the hog farm lawsuits upon itself.

When Aneja agreed to join the effort, he showed no interest in traipsing around another hog farm. But John Hughes twisted his arm, insisting that something might have changed.

Aneja laughed out loud. "John, think about it. Lots of hogs. The slatted floors. The shit goes through. Cinderblocks. Metal sheeting. How could it be different? Believe me. It's going to be the same. And the closer you get, the worse it's going to smell."

He's right, especially about the smell. That's one thing that Joey Carter can't disguise.

Unlike others on the team, John Hughes hasn't spent weeks of his life down east. He's been chained to his desk in Salisbury, drafting motions to clear a path for the truth. As a result, he's never experienced what Elsie Herring likes to call the "live" scent of Smithfield's business. The smell of Joey Carter's hog sheds hits him like a fist. It's earthy, like when his dog needs a bath, but distilled a thousand times. It's the smell of spilled feed and wet feed, hog breath and body odor, excretions and feces, urine and water, all blended together. It's a memory that will motivate John in the trenches at trial, when he's pulling all-nighters in his living room, fielding the paper churn of the McGuireWoods defense machine and returning fire, ream by bloody ream.

The hours pass too quickly, and the intermittent rainfall impedes the use of the air-sampling equipment. Shane Rogers and his fellow scientists work as efficiently as they can despite the weather and the constant intermeddling of Jennifer Clancy and the other industry minders.

Corey Robinson, who has never met a person he couldn't talk to, finds the spectral silence of the minders bizarre. As they hover around him, he wants to inquire, "What are you thinking right now?" But they wouldn't answer him if he asked, so he keeps his own company and concentrates on framing his shots.

As the hogs go about their business, the floors of the barns lose their morning gleam, and Corey dutifully captures the waste as it multiplies and the hogs as they roll around in it. The dark stains that spread across their hides look like mud. But there is no mud in a CAFO. Only shit.

When the light of day fades to dusk, Shane and the scientists scramble to collect their final samples, and Corey snaps his parting photographs. A woman named Ana from the Johns Hopkins team is inside the last of the four hog sheds on Carter's north operation. The gloom under the roof is so thick that she can barely see where to step. The former police chief is there with her, like a kid stuck in detention, pretending interest while eyeing the door.

At last, Ana says, "We're done. It's too dark to see in there."

"You're really done?" Joey Carter asks.

She nods and walks away. A minute later, she looks over her shoulder and sees a yellow shaft of light spilling out of the barn. She never thought to ask if the hog sheds had lights. And Carter never flipped the switch.

The site visit team piles back into the RV and leaves the grower and the industry minions behind. The smell of the hog barns, however, won't relent. It's on their skin, in their clothes and equipment, and all over the rental vehicle. It trails them down I-40 to Wilmington, and fills the house in Wrightsville Beach like a putrid fog. By the time they get home, they are mostly inured to it. But Daniel Wallace isn't. He didn't spend the day on Joey Carter's property. He's been driving coolers full of Pig2Bac samples to the FedEx office for overnight delivery to the lab.

When Daniel walks into the house, thinking about dinner, he is overpowered by the stench. He sees Shane and Corey unloading their equipment and has an idea. He asks Shane to pull out his VOC meter and take readings of Corey. The readings jump from near zero in the stale air to nearly 497 ppm (parts per million) near Corey.

Shane repeats the experiment with Ana, who spent all day inside Joey Carter's barns. The VOC meter spikes again. He holds the meter up to their equipment and the numbers rise, though not as high. They walk out to the driveway and test the surfaces in the RV. The meter confirms what their noses smell. It's as if someone took a giant can of paint and sprayed it all over them. Shane takes pictures of the meter to show the jury. And then he and the rest of the team throw their clothes in the washer with a double dose of detergent and make a beeline to the shower.

The next morning, they're back on-site, this time at Billy Kinlaw's farm in Bladen County. The day is damp and cold, the air as moist as the clouds. As before, the weather hampers the work of the scientists, but the conditions offer Corey a meteorological gift. The temperature gradient between the toasty barns and the chilly atmosphere interacts with the elevated humidity to create a blanket of fog inside the hog houses. The vapor is rancid. It clogs Corey's lungs and coats his face and equipment like putrescent dew. He speeds through his shooting and escapes outside, where the smell isn't as overpowering. It is there that he sees it: The fog is rising from the vents in the barn like chimney smoke. The video footage he captures in the next few minutes will prove as effective in the courtroom as Shane's Pig2Bac findings.

In his lens, the odor is visible.

✳

With Christmas fast approaching, the team bids farewell to one another and disperses on the four winds—Shane to upstate New York, the Johns Hopkins scientists to Baltimore, Corey to Colorado, and Mike Kaeske to Utah. Meanwhile, Daniel Wallace and John Hughes and the rest of the Wallace & Graham crew make the trek back to Salisbury.

The holidays, however, are not quite a reprieve. Try as they might, they can't escape the reek. At Corey's Christmas party, he shows off his camera to a few of his buddies. The smell of the hog barns is like a halo around it. One of his friends suggests he file an insurance claim and purchase a replacement. Surely, his friend says, you can't use that again.

Corey keeps the idea in his pocket, but tries an experiment first. He places the camera outside in the golden Colorado sunshine. He gives it time, allows the intense solar radiation to burn the VOCs and bioaerosols off the glass and plastic surfaces. The experiment is successful. The camera is saved. After two months in the sun.

Shane's experience is more personal. He smells the odor on himself. It's like a ghost in his head, a schizophrenic whisper. He detects it at random moments at home and at his office at Clarkson. He tries everything he can think of to combat it. He rewashes all of his travel clothes, hypothesizing that the odor particles might have attached themselves to the drum in his washing machine or dryer. He showers multiple times a day, imagining that the VOCs might still be trapped in his hair follicles. When the scent doesn't disappear, he flushes his nose with nasal decongestants and treats his skin with lotions and essential oils. When all else fails, he begins to wonder if it is a phantom smell, a creature of psychology not physiology.

It takes the query of a colleague to solve the riddle. He is in his office at Clarkson one day during the holiday break when she pops in to say hello. She wrinkles her nose. "What's that smell?" she asks, not knowing that he has been asking the same question for days on end without an answer. It is then that he realizes that he has missed something: his reading glasses. He wore them every day in hog country, and he has been wearing them every day since. He never thought to disinfect them. He removes them from his head and holds them out to his colleague, who is standing ten feet away. Her face contorts with displeasure. *Extraordinary,* he thinks. That evening, he asks his wife about it, and she confesses that she smelled it, too, but figured it would dissipate over time. Shane tosses the glasses in the trash.

After two weeks and a thousand miles, he is finally free of the stench.

CHAPTER 20

COMPANY TOWN

We hang the petty thieves
and appoint the great ones to public office.
—*Aesop*

**Salisbury
and Raleigh,
North Carolina
March 2017**
Most people think that the company town is a creature of industrial yore—Detroit in the heyday of General Motors; Pittsburgh after the merger of Carnegie and U.S. Steel; Pullman, Illinois, in the days of the luxury sleeper car; and Hershey, Pennsylvania, the fantasia of chocolate. None of those monopolies survived the economic dislocations and sociopolitical transformations of the twentieth century. The less notable company towns, too—the coal towns and lumber towns and mining towns scattered across the rural American landscape—died away as the country grew more educated and mobile, as opportunity expanded from coast to coast.

Not so in agriculture.

In the last half century, the company town has made a quiet comeback, thanks to the hyper-consolidation of the Big Ag conglomerates and the near-slavish dependency of contract farmers on the market systems controlled by them. This is the dynamic that turned the old tobacco lands between Raleigh and Wilmington into Murphysville. And hog country is not alone. There are echoes of this same Oz-like influence in rural territories across the American heartland, from the plains of Oklahoma and Nebraska up through the Mississippi River Valley into

Missouri, Illinois, Iowa, Minnesota, and the Dakotas. In these places, the fortunes of countless people, and the towns they love, rise and fall on the whims of a single agribusiness corporation, or a tightly knit group of them, whether the industry be pork or chickens, turkey or beef.

Rarely, however, has one company amassed enough influence to take the reins of an entire state legislature. In the spring of 2017, however, Smithfield Foods makes a play for the North Carolina General Assembly. Its goal is singular and undisguised: to drive a stake through the heart of the nuisance suits before Mona Wallace and Mike Kaeske can seat the first jury in Judge Britt's courtroom.

The agitators who lead the advance in Raleigh are the same ones who championed the Right to Farm amendment before the suits were even filed: Brent Jackson, the state senator and food broker turned majordomo of Big Pork, and Jimmy Dixon, the Republican firebrand from Duplin, with the ham-hock visage and the ivory duckbill bouffant.

As in 2013, they have partisan allies in every crack and crevice of the General Assembly. The Republicans hold a supermajority in the House, 75 seats to 45 for the Democrats, and in the Senate, 35 seats to 15, which means that, even though the new governor, Roy Cooper, is a Democrat, his veto is ceremonial. In the last legislative session, the Republican supermajority achieved a measure of global notoriety—infamy, to many—with its transgender bathroom bill. Put simply, the party of Jackson and Dixon can do whatever it damn well pleases.

On March 23, 2017, the same day that the discovery period closes in all five cases slated for trial, Jimmy Dixon introduces a bill in the state House that would put a choke hold on the kinds of damages available to plaintiffs in farm nuisance suits. It would also, in a provision without precedent, apply to existing litigation.

The clerk gives it the name HB467.

On the plaintiffs' side, Bill Graham, Mona's partner, is the first to hear about it. He has ears on the ground in the General Assembly, friends and associates he collected during his erstwhile run for governor. He learns of the bill, in fact, before Jimmy Dixon makes it public. His people inform him that the industry is throwing everything behind it, and that they have support from the leadership.

A few days after the bill is introduced, Graham takes a trip to Raleigh and makes his rounds in the General Assembly. No door is closed to him, no politician out of reach. He's a gifted glad-hander with golden boy good looks and Hollywood charisma. Tall and trim, with a frame that compliments a suit, he has a smile that seems to sparkle and a down-home twang as smooth as a glass of Pappy. Like Mona, he's a phenomenally successful lawyer. But he has never lost touch with his roots. He spent his formative years in rural Harnett County and worked in a cotton mill while putting himself through college. He knows what it's like to prune tobacco and ride a combine, clean looms and blow down HVAC systems. Some people look at him and see a silver spoon. But Bill Graham wasn't born to privilege. He's a country boy at heart.

He finds Jimmy Dixon huddling with the Speaker of the House, Tim Moore, in the office of David Lewis, the House representative from Harnett County and one of the co-sponsors of HB467. He knows the storyline that Dixon has been spreading around, that he and Mona and Mike Kaeske and Lisa Blue are painting a bull's-eye on the little guy, putting the squeeze on the state's hardworking family farmers. Graham is a card-carrying Republican. He understands what makes Lewis and Moore tick—their conservative economic principles, their suspicion of regulations, regulatory agencies, and trial lawyers. Dixon he'll never convince. The man has been in the industry's back pocket for years. He's taken $115,000 in political donations from the big integrators and other industry-aligned groups—a heady sum, given how inexpensive it is to run a state House race in hog country. But the others are still in play.

Jimmy Dixon's greeting isn't kind: "You guys are just after money."

Graham summons his most reasonable tone. "Every civil suit has a claim for monetary damages. But that's not what this is about. Some of your constituents have been harmed."

Dixon, however, is itching for a fight. He launches into a condescending lesson about the hardships of life on a farm.

Eventually, Graham grows tired of the harangue. "I've got an idea, Representative Dixon. Why don't you let me tell you what it's like to work in a cotton mill? What difference does that make? These people were harmed. You need to do the right thing."

When Dixon just stares at Graham bug-eyed, the Salisbury lawyer glances at Lewis and Moore, making sure they're paying attention. "If we win—which is a big 'if,' at this point—none of these farmers you're talking about will be paying the freight. It's going to be the Chinese. They're the ones calling the shots. Why are you protecting them?"

Dixon ignores the question, though later in the press he will use Graham's reference to Smithfield's Chinese owners to accuse Mona and Bill of seeking a windfall of foreign cash. Rather, Dixon tries to flip the script. "Why'd you *really* file all these lawsuits?" he asks.

Graham smiles. "You don't know?" It's exactly the opening he was looking for. With Lewis and Moore watching, he lets Dixon have it.

"Jimmy," he says, "let me break this down for you. These people tried back in the nineties to get the government's attention. That didn't go anywhere. They tried the local government. They tried the county government. They tried the state government. They tried the federal government. They tried everything. And you know what? When you wear out your welcome in the legislative branch, and you wear out your welcome in the executive branch, the courthouse is the only place left to go." Dixon's lips stretch into a pale scar, but Bill Graham isn't finished. "These people are powerless. We know what the industry did. Look at where the farms are. Almost all of our clients are Black."

When Bill Graham puts race on the table, the conversation plunges off a cliff. Dixon won't even engage the point, and Graham is smart enough to walk away. In the days to come, the Duplin politician will fall all over himself denying that the largest concentration of hog CAFOs are in low-income communities of color. He will never admit that this story is about civil rights. In his mind, it's about family farmers and greedy trial lawyers.

And he, Jimmy Dixon, is on the side of the right.

✻

With the hog barons storming the legislature, it isn't long before Mona Wallace joins Bill Graham on the field. The same week that Bill meets with Jimmy Dixon, Mona gets a call about HB467 from Leigh Lawrence, legislative aide to Representative Billy Richardson.

Billy is a practicing attorney, a veteran politician, and the child of parents who embodied the spirit of social justice. His father, a banker, hired the first Black manager at his bank. His mother, a guidance counselor and self-proclaimed "radical," rescued kids from abusive situations and put them up in Billy's room. Many of these kids were Black. As a state representative from Fayetteville, Billy understands Smithfield's game. He sees the strategy that its sponsors and lobbyists have adopted.

He vows to oppose them with everything he has.

Billy also happens to be a fan of Mona Lisa Wallace. To him, she's a "national treasure." He urges Mona to talk to Skip Stam, a former Republican legislator and one of the savviest constitutional scholars in the state. Billy thinks that property rights might be the key to defeating HB467. While the Republicans hold a supermajority in the General Assembly, the most conservative wing of the GOP is as zealous about guarding home and caste as they are about opposing abortion and transgender rights. If Mona can convince Skip Stam to lend a hand and frame the debate in those terms, some of the Republicans might break ranks with Jackson and Dixon and aid the Democrats in scuttling the bill.

With the House Judiciary Committee scheduled to take up HB467 in mere hours, Mona drives through the pouring rain to meet Stam at his office near Raleigh. He's intrigued by the bill, especially Jimmy Dixon's attempt to apply it retroactively to the lawsuits. He's a lawyer's lawyer, the kind of guy who gets a rush cracking open a centuries-old law book and searching for insight.

To ground his thinking about the bill, Stam defaults to Blackstone—naturally. As Mona waits patiently across his desk, Stam dusts off a volume from the legendary jurist's *Commentaries on the Laws of England* and consults the entry for "nuisance." His eyes light up. It turns out that the seminal nuisance case in the English common law is about hogs.

Way back in 1610, a man named William Aldred claimed that his neighbor, Thomas Benton, had erected a pigsty too close to his property, such that the stench from the hogs made his house unbearable to live in. The judges on the King's Bench found in Aldred's favor, holding that "an action on the case lies for erecting a hogstye so near the house of the plaintiff that the air thereof is corrupted." The court wrote that a man has "no right to maintain a structure upon his own land, which, by reason of disgusting smells, loud or unusual noises, thick smoke, noxious vapors, the jarring of machinery, or the unwarrantable collection of flies, renders the occupancy of adjoining property dangerous, intolerable, or even uncomfortable to its tenants."

Stam is delighted by this discovery, and Mona is delighted by his delight. He tells her that the retroactivity provision in HB467 is unconstitutional. He's fought battles like this before. It is one thing to tweak the law in a way that will apply to cases down the road, another thing to reach back in time and pluck vested rights out of the hands of people who have relied on them. It's especially egregious to pilfer rights from plaintiffs in the middle of a lawsuit to shield a favored industry from sanction. It's crony capitalism and legislative capture at their worst.

There is also the minor problem of precedent. With HB467, Smithfield and its minions are taking aim at four hundred years of common law. They want nothing less than to rewrite the definition of nuisance to prevent the neighbors of an agricultural operation from recovering a jury award commensurate with the harm. They want to shrink the broad concept of damages in a nuisance case to the loss of property value alone.

To a bewigged traditionalist like Skip Stam, this is sacrilege. It doesn't matter that he's a Republican. If the King's Bench and William Blackstone say that people have the right to clean air, then, by God, people have the right to clean air. He's all in.

A couple of days later, Stam works up a "Dear Colleague" letter enumerating the flaws in the bill and emails it to the chairs of the House Judiciary Committee. The following morning, he and his wife board a flight to France. Little does he know that the furor he has just unleashed will follow him across the Atlantic.

Back at the statehouse, the pork industry's favorite surrogate, Jimmy Dixon, is laboring tirelessly to advance the bill to the floor. At his behest, the Judiciary Committee takes it up less than a week after it is introduced. The bill's opponents are just as well organized. They come out in droves, packing the committee room in open rebellion against Dixon and the hog lobby. Elsie Herring is there, along with Randy Davis, a white plaintiff from Don Webb's group. Larry Baldwin is there representing the Waterkeeper Alliance, as is Naeema Muhammad from NCEJN. Even John Hughes and Bill Graham make the trip over from Salisbury. The show of force puts the brakes on Dixon's runaway train. Instead of transmitting the bill to the full House without delay, the committee is forced to debate and deliberate.

Dixon, who has a flair for the grandiose, leads with a quote from Abe Lincoln. The quote itself—that politicians have to pay attention to farmers because farmers constitute the largest voting bloc in the electorate—is obsolete in 2017, but Dixon adapts it for his purposes. "Farmers no longer cast the most votes. But guess what, Ladies and Gentlemen? Farmers still feed everybody that votes. And if there's anyone in here who believes that food comes from the grocery store, line up after this and I'll give you a spanking. Food comes from farms."

Dixon then pleads the bill's merits. It isn't about reining in punitive damages, he says. It's about reining in the trial lawyers. As he tells it, the lawyers suing Smithfield are only interested in extorting a settlement. He recounts a story about his "good friends" at Prestage and Goldsboro, two of the integrators still standing, who were sued in Mississippi and Indiana and won in court, but were left with "exorbitant" legal fees. This is the sort of egregious legal abuse that HB467 will help prevent.

It's a serviceable speech. But the audience is savvy enough to see through the ruse. It turns out that the precise species of damages that Jimmy Dixon wants to toss in the dustbin are the *only* damages that the plaintiffs are claiming in court. In an effort to streamline the litigation, Mona's team agreed to waive compensation for lost property value and seek only "annoyance and discomfort" damages—the plaintiffs' lost quality of life. Shortly after Mona and Mike cemented this commitment, Dixon introduced HB467. Were the bill to be enacted as written, the damages that Elsie Herring and Randy Davis and Don Webb and their five hundred co-plaintiffs could claim from any jury verdict would be reduced to zero. That would be true of punitive damages too. In North Carolina, punitive damages are capped at three times compensatory damages. And, as any second grader knows, three times zero is zero.

Dixon also has the sympathy equation inverted. The true combatants in the litigation aren't the plaintiffs' attorneys and the farmers who feed America. It's ordinary homeowners—*his constituents*—arrayed against a global corporation owned by Chinese plutocrats. But telling the truth about the war would complicate Dixon's legislative enterprise. So he omits the plaintiffs and the hog company from his story, and he reacts indignantly when some on the committee suggest that Smithfield's billionaire owners can foot the legal bill.

"I'm going to use an inordinate amount of restraint," he says. "These sixty-nine farms, these people are red-blooded, hardworking Americans that have clawed to get to where they are at. These people cannot be separated, and to put forth the proposition that it's fair because it is a Chinese-owned company and they can afford it . . . We are looking at what is fair, not what a company can afford."

The first citizen to address the committee, a nurse from Winston-Salem, raises the banner for the neighbors. "What is the fair market value of a person's life?" she asks. "Their peace of mind; the right to enjoy the property they worked hard for and saved for or inherited from their grandparents. We quoted Abraham Lincoln; why don't we quote Moses? 'And the Lord breathed into him the breath of life.' If we are talking air, we are talking life."

Larry Baldwin of the Waterkeeper Alliance takes the critique up a notch. "The CAFO industry is one of the most insidious industries that I know of. Their tactics, the things that they do to their communities, particularly African Americans, communities of color, low income, Hispanic, Native Americans . . . This is about race. This bill has got to go. It is not about protecting people. It is about protecting the industry."

Eventually, Elsie Herring steps up to the microphone. She's done this so many times before, told the story of her mother's land, the way the hog farmer poisoned it and siphoned joy from Beulah's final years. She isn't intimidated by the powerful men behind the dais, by the judgment she sees in their eyes. And she definitely is not afraid of Jimmy Dixon.

"My name is Elsie Herring," she says in a voice strong and steady. "I come from Duplin County. 'Hog Heaven.' We have over 2.2 million hogs in our communities. We tried every avenue available to us to bring attention to the conditions we've been forced to live under. And we are forced to live with animals and their waste. This has been ongoing for decades now. By this bill being presented, it is taking away the last hope that we have."

Other speakers come after her, all opposed to the bill. But Jimmy Dixon is unfazed. He will never give credence to the complaints of people like Elsie. In another setting, he will suggest that the plaintiffs are confused, at best, and mendacious, at worst. He will never concede that the Murphy men have made the lives of hundreds of his Black neighbors a living hell. He is a company man like Don Butler, as firm in his loyalties as if he were on Smithfield's payroll. But he is not in charge of the

General Assembly. There is an order to the work of the legislature, a way the sausage gets made. And that's the way Jimmy Dixon plays.

The Judiciary Committee tables the bill and sets another hearing for the following week. What happens next, however, doesn't bear much resemblance to the business of government.

It looks like P. T. Barnum has taken up residence in the statehouse.

CHAPTER 21

THE PEOPLE'S CIRCUS

No man's life, liberty, or property are safe
while the legislature is in session.
—*Gideon J. Tucker*

**Raleigh,
North Carolina
April 2017**

In the first week of April, Mona Wallace and Bill Graham set up a satellite operation in Raleigh. Billy Richardson offers them his chamber as a forward operating base. It's a tiny two-room suite, with a doormat-sized reception area, a desk for Billy's legislative assistant, Leigh Lawrence, and an office that Billy keeps charmingly cluttered with books, papers, and memorabilia from his years of public service.

Mona lives there by the phone, along with Mark Doby, her aide-de-camp for the HB467 effort, when they aren't out casing the marble hallways of the General Assembly and cornering representatives in the building's nooks and crannies. A lifelong Democrat, Mona works the left flank of the statehouse, with wheel-greasing from Billy and the environmental and civil rights caucuses, while Bill Graham and his public affairs team whip votes on the GOP side, wielding Skip Stam's "Dear Colleague" letter like Holy Writ.

They score another coup when Robert Orr, a former state supreme court justice, and Republican lion, opines that the bill is a constitutional abomination. In a carefully crafted letter, Orr argues that HB467 would amount to an unlawful taking of property—in more colloquial terms, a snatch-and-grab—in violation of the North Carolina Declaration of

Rights, which traces its origin to the founding of the state. The John Locke Foundation, a center-right think tank, also tosses a brand at the bill: "Permitting the legislature to intervene in pending litigation in a way that clearly favors one party while harming the other is a dangerous precedent that threatens not only the right to due process of law, but also the separation of powers."

Under normal circumstances, such rousing condemnation from GOP luminaries would be a check on the ambitions of the bill's sponsors. But Jimmy Dixon and his merry band of hog populists are dead-set on doing the industry's bidding, and they don't fret the lectures coming from the party faithful. Instead, they focus on shepherding the bill through the gauntlet of committee and delivering it to their collaborators on the floor. Before they put the bill to a vote, however, they must grin and bear another public hearing in the Judiciary Committee.

The people come with knives out, as does a Black legislator named Amos Quick.

Quick is a jewel-eyed, silver-tongued Baptist preacher who spent years running the Boys & Girls Club in Greensboro and serving on the Guilford County Board of Education before taking the pulpit and winning a seat in the General Assembly. Although urban Greensboro is a million miles from hog country, Quick is acquainted with life down east. He got his college degree from UNC –Wilmington and he has family on the coastal plain. Moreover, as a Black man, he is all too familiar with the system of racial prejudice that has advantaged white people at the expense of people of color in every aspect of American life since the abolition of slavery. He is also a freshman Democrat, eager to make the People's House actually work for the voters. In the week since the last hearing adjourned, he has done a little due diligence on the bill, and he has some questions for his esteemed colleague, Mr. Dixon.

First, says Quick, isn't HB467 nothing more than a thinly veiled attempt by the hog industry to undercut the lawsuits against Smithfield pending in federal court?

Dixon, to his credit, doesn't shroud the truth. Yes, the bill is about the Smithfield cases. But it's really about protecting the growers. They are inseparable from the company.

All right, replies Quick, then isn't the bill discriminatory? It would take away the right of mostly Black neighbors to sue an industry that has already discriminated against them—wittingly or unwittingly—by clustering industrial hog operations in their communities.

Jimmy Dixon's hackles go up. "That's absolutely incorrect."

"Can you correct me, please?" Quick responds, no doubt anticipating that his colleague from Duplin will at least dignify the question with a substantive answer.

But Dixon isn't interested in talking about discrimination, historical or contemporary. Instead, he goes off on a circumambulatory rant about family farmers. He tells Quick about the thirty-three poultry houses and the swine facility that he used to own, about what a joy it was to stroll through those facilities with his grandchildren on his shoulders. Ultimately, he opines that Quick doesn't know what he's talking about.

Quick tries a different tack, the well-trodden path of property rights. To accentuate the point, he raises the specter of hog feces in Mary Tatum's kitchen. Surely people like her should have the right to sue for damages without contending with legislative shackles. This is one of Billy Richardson's principal arguments, one he's been parading about the statehouse with a fervor that would make his radical mother proud. He's borrowed a page from Shane Rogers's Pig2Bac findings and weaponized it against HB467.

Jimmy Dixon takes refuge in denial. The notion that hog waste is getting into people's houses is a fiction. He won't believe it until he sees it. He invites Quick to take a trip down east and show it to him. "I'll tell you what," he says, "whosever home that is, they will not have a stronger defender than I." The real problem here is not the hog farms but the plaintiffs' lawyers. They're the ones blowing all this out of proportion.

Dixon's invitation is, of course, a sleight of hand and utterly disingenuous. If he cared at all about the claims of the neighbors, he would not be championing a bill meticulously crafted to deprive them of their day in court. But this meeting isn't about getting to the truth. It's a piece of political theater. And Dixon is a capable showman. He has the votes to push the bill forward. All he has to do is give his opponents and the public the illusion of being heard, and then he and his compatriots in the committee can ignore them and send the bill to the floor.

Unlike at the first hearing, the audience is not united against the bill. The people who rise to speak are a picture of a community divided, riven down the middle by Boss Hog.

There's a man who works at Smithfield's Tar Heel wastewater plant. He has friends who are hog farmers. He *knows* that 99 percent of them are doing the right thing.

There's a military veteran who bought land down east intending to build his family's home on it. But then a hog operation went in next door, and his wife couldn't tolerate the stench. The man never built the home. His dream died.

There's a hog farmer from Duplin, who was named in one of the original state court lawsuits. He's worked hard, he says. He's a good neighbor. He doesn't want to take away anybody's property rights. He just wants to be left alone. The state has already regulated him enough. He supports Jimmy Dixon's bill because it will give him and his fellow growers peace of mind.

When the hog farmer takes a seat, Don Webb shuffles to his feet. He's getting up in years, and his once-strapping body is starting to fail him. But the blaze of incontrovertible conviction is still burning in his eyes. He's here to talk the truth.

"I'm a *former* hog farmer," he says in that inimitable baritone, "and when I found out what I was doing to my neighbors, I got out of the business. I was making money, but then my neighbors came to me and said, 'Don, can't you do something about what you're doing?' My hog pen was as clean as you could have it. But it was a feces and urine factory. That's what I was doing to American citizens."

Webb's cadence builds like a thundercloud. "I'm a human being. I'm an American. And Americans should not have to smell somebody else's feces and urine. That's what they want to force in this bill. Read the Constitution. If you want to play with my constitutional right to sue, if you want to take that right away from me and other people, you got no right to do it, and you know it. Let me tell you something, you know you're wrong."

He's just getting started when his two minutes expire. He's accustomed to speaking on the stump, to giving the fire inside him free rein until it burns itself out. He tries to keep going, but the committee chairman cuts him off and acknowledges the last speaker from the gallery, Mark Dorosin, a lawyer from the UNC Center for Civil Rights.

Without saying so, Dorosin offers Amos Quick the clarification that Jimmy Dixon wouldn't. At its core, he says, this dispute is about race.

If Jimmy Dixon's bill is made law, it will only serve to exacerbate the racial disparities down east.

Dixon, however, has his hand on the decision lever, and the committee is behind him. The chairman doesn't even pause to let Dorosin's words sink in before he calls for a vote.

"All those in favor signify by saying, 'aye.'" The ayes ring out. "Those 'nay.'" The nays trickle in. "The 'ayes' have it. We are adjourned."

✳

The full House takes up the bill the very next day.

It's a Thursday session and the calendar is jammed with pending legislation. Although the rulebook of the General Assembly is dominated by esoterica, the three-step of passing a bill is straightforward. The "first reading" is ministerial, nothing but an announcement that a new bill has been introduced. The "second reading" happens after the committee assigned to review the bill refers it back to the floor with amendments, if any. The second reading requires a vote of the full House. If members wish to debate the bill, they raise their objections at this stage. After the vote takes place, the Speaker then calls for the "third reading" and the final decisive vote. Usually, this vote is pro forma. But not always. Not when the Speaker calls the second reading out of order.

That is what happens with HB467.

In retrospect, it looks like a setup, a conspiracy between the bill's sponsor, Jimmy Dixon, and the Speaker, Tim Moore, to catch the opposition off guard and set up the third reading. But in the moment, there is nothing but chaos and confusion.

The legislative calendar is set in advance. All of the members receive a copy of it. They know when the bills they care about will come up for a vote. Since the session can run on for hours, and many members are extroverted and elderly, few remain at their desks for long stretches. There is much standing and wandering about. Often, members meet in the wings for bouts of posturing and horse-trading. Meanwhile, the Speaker drones on at the podium, his words echoing in the background like an announcer at the racetrack.

An hour and fifteen minutes into the session, after debate on a bill to increase funding for firefighters and first-responders, Tim Moore throws a wrench in the gears. He skips over something like a dozen pieces of legislation, and, in the hurried voice of an auctioneer, says, "House Bill 467, the clerk will read." There is an extended pause while the clerk scrambles to locate the bill. Eventually, he reads the names of the sponsors—Jimmy Dixon, David Lewis, Ted Davis, and Jay Bell—and the title: "An act to clarify the remedies available in private nuisances against agriculture and forestry operations."

In an ordinary session, when presented with a major piece of controversial legislation, the Speaker would recognize the sponsors to hold forth about the bill's merits and then open the floor for debate, which would likely drag on for a while. With HB467, however, Moore bypasses all of that and directs the clerk to open the vote, throwing the entire chamber into muted consternation. Members who are at their desks glance around in bewilderment. Those who are away handling other matters race back to their seats to record their votes.

Billy Richardson is one of those on his feet. He is at the rear of the gallery, absorbed in unrelated business, when the second reading takes place. He doesn't realize what is happening until the vote is underway. He strolls back to his desk, a strategy forming in his mind. He cares about only one thing: preventing the third reading.

The clerk gives the members a mere twenty-six seconds to record their support or opposition. Then the Speaker closes the vote and calls out the result: 70 in favor, 42 against.

"Objection!" Billy cries out, as Moore attempts to steamroll toward the final reading and the decisive vote. "Objection!"

Moore sounds a note of surprise. "Having been objected to, it remains on the calendar."

Lodging his objection in the nick of time, Billy Richardson has bought Mona Wallace and Bill Graham a brief reprieve. HB467 will not be called again until the next session, on Monday evening. The bill's opponents have the benefit of the weekend to make a last-ditch push to strip the "pending litigation" language from the text.

In the wake of Billy's objection, Representative Garland Pierce, a Black preacher from the rural southern part of the state, rises from his desk, his forehead pinched in puzzlement. "Was there discussion or debate on the bill?" he asks the Speaker politely.

"There were no lights on," the Speaker intones, referring to the lights on each desk that signal a member's desire to be heard.

Pierce's face contorts in disbelief, as if to say, "You've got to be kidding." But he maintains his decorum and defers to Moore. This is the second time in as many days that a Black representative has challenged a white colleague about a perceived injustice and the white representative has responded with open condescension.

Pierce's perplexity about the second reading, however, is widespread. Like popcorn going off, six different House members rise to change their votes on HB467 from "aye" to "nay." From their frowns, it is obvious that they believed they were voting on something else.

Thus the stage is set for a showdown on Monday night.

For Mona Lisa Wallace and Bill Graham, the stakes could not be higher. After spending four years and millions of dollars of their own money preparing the hog farm cases for trial, they have ninety-six hours to convince enough House Republicans to turn against their own party, set aside their affection for agribusiness, and vote to uphold the property rights of poor, rural Black people down east. Otherwise, the hog farm cases will be worth pennies on the dollar.

This isn't a job for the faint of heart. They need a genuine miracle.

CHAPTER 22

AMENDMENT ONE

Corruption is nature's way of restoring our faith in democracy.
—*Peter Ustinov*

The weekend is a whirlwind of noise. With ringleading from Billy Richardson and strategic assistance from Skip Stam—who is still in Paris—Mona Wallace and Bill Graham hatch a plot to introduce an amendment to HB467 before the Speaker can call for a vote on the third reading. The amendment is laser-guided. It targets only the retroactivity provision and leaves the rest of the bill untouched. They can argue the substance of the rule change when the bill goes over to the Senate. The only ground they stand a chance of gaining at the moment—and that chance is slight—relates to the "pending litigation" language. If that language dies before the bill makes its transit to the upper chamber, it is unlikely to be revived. If, on the other hand, it survives the full House, even Governor Cooper won't be able to stand in its way.

To make the amendment attractive to Republicans, however, they need the right sponsor. Billy Richardson is a Democrat. And Skip Stam, for all his conservative bona fides, is no longer in office. They search for a Republican of character to put his stamp on the amendment.

They find such a man in John Blust.

Blust is an attorney and former U.S. Army captain from Greensboro. Like Skip Stam, he is a devout conservative whose truest allegiance is to the rule of law, not to any party or clique. He is a devotee of Churchill, who said, "The truth is inconvertible. Malice may attack it, and ignorance may deride it. But in the end, there it is." After taking a look at HB467, he decides he can't support it. It is not in the interests of the people he was elected to serve. He is reluctant to face the hog barons' howitzers. But his conscience demands it.

He agrees to sponsor Amendment One.

His defection is met with derision from the Dixon wing of the GOP. On Sunday, as Skip Stam and his wife are flying home from Paris, Pat McElraft, a blustery Republican from Emerald Isle, takes Blust to task in an email to the GOP caucus. After trotting out one of the industry's favorite screeds—that radical environmentalists are behind the opposition to HB467—she argues that the bill is a critical bulwark against the anti-capitalist, anti-agriculture left.

While the intramural conflict rages within the GOP, Mona and Bill make their final pitch to representatives on both sides of the aisle. The situation is so precarious that they're not afraid to beg, to plead their clients' case, even to show glimpses of the skin they have in the game.

No matter how loudly Jimmy Dixon and the hog lobbyists bloviate, this contest isn't about the trial bar. It's about the hundreds of citizens whose health and quality of life the hog barons have treated as disposable for more than a generation. Juries put a price tag on pain and suffering. They force the bean counters inside recalcitrant corporations to factor the human and environmental costs of production into the cost of doing business. For far too long, the hog barons have required everyone else to pay the price of their pollution. No more. HB467 must be amended. Otherwise, Smithfield will never pay its fair share.

As persuasive as the argument sounds to Mona and Bill, the math they face is daunting. If all 120 House members show up and vote, they need 16 Republicans to join the 45 Democrats to approve the amendment, assuming there are no Democratic turncoats. They take no vote for granted. They accept every meeting. As the afternoon softens into evening, they count the votes they have in hand. Many legislators are still undecided. The fate of the amendment—and the litigation—is going to come down to the speeches on the floor and the consciences of the wavering members. Until the votes are locked, there is no way to predict the outcome.

The hog lobby, meanwhile, has been working to stack the deck. Along with consolidating Republican support, they have summoned hundreds of growers and industry boosters from down east, busing them in and packing them into the visitors' mezzanine above the House floor. When Mona and Mark Doby climb the stairs, looking for seats, they are astonished to find the gallery full. They try every entrance until, at last, a friendly security officer recognizes them and carves out a space among the Smithfield faithful. Glancing around, they feel the weight of the stares, the pent-up energy and fear. It isn't obvious that these folks understand the substance of Jimmy Dixon's bill. But they surely comprehend the significance of the occasion.

For both sides, the stakes are existential.

At last, the hour arrives, and the House members take their seats. Although Mona and Mark are alone in the audience, their colleagues back at Wallace & Graham are tuned in either to the television broadcast or the Internet audio feed. Across the country, Mike Kaeske and Lisa Blue are listening in, too. Everyone's nerves are frayed. They have invested years in this litigation. They have built a case that could actually go the distance. Yet in a single night, with a single vote, Smithfield's allies in the statehouse could take it away from them.

The legislators rise for the prayer and the Pledge of Allegiance, and then the House Speaker, Tim Moore, assumes the podium and the session gets underway. When the time comes to debate Jimmy Dixon's bill, the representative from Duplin stands beside his desk and takes up the microphone. His crown of alabaster hair is perfectly coiffed, his reading glasses are perched on his nose, and he's dressed in his Sunday best—a dapper navy suit paired with an understated yellow tie and augmented by two lapel pins that signal his patriotism and state pride.

"Colleagues," he begins, "this has been one of the bills that gives us all some degree of anxiety." His speech is extemporaneous and more than a little meandering, but his message is aimed at those in his own party who are thinking about defecting. He's not a lawyer, he says, and this is not a courtroom. In putting forward his bill, he's relying only on common sense. North Carolina's hardworking farm families are in peril.

The General Assembly must act to protect them, even if that action has an effect on pending cases. Sure, there's a debate about whether the retroactivity provision is legal. But he's not interested in the legalities. He's read more than he ever wants to read about nuisance lawsuits around the country. He'll let the lawyers explain why the bill can apply to the lawsuits pending in Judge Britt's courtroom.

Instead, he talks about his own farm. "I have been permitted to dispose of my waste in very specified manner, and I want to testify to every single one of you in this chamber, these allegations are at best exaggerations, and at worst outright lies. When you talk about spraying effluent in people's houses and on their cars, that does not exist. I've been down there. I've lived it." As if to cement his veracity, he invokes his family. "My children and grandchildren have played around the lagoons. And we've sprayed our effluent properly."

Dixon takes another swipe at the plaintiffs, says they're being "prostituted for money," despite being "wonderful, *wonderful* people." The way he repeats the word feels like a psychological tic, a fleeting rebellion by his superego against the darker instincts of his id. But that's all the kindness he's willing to extend them. He attacks their lawyers, talks about the "Learjets" they are flying in from Texas to profit off of North Carolina's citizens. He concedes that a hog farm is no flower garden, but offers an invocation in its defense: "Every single one of us should, on a regular basis, get down on our knees and thank our Heavenly Father that there are people who are willing to put up with the circumstances of production so that we can enjoy the benefits of consumption."

For his closing, Dixon slips into grandiloquence. "Ladies and gentlemen, there is more at stake than you realize. There are enemies to agriculture, especially livestock agriculture. Extreme environmentalists and animal rights people have joined together and become allies to those who would take advantage monetarily of the very folks they propose to represent." He pauses, surveying the House floor. "Ladies and gentlemen, please vote for this bill."

After Jimmy Dixon's bombast, his co-sponsor, Ted Davis, sounds like a prude. He tries on a variety of arguments, as if modeling on the runway, then settles on this one: Judge Britt needs the legislature to clarify the damages that are available in North Carolina nuisance suits. The old judge said as much way back when he overruled Smithfield's motion to dismiss. "The fact that he could not make that decision meant that the cases were put on hold," says Davis, "and they're still on hold." In effect, Judge Britt needs the help of the General Assembly.

As soon as Davis yields the floor, Darren Jackson, a Democratic lawyer from Wake County, blows this argument into the next life. He holds up a docket sheet from the federal court, showing that the cases are not on hold. The parties have been litigating them in earnest for the last two years. Other members join him in inveighing against Jimmy Dixon's bill. Some defend the ancien régime—the common law of nuisance tracing its origins to William Aldred's case and the King's Bench. Some focus entirely on the "pending litigation" language.

Eventually, John Blust stands up and introduces Amendment One. His gray suit blends naturally with his silvering hair and offers a striking contrast to his Carolina blue tie.

"Farmers are a very romantic, sympathetic group of figures," he opines, "but we all know that much of the agriculture today—because of economies of scale and equipment—is not your family farmer. These are giant hog operations that have environmental consequences."

A disgruntled Jimmy Dixon interrupts him. "How many of these farms have you been on in your life?"

Looking flustered, Blust concedes that he's never been on a hog farm before. But he's smelled them. Then he realizes that Dixon has lured him down a rabbit hole. The bill isn't about the farms or the farmers. It's about the property rights of North Carolina landowners.

Dixon interrupts him a second time, asking whether Blust understands the concept of "integrated livestock operations." The subtext is plain. This isn't Blust's area of expertise. He should leave the regulation of agriculture to industry men. Blust, however, is ready for him. He's not going to yield to any more questions. Dixon is wasting time on trifles.

"I have other objections," explains Blust, "but to do away with the most onerous part of this bill—that we are involving ourselves, as a legislature, in picking a winner in a lawsuit—I would like, Mr. Speaker, to be recognized to send forward an amendment."

Tim Moore admits the amendment, and the clerk reads it into the record. The language is formalistic, but the meaning is clear. Even if the General Assembly adopts HB467, thereby torching four centuries of legal precedent, the newly circumscribed law of nuisance won't apply retroactively. In Judge Britt's courtroom, Smithfield will be on its own.

As soon as Blust cedes the floor, Jimmy Dixon claims it. The Duplin representative has a saying that he's shared around the General Assembly, a maxim of public speaking that he honors more in word than in deed: "Be sincere, be brief, and be seated." When it comes to Amendment One, he respects his own creed. "Members," he says, staring down the Republicans in the back bench, "it's very obvious what this would do. Vote red. Vote no on the amendment."

Over the next few minutes, a slew of other members, including prominent Republicans, give Dixon's position an unapologetic thrashing. A former state court judge compares it to Roy Williams, the legendary UNC basketball coach, asking the NCAA to move the three-point line forward a few feet during the national championship to end a shooting drought. In an effort to save face, Jimmy Dixon tosses his maxim about brevity in the dumpster and rises a third time.

"Let me tell you," he says, peering over his glasses, "the North Carolina Chamber of Commerce, the North Carolina Farm Bureau, the North Carolina Pork Council, the North Carolina Farm Families, the North Carolina Poultry Federation support this bill exactly like it is. Let's give a little bit of leave to the folks who feed us on a daily basis."

When, at last, the Speaker puts the question to the House, all sound in the chamber dies away. For Mona and Mark in the mezzanine—and for the rest of their team tuning in remotely—the silence is as taut as a piano string. The scene is a kind of public reckoning. Before the plaintiffs are permitted to tell their story to a jury, they must survive the judgment of the State of North Carolina, as expressed by a body politic that has never been more beholden to corporate power than it is today. Although the hog barons are not in the room, they are present by proxy, their influence etched into the pensive faces of hundreds of growers sitting and standing in the gallery, their will effectuated by their political handmaidens from down east.

This is Jimmy Dixon's shining moment. Can he rescue Smithfield from the gavel?

All eyes turn toward the scoreboard suspended above the House floor. The names of the members are stenciled in white on a black background, like flights on an airport display. The silence extends, seconds piling upon one another, until the Speaker says: "The clerk will lock the machine and record the vote." It is then that color suddenly appears on the scoreboard. The white letters flash to green or red, depending on each member's vote.

Of the 120 members, five are missing from the chamber, which alters the math. A majority is now 58, not 61. Ordinarily, the Speaker, Tim Moore, abstains from voting, unless he is required to break a tie. Moore ignores this unwritten rule and votes with Jimmy Dixon. But even his support isn't enough to hand Smithfield the win.

The final tally is breathtakingly narrow: 59 to 56.

If Mona and Mark were anywhere other than in the House chamber, they would exult with a cheer. As it is, they release the tension in a hearty exhale. Despite all reports of its demise, democracy is still alive.

Then again, so is HB467.

The amendment's passage has simply excised the most controversial portion of the bill. The bill itself is still up for debate. By now, however, the result feels like a fait accompli. Only two members rise to comment—Garland Pierce, the Black preacher from Scotland County, and Pat McElraft, the Republican from Emerald Isle, who contends that whatever unpleasant odors may issue from Smithfield's hog farms, it is the "smell of freedom." As if to add an exclamation point, she raises her eyes toward the gallery and intones, "God bless you, farmers."

Unburdened by the retroactivity provision, the bill cruises to an easy victory. It meets a similar reception in the state Senate, where Brent Jackson shepherds it to passage by a wide margin, despite two weeks of impassioned lobbying by Mona and Bill and Skip Stam.

In North Carolina, now, the common law of nuisance is mostly a dead letter, at least when it comes to industrial farming and forestry operations. But the failure of Smithfield's elected cabal to poison the cases in Judge Britt's courtroom means that the company built by Wendell Murphy and Joe Luter and now owned by Wan Long has no choice.

To win, it must defeat Mike Kaeske.

PART FOUR

CONFRONTATION

Battle is an orgy of disorder.
—*George Patton*

CHAPTER 23

FIRST WORDS

It all depends on how we look at things,
and not how they are in themselves.
—Carl Jung

Park City, Utah,
and Salisbury,
North Carolina
July–December 2017

Every trial comes down to two things: the jury and the opening. That's the way Mike Kaeske sees it. The jury is Lisa Blue's specialty. She sees through people as if they're made of glass. It's the gift of hardship, the by-product of empathy born of self-doubt and struggle—with her dyslexia and learning disabilities; with being a Jewish girl in Atlanta in the sixties, raised by the first white doctor in her area to treat Black patients; with seeing her synagogue bombed on her sixth birthday; with watching the battle for civil rights play out on her own streets. She knows other people so well because she knows herself. When jury selection comes, she will be Mike's skeleton key, his best chance of launching the trial phase with an auspicious panel.

But the opening? That's his to write.

He's obsessive about it, as he is about everything in his carefully constructed life. He wants it to sing like an aria, to come alive before the bar like a grand monologue on the stage. He believes in the rhetorician's adage about primacy and recency, the importance of first and last words. The opening is his first opportunity—and that of the plaintiffs—to make an impression on the jury. And the jury is primed to remember it because, at that stage, they are a blank slate. They are energized by the anticipation of drama, of witnessing a big federal trial. The ennui hasn't set in yet, the glazed eyes and bored stares. Kaeske's goal is to take the jury's blank slate and limn the whole world in indelible ink, such that by the time Mark Anderson rises to counter him, there won't be room left for a different picture. For the defense lawyer to sound coherent, he will have to color between Kaeske's lines.

That's the benefit of going first, and Mike Kaeske is a master of it.

Most laypeople mistake the opening for an argument. It is not. It is a story, a marshalling of the facts and evidence before the first witness is sworn, before a single document is admitted to the record. Kaeske has an instinct for narrative structure, an understanding of the way story works in the human heart. He knows how to make the jurors connect with his protagonist, how to hold up his clients like a mirror so the jurors can see a reflection of their own humanity. He's also keenly aware that every good courtroom story requires a villain, ideally one with a human face. Kaeske has devoted a lot of thought to this one. None of the company men he deposed fits the bill. Neither does Ken Sullivan, Smithfield's current CEO, or Wan Long, the Chinese billionaire half a world away. The natural villain in his play is the first hog king, Wendell Murphy.

Kaeske knows that once he starts putting on evidence, the trial will bog down. There will be objections and delays, tedium and boredom. Simplicity will give way to complexity, and, as it does, Smithfield's defense team will convert that complexity into reasons for the jury to doubt. The story he delivers in the opening, therefore, must be tightly woven and hold together seamlessly. It must appeal to the heart while adhering to the law. It must answer the questions that accompany every juror into the jury box that first time: Why have you brought me here? And what wrong do you need me to right?

There is a theory that Mike Kaeske has long employed in writing his first words to the jury. At the core of the theory is a rule, a restatement of the law of the case, which the judge will recite in his jury instructions at the conclusion of the trial. The rule must be plainspoken and uncontroversial. It must be self-evident even to the defendant. Once you have the rule, you have the cornerstone of your story. You have the wrong.

In July of 2017, Kaeske invites two people to join him on his Park City mountaintop to build the hog farm opening. One of them is Daniel Wallace. Over the past two years, Daniel has become Kaeske's unofficial wingman. Whenever Mike needs help with some dimension of the case, he calls up Mona and she dispatches Daniel. Last autumn, they prepared for the depositions of the company men on the trail in Cedar Mesa. After the New Year, they crammed for the expert depos on the ski slopes. The camaraderie they have developed goes beyond work. Along with being a mentor to Daniel, Kaeske has brought him into his inner circle of friends.

The other person Kaeske involves in shaping the opening is Sophie Flynn. An uber-bright twenty-something and a rising star in global public health, Sophie is only a few years out of Brown University, but already her résumé is half a mile long. Along with editing AIDS research, promoting renewable energy, and helping low-income people get access to community services, she's now the executive director of GHETS (Global Health through Education, Training, and Service), a nonprofit working to advance women's health in the developing world. She came to Mike on the recommendation of Dr. David Egilman, who teaches medicine at Brown and chairs the GHETS board.

To the plaintiffs' bar, Egilman is the equivalent of a Nobel laureate—fearless, relentless, and scary smart. To corporate malefactors in Big Pharma, he is the Boatman on the River Styx. Early on in Kaeske's association with Mona, he reached out to Egilman to serve as a trial witness. Egilman had other commitments, but he offered his son, Sam, to support the effort. He also introduced Mike to Sophie.

It's a brilliant match, and fateful in many ways. Sophie is everything that Mike Kaeske could ask for in a trial collaborator. She's cheerful, eager, and endlessly energetic, and, like him, she has an eidetic memory. She's able to retrieve the most obscure details from documents and testimony as if they are floating on the surface of her mind. Beyond that, she's profoundly committed to the cause. She and Daniel Wallace forge their own bond, as moons in orbit around Kaeske's planet.

Together, they write the opening.

They tinker with it for days on end, sitting on the terrace outside Mike's dining room, as the sun shines down from the spotless blue sky and the leaves of the aspens quake in the high-altitude breeze. Their exchanges are dialectical, evolutionary. They work through the first words line by line, searching for a rule that will draw the jury into the moral equation, that will present the wrong not merely as a violation of the plaintiffs' rights but also as a breach of the social order. If the jury takes the case personally, if they believe the outcome matters to them and to the people they love, they will be more inclined to deliver justice to the plaintiffs.

But how does one personalize the odor from an industrial hog operation for city people from Raleigh? Many will have little knowledge of hog country. Most will have no desire to find out for themselves. To them, the plaintiffs' communities could just as easily be in Iowa. Mike, Daniel, and Sophie study the jury instructions for the law of nuisance. The rule arises as if conjured. It isn't as mellifluous as some that Kaeske has devised, but it does the trick.

A company must never substantially and unreasonably interfere with its neighbors' use and enjoyment of their property. If a company does substantially and unreasonably interfere with its neighbors' use and enjoyment of their property, the company is responsible and must pay for the harm.

From there, the three of them begin to assemble the pieces of a story. The outline is rough at first, but the body of text that emerges from their collaboration is solid enough to give Kaeske something to revise. And revise it he does, over the next six months. In a typical case, he devotes 120 hours to the opening. For the hog farm cases, he whittles and chops, elaborates and condenses, until he's poured 1,600 hours into the document. Then he commits it to memory, all two plus hours of it, until the words have taken up permanent residence in his brain.

He practices the opening on his friends, and debuts it for another focus group in Raleigh. Everyone on Mona's team, indeed, everyone who is anyone in his life, hears him deliver it from beginning to end, often multiple times. His friends will tell stories about the experience later on, laughing at the memory of their buddy Mike holding forth about hog odor in his living room to everyone who would listen. Mike's goal is perfection, and any person possessed of a thinking mind can give him feedback. He has never written anything like this before. He wants to nail Boss Hog to the wall. He wants to seal the verdict before the trial begins.

The reviews trickle in as the aspens turn golden and the first snowflakes fall. People search for superlatives, deliver their highest praise. At this point, the opening is just words on the lips of an itinerant lawyer strutting about his house in jeans and a T-shirt. Before the jury, it will be a full-scale audiovisual production.

Mike Kaeske will make it unforgettable.

✳

In early November, Judge Britt issues an omnibus order denying Smithfield's motions for partial summary judgment on nearly every point. A month later, the old judge hears arguments on the hog giant's motion for severance—to try each household separately.

It's a classic defense move: narrow the lens and increase the zoom until the jury can see only individual trees, never the whole forest. In this case, severance would also turn the litigation into a trial by ordeal. It would split the five discovery pool cases into fifty-one individual trials. Smithfield's lawyers argue that every household is unique, and that trying the cases by neighborhood, or in groups of eight to twelve plaintiffs, as Mona and Mike prefer, would encourage juries to deliver broad-brush verdicts. Underlying Smithfield's position is a curious assumption—that only a few household-specific verdicts will be enough to compel the hog giant to come to the bargaining table and broker a global resolution.

The judge, however, isn't convinced. After Smithfield's lawyer leaves the podium, he asks Mike Kaeske: "Do we know that there is going to be any global resolution?"

"We do not," Kaeske replies.

"Doesn't the court have to assume that we're going to have to try these cases?"

"I think so," says Kaeske.

As the hearing progresses, Britt works his way toward a compromise. He will allow the defendant one chance to try a single-household case—any household of Smithfield's choosing—but the remainder of the discovery pool cases will be tried in neighbor groups of eight to twelve. The inaugural trial group will be the plaintiffs' choice; Smithfield will select the second group; and so on until all the plaintiffs in the discovery pool are accounted for. The first trial will commence on April 2, 2018. The second trial will begin two weeks after the first concludes. And subsequent trials (perhaps as many as a dozen) will be scheduled at a rate of one per month until all the bellwether cases have been tried to verdict—or the parties negotiate an armistice. It is an exhausting proposition for the eighty-five-year-old judge, but he embraces it with aplomb. Judge Britt loves the bench. Everyone who watches him knows it.

The choice of the first case is reflexive for Mike Kaeske. He wrote the opening for the *McKiver* group in Bladen County and the massive 15,000-head hog operation run by Billy Kinlaw. He works with Mona's team to assemble the slate of plaintiffs. They land on ten out of the total of twenty, including the matriarch, Joyce McKiver.

Unsurprisingly, Smithfield's defense team selects Joey Carter, the former Beulaville chief of police, to be the company's standard-bearer. Of the *McGowan* group, they pick the two-member household of Elvis and Vonnie Williams. With the Williams family, distance and history are on Smithfield's side. Not only is their property one of the farthest from the hog farm, but Elvis moved to the neighborhood in 1989, after Carter built the first two barns on his south operation, and Vonnie followed suit in the early nineties after she and Elvis tied the knot. The timeline will allow Mark Anderson to argue that they came to the nuisance, that they bought their home knowing the farm was there.

Mona and Mike place *Artis* in the third spot, and create a lead group out of neighbors who live mere yards away from Dean Hilton's hog operations—such as the gardener, Jimmy Jacobs—and neighbors whose homes are a mile away—such as the siblings, Joyce and Willie Messick. As they conceive of it, the stories told by the closer folks will reinforce the tales told by the more distant neighbors in the eyes of the jury.

For trial four, Smithfield flags *Gillis* and lumps together eight plaintiffs who live the farthest away from the company-owned Sholar farm—no one who can attest to what it's like to live a few hundred feet from five hog barns and two gigantic cesspools.

For the fifth trial, Mona and Mike return to Joey Carter's neighborhood, but choose a more diverse group of plaintiffs, including Linnill and Georgia Farland.

With the trial methodology established and the calendar taking shape, the lawyers take their leave of the field for an all-too-brief holiday ceasefire. Before the team at Wallace & Graham parts ways for the break, Mona and Bill Graham gather everyone together for the firm's annual Christmas party. They hold it at Santos Chef, an Italian place in downtown Salisbury.

It has been a grueling two years since Mike and Lisa came onboard and discovery began in earnest. All of them are bloodshot and bone-tired. They have crawled around the hog country mud, spent days breathing the fetid air in the growers' barns, and scraped hog feces off of the neighbors' houses, all while enduring near-constant surveillance from the industry. They have culled through hundreds of thousands of pages of Smithfield documents for those few "case crackers" that could sway the jury. They have papered the walls of the federal court with motions and memoranda to keep pace with the McGuireWoods printing press. And, thanks to Jimmy Dixon and his cabal from down east, they have lived out of tents in the statehouse and barely survived a political assassination attempt. If the Fates were kind, the New Year would usher in a reprieve. But looking ahead, there is no end in sight.

When the ball drops on 2018, they will face a gauntlet even more daunting than the one they have endured. Each trial will last three to five weeks. Many of them will spend those weeks living out of apartments away from their spouses and children. As John Hughes will later reflect, there is something monstrous about a federal trial against a corporate Goliath with bet-the-firm stakes. Now multiply that by three or four or five such trials in a span of months, and, suddenly, the monster doesn't just look frightening. It looks mythic.

Seeing the thousand-yard stares in the eyes of his crew, Bill Graham rises to deliver his year-end speech. He surveys the faces around the restaurant: Mona, with her sand-dollar eyes and champagne-sparkle smile. Linda Wike, as faithful a paralegal as there ever was. John Hughes, the professor's son, with his endearing shaggy-dog look and fathomless mind. Mark Doby, the client whisperer who bleeds Tar Heel blue. Whitney and Daniel, the Wallace duo that Mona is grooming to succeed her. They have the talent, loyalty, fraternity, and decency to carry the firm into the future. One day, they will give this speech.

As he reaches for the words to rally the troops, Bill Graham is every bit the governor he might have been. This year, unlike previous years, he's been with the team on the front lines. He's fought beside them in the trenches. He's seen the hog kingdom breathe its fire. But he's been in the game longer than any of them, except Mona. He knows that their exhaustion will pass like everything else in life. Yet the importance of their work will endure.

"This is not just a case," he says. "This is a cause. We are fighting one of the most powerful companies in the world. Smithfield created an entire grassroots organization to speak out against our lawsuits. We need to remember that we are professionals. We are fighting for people who don't have the power or the platform to tell their stories. Your training, your knowledge, your experience can level the playing field with a multibillion-dollar corporation. Whatever they say in the press, this case is going to be decided by a jury in Raleigh."

He meets the eyes of his colleagues and friends, sees the dignity in them, the flames of passion and courage. He believes they can do it. He believes they can win. All they need is perseverance and strength.

"This is why you went to law school," he says, in valediction. "This is why you do what you do. Keep fighting the good fight."

CHAPTER 24

CLOUD OF WITNESSES

Act, and God will act.
—*Joan of Arc*

**U.S. District Court,
Raleigh,
North Carolina
April 3, 2018**

There is a smell to a springtime battlefield in the hours before it is baptized with blood. The fresh scent of sun-ripened grass, the complex minerality of wet soil, the wine-bright crispness of dew, and the heavy musk of bodies, of sweat and breath mingling in the air, weighing it down with portent. In Judge Britt's courtroom, on the first day of the *McKiver* trial, all the bodies are washed and many perfumed, and the air is recycled by machinery and conditioned by chemistry. But one can still smell it, a faint whiff of condensed humanity. It is a reminder that everything that happens here, in this temple of justice, will be attended by a cloud of witnesses—the twelve jurors seated in the box, the judge up on his bench, the clerks and lawyers at their tables, and the hundred-odd spectators in the gallery. Everyone is in place, expectant, waiting.

This moment is a commencement. It is also a culmination. Its meaning has as many facets and dimensions as the people gathered to commemorate it. Although she is not a plaintiff in this case, Elsie Herring is in the audience. She wouldn't miss it for the world. She's seventy years old now. Time has mellowed her a bit, bequeathed her patience and perspective. But it hasn't changed her essence. She's still as feisty and opinionated as she ever was. She's lived by herself for the past twelve years with only her dogs for company. But she's never really been alone. She sees her mother in her own rhythms, Beulah's hand in the habits of her life. She calls upon her regularly: *What would you do, Mama? How would you handle this?* Beulah's spirit is like a warm hand on her heart. Wherever she goes, her mother is never far away.

A thought comes to her as she sits in stillness on the bench seat, surrounded by so many familiar faces. Before her mother died, Beulah told Elsie not to worry, that there would come a day when God would fight for them. "On that day," Beulah said, "the hog farmer won't be able to do a thing about it." In the courtroom, Elsie smiles. *Mama,* she thinks, *that day is finally here.* The truth of their suffering, the truth Elsie has sacrificed so much to tell, is going to be delivered to the jury. The hog barons have never feared her voice, never taken her seriously.

But they are afraid of this jury.

Don Webb is there with Elsie in the gallery, as is Rick Dove. It's been twenty-five years since Don and Rick first mused about finding a lawyer to bring a nuisance action against the industry. It is hard to believe that they are actually here, in this federal courtroom, with some of the best lawyers in the country on their side, with TV cameras outside the courthouse and a security team milling about in the hallway. They watch as Mike Kaeske stands to address the jury. He's a hero in their book, a superstar. As is Mona Lisa Wallace. They love her like a sister. They will always feel indebted to her for taking this on, for investing so much in their cause.

For Mona herself, the moment isn't an occasion for reflection. She is rooted in time, rooted in the present. When Mike rises from the seat beside her, she knows every turn of phrase in his opening, every slide and video and photograph. She knows how religiously he prepared for this day. But she has never seen him perform it in a packed courtroom, with journalists scribbling on their pads, with hog industry heavies all around, with Smithfield's lawyers waiting to pounce, and with the jury listening to his every word. Despite his laid-back demeanor, she knows that his stomach is twisted in knots. She's nervous, too. In her four decades of practice, she has never seen a trial like this, where the whole world, it seems, is looking on. There is no room for error. Mike needs to capture the jury right out of the gate.

She watches the faces of the jurors as he lays out the Good Neighbor rule: *A company must never substantially and unreasonably interfere with its neighbors' use and enjoyment of their property* . . . All but one of them are white, thanks to the defense team's use of three of its six peremptory challenges to strike Black people from the panel. Lisa exhorted Kaeske to make a *Batson* challenge, to allege racial profiling. But he abstained, making a split-second decision not to bog Judge Britt down with a highly contentious motion that few judges ever grant. He regretted the decision almost immediately, but that's life in the fluidity of a federal trial. All that matters now are the twelve people in the box in front of him. They are watching. They are listening. They are waiting to hear the story.

And like Demosthenes in the Athenian assembly, Mike Kaeske does not disappoint.

His opening is equal parts oration and presentation. Along with his boyish good looks and radio-DJ voice, he is aided by a giant floor-to-ceiling screen that Judge Britt allowed the plaintiffs to erect along the wall opposite the jury, over vociferous objections from the defense. In addition, he has the help of Paul Malouf, a trial technology wizard, who keeps all the megabits and binary code flowing along through wires and air with a minimal number of bugs.

Mike dives into the history, not of the plaintiffs but of the industry. He tells the jury about the 18,000 individual hog farms that dotted the coastal plain of North Carolina back in 1972, with an average of 75 hogs each. Then along came Wendell Murphy with his grower contracts. The family farms started to die off, even as overall production expanded, and more and more of the hog business migrated to the integrators like Murphy Family Farms.

In 1982, Murphy designed the "1224," a barn that could house 1,224 hogs under one roof. The 1224s proliferated, minting money for Wendell Murphy. But this rapid expansion had an underside. A full 1224 produces as much waste as 6,000 people. An operation with four or five 1224s produces the daily waste of a town of 30,000. Where did Murphy and his growers put all that untreated waste? They flushed it out of the barns and into open-air "lagoons."

For color, Kaeske throws in comparisons. Each lagoon has enough hog waste to fill thirty water towers, to cover fifteen football fields one foot deep, to blanket a two-lane road six inches deep from the courthouse to the Raleigh-Durham Airport, with enough left to circle the terminal three times. And what did Murphy and his growers do when the pits got too full? They hooked them up to jet-propulsion guns and turned once-productive fields into wastelands. Two hundred gallons per minute, dozens of feet in the air, the dirty pink composite of feces and urine misting and aerosolizing and drifting on the wind into the surrounding neighborhoods.

Kaeske illustrates this with a video.

He leads the jury through Wendell Murphy's tenure as a legislator, the laws he authored and promoted to grow the industry and shield it from taxation and regulation, and then to fund the Pork Council, which worked to consolidate the industry's power and stifle dissent. This dissent came from many quarters—from neighbors, from county zoning and health boards, from activist groups, from doctors and epidemiologists, from the media, and, eventually, from the state itself. In 1995, the Raleigh *News & Observer* won a Pulitzer Prize for its reporting. Yet Murphy and the industry marched on, unrepentant, until their expansion threatened a storied golf course. At last, the authorities drew a line in the sand, imposing a moratorium on new construction. But the 2,000 lagoons and sprayfields scattered across mostly rural, low-income communities of color were grandfathered in. Even when the state's flagship university confirmed the danger of hog waste to human health, the government allowed the cesspools and spray guns to remain.

The Smithfield Agreement, negotiated by the state attorney general, offered a chance for a hard reset, but the industry's representatives hobbled the process, demanding that any new technology be revenue-neutral. They allowed the most promising innovation, Super Soils, to slip into senescence, relegated to the ash heap of revolutionary ideas that might have transformed people's lives. Oh, and by the way, Kaeske says, this same Smithfield that labeled Super Soils too expensive? The Chinese bought the company for $7 billion in 2013. Three years later, in 2016, this same Smithfield sold $2.7 billion worth of pork.

Having told the story of the hog kings, Kaeske zooms in on Billy Kinlaw's farm. It's an old Murphy Family Farms operation, built just up the road from a Black community with deep roots in the land. While the farm is Kinlaw's in name, it is Smithfield's in practice. The grower doesn't own the 15,000 hogs in his sheds. He doesn't decide when they come or go, doesn't elect when the dead trucks collect the corpses of the hogs that die in his care.

Sometimes, the trucks trundle down the road in the wee hours of morning. One night, eleven tractor-trailers visited the Kinlaw operation between 12:28 a.m. and 5:33 a.m. All of them passed within fifty feet of the plaintiffs' bedroom windows. Those are Smithfield's trucks, Kaeske says, not Billy Kinlaw's. The flies and buzzards that haunt the community, those are Smithfield's flies and buzzards. And the odor that often permeates the air around Kinlaw's farm, that's Smithfield's odor.

Smithfield has known the truth for decades. It has even maintained an archive of media stories and research articles about the problem. Smithfield has the technology to eliminate the problem. It has the money to eliminate the problem. Yet it chooses to do nothing. Almost by definition, Smithfield has violated the Good Neighbor rule.

Next, Kaeske takes the jury on a tour of the barns. He shows them the shit-caked hogs, intelligent animals crammed into cages and left to wallow in their own excrement. He tells them about the chemicals and odorous compounds in their manure, about the bacteria and pathogens that can travel for miles on the wind. Then he personalizes it, lets the jury see how the plaintiffs have been forced to live.

"Imagine, you've had a busy week," he says. "Your chores are backed up at home. You tell yourself, 'On Saturday, I'm going to mow the yard before it gets too hot, and wash the car in the heat of the day, and in the evening when it cools off, we'll have friends over from church for a barbecue.' When you wake up Saturday morning to the beautiful North Carolina blue skies, you go outside and get your mower. You make three passes into doing the yard and it hits you—feces, urine, hog. You're annoyed. You get upset. You go in the house and sit down and watch the game. You hope the odor passes. A couple hours later, you go back outside. The odor is gone. You finish the yard, pull the car out, get the bucket and rag and turn on the hose. It hits you again. You can't stand the smell. You go in the house and slam the door and call your friends. 'We're not grilling out over here tonight. It smells like hog. You never know when the odor will come. You never know when it will stop. You never know how bad it will be.'"

This is life in the hog kingdom. This is Smithfield's world.

Kaeske names the experts he will call. Dr. Shane Rogers from Clarkson, the former EPA scientist and expert on fate and transport. And Dr. Steve Wing, the famed epidemiologist from UNC, now deceased. Kaeske talks about the Pig2Bac marker, tells the jury about Shane's findings around the plaintiffs' homes. "It doesn't take a scientist to know that if hog feces is on the side of your home, then it's in the air you're breathing and smelling, too, and on your car parked outside, and on your clothesline, and on your mailbox, and likely in your home, as well."

Mike Kaeske tells the jury about his clients, about the community matriarch, Joyce McKiver, who is now as old as Judge Britt, and about her children and grandchildren, all her kin who have made a home on her ancestral land. He tells them about the longleaf pines, the big blue skies, the rivers and streams and woods that many of them have loved since they were young. "The folks in this community were living their lives on their own little piece of America long before Smithfield came along," he says. They remember the days when they could sit on their front porch and greet their neighbors without being accosted by hog odor, when they could till their gardens and tend their flowers without worrying that a plume of stench from Billy Kinlaw's cesspools might camp out in their front yard. They remember how it was before.

But that's not the way it is now.

Pivoting smoothly, Kaeske tells the jury to beware the hall of mirrors that will be Smithfield's defense. Beware the illusion of the family farmer that the company has spent millions of dollars to conjure. The hog barons have taken extraordinary pains to portray themselves as the benefactor of the family farmer. It's a public relations ploy. It's also wildly ironic. It was the industrialization of hog production led by Wendell Murphy and Joe Luter that put 15,000 actual family farmers out of business.

Beware, also, the economic excuse. "We're good for the economy," they'll say, "and we employ thousands of people." All of that is irrelevant to the law. The suffering that the industry has heaped upon Joyce McKiver and her neighbors is not merely a sunk cost on society's balance sheet. It is a direct consequence of Smithfield's business model.

Smithfield must pay for the harm.

Beware of the bacon excuse, Kaeske adds. "Sure, they make pork. We don't want to stop eating pork, and there is no reason to. Smithfield can still contribute to the economy if they're using alternative technology. In fact, they'll contribute more." The new technology will bring in more jobs to North Carolina. The clean-up effort will infuse the community with Smithfield's cash, money that might otherwise have been shipped to the company's owners in China.

Beware, also, the regulation diversion. Whatever regulations may exist to curtail the excesses of industrial hog farming, they have not prevented harm. And neither Smithfield nor its contract growers have a permit from the state that allows them to break the Good Neighbor rule. The law of nuisance stands apart.

Lastly, beware the excuse that the neighbors never complained. Kaeske takes a moment to introduce the neighbors who are sitting in the gallery. He shares little anecdotes about their lives. He wants to etch their faces into the jury's consciousness—all of them Black in a courtroom full of white people—before offering an explanation.

"Most of these folks never considered that they could complain, or that complaining would do them any good," he says. "Until this lawsuit, they didn't think that they had a voice. You'll see. They'll tell you straight. Some will tell you they didn't think it was their place to complain, or that they had the power to complain. But let's say you decided to complain to the Smithfield grower, what's he going to do about it? He's following Smithfield's rules, and they don't pay him enough to do anything different." The same logic applies to Smithfield itself. "People started complaining about Smithfield's hog operations decades ago, and it's never done any good. Smithfield doesn't need to hear more complaints to know there is a problem."

Having been on his feet for over two hours now, Kaeske comes to rest before the jury box. "One of our most basic constitutional rights is our ability to own, use, and enjoy property," he says. "What is the value of the interference? You'll hear that to the neighbors, many of whom inherited the property, they don't want to leave this land. And it's not just the value of their property that's lost, it's the value of the enjoyment of their property." Kaeske surveys the faces of the jurors. "The value of your property, you will hear, is not what you pay for your property. The value of your property is in your ability to use and enjoy your property."

There's a glimmer in Kaeske's eyes when he makes his final pitch.

"Lawsuits can cause change. They can. We all know that. My clients' hope is that the way you value the harm with your verdict will cause it to change."

When he sits down again, Mona Wallace lets out the breath she didn't know she was holding. She glances around the gallery and sees the glow in people's faces, her clients' sense of vindication, the smiles her colleagues are trying to hide. Although this is only the first act of a lengthy contest, she allows herself the momentary luxury of joy.

She's proud of all of them, especially the plaintiffs. Most of them have never been in a courtroom before, let alone one like this, with the glare of the media spotlight in their eyes and the power of an entire industry arrayed against them. It takes courage just to file suit. But they have done far more than that. They have endured intrusive depositions and inquiries into their personal lives. They have waited and trusted and persisted for years in believing that her team could do it, that they could be the voice of their community and bring their story to life.

She's proud of Mike, too—for giving it everything, and for delivering. When she met him in New York in 2015, she wasn't sure what to think. But she trusted Lisa's assessment of his talent and John Hughes's appraisal of his character, and decided to take the risk. When he started winning big motions, her confidence grew. Yet a federal jury trial with years of effort and millions of dollars on the line is a crucible unlike any other. It exposes every weakness, calls forth the dross from beneath the shine. There was no dross in his opening. It was a virtuoso performance. In a soliloquy as long as a Quentin Tarantino film, he never once lost the plot, never lost his train of thought, and never made the story about himself. He swung for the fences and hit the ball into the upper deck.

We made the right choice, she thinks.

Behind her, Elsie Herring is feeling something even deeper. She hears Mike's last words like a vibration in her soul, a pure note of music stirring her to hope. For more than a third of her life, she has been praying and agitating for change. Yet the world has resisted her entreaties, and change has never come. Perhaps this time it will be different. Perhaps here in this hallowed hall, the wrong that she has carried around like a wound that just won't heal will find its remedy.

Perhaps the truth, at long last, will set her free.

CHAPTER 25

BLOODSPORT

No man is above the law and no man is below it; nor do we ask
any man's permission when we ask him to obey it.
—*Theodore Roosevelt*

**Raleigh,
North Carolina
April 3–11, 2018**

The *McKiver* trial lasts three weeks from
opening statement to closing argument. It's
a forced march of exhausting days and near-
sleepless nights. The adrenaline and endor-
phins, the tightrope nerves and tumbleweed
emotions, and the trove of common memories
forge a bond among the plaintiffs' team that will endure for years afterward, perhaps forever.

So does living together. Instead of booking rooms at a downtown
hotel, Mike and Mona rent four apartments in a building miles away
from the city center. It's a more comfortable living arrangement, given
the length of time they're going to be in town, and it affords them an
additional layer of security. When they aren't at the courthouse, no one
outside the team knows where to find them—not the media, and definitely not the allies of Smithfield.

In all of Mike Kaeske's career, he's never lived in such proximity to
his trial team. The apartments feel like a terrarium, a self-contained universe sealed off from the world. The three-bedroom unit he shares with
Haven, his goldendoodle, Tük, and Sophie Flynn doubles as the team's
"war room." It is their psychic center of gravity, where Kaeske expurgates
his doubts every morning before the trip to the courthouse, with aid

from Haven, Lisa, Sophie, and Daniel, and where he battens down every evening with Mona and the crew to debrief, share a takeout dinner, and draw up the next day's battle plan.

A trial, in its performative shape, is a cross between Broadway theater and North Hollywood improv. The production is scripted, yet everything is subject to last-minute change. Since Mike prefers to try cases on his own rather than share the workload with other lawyers, he has to ponder every question himself from all points on the compass. He has to wrestle through every contingency and know the order of proof like his own life story. If he falters, if the defense team catches him by surprise, the jury will see it and notch a demerit on their mental scorecard.

He vows never to be caught by surprise.

In the war room, he thinks out loud in a stream of consciousness, bouncing ideas off Sophie and the other team members like Roger Federer warming up before a match at the U.S. Open. His intensity is at the red line; his criticism is frequent and unsparing. If an idea doesn't work, he scraps it and moves on. If a concept is solid but out of sequence, someone writes it on a sticky note and pastes it on the wall. As the days give way to weeks, the wall turns into a pink-and-yellow checkerboard of words and phrases, themes and concepts, that are constantly being reorganized and replaced. Though some of the team members find it enervating—even, at times, a cause for wounded feelings—Kaeske thrives on the intellectual combat. He needs it to keep his mind sharp, to maintain his edge, and to stay ahead of Smithfield.

To handle the stress, the team develops a culture of playfulness. Humor is an unofficial currency, and inside jokes proliferate. The welcome mat outside Mike's apartment bears the inscription WELCOME TO THE SHITSHOW. It's his philosophy of trial practice—that everything that can go sideways will go sideways, and if it doesn't this time around, it will next time. Karma is an unforgiving bitch, so it's best to see her coming. Lisa Blue adds to the laconic atmosphere a dash of her own snark, handing out mugs emblazoned with the silhouette of two hogs locked in coitus, with the epigram MAKIN' BACON. As caustic as he can be in a sparring contest, Kaeske has a capacious sense of humor and is always ready for a laugh.

He is also a fitness fanatic, as is Lisa. Every morning at six o'clock, they meet in the gym for half an hour on the elliptical. Daniel Wallace joins them. Since Mike is a light switch, and at trial he is always "on," he focuses on the case as soon as the cobwebs clear. After working up a sweat, the three of them shower and dress and gather again in the war room. Haven—who is a saint by unanimous attestation—has Kaeske's shirt ironed and his ensemble ready to go as soon as he returns from the gym. A creature of extreme habit, Mike wears only one brand of shirt (Tom Ford), and only one color of suit (blue). In fact, just about everything in his closet back home—jeans, T-shirts, ski jackets, hats, backpacks—is some shade of sea or sky.

If humor and exercise are Kaeske's relief valves, music is his therapy. He's a huge fan of Mumford & Sons. He can sing every word of Citizen Cope. His latest crush is the Revivalists. He's a compulsive concertgoer. The only thing better than listening to the right song is seeing it performed live. When the Revivalists play the Red Hat Amphitheater in Raleigh, he will be there, singing "Wish I Knew You" with David Shaw and the band, as will half the trial team.

As a musician himself, Shane Rogers shares Kaeske's devotion. It's one of the many commonalities that fire their friendship. After Shane endures a grueling two-and-a-half-day ordeal on the stand, Mike texts him a note of thanks along with a song: "She Sells Sanctuary" by The Cult. It's a blast from the past for Shane, something he listened to as a young man. After Shane testifies in a later trial, Kaeske will send him "Age of Consent" by New Order, another old favorite. Kaeske's song selections are spot on. It's as if he is in Shane's head.

Music is a salve for John Hughes, too. As the designated scrivener, he spends almost no time in Raleigh. Rather, while Mike is examining witnesses, and Mona is passing him ideas from the chair, and Sophie is managing the storehouse of exhibits, and Lisa is watching the jury, and Whitney, Daniel, and Mark Doby are scribbling notes, and Linda Wike and Rene Davis are handling logistics for the clients (hotel reservations, wardrobe issues, lunch orders, etc.), the professor's son is camped out in his makeshift home office in Salisbury. He eats junk food like a teenager, never changes his clothes, and keeps bizarre hours, working through the night and sleeping in short bursts during the day. For eighteen or nineteen hours at a time, he is glued to his laptop, fingers pecking away. He listens to music as he writes—everything from Led Zeppelin to sitar arrangements from half a world away.

The whole scene drives his wife, Jenny, crazy. She understands the obsession of his craft. She's a writer, too. But she hates the toll it is taking on him, the roller coaster of emotions and the friction that arises between John and Mike, who has to argue John's motions before Judge Britt. She dislikes the cloying funk in the air. She's disgusted by his dorm-room diet. Most of all, she loathes the fact that John is always distracted, that even on weekends he's lost in the law, that when their little dachshund dies in the middle of the trial, he barely takes a moment to grieve. But she's a patient woman. She knew the man she was marrying, and she gives him the space he needs. As a writer, at least, she's glad to see him pouring his soul onto the page.

Of the sixteen days that the *McKiver* case is on the docket, the plaintiffs use ten days to meet their burden of proof. Their first two witnesses are Steve Wing, testifying posthumously by video, and Shane Rogers. As a one-two combination, the scientists are devastating.

Wing communicates to the jury with almost priestly authority. In the courtroom, the last words of a dying man ring like a celestial pronouncement. That he agreed to testify at such a late stage out of the goodness of his heart and not for money gilds his words in gold leaf. All doubts about his credibility—if any once existed—are dispelled.

Then Shane Rogers takes the stand. With painstaking clarity and detail, he describes his findings from Joyce McKiver's neighborhood. While he is discussing the Pig2Bac marker—the inevitable companion of hog feces—Kaeske plays for the jury a gorgeously produced animation of Pig2Bac-bearing particles rising from the hog barns, wafting on the wind, and coming to rest on the neighbors' homes. In describing his visit to Kinlaw's hog operation, Shane shows the jury photos and videos of Smithfield's filth-stained hogs and of himself in a small boat, dressed in a hazmat suit, floating on the morass of a pink-brown lagoon. He underscores the visuals with his own hog odor story: the rancid eyeglasses that dogged him for weeks.

As a visual aid to Shane's testimony, Mike Kaeske trots out a life-sized display model of a three-hundred-pound market hog that Lisa purchased online and the team caked in mud. Mark Anderson, as if hoping to diminish the grossness of the reproduction, christens the pig "Wilbur." But the giant hog bears no resemblance to Charlotte's friend. It looks like a manure-covered monstrosity.

By the time Shane vacates the stand, he has left the jury with a smorgasbord of vivid impressions, chief among them that Smithfield, along with being king of the hog kings, is also the undisputed king of shit. One can almost hear the jurors' vomit reflex engaging.

After framing the case with his experts, Mike Kaeske weaves the rest of his witnesses like threads on a loom. The plaintiffs, almost all of them kin to Joyce McKiver, are at once nervous and eager to testify. They have been a constant presence at the trial, their countenances lending gravitas to the testimony of the experts. Now, at last, they have a chance to speak. One by one, they take their turns in the witness chair, trying their best to conceal the trembling in their hands.

While each of the plaintiffs contributes a unique splash of color, Daphne McKoy, the youngest of Joyce McKiver's children, distills her family's pain to its purest essence. A social worker and single mother of two teenagers, she is a cherubic woman with eyes that exude kindness, shoulder-length hair embellished with a wavy beach curl, and horn-rimmed glasses that lend her soft features a distinguished touch. She was born in the neighborhood and has lived there most of her life. She lays out the story in detail—the flies, the trucks, the buzzards, and the hogs. She is on the stand for three hours. It is a nerve-racking experience, but her summation lands like a thunderclap.

"My father was a sharecropper. We didn't have a lot, and what he did leave to his family was that little piece of land. They gave that land to me, and I grew up there. Now that my kids are growing up there, they don't have the same upbringing I had. All they've known is trying to play outside, having to cut it short because it stinks. Or they're getting ready to go to school, and I'm like, 'Oh, it stinks so bad out here.' So they're not getting the sentimental value that I got out of the land. I would like for you to know how helpless I feel as a mother to hear them complain about how the kids say, 'Your house smells—'" Daphne chokes up. "'Your house smells like a trash dump,' or 'You don't want to have your friends over because of the smell.' I just want you to know how hopeless and helpless it feels. So I'm here now, and it's been a long process. It's been years. I'm just hoping that there is a change."

When she steps down from the stand, the entire courtroom is silent. Her words are pennies cast into a fountain, the wishes and prayers of her family for dignity, for surcease.

*

In time, Kaeske summons a quartet of company men, surrounding them
with Daphne's neighbors to create a kind of mural of the hog kingdom's
tyranny. He calls Kraig Westerbeek and John Sargent by proxy, playing
the jury compilations from their video depositions. But Don Butler, the
industry's leading front man, now retired, and Gregg Schmidt, the president of Murphy-Brown, he subpoenas to testify live, as adverse witnesses.

A public relations guru and multi-tour veteran of the hog wars, Butler is a smooth operator on the stand. He is calm and composed, his
voice measured, his words carefully chosen. Over the next day and a
half, Mike Kaeske unravels him. In Kaeske's view, Butler is not just a
partisan but a propagandist. He's been around the industry longer than
any of his colleagues. He knows that what the neighbors are saying is
true, yet he persists in denying it. Indeed, he spent his career as the
industry's leading mercenary, fighting at every level of government to
deprive the neighbors of justice. It's Butler's hidebound recalcitrance, his
bad-faith denial of reality, and his role in wielding the industry's axe,
that Kaeske wants to highlight for the jury.

Like a swordsman, Kaeske keeps his distance at first, circling Butler
almost lazily and tossing out uncontroversial queries about Smithfield,
its corporate structure, and the Shuanghui buyout in 2013. He waits for
his moment, then makes a swift cut. The subject is one of Wendell Murphy's pet laws, which stripped localities of their power to use zoning laws
to regulate the hog industry. Butler, who was running public affairs for
Carroll's Foods at the time, was one of the chief exponents and enforc-
ers of this law. Yet when Kaeske asks about Carroll's use of litigation to
bring the counties to heel, Butler flatly denies that he was involved.

Until Kaeske shows him a letter he sent to the Bladen County Board
of Health, threatening to sue if they required a health inspection for hog
operations. And a memo Butler sent to Carroll's president, Sonny Faison, recommending that they take Robeson County to court over new
hog farm regulations. Impeached by his own words, Butler's memory
suddenly improves.

Kaeske's next cut is even deeper. He shows the PR man a newspaper
clipping from Butler's own Bladen County back in 1995, in which a
neighbor complained that the hog odor wasn't just an outdoor nuisance;

it had gotten into his home. Kaeske asks Butler if he believes that odor from an industrial hog operation can seep into a neighbor's home.

"Inside their home?" Butler asks. "No, I don't believe that."

"So this man," Kaeske replies, holding up the article, "when he said, 'I have smelled it in my home twice this week,' you don't believe he was telling the truth?"

Butler tries an evasive maneuver. "I can only answer that, sir, in the experience of my life. I've been close to hog farms a lot. I've never smelled it inside my home."

"Well, to be fair," Kaeske says, "you don't smell at all, correct?"

Butler's face, well-tanned from the sun, turns a shade of purple that Kaeske has never seen on a human being. The color suffuses his head and neck. "I *do* smell," he retorts. "I have a diminished sense of smell that occurred several years ago, approximately six or seven years ago due to a medical event. But prior to that I had a normal sense of smell."

This is a point that Kaeske hammered in Butler's deposition. Butler claimed that he lost much of his olfactory sensitivity after a seasonal cold. As a medical explanation, it is plausible. Some viruses can impede one's sense of smell. Yet given Butler's occupation, it is hardly the only possible culprit. At his deposition, Kaeske inquired whether his constant proximity to hog farms, with their dust, chemicals, and pathogens, might have impacted his nose. Butler denied it. At trial, Kaeske doesn't belabor the details. Instead, he allows the fact of Butler's departed sense of smell to linger in the air, casting doubt upon the man's entire testimony.

Returning to the article, Kaeske shows Butler where neighbors complained that the hog odor prevented their children from playing outside. "Do you believe that industrial hog operations like Smithfield's Kinlaw industrial hog operation have the ability to release odors into the neighborhoods strong enough that children would be unable to play outside because they don't like the hog farm odor?" he asks.

Butler is unmoved. "No, I do not believe that."

Staying light on his feet, Kaeske wears the PR man down with papers from Smithfield's archive, papers that document the work of activists and the findings from industry-sponsored focus groups, and media articles from the height of the hog wars. Butler fights back vigorously, admitting what he must admit—that odor increases on humid days and that a thousand hogs in a barn produce a smell—but denying the premise that an industrial hog operation could ever be a nuisance. It's his view that only a small group of neighbors were doing all the complaining, that the media is biased against the industry, constantly recycling dated stories with a negative bent, and that when Smithfield received legitimate complaints, it responded to them.

"If my neighbors ever came to me and complained about a problem, I would fix it," he assures the jury. "And that's been the position of the company I've worked with for my entire career."

Kaeske senses the man's overreach and puts his weight into a countering thrust. "Has Smithfield or any of its related companies ever eliminated the lagoon and sprayfield system in North Carolina due to the complaints from neighbors?"

"Have we ever closed . . . ?" Butler says, struggling to recover. "Is that what you're asking me? Have we ever closed a farm due to the complaint from a neighbor?"

"No." Kaeske shakes his head. "I don't want to close any farms. No. Has Smithfield ever eliminated the lagoon and sprayfield system in response to complaints from neighbors?"

"No, because that would be the same thing as closing the farm."

Kaeske allows a trace of umbrage into his voice. "No, it wouldn't. There are methods that can be used to eliminate the lagoon and sprayfield system, aren't there."

Backed into a corner, Butler purples again. "No," he replies forcefully.

Kaeske presses harder. "You know that there's technology that will eliminate the lagoon and sprayfield system, correct?"

Butler doubles down. "No, I don't."

This is another mistake. It exposes Butler's flank in a way that Kaeske will exploit later on. For now, though, Kaeske has other priorities.

He asks: If Smithfield were genuinely committed to addressing the concerns of the neighbors, why didn't it take the opportunity to do so after it got sued? Lawsuits are complaints, aren't they? That word is literally the title of the document. Butler takes cover behind his lawyers. He did nothing, he claims, on the advice of his counsel. Mark Anderson lodges a vehement objection, which Judge Britt sustains.

But the point remains: Butler did nothing.

If Smithfield really wants to hear the neighbors' opinions, Kaeske continues, has it created a hotline and posted it on its hundreds of trucks to make people aware that if they have a problem, they can complain? Butler admits the company has never done that. But there's a toll-free number on the Smithfield signs outside every farm.

"It is not difficult to get in touch with Smithfield Foods in southeastern North Carolina," Butler says. "If you want to get in touch with Smithfield Foods, it's not difficult."

This is yet another miscue, and Kaeske takes advantage of it. "Now, let's say it's Saturday and my clients are trying to have a barbecue, and they get the smell of the hog odor so bad that they don't want to be outside anymore, what are you saying they should do?"

Butler fumbles for a response. "Well, that's a dilemma. I don't know." He goes on to say that Smithfield has instructed its hog farmers to avoid spraying when they know their neighbors have planned an event. But that's not Kaeske's question. He's asking about a spontaneous gathering. Who are the neighbors supposed to contact? Suddenly, Butler recalls that Smithfield has a 24/7 complaint line listed on its website.

"Anybody can call it," he explains. "They can leave an anonymous complaint about whatever they want related to Smithfield."

"And tell the members of the jury when that went into effect," Kaeske says.

"I don't know the exact date."

"You do know that didn't go into effect until after this lawsuit was filed, correct?"

Anderson objects, but Butler answers anyway: "I don't remember the date."

Kaeske refuses to let this go. "You know as recently as two years ago there was no phone number anywhere on the Smithfield website for complaints?"

"Objection!" says Anderson.

"Overruled," replies Judge Britt. "If he knows."

"I don't know," Butler admits.

Another strike of the blade, another splotch of blood. But Kaeske won't be satisfied until he exposes this "complaint" system as a sham. So he puts it in context, presses the hypothetical about the Saturday barbecue. With Butler's reluctant help, he establishes that even if a neighbor tried to complain, the best the company would do is send someone from environmental compliance out to inspect the farm and talk to the hog farmer. But by then the barbecue would almost certainly be over, and the smell might very well be gone. If Smithfield really wanted to combat the odor, it could require its hog farmers to measure the odor. But it's never done that, as Butler attests. Finding his back once again against the wall, the PR man passes the buck to the state. The neighbor, he says, should call the Division of Air Quality, which has regulatory authority over hog farms and can investigate odor complaints and impose fines.

"You just told us you'd fix it," counters Kaeske.

"I said we'd do everything in our power to fix it," Butler rejoins.

This is the shape of Butler's charade: Deny until cornered, feign concern, then offer half-baked solutions that fall apart on inspection.

Kaeske takes Butler back to the late nineties. After the legislature imposed a moratorium on new hog farms, it decided to enact odor regulations in response to neighborhood complaints. The committee tasked with writing the regulations asked the regulators at the Division of Air Quality for help with the drafting. The hog barons, however, were not content to watch from the sidelines. They created a "producers working group" and offered their own comments to the drafters. In the view of DAQ, there were a variety of possible methods to measure objectionable hog odor—odor panels, scentometers, electric noses, and citizen complaints, with a complaint system being the least efficient. Unsurprisingly, the hog industry signaled its strong preference for a complaint system, and Don Butler, more than anyone else, made that public case.

Kaeske ramps up the attack. "You understand that if it's based on complaints, that's putting the burden on the people who are getting interfered with to figure out how to complain, right? It's putting the burden on the people who have to smell the odor, right?"

Again, Butler ducks, saying the complaint process was meant to empower the citizens and give them a chance to be heard. "Problems that we don't know about can't be addressed."

"You know that hog operations create hog odor that leaves the property," Kaeske retorts. "You wanted a system that required people to go figure out how to complain."

Mark Anderson rises to his feet. "Objection!"

"That's what you wanted, correct?" Kaeske demands.

At last, Judge Britt puts his hands between them: "Sustained."

There's one final area of inquiry that Kaeske wants to make before he releases Butler, one last series of cuts and strikes before he lays down his sword. He isn't aiming for a death blow. He wants to leave the man staggering, weeping blood. He wants the jury to feel no pity for him as he retreats down the aisle. He wants them to remember him as the living, breathing face of an industry that has shown no mercy, that has rigged the economic and political systems of an entire state to enrich and protect itself, and that has denied hundreds, perhaps thousands, of mostly Black landowners their human rights, denying Daphne McKoy's children a homeplace that they can be proud of, that they might return to one day, like their mother did.

"In 1999," says Mike Kaeske, "there came a time when the governor of the state of North Carolina decided because of the problems, including odor, associated with the lagoon and sprayfield system that the system needed to be eliminated in the state, correct?"

"I think that was his belief," Butler concedes.

Kaeske shows the PR man the press release from Governor Hunt's office in which he called for a ten-year conversion of hog lagoons to new technology. He asks Butler whether the governor was right to consider hog lagoons a source of air and water pollution.

Butler doesn't budge. "That was the governor's opinion."

"But was it true?"

Hemmed in yet again, Butler gives an inch. "There might have been some instances of that, but it was not widespread."

"So you disagree?"

"I do."

Kaeske then presents him with the Smithfield Agreement. He offers the jury a primer on the agreement's terms, by way of admissions from Butler. Under the agreement, Smithfield—not the state—would pay to install on all of its hog farms any new waste-management technology that the NC State researchers found to be environmentally superior to lagoons and sprayfields, and also operationally and economically feasible. The company could not offload the cost of upgrading its contract farms onto the growers.

Kaeske puts his next question bluntly: "Technology was found that solves all these problems both technically and operationally, correct?"

Butler is savvy enough not to hide. "The designee did identify a couple of technologies that met these requirements." Super Soils was one of them. But, he adds, the technologies only met the specifications necessary to be implemented on *new* farms, not existing farms.

Kaeske keeps Butler focused on Super Soils. "If I want to go build a new hog operation right now, this process determined that Super Soils is operationally, technically, and economically feasible, and it would be permitted by the State of North Carolina, correct?"

"For new or expanded farms," Butler affirms.

"All right," says Kaeske, pivoting quickly. "Now, back to conversion of existing farms. The only outstanding issue was money, correct? It was technically feasible. It was operationally feasible. The only issue was money. If you wanted to pay for it, you could do it, right?"

Butler admits this. But under subsequent questioning, he denies the premise—that Smithfield could, if it chose to spend the money, implement Super Soils on all of its existing farms, its company-owned farms and its contract farms alike. "We're not going to put in technology or ask our growers to, if we know it's going to put them out of business."

This is the sticking point. It's been Smithfield's mantra for a decade now. Kaeske knows he won't convince Butler to abandon it. But he can force the PR man to admit that the findings of the economic subcommittee were skewed by industry influence. Out of eleven members, five were industry insiders: Bart Ellis, from Smithfield Foods; Dave Townsend, from Premium Standard Farms; Bundy Lane, from Frontline Farmers; Richard Eason, from Cape Fear Farm Credit; and Dennis Dipietre, an economic advisor to PSF. And all of them banded together to advance a feasibility standard that ruled out Super Soils and everything else.

"Their opinion," says Kaeske, "was that we're not willing to pay one dollar more, correct?"

"That was their conclusion," Butler concedes.

"There is no doubt that if Smithfield wanted to use Super Soils on its contract grower operations, it could afford the money to pay for it, correct?"

Butler avoids the trap. "Smithfield is bound by the terms of the agreement and is still good for those commitments. We didn't make any commitments beyond the agreement itself."

"Sir, you didn't answer my question. Set the agreement aside. The technology exists in the world. Do you agree that Smithfield should be socially responsible?"

Butler's skin takes on its purple sheen. "Yes, I do."

"You agree that Smithfield should be environmentally responsible?"

"I do."

"You agree that Smithfield should be a good neighbor?"

"I do."

"This technology exists, and if Smithfield wanted to use it at any one of its corporate farms or at one of its contract grower farms, Smithfield can certainly afford the money to use it."

Again, Butler tries to dodge, claiming that he visited the test sites for the new technology and that none of them made a significant difference in the odor level. Kaeske asks the question about affordability yet again, forcing Butler to answer.

"Not if it's going to drive us out of business, no," he says.

The trap closes. Ever the professional, Kaeske doesn't allow his glee to register. But he has Butler by the throat. "How much did Smithfield make in profit last year?"

Mark Anderson tries to intercede, but Judge Britt overrules him.

"I don't know," Butler says.

"Approximately $2 billion, correct?"

Again, Anderson objects, but the judge declines to intervene.

Kaeske uses the opportunity to underline the number: "Profit of $2 billion, correct?"

If any of the jurors were drifting before, they're definitely paying attention now. The mention of $2 billion—that's "billion" with a "b"—echoes in the chamber like a secret chord. No wonder Smithfield's trial counsel wanted to prevent Mike Kaeske from saying the words.

"I think that's approximately correct," Butler allows.

"Okay. So if Smithfield wanted to take some of that profit and use it to implement this technology that was determined to be technically and operationally feasible and was determined to substantially eliminate the odor created by the lagoon and sprayfield system, Smithfield could afford to do that with its $2 billion in profit, correct?"

The answer is self-evident, but Don Butler still says, "No."

The point scored, the wound suppurating, Kaeske leaves it there.

"Mr. Butler, I have one more document that I want to show you and the members of the jury." It's a memorandum dated February 1, 1999, written by Butler himself. "Mr. Butler, have you ever heard anyone say, 'I believe it is a foregone conclusion that we will be forced to transition to different waste-treatment technology over the next few years'?"

"Yes," says Butler, looking weary and miserable.

"You've said that, correct?"

"I did."

"It's now been nineteen years since you said that, correct?"

"It was written in 1999."

"And you've postponed the elimination of the lagoon and sprayfield system that creates those problems for nineteen years, correct?"

Butler's face is fuchsia. "Because technologies have not been identified that were . . . that met the criteria for conversion." When Kaeske hits him with the $2 billion again, he tries on a last-ditch excuse: "If we had known about a technology that we believed was truly better and would allow farmers to remain in business, we would have adopted it and implemented it."

If ever a string of words rang hollow in a courtroom, these do.

"One last thing," says Kaeske. "When you say 'allow farmers to remain in business,' there is absolutely nothing about your relationship with Mr. Kinlaw or any one of the other contract growers that prohibits you from paying for that technology to be used on his operation, so that he doesn't have to pay for it, correct?"

"Correct."

"And, as a matter of fact, your contract with the contract growers actually gives you the right to dictate the facilities of the grower, correct?"

Butler tries to push back, but Kaeske doesn't care. He's sick of the PR man's sanctimonious bullshit, and if his instinct is right, so is the jury. Mark Anderson can try to rehabilitate him, to bind up his wounds and conceal the blood, but no amount of bandaging can undo the damage. The truth is obvious to anyone with a functioning conscience.

Kaeske turns away and catches Sophie's eye, then Mona's. He looks up at Judge Britt, who is peering at him over his eyeglasses. Kaeske's lips spread into a smile.

"Your Honor, I pass the witness," he says.

CHAPTER 26

A TRAITOR TO HIS KIND

Nothing in this world is harder than speaking the truth.
—*Fyodor Dostoevsky*

Raleigh,
North Carolina
April 13–16, 2018

There are few symbols more flag-draped than the citizen farmer. Ruggedly independent, dependable, hardworking, and wholesome, a farmer, as we Americans envision him, is as devoted to the land as he is to his family. He is a patriot, a God-fearing man with an unerring moral compass. The farmer archetype is so gilded now that it has translated into myth, especially for post-industrial city dwellers. But that is the source of its enduring power. And that is why Smithfield placed the silhouette of a farmer on its heraldic crest. To win over the jury, Mike Kaeske must expose the company's fraud without trampling on the myth. It's a delicate dance, but he knows he can do it.

He calls Billy Kinlaw to the stand.

The hog farmer is an old man now, nearly eighty. He's not much of a farmer, really. He's a retired insurance salesman and real estate broker who happens to raise hogs for Smithfield. But he's a decent man, and he cares about the land. He didn't want to build the hog operation in Joyce McKiver's neighborhood. He had a piece of inherited property that he wanted to use instead, a plot without homes around it. But Wendell Murphy's people weren't fond of the site. In their view, it was too close to another hog farm. They exhorted him to buy the patch of forest where Daphne McKoy and her siblings played as children and build the hog farm there. He took their advice and borrowed the $1.3 million he needed to erect twelve barns and three lagoons according to Murphy's plans. Then he signed his first contract to grow hogs. That was in 1994.

As the years passed, he left Murphy and grew for Prestage, then Premium Standard Farms, then Smithfield when it acquired PSF. He strongly preferred the PSF contract. The transition to Smithfield cost him $80,000 in annual income. He's been in the hog business for twenty-four years, yet these days his operation barely makes a profit. Kinlaw, in his down-to-earth way, tells the jury that his farm pays for his pickup truck, gas money, and life insurance. While Smithfield rakes in billions, he can't pay himself a salary. From the way he puts that striking fact—and then elaborates on it during Mark Anderson's deferential cross-examination—the jury sees what Mike Kaeske saw at Kinlaw's deposition a year ago. Unlike Joey Carter, the former police chief of Beulaville, and Dean Hilton, the real estate investor, Billy Kinlaw is no friend of Smithfield's. He even admits that Joyce McKiver complained to him about the odor. He might not be the paragon of a citizen farmer, but he steps down from the witness stand with his honor intact.

After the hog farmer departs, Mike Kaeske summons his "boss," Gregg Schmidt, president of Murphy-Brown. Of all the Murphy men, Schmidt is the only one that Kaeske respects. Unlike Don Butler, John Sargent and Kraig Westerbeek, all of whom performed verbal gymnastics under oath to avoid a collision with the obvious, Schmidt has never traded in farce or played footsie with reality. He is loyal to his employer, but he seems genuinely conscientious.

Much of Schmidt's testimony overlaps with Don Butler's. But the Murphy president offers an additional morsel about the Smithfield Agreement. In his deposition, he admitted that he could snap his fingers and implement Super Soils on all of Smithfield's hog farms. In front of the jury, he waffles a bit. Kaeske, however, forces Schmidt to read his prior testimony to the jury. Squirming, Schmidt concedes that neither he nor anyone at his company has spent any time examining whether the third generation of Super Soils, Terra Blue, could be implemented without undermining the company's profitability.

Following this thread, Kaeske asks Schmidt about the salaries of Smithfield's executives. "Could you tell the members of the jury over a period of, say, five years, from 2010 to 2015, how much money the Smithfield CEO got in compensation?"

Schmidt doesn't know offhand, but he says it's in the public record.

Kaeske has the figure. "Does $133,400,265 sound like the amount of compensation for the president and CEO of Smithfield from fiscal year 2010 to 2015—$133 million for that one man?"

The enormity of the number gives Schmidt pause. "I think probably, Mr. Kaeske, that has something to do with the sale of Smithfield at the time. So maybe it is reasonable in that regard."

Kaeske doesn't allow the excuse to stand. He establishes that in 2011, two years before the Chinese buyout, Larry Pope, then CEO, took home $20 million in compensation. In 2012, Pope earned $16.5 million. Also, between 2010 and 2015, Smithfield's four top officers—its CEO, CFO, COO, and Murphy-Brown's president—took home over $245 million.

Kaeske wields that figure like a hammer. "Do you know how many contract grower farms Smithfield could install Super Soils on for $245 million?"

Mark Anderson objects, but Judge Britt overrules him.

"No, I don't," Schmidt concedes.

Over the next few minutes, Kaeske guides him through the math. It turns out it would cost $3 million to install Terra Blue on Billy Kinlaw's operation. Three million compared to $245 million in compensation to four executives over five years.

But there's a solution that would cost even less: lagoon covers.

In Missouri, Premium Standard Farms installed covers on its lagoons pursuant to the consent decree. Schmidt admits that PSF didn't collapse under the cost of those improvements. He also admits that impermeable covers, if deployed in North Carolina, would eliminate lagoon odor and ward off rainwater, thus reducing the frequency of spraying.

Kaeske establishes that the cost of a simple cover, with a six-year life, is $116,000. By contrast, the cost of a long-lasting high-density polyethylene (HDPE) cover is $243,000. But that cost is more than offset by the subsequent savings. Over a twenty-year period, an HDPE cover can save a farm as much as $638,000. And that doesn't take into account the income that could be generated by harnessing methane from the manure and converting it into electricity.

"If it costs $243,000 to cover the lagoon and install the flare and all that kind of stuff," says Kaeske, "Smithfield could certainly afford to do that at the Kinlaw operation, correct?"

"In one instance, sure," Schmidt allows.

Since the Kinlaw farm has three lagoons, the total cost for the covers would be $750,000. Kaeske uses the modified number to press the point: "Smithfield can afford that?"

"To make the payment, yes."

"How many lagoons service Smithfield's hogs in North Carolina?"

"I don't know the exact number," Schmidt replies. "But we have close to two thousand sites in North Carolina. Each one of those would have a lagoon."

"Some would have more than one," Kaeske clarifies. "Let's just use two thousand. Two thousand times $243,000 is approximately $500 million. So the cost to do this at every one of the facilities where Murphy-Brown keeps its hogs is $500 million, right?"

Schmidt agrees. "I think the math is reasonable."

Kaeske then compares this to Smithfield's profit. Schmidt clarifies that the $2 billion figure from last year is for WH Group, the Chinese parent company. The operating profit of Smithfield Foods was close to $1 billion, and the after-tax profit was $640 million. So the cost to install HDPE covers on all Smithfield's lagoons in North Carolina equals three quarters of the company's after-tax profits for one year, and a quarter of the Chinese parent's annual profits.

Finally, Mike Kaeske confronts Schmidt about the origin of NC Farm Families. He shows the Murphy man the email from Keira Lombardo, the company's senior vice president of corporate affairs, to Ken Sullivan, Smithfield's CEO, late in 2015. He gets Schmidt to admit that NC Farm Families was the vehicle that Smithfield and the Pork Council created to battle the nuisance suits and to rally the growers. He then asks Schmidt about the $4 million advertising budget. Schmidt admits that Smithfield contributed $1 million to the effort.

"Do you know how many Super Soils systems $3.9 million would have paid for?" Kaeske asks.

"No, sir," Schmidt replies.

"Do you know how many covers $3.9 million would have installed on contract farms?"

"We'd have to do the math, but offhand, I don't know."

Kaeske leaves the calculations undone. His point isn't the numbers; it's Smithfield's disjointed priorities. The hog giant will pay its executives hundreds of millions of dollars and throw millions more into a public relations campaign to fight the neighbors in court—to say nothing of the millions it is paying its lawyers—but it won't shell out a copper penny to upgrade its medieval waste-management technology.

❋

On April 16, the tenth day of the trial, Mike Kaeske calls the plaintiffs' final witness. The man's appearance at the rear of the courtroom causes a stir on the industry's side of the gallery. He makes his way up the aisle slowly, tensely, the glares from his brethren like heat on his neck, their unspoken questions reverberating in his mind: *What are you doing, Tom? Aren't you supposed to be on our side?* Their disapproval comes as no surprise. It's why his son tried to discourage him from doing it, and why he struggled as long as he did with the request that Mona Wallace danced around for two years and that Mike and Lisa Blue finally made explicit on a visit to his farm in the summer of 2017.

They wanted Tom Butler to tell his story on the witness stand.

Tom remembers that visit vividly, the way Mike and Lisa sat in his office behind the hog barns and talked to him for two hours about the cases. He had stayed in touch with Wallace & Graham after meeting Mona in early 2015, and then, serendipitously, he had bumped into her at an environmental summit at Duke in the autumn of 2016. Seeing her again reinforced his instinct that he could trust her, as did the spontaneous praise she received from the podium. Michelle Nowlin, a Duke law professor and luminary in the environmental movement, pointed Mona out to the audience and described the nuisance litigation as a potential watershed in the decades-long fight to humble Boss Hog. A few months later, Mona connected Tom to Mike by telephone, and Tom invited Mike out to the farm for a longer conversation.

Tom felt the gravity drawing him into their orbit, the inexorable drift of his trajectory toward theirs. After crossing paths with Mona at Duke, he had hosted a group of EPA officials at the farm, introducing them to fifteen of his neighbors, including the one who had first raised a concern about the odor. The EPA was in the process of investigating a Title VI complaint against the state, alleging that its hog farm permitting system was disparately impacting people of color, subjecting them to a greater nuisance than white residents. At that meeting, Tom's neighbors gave full vent to their disgust. They told the EPA investigators that their children hated the hog odor the most. The stories of the kids tugged on Tom's heartstrings, solidifying his commitment to reform.

For ten years, he had upgraded his farm on his own initiative, without any help from Prestage. He was now so deeply in hock to his lenders that he would likely die in the red. Yet his lagoon covers and anaerobic digester were only partial solutions to the problem. The only genuine panacea—a real-time treatment system that would convert the solid waste into fertilizer and the liquids into potable water—was still in the prototype stage, unaffordable to growers like him.

It didn't have to be this way. Had Smithfield invested in Super Soils a decade ago, the price of the technology would have fallen enough for it to be deployed across the state. Tom's neighbors and their children wouldn't be suffering the effects of the odor anymore. Neither would the neighbors in Mona's lawsuits, or the complainants in the Title VI action, or people like them across hog country. The industry had only itself to blame for the mess it was in. Yet without some kind of reckoning, the hog barons would never admit it.

It was in this frame of mind that Tom Butler welcomed Mike Kaeske and Lisa Blue to his farm in July of 2017. They showed concern for the position he was in. They appreciated the risk of speaking out against the industry. Prestage could take away his hogs, damage his reputation, and yank his contract. What Mike and Lisa didn't know is that Tom had already received a token of the industry's wrath on account of his transparency with the media. For three weeks, Prestage had left him with fewer than 1,000 hogs on his 8,000-head farm, as if to prove his vulnerability, to remind him who's boss.

Tom knew what testifying could cost him, as did his son, who was with him when the lawyers arrived. His son was legitimately fearful. It was one thing for Tom to speak to journalists and host students and activists at the farm. It was quite another for him to swear an oath in court and testify in support of a nuisance lawsuit against the world's largest hog producer. As a witness, he wouldn't just be a contract grower espousing an unconventional take on agriculture. He would be in open rebellion against the hog kingdom.

He would be a traitor to his kind.

Tom didn't make any promises that day, and Mike and Lisa didn't ask for any. But he did allow them to add his name to the voluminous list of potential witnesses they were compiling for the court, with the proviso that they would bracket it with the names of other growers, so that the defense lawyers wouldn't single him out. Smithfield's legal team never subpoenaed Tom for a deposition. Indeed, Mike and Mona weren't obligated to inform them that Tom would be testifying until forty-eight hours before he took the stand. The notice, when it came, must have struck Mark Anderson like a bolt from the blue.

But the decision wasn't sudden for Tom Butler. By the time he made it, it felt inevitable. He told his son and daughter that if things went sideways, they could inform their friends that he had Alzheimer's. He meant it as a joke, but in a way, he could not have been more serious. He had no idea what would happen when he showed up at the courthouse, no idea what the industry would do to him after he hoisted the enemy's colors and unleashed his broadside.

Walking to the witness stand on April 16, he still can't fathom what the fallout will be. He offers Mike Kaeske a subdued smile and raises his right hand before Judge Britt, solemnly swearing to tell the truth, the whole truth, and nothing but the truth, so help him God. He's dressed casually in slacks and a polo shirt, with a fleece vest over the top. He looks out over the sea of faces, and his heart sinks. He sees hatred in the eyes of people he once considered friends. His bosses, Bill and John Prestage, are sitting in the front row, staring back at him implacably. He looks at Mona, then gazes beyond her at the plaintiffs. Although they are strangers to him, they are the reason he is here. The world needs them to prevail. The jury needs to believe them.

The day of reckoning must come.

Mike Kaeske guides him through his story: His family farm in Harnett County, 120 acres of money crop. The sunset years of King Tobacco, then the transition to hog farming. His education at East Carolina. His marriage of fifty-one years. His two children and three grandchildren. His calling as a farmer, his simple love of growing food for people. His partnership with his brother. The HDPE lagoon covers he installed in 2008. The biogas digester that harnesses methane from the lagoons. The composter that replaced his dead boxes and eliminated his buzzard problem. He's a storyteller by nature; he could talk to the jury all day. But Kaeske keeps him focused on the parts of the narrative that the jurors need to hear.

Tom talks about his neighbors, about the one who had the temerity to complain to his face, and the others whose distaste trickled back to him through the grapevine. He tells the jury what his neighbors told the EPA—that the lagoon covers made the farm seem to disappear, until the next time he had to spray. He admits that he can smell his hogs at his own home three-quarters of a mile away. Sometimes, when the odor moves in a plume, it smells like his house is beside the barns.

He tells the jury that when he first got into the hog business, he was naïve about the waste. "We grew up with eight or ten pigs, three or four mules, ten or twelve cows, and a few chickens. That was my experience with animal agriculture. We never thought for one minute about the difference between eight or ten hogs and 8,000. The waste we produce, we never thought about that. We never thought about storing all of that waste and getting rid of it, and, especially, we didn't think about the odor associated with it." In his experience, the most pungent odor from a hog farm is the lagoon odor, because of the plume effect. He has witnessed people on his farm becoming visibly nauseated by it.

He talks about his personal investments in waste-treatment innovation and the industry's failure to offer any meaningful support. He is always looking for new innovations to reduce the odor. Currently, he has an experimental "wind wall" behind his barns that researchers from NC State installed to cut down on the odor emitted from his fans. His dream is to process the hog waste on a daily basis so that no manure ever sits still, to filter it and refilter it and treat it and turn it into a value-added product. He has had some issues getting financing for that technology, but he is close. He believes the obstacles will be overcome.

Kaeske zeroes in on the heart of his testimony. "Sir, from your experience trying to make things happen to get rid of the odor, do you feel like the industry is going to change?"

"They will change when they have to," says the hog farmer, as if he's been waiting a long time to say these words, "when they're forced to by rules and regulations."

Kaeske puts his next question gently. "Is it hard for you to testify here today?"

Tom looks at the jury. "It's one of the hardest things I've ever done. You are kind people, but I'd rather be anywhere else in the world except here today. I thought about it a long time before I agreed to testify and tell my story. But it's important to me to get the truth out. I've heard this rhetoric over and over that we don't have an effect on our community. Well, we do. And that's from twenty-three years of experience."

Kaeske smiles. "I pass the witness."

Mark Anderson's cross-exam is a study in half-hearted chiseling. The industry has no countermeasure to use against Tom Butler. The best Anderson can do is point out that Kraig Westerbeek and others from Smithfield have visited Tom's farm and shown interest in his biogas digester. Also, when the legislature considered suspending subsidies for energy produced by swine-related biogas, the hog farmer joined forces with Westerbeek and Don Butler to lobby against it—and won.

That said, the defense lawyer's questions allow the hog farmer to take another swipe at the industry. He calls himself Prestage's puppet. His relationship with the integrator is servile. When Anderson tries to suggest that his neighbors might have threatened to sue him over the odor, the hog farmer corrects him. No one in his area has ever threatened to file suit, but should they wish to, he believes they should have the right.

On redirect, Mike Kaeske keeps his inquiry brief. "Mr. Butler, do you get paid enough for the hogs that you raise to be able to do these things that you're trying to do?"

"No," Tom replies.

"Prestage pays you. Is that right?"

"Yes."

"And Smithfield pays Prestage. Is that right?"

Anderson lodges an objection, but Judge Britt overrules him.

Kaeske rephrases the question: "Who is it that's making a profit off of the hogs that are grown at your facility?"

"Smithfield," says Tom.

"Do you think it's fair that the people making the profit off the hogs leave it to the grower to try to figure out how to deal with the waste from their hogs?"

"No," replies the hog farmer.

After a brief re-cross from Anderson, Kaeske wraps up the exam. "Just one other thing. You were asked about other growers trying to do the things that you've done. Has this been a hard process for you or an easy process?"

The look in Tom's eyes underscores his answer: "Very difficult."

"Mr. Anderson asked you whether you encouraged other growers to get involved. What was the reaction that you got from people?"

Though Kaeske asks the question lightly, for Tom Butler it's a loaded gun. The truth is that he has tried everything to inspire other growers to join his dissident campaign. *If only we could get ten growers,* he's often thought, *then Smithfield couldn't stand against us.* But he's never found anyone willing to confront the hog barons, let alone a coalition of nine. The road he's walked these many years has been a lonely one.

"Well," he says, "they told me the same thing that I'm aware of. We don't have enough money. And I've heard industry people say that there is just not enough money in the contracts to do this type of work. Until you get something like a policy or an endorsement from your integrator that will support you, you're just not going to go out on that limb."

That's all Kaeske has for him. It's all the jury needs to hear. But Judge Britt has a couple of questions of his own.

"Has it been your experience over the years in dealing with your hog farm," says the judge, "that different people perceive hog odors the same or differently?"

"Differently," Tom replies. "Individuals are different. Like I was saying about the visitors, we noticed different reactions."

"Do you feel that detection of hog odor is subjective, or can it be objective?"

Tom Butler's voice doesn't waver. "It can be objective."

With this pronouncement ringing in the air, Mike Kaeske rests the plaintiffs' case. As Tom climbs down from the stand and strolls out of the courtroom, the trial lawyer watches him go with a mixture of admiration and affection, as do Mona and her team, and all the neighbors looking on. He is the linchpin of all their efforts. Without his testimony, the entire litigation could be dismissed as a partisan conflict between warring tribes, where the truth is a kind of cultural Rorschach test. With his testimony, however, the inkblot distills into a discernible shape.

The scales of judgment.

CHAPTER 27

SEE NO EVIL, SMELL NO EVIL

You can't wake a person who is pretending to be asleep.
—Navajo proverb

**Raleigh,
North Carolina
April 16–23, 2018**

What can a corporation as thoroughly indicted as Smithfield say in its own defense? It could take a page out of Jimmy Dixon's playbook and decry the plaintiffs as liars. But in a courtroom where the jurors can simply turn their heads and see Joyce McKiver and Daphne McKoy sitting in the gallery like supplicants in church, such bloviating could backfire. Far better to drown out the plaintiffs' case with the white noise of untroubled community members, buttoned-up company employees, and credentialed experts and academics, all of whom, in one way or another, tell a countervailing tale in which hog odor is a passing feature of rural life, and industrial food production a creedal dogma in America's civic religion.

The community witnesses summoned by McGuireWoods paint a picture of a virginal landscape, a sanctuary from the frenetic world. There's a horse trainer, Ted Carson, who sells Arabian breeding stock to collectors from around the globe. There's a game warden, Michael Nunnery, who works for the North Carolina Wildlife Resources Commission. There's a couple, Gigi and Mark Enloe, who are longtime friends of Billy Kinlaw. And there's a chiropractor, Dr. Danny Ellis, who owns property beside the hog farm. In contrast to the plaintiffs, all of whom are Black, every community witness for the defense is white. Their stories take roughly the same shape. They know what the hog odor smells like. They have experienced it on and around Billy Kinlaw's property. But it's never been pungent enough to impact them.

With everyone but Dr. Ellis, Mike Kaeske is gentle, even deferential, on cross. But he elicits some crucial facts. Whenever Ted Carson is planning to host horse buyers from out of town, he asks Billy Kinlaw not to spray. And the hog farmer politely abstains. Even with that precaution, however, Carson's guests have occasionally smelled the odor. The game warden, Nunnery, is an outdoorsman, and Kinlaw lets him use his farm like a sportsman's paradise. Nunnery also lives on the other side of the highway, and his kids have never had to smell the odor at home. The couple, Gigi and Mark, are troubled by the war the litigation has brought to their community. But they have never lived as close to Kinlaw's farm as the plaintiffs do. While the odor may not bother them, they know it's a problem for other people.

When Dr. Ellis takes the stand, Mike Kaeske watches him carefully, wondering if he will speak candidly or shade the truth. He dissembles, drawing Kaeske's ire. The chiropractor owns almost a thousand acres of timberland beside Kinlaw's farm, along with two miles of frontage along the Cape Fear River. There's a cabin on the property, down by the water. He's thinking of building a home there after his kids leave for college. He is acquainted with some of the plaintiffs. He's chatted with them on occasion. His experience with the odor has come mostly from dead trucks on the road. Once in a while, he gets a whiff of it in the air, usually when Kinlaw is spraying, but it doesn't annoy him.

Dr. Ellis's tale of the good life along the river contrasts sharply with the story of another local landowner, Dale Bollinger, who owns a cabin across the water and who testified for the plaintiffs. Some of the jurors are no doubt thinking of him as Ellis speaks. Bollinger's testimony was radically different from that of the chiropractor. Sometimes, when the wind comes out of the north, the odor from the farm is so strong that it burns Bollinger's nose and makes his eyes water. The odor has gotten worse over the past ten years. There have been times when it has driven him and his wife and daughter inside, both at the river cabin and at his home a short distance away. One season, the odor was so offensive that he found Kinlaw's operation on the Internet and called the hog farmer to complain. When the odor persisted, he filed a complaint with the state. The regulators paid Kinlaw a visit but took no corrective action. They told Bollinger that Kinlaw's farm is one of the cleanest in Bladen County, and that they smelled nothing objectionable on-site. A year later, Bollinger filed another complaint, again to no avail. Since then, his family has had to live with the stench. Sometimes, the people who rent the river cabin leave negative marks on VRBO, an online vacation-rental marketplace. The issue is episodic and periodic, Bollinger said, governed by weather conditions. It all depends on the prevailing winds.

Dr. Ellis, by contrast, hasn't had any problems like that. Or so he tells the jury when Mark Anderson questions him in his direct exam.

On cross, Mike Kaeske draws his blade. He makes a show of searching for a piece of paper. It's a memo that Mark Doby wrote after he had a telephone conversation with Dr. Ellis. Kaeske doesn't show the chiropractor the memo. Instead, he turns it into a question.

"Have you ever thought to yourself, 'My biggest thing that's difficult to bear at times is just—and I don't blame the folks around there—is the stench from the sprayfields. It's pretty intense. There are some days when it's so humid and when they spray it's strong enough to burn your eyes.' Have you ever thought that?"

The question leaves Ellis visibly unnerved. He makes an attempt to clarify: "There have been times when they do spray, like I said, when you initially go in and I'm there at the gate, and it's a warm, humid day, that the spraying can be pretty intense, so—"

Kaeske interrupts him. "Do you remember saying that out loud?"

Ellis starts to stammer. "I do remember talking . . . having a conversation with . . . Mr. Doby called me several times . . . —too many times to count . . . It was very—"

Kaeske is relentless. "Sir, do you remember saying that?"

Mark Anderson is perturbed. "He should be allowed to answer, Your Honor."

While Judge Britt ponders the objection, Ellis tries to cover himself with fig leaves. He recalls the conversation with Mark Doby but doesn't remember saying those exact words. He thought Mark's entrée was misleading, that there was some kind of problem with his property. When he called Mark back, they got to talking about the hog farm, and he admitted smelling the odor.

Kaeske looks at the memo again. "Do you remember saying 'They could be sitting out on the front porch and when those AG Protein trucks go by, it's unreal. It will take your breath away. I can definitely see how it impacts their life.' Do you remember saying that?"

"Not specifically, no," says Ellis cagily.

Kaeske asks the chiropractor if he believes the statement is true, that when the plaintiffs are sitting on their porches and the dead trucks go by, it's unreal, that it will take their breath away and impact their lives. Again, Ellis pleads his faulty memory, then admits the odor from the dead trucks can be intense. And, yes, they don't drive by his house. And if he wanted to build a house on his property, he could build it a mile away from Kinlaw's farm. He is not trying to contradict what the neighbors have said. He doesn't dispute that people have the right to enjoy their properties the way he enjoys his property. That's obvious.

With Ellis dangling by his fingertips, Kaeske turns him into a signpost for the jury. "If there was a way that Smithfield Foods or Smithfield Hog Production Division could make it so that there is no smell that ever comes out of that hog operation that interferes with anybody, that would be a good thing for everybody in White Oak, right?"

Ellis doesn't know what to make of this. "Sounds like a perfect world, but I mean, I suppose. I mean, I—"

"You would vote for it, wouldn't you?"

"I don't know. I mean, I . . . You mean that you never smell a farm?"

"No," Kaeske says. "If you could substantially eliminate the odor from that farm and eliminate the spraying from that farm, and they could afford to do it, that would be a good thing for the neighborhood, right?"

"I suppose it . . . I mean, I . . ." Ellis is in free fall now. "I know when I went to NC State, that was the preferred method at the time. I remember them always, you know, hailing that method and, I guess, things . . . Maybe it's changed, I don't know. I mean, I don't know whether I would vote for it or not. I mean, I don't . . . I mean, this . . . My honest answer, I don't know. You know, I mean, I guess it would be nice. I mean, I don't know how to answer that."

Mike Kaeske is laughing inside. "Thank you, sir, for your time."

※

The Murphy-Brown employees—one field specialist and two top-tier managers—give the jury a certain view from inside the kingdom. They love their work. They are proud to participate in feeding the world.

Standing on its own, it's believable testimony. Smithfield does compensate its managers well. Also, the company is on the cutting edge of nutrition and animal science. Its people are always searching for better genetics and more efficient feeding systems—whatever will breed more piglets, fatten hogs faster, and deliver Smithfield's customers the tastiest cuts of pork. In short, whatever will make the company more profitable. Also, these folks genuinely seem to care about the animals.

At the end of the day, however, Smithfield's hogs aren't a millions-strong herd of storybook Wilburs. They are genetically engineered cogs in the meatpacking machine, units of product for sale, calories of protein for the moms and pops and kids worldwide who eat Smithfield ribs and Eckrich smoked sausage, Farmer John bacon and Nathan's Famous hot dogs, Cook's ham, Kretschmar lunchmeat, and all the rest.

Smithfield's expert witnesses, on the other hand, are a study in sharp contrasts. The first, Dr. Todd See, a specialist in animal science at NC State, adheres to the Hippocratic Oath. He does no harm. Indeed, he gives the industry a dose of credibility—for a time.

He pores over soil reports from Billy Kinlaw's operation and talks about nitrogen and phosphorus levels. He gives the jury an overview of lagoon design and anaerobic digestion. He says the Pepto Bismol color is a good thing; it means the bacteria is working. He informs the jury that his research farms at NC State are still using lagoons and sprayfields because alternatives like Super Soils are too costly and complex. In sum, he says, Kinlaw's operation is functioning as designed. Its odor levels should be about as low as a hog CAFO can produce.

As effective as Dr. See is as a witness, he is also a readymade target. On cross, Mike Kaeske asks him about his relationships with the industry—the Pork Council board seat that he's occupied since 1998; his friendship with Don Butler and Kraig Westerbeek; the research dollars he gets from the Pork Council; even the fact that the young woman serving as the public face of NC Farm Families is engaged to marry his son. His neutrality thus impeached, Kaeske pushes him about the smell of a hog operation, asks him if the odor respects property boundaries. See, of course, concedes that it doesn't. But the odor of a swine farm doesn't bother him, he says. He just doesn't see the problem.

If the animal science specialist manages to leave the courtroom with his dignity intact, the hog giant's second expert, Dr. Jennifer Clancy, does not. The microbiologist-cum-litigation-consultant is like Chernobyl on the stand, an irremediable disaster.

Her assignment at trial is much the same as it was at the hog farm site visits in 2016—to undermine, contradict, and attempt to refute the testimony of Shane Rogers. Unfortunately for Smithfield, Dr. Clancy is not an expert on odor or the fate and transport of chemicals. She is standing in for Smithfield's *real* odor expert, Dr. Pamela Dalton.

Dalton's absence is a sore spot for the company. She's an old Smithfield hand, a veteran of the Missouri litigation and a sympathetic voice for the industry. At the company's behest, she conducted a study of the McKiver neighborhood using a device called a "Nasal Ranger" and a team of "sniffers," after which she wrote a report opining that the odor emanating from Kinlaw's farm isn't significant enough to constitute a nuisance. Judge Britt, however, found fault with her methodology. He ruled that because the Nasal Ranger relies on human judgment, it isn't an objective measuring stick for odor. For Dalton to offer opinions to the jury on that basis, she would transgress both law and science.

With Dalton's findings whittled down to splinters, Smithfield had little choice but to rely on its backbencher, Clancy, to suggest that hog shit doesn't really stink—or, if the judge won't allow it, then to attempt to discredit Shane Rogers.

Most of Clancy's testimony on direct is an eye-glazing reprise of her expert report, which reads like a literary critique written by the world's most priggish schoolmarm. Her evaluation of Shane is plodding and pedantic. The duplicate samples he gave her at the farms weren't labeled, she says. And Shane didn't perform every kind of sampling at the Kinlaw farm that he did at other facilities. Also, the samples Shane *did* take weren't proper. Shane's team put their gloves on wrong. They might have introduced contamination. Moreover, Shane didn't number the samples to clarify where they were taken. And Corey Robinson frightened the hogs with flash photography. Having said all that, Clancy admits that she did no sampling or testing of her own, and that her sole responsibility on-site was to observe the plaintiffs' team and ascertain whether they were following protocol. At Mark Anderson's prompt, she offers a definitive opinion: Shane's work was not appropriate.

For Mike Kaeske, there are moments in every trial when all the anxiety and exhaustion and sleeplessness and calculation bleed away and only pleasure remains. This is how he feels when he stands up to cross-examine Jennifer Clancy.

He dangles a lure, gets Clancy to admit that, as a scientist, she knows how to take tests. Then he knocks the wind out of her. Whatever expertise she may have in microbiology, she's clueless about industrial hog farms. Before Smithfield hired her, she had never paid a visit to a hog operation. Indeed, she knew *nothing* about hog operations. She had never studied them or written about them or been consulted on the topic. She was a greenhorn, a neophyte, as fresh out of the drawer as the Crocodile Dundee outfit she wore to the first site visit.

And her elaborate critique of Shane Rogers's inspection protocol? She invented it after the fact. Shane didn't furnish the defense team with his protocol until two and a half months *after* the site visits. Clancy says she doesn't remember when she first saw the protocol. But she watched Shane carefully as he took his samples and made detailed notes.

Kaeske wears his skepticism openly. "You made detailed notes?"

"I made notes."

"Did you make *detailed* notes?"

Clancy backtracks. "Well, I don't know how detailed my notes were. I made notes as I do. Any time I would be watching a sampling operation, I would make notes."

When Kaeske asks her how she recorded her notes, she says she used her phone and maybe a notebook.

"And your cell phone and maybe your notebook, those were your scientific data collection devices, right?"

Again, Clancy backs away. "Well, I didn't collect any data."

"You've got a lot of commentary, right?"

"Correct. But that's not—it's not scientific data."

"Okay," says Kaeske. "So what you've told the members of the jury about what you observed, that's not scientific, correct?"

Clancy tries to duck the question. She retorts that she's a scientist.

After a bit more jousting, Kaeske lands a blow that lays her flat on her back. "And your job—what you were hired by Smithfield to do—was to go watch somebody conduct science and then be critical about it later in written form and oral form to a jury, correct?"

Anderson is on his feet. "Objection!"

"Sustained," says Judge Britt.

Kaeske rephrases the question, forcing Clancy to admit the truth. Those meticulous notes she took, she lost them. She dropped her phone in one of the barns and it broke. At another site visit, her phone got wet and stopped working. She couldn't retrieve some of her notes. She tries to spar with the trial lawyer over what, exactly, she lost. She still has something marked "new notes," but she's missing the old ones and can't say what happened to them.

By now, Mike Kaeske is floating on air. He asks her about the equipment she denounced Shane for *not* using at the site visits. She admits that she's never used any of it before herself. And Pig2Bac? She's never tested for it or processed it in her lab. Oh, and she isn't competent to test for hydrogen sulfide, ammonia, or volatile organic compounds. She admitted that in her deposition. Still, she felt qualified to criticize Shane for the way he performed those tests.

When Kaeske hands her off to Mark Anderson, the defense lawyer tries to rehabilitate her with a jargon-rich colloquy on chains of custody and controls, called "field blanks," which are designed to prevent sample contamination. She sounds smarter, more capable, more in control. At least some of the errors she noted in her report were legitimate. But then, inevitably, Kaeske takes the floor again. After a few tedious exchanges, he strikes at the heart of her credibility.

"We were obligated to provide you duplicate samples, correct?"

"Yes," Clancy admits.

"And those duplicate samples you threw in the trash, right?"

Clancy tries a dodge. "I didn't analyze the samples."

"You threw them in the trash?"

"We didn't analyze the samples and they were disposed of properly."

"Dr. Clancy, how much have you been paid for your testimony in this case?"

Anderson tries to object, but the judge requires her to answer.

She tells the jury that she has charged Smithfield $350 an hour.

"And at the time of your deposition you had been paid $90,000. Is that correct?"

The amount, stated so baldly before the jury, makes Clancy uncomfortable. "If that's what I had testified to . . . I don't have . . . I don't remember the invoices, so—"

"Since that time, how much have you billed?"

"I have probably billed another $100,000 to $125,000," concedes Clancy. "But again, I'm not absolutely certain of the number."

Kaeske has nothing against high-priced experts. They're part of the scenery in every major litigation. And the most eminent scientific witnesses are worth every penny. But for Jennifer Clancy, a glorified hall monitor who had never been on a hog farm before, who did no sampling or testing of her own, who lost her notes, who had no familiarity with Shane's equipment, who didn't have the competency to perform the lab tests Shane's samples required, and who took the samples Shane gave her and tossed them in the trash, the number feels obscene.

With a flourish, Kaeske goes for the coup de grâce: "So you've been paid something more than $200,000 for your criticisms of Dr. Rogers in this case?"

Anderson objects, and Kaeske reframes the question: "You've been paid more than $200,000 for your testimony in this case?"

"Yes," says the microbiologist.

By the time Kaeske sits down again, Dr. Clancy is the picture of a ruined witness.

In the four trials to come, she will never be invited back.

✳

Smithfield's last witness is Kraig Westerbeek. He's the company's representative at the trial, and, as such, he's had the benefit of being in the courtroom from the beginning. Of course, the jury has already heard from him, back when Mike Kaeske played excerpts from his video deposition in the plaintiffs' case. But that's not the Kraig Westerbeek that Mark Anderson wants the jurors to remember. So he shows them a picture of Westerbeek with his wife and daughters at the home of his father-in-law. What's in the background? A sprayfield. Anderson shows the jury a picture of Westerbeek's girls at church. Behind them, in the sun-washed distance, is another sprayfield. In fact, Westerbeek's home in Duplin County is only half a mile from a hog farm. Anderson puts an aerial view of the area on the monitor. From the photos, it is clear that, in Westerbeek's world, hog farms are all around.

Anderson asks him about his work at Murphy-Brown. Westerbeek's expertise is in agronomy and environmental science. He offers the jury an overview of nutrient management, irrigation zones, and land application—the technical terms for spraying. There is a mathematical balance on the nutrient side. What comes out of the animal needs to be absorbed by the crops and soil. Each hog farm has its own "waste utilization plan," which Westerbeek has a hand in creating. Hog farmers must abide by the plan and keep records of their spraying.

In time, Westerbeek changes gears and talks about the frontiers of waste management, the experiments NC State performed under the Smithfield Agreement and the potential of biogas digesters to convert the methane collected from thousands of hog lagoons into usable energy. He talks about the company's environmental policy and compliance standards, about its partnership with the EPA to measure ammonia and hydrogen sulfide emissions on company-owned farms, and about its efforts to reduce its carbon footprint. These days, Westerbeek spends most of his time on renewable energy projects. That's the takeaway he seems to want to leave with the jury. Even though Smithfield is in the business of slaughtering hogs and spraying their waste on the land, the company is concerned about sustainability.

On cross, Kaeske asks Westerbeek how long he has lived in Duplin County.

"Well," says the Murphy man, "I grew up in Sampson County, and I graduated from college when I was twenty-one and I'm forty. I would say approximately twenty-five years."

"And Duplin County," Kaeske says, "that's the number one densest hog county in the whole country, right?"

"That's what I'm told."

Kaeske's voice takes on a trace of incredulity. "You've never in your whole life smelled offensive hog odor off of a hog property, correct?"

"Not offensive odor, no, sir," says Westerbeek sanguinely.

As he did in his deposition, Kaeske throws the science at him—

the peer-reviewed articles from Duke, UNC, and Yale about the health effects of hog odor. Westerbeek disagrees with all of it. To him, it's misguided drivel.

"And you don't believe that hog odor can interfere with people's lives, correct?"

"No, sir," says Westerbeek. "That's not been my experience."

"And you don't believe that offensive odor gets off the Kinlaw property, correct?"

"Once again, I've never experienced offensive odor off site, so I would say the same. That's been my experience at Kinlaw as well."

Kaeske's next cut is deep. "And my clients are supposed to complain to you, who doesn't believe in anything, right?"

"Objection!" cries Mark Anderson.

"Overruled," says Judge Britt.

If Westerbeek's pug-nosed agnosticism about hog odor hasn't already alienated the jury, his response to this question surely does. It's glib; it's cheeky; it's laugh-out-loud absurd.

"Yes, sir," he says. "We have a complaint system . . . If they have an issue, we would love for them to let us know about it, absolutely."

Mike Kaeske stares at him in amazement. As if twenty-five years of advocacy by Elsie Herring, Don Webb, Rick Dove, Gary Grant, Devon Hall, and Naeema Muhammad have not been enough. As if all the community forums put on by REACH, NCEJN, Waterkeepers, and their allies have not been enough. As if all the epidemiological studies, all the picketing at the statehouse, all the billboards and pressure campaigns have not been enough. As if the countless complaints published in news articles and books and aired on television and in documentaries have not been enough. As if twenty-six lawsuits and five years of litigation are not enough. Murphy-Brown has a complaint system. It would love to hear from the neighbors about their problems. In serving up such a whopper, Westerbeek negates every other word he said. It's as if he has donned a red cape and top hat, waved a magic wand, and made himself disappear.

On that auspicious note, Smithfield rests its case.

—

CHAPTER 28

PITCHFORKS
ON THE DOORSTEP OF JUSTICE

Wherever there is a crowd, there is untruth.
—*Søren Kierkegaard*

On Tuesday, April 24, Mike Kaeske and Mark Anderson deliver their closing arguments in front of a standing-room-only crowd. For Kaeske, the goal of the closing is to give the jury a target, a weapon, and the moral persuasion to use it. He hits all three points with his trademark panache, especially on rebuttal, after Anderson yields the floor. Equal parts oratory and performance art, the rebuttal is all gut and feeling and extemporaneous rhetoric, unlike the initial closing, which is choreographed to address issues of fact and law. It's one of the advantages that the adversarial system gives the party bearing the burden of proof.

The plaintiffs get the last word.

Mike Kaeske kills it. He brings the long war into the courtroom, distilling the jury's decision down into binary choices—the hog barons versus the common folks, human dignity versus the god of Mammon. "Today, you are more powerful than the governor of North Carolina," he contends. "You are more powerful than the attorney general of North Carolina. And you are more powerful than that corporation. You can make a decision today to deter them from this conduct, to speak to them in terms that they can understand so that they will make this change, for the citizens of this state and for our environment. You've heard the evidence that allows you to do it, to fight for these people. We have been fighting for these people. It's your turn to fight for these people."

When he sits down, there are tears in the gallery, but Mike Kaeske's eyes are dry. He's left his heart on the field. So has Mona. So has everyone on the team and all their clients. Now they must wait, their fortunes in strangers' hands. Whatever the jury comes back with, it won't be the end of the story. It will only be the end of the beginning. In a few weeks' time, all of them will be back in this courtroom watching Mike deliver his opening to a new set of jurors in the *McGowan* trial. A month after that, they will try *Artis,* then *Gillis* and the second *McGowan* group. Without the cumulative power of multiple verdicts, Smithfield will never kneel. But this first verdict matters. It's the bellwether of the bellwethers.

What happens here will set the tone for everything else.

The jury deliberates for nearly two days. Mike and Mona and the rest of the team shuttle between the courthouse and the apartments, busying themselves with trifles and staring at the clock. The void of quiet gnaws on them. They see in the jury's request for clarification about the difference between compensatory and punitive damages the chance of a nominal verdict, a small-dollar award that Smithfield would surely interpret as a victory. But no one dares to speculate, at least not out loud. When the jury is deliberating, Mike Kaeske is as superstitious as Wade Boggs eating his pre-game chicken. Predictions are verboten. Only a fool would tempt the Fates.

The verdict lands just after two o'clock on Thursday afternoon. Per the form Judge Britt sent back to the jury room, the verdict has a four-question structure. The first question derives from the Good Neighbor rule: "Did the defendant substantially and unreasonably interfere with the plaintiff's use and enjoyment of his or her property?"

In the blank by the name of each plaintiff, the jury answers "YES."

On the right side of the gallery, where the neighbors and lawyers are holding hands and waiting statue-like, fingers squeeze and grips tighten with joy and anticipation.

The judge continues: "What amount of damages, if any, is the plaintiff entitled to recover from the defendant?"

In the blanks, the jury foreman wrote: "$75,000."

For the neighbors, this is vindication. The jury saw them. It heard their pleas for justice, and it delivered. It's also a tidy sum of money, more than most of them have ever seen.

Mike Kaeske, however, feels the sting of disappointment. It could have been worse, but it's hardly auspicious. Without any framework to quantify the harm, the jury conjured a number out of thin air. Perhaps they tried to guess the assessed value of the neighbors' homes. Maybe they speculated about the salary of a teacher or social worker in Bladen County and doubled it. Wherever the number came from, they set the bar low, not high. Kaeske sees that as his own mistake. He didn't give them a foothold in his closing. He could have made a numerical ask, but he didn't. He vows not to make that mistake again.

Judge Britt reads out the third question on the verdict form: "Is the defendant liable to the plaintiff for punitive damages?"

Beside each name, the jury replies "YES."

At the sound of the final question, the air in the courtroom seems to crackle, as if charged. "What amount of punitive damages, if any, does the jury in its discretion award to the plaintiff?"

In its discretion. With those words, the law places a sledgehammer in the jury's hands. Punitive damages, by design, are supposed to be unconstrained. They are intended to channel a jury's wrath, to allow a group of citizens to punish the most egregious wrongs with a blow heavy enough to inspire repentance. But these days, the hammer comes with an invisible chain. At the behest of corporate lobbyists, many state legislatures have tethered punitives to compensation, limiting the dollar value of a jury's punishment to three times its compensatory award. Jurors, however, have no idea of this, and the lawyers are not allowed to inform them. The judge imposes the cap after the jury is dismissed. An argument could be made that this is a violation of due process, that leaving the jury in the dark undermines both the purpose and the effect of the exercise. But that argument has yet to prevail. So juries wield the sledgehammer in ignorance. What is the price of justice? they ask themselves. What level of pain will compel change?

For each neighbor—Joyce McKiver, Daphne McKoy, and on down the list to the last—the jury answers, "5,000,000."

Five million times ten. Fifty million dollars.

For the plaintiffs and their lawyers, the verdict is a rhapsody, an electrifying blend of high notes and thrumming chords that brighten their faces and bring relief in a rush. For years, Mona and her team at Wallace & Graham have been saying, "Just get us to a jury. We want them to tell us if we're right." This verdict is a validation.

Elsie Herring feels the same way when she hears about it from Naeema Muhammad. She was in the courtroom for the closings, but since she's not a plaintiff in the *McKiver* trial, she returned home to wait for the jury's decision. On the afternoon of April 26, she's standing in her nephew's yard, across the street from her house. It's a bright spring day, not quite warm, but warming. The air is clear. The hog farmer isn't spraying. Elsie takes Naeema's call because she has an intuition that it might be about the trial. When she hears about the jury award, she feels a little thrill. Fifty million dollars. At last, a measure of justice.

John Hughes hears about the verdict by text message from Mark Doby. Mark doesn't give him much, just a sketch of the numbers. But that's enough. He feels a profound sense of satisfaction. The verdict affirms both the moral significance and the value of the case. The cap on punitives is a problem. It will constrict the total award to just over $3 million. But even with the reduction, the judgment is explosive.

Down east in hog country, the verdict lands like a well-aimed mortar shell. Amid the smoke and wreckage, the friends of Smithfield gnash their teeth. They feel as if they've been cheated, as if Judge Britt denied them a fair trial and a jury of city slickers condemned their way of life. A lot of folks seem not to appreciate the statutory cap. Fifty million is the headline that ran in the *News & Observer,* and fifty million is what sticks in people's heads. To the subjects of the hog kingdom, a $50 million award for only ten plaintiffs, when there are nearly five hundred more waiting in line behind them, is like a midnight visit from the Ghost of Christmas Yet to Come. That's $2.5 billion in potential exposure.

There's a chance these lawsuits could bring down the sky.

The day after the verdict is read, Smithfield issues a scathing four-page press release. Instead of delivering boilerplate protestations of innocence like a typical corporate defendant, the company goes on the offensive, indicting the plaintiffs' lawyers, the judge, and the judicial process itself. It decries the lawsuits as a "money grab by a big litigation machine" and an "outrageous attack on all animal agriculture," including "thousands of independent family farmers." And it castigates Judge Britt for "fundamental unfairness." In an unprecedented move, Smithfield attempts to relitigate some of the judge's rulings in the court of public opinion. At least, that is how the statement reads on its face. Mona and Mike soon adopt a darker view: Smithfield hopes to influence the thinking of future jurors.

For the most part, the media ignores the hog giant's attack on the judicial system. But others within the Big Ag firmament soon join the outcry. The Pork Council rails against the lawsuit, calling it "an ongoing, coordinated and unfounded attack on agriculture that endangers thousands of jobs and economic activity across the state." In a blog post, NC Farm Families asks, "How does this end? The answer to that question matters to the lives of thousands of farmers. And the wrong answer could fracture a pillar of North Carolina's economy." Indeed, no less a personage than the U.S. secretary of agriculture, Sonny Perdue, calls the *McKiver* verdict "despicable," despite admitting that he is unfamiliar with the case. "It's horrible if that's the kind of money that people are awarding," he tells a gathering at the USDA. "I feel certain that kind of award has to be overturned."

It's not clear whether he's auguring an intervention by the Fourth Circuit Court of Appeals, but the idea that the verdict might not be written in stone, that it might be thrown out by a higher—and friendlier—authority, resonates in febrile minds down east. Before long, the notion of "waiting for the Fourth Circuit" will become a kind of invocation, a prayer among the hog country faithful for shattered stars to realign.

Two weeks after the Perdue denunciation, Boss Hog's bedfellows in the state legislature waltz onto the field again. According to Brent Jackson and Jimmy Dixon, the law of nuisance is still far too accommodating when it comes to agricultural operations. They champion yet another revision to the Right to Farm Act.

The bill—codified as S711—takes the universe of potential farm nuisance claims and shrinks the legal funnel until the odds of any particular claim surviving a motion to dismiss are about the same as winning the lottery. Where before neighbors had three years to file a claim after the onset of a nuisance, now they have only one year, and the trigger for the limitations period isn't the appearance of the nuisance but the day the lights went on at the farm, unless some "fundamental change" occurs, altering the farm's operations later on. Since upstart hog farms are effectively banned in the state, and since the language of the "fundamental change" exception would exclude almost every imaginable modification in farming practice, it is hard to conceive of a future nuisance claim that would not be gutted in the S711 abattoir.

But this is precisely Jackson and Dixon's objective. The bill explicitly references the hog farm litigation and criticizes Judge Britt for erroneously interpreting the law. The bill also takes aim at punitive damages, limiting their availability to instances in which the farm at issue has been subject to a criminal or civil enforcement action by the state or federal authorities. There's more, too. The bill would place a substantial portion of the state's hog farm records inside a locked vault, prohibiting neighbors, attorneys, journalists, and the public from conducting the sort of archival review that delivered Mona's team so many critical nuggets of evidence. For future plaintiffs, there is no plausible way forward.

This naked act of legislative protectionism is such a windfall for the hog barons—and Big Ag in general—and so callous toward ordinary citizens that it compels John Blust, the yeoman hero of the battle over HB467 the previous year, to deliver a remarkable fourteen-minute rant in the House chamber when S711 comes up for its third reading.

"We are taking a side," he fulminates. "We're saying that we in the legislature, we know better than the court, we know better than the facts, we know better than the law. We're going to protect one litigant, and we're going to say to the other, 'You don't matter. You don't count.' And it's because the one side has the ear of the powers that run this institution."

Blust indicts his own colleagues, tossing out adjectives like "biased" and "wicked" like grape shot and arguing that the level of coordination between the House leadership and the pork industry is emblematic of a legislature that has been compromised.

He is dumbfounded, too, that the bill's proponents would cast aspersions at Judge Britt, yet refuse to admit their own manifest unfairness. At the core of his disgust is the fact that none of his Republican colleagues will tell him what Judge Britt did wrong. They will accuse the plaintiffs of committing perjury on the stand, but they won't say how exactly the judge subverted the law. Nor will they explain how S711 offers a necessary correction. "It's an emotional play," he contends. The bill's sponsors have couched it as protection for family farmers and suggested that anyone who doesn't vote for it is a bad person.

Blust also takes aim at Jimmy Dixon's anti-lawyer screed. "I'm a little taken aback that the politicians are casting stones at the lawyers," he says with a trace of humor. "We are the People's House and the People's legislature, and we ought to do business in a deliberative fashion that befits the trust that's been bestowed upon us by the People. That ought to be an ironclad guarantee that we take seriously at all times."

Directing his frustration at the House Speaker, Tim Moore, he says, "This bill has never been explained." The law *already* favors Big Ag. He draws on a biblical analogy. After Moses told Pharaoh to let his people go, the ruler of Egypt responded by forcing the Israelites to make bricks without straw. That's what Smithfield's allies are doing here.

Before he yields the floor, Blust offers his colleagues a better way. Why not pass a law mandating that Smithfield implement the waste-treatment technology that would bring an end to the nuisance itself? "That's the best way to stop these lawsuits going forward," he opines.

But the House isn't listening to John Blust. It is in thrall to Jimmy Dixon, as the Senate is to Brent Jackson. Both chambers pass S711 with overwhelming support, and then, when the governor has the audacity to deploy his veto pen, Smithfield's surrogates muster the votes to override it. Though none of the legislators actually says it out loud, their message reverberates in every nook and cranny down east:

"If you live near a polluting hog operation or poultry operation or dairy farm and you haven't already filed suit, you're shit out of luck."

Having poisoned the well of future litigation, the hog kingdom turns its cannons once again toward Judge Britt's courtroom. In an interview with the *Wall Street Journal*, Ken Sullivan, Smithfield's CEO, calls the lawsuits an "existential threat" and suggests that if the verdicts keep coming, Smithfield may be forced to leave the state.

To outside observers, including the plaintiffs' legal team, the threat rings hollow. Just ten months ago, Smithfield announced a new $100 million investment in its Tar Heel slaughterhouse. The company's fate is economically intertwined with that of North Carolina. North Carolina is the second-largest hog producing state in America, behind Iowa. And North Carolina's hog farms are closer together—and closer to the slaughterhouse—than Iowa's. That proximity is one of the efficiencies that animates Smithfield's production machine. Its facilities are not mobile. They can't be transported down the highway. They are rooted in the dirt. Leaving the state would undermine the company's entire business model. Yet down east in hog country, Sullivan's words sound like an air-raid siren. His threat brings out the mob.

In the days immediately preceding the *McGowan* trial, the staffs at Wallace & Graham and the Kaeske Law Firm observe strange traffic on their websites and unpleasant comments on social media. They ignore the chatter, imagine it harmless. It is not. It is a low-pressure system over a super-heated ocean. Before long, it will give birth to a storm.

On the first day of the trial, after Mike Kaeske delivers his opening to a new panel of twelve jurors, Andy Curliss, head of the Pork Council, writes a blog post that fuels the frenzy down east. He gives it the title "Eastern North Carolina Is Under Attack" and pushes the rhetoric to the edge. He fingers Kaeske by name, branding him a "Texas lawyer" and insinuating that he is peddling a lie for the sake of greed, a lie that could put hog farmers out of business.

Curliss paints a picture of a region under siege. While Duplin County is "heaven on Earth" to most of its people, he writes, miles away in a distant city, an out-of-state lawyer is slandering hog farmers to line his pockets with cash. And thanks to Judge Britt, the jury will never get to see what life is really like in hog country—the weddings and cookouts, the reunions and ball games, the kids bouncing on trampolines and shooting hoops, all within sight of the hog farms that lie in every direction. "All of that is under attack by the Texas lawyer," Curliss concludes. "If he succeeds, he'll win some money. And all of North Carolina will be hurt."

The post goes viral in hog country.

The following day, June 1, Curliss launches another broadside. Again, he calls out Kaeske by name and throws around the term "Texas lawyer" like a slur. This time, however, he alleges that Kaeske is twisting the facts. The Pork Council's CEO says it isn't right for Kaeske to claim that the neighborhood along Hallsville Road (the home of the Farlands and Woodell McGowan) predates Joey Carter's hog operation, when the only plaintiffs in the trial, Elvis and Vonnie Williams, didn't buy their property until after Carter launched his operation.

This second post is short and punchy, and it leaves his readers with the impression that Mike Kaeske is a master provocateur and prevaricator. Since most of the Pork Council's followers aren't observing the trial, they don't have the means to fact-check Curliss's assertions, even if they wanted to. Were they in the gallery, however, they would know that it is Curliss, not Kaeske, who is contorting the truth.

In his opening, Kaeske told the jury that Woodell McGowan's aunt, Lillie Belle Hall, started selling her land in 1970; that Al Davis and his family built their home in 1970; that Cartha Williams built hers in 1971; that Elaine Carlton moved into her home in 1971; that Linnill Farland built his home in 1971; that David Carter and his family bought their land in 1971 or 1972; that Perry Miller moved into his home in 1972; that Barbara Gibbs built her home in 1973. All of this construction happened more than a decade before Joey Carter built his first hog barn. As for Elvis Williams, he moved to Hallsville Road before Carter expanded his south operation and broke ground on his north operation. His wife, Vonnie, joined him several years later.

These are not twisted facts. They are undisputed facts.

Yet Andy Curliss's readers believe that a Texas lawyer is manipulating the truth and deceiving the jury. They believe that everything precious in their rural world is under attack. They believe that the largest employer in the coastal plain and the source of so many of their livelihoods might abandon the state if these greedy lawyers keep winning.

In the face of such an incendiary narrative, the people of hog country lash out.

At 8:55 p.m. on Friday evening, the first of June, after only the third day of the *McGowan* trial, a man by the name of Richard Mole sends an email to Mike Kaeske through his firm's website: "Stay your sorry ass out of North Carolina, you piece of shit. Get your clients to get the fuck out of here also and never come back. We don't play with people like you."

At 7:27 the following morning, Saturday, June 2, the Kaeske Law Firm receives a web message from someone calling himself "American As

Can Be." The subject header is "Pigs" and the return address is obviously fake. The email reads: "Leave Those Pig Farmers Alone Asswipe. We Already Know the Purpose of Your Actions. Once Done It Will Never Be Undone. . . ."

Kaeske's associates in Texas forward the emails to him in Raleigh, and he shares them with Mona and the trial team. While he's troubled by them, he's not really afraid. No one outside their team knows where they are staying. A dedicated assailant could follow them back to their apartments, but it's hard to imagine the authors of these emails mounting such an operation.

Mona, by contrast, is unnerved. Whereas Mike lives out west, North Carolina is her home. Her family and employees live just up the road in Salisbury. The threats remind her, hauntingly, of something that happened a couple of weeks after the *McKiver* verdict. Try as she might, she can't make sense of it. It was a Friday evening, and she was at home babysitting her granddaughters—Whitney's kids—while Lee was away for the weekend. She and the girls were watching TV together in the family room. Walled in by windows, the room looks out over her backyard. In the distance, through the trees, is a golf course.

Around 9:30, she saw a blaze of lights sweep down the fairway from the clubhouse. A whole line of golf carts stopped just outside her fence and turned as if to paint her house with light. Their headlamps speared the trees and cast weird shapes across the ground. She told her girls to stay put and walked quickly to the side door and out onto the driveway. She looked up the path leading to the golf course and saw that the carts were there too, shining their lights toward her. She went back inside, locked the doors, and called the police. Perhaps it was nothing, just a night game on the course. But she couldn't be sure. Her office was receiving ominous calls. The Pork Council was spotlighting her firm on the Internet. She knew how much the hog barons hated her. If the Murphy men had an enemies list, she and Mike Kaeske were at the top.

On Monday, Kaeske shows the emails to Judge Britt. The judge takes them seriously. "That's a direct threat," he says, in chambers, lawyers from both sides present. "I'll turn that over to the Marshal and the FBI."

Kaeske, however, has a broader concern. He's worried about the sanctity of the trial. He places the threats in context, tells the judge about Andy Curliss's blog posts, especially the first one, on May 31, which Kaeske likens to a "whistle being blown." He has reason to believe that witnesses are being intimidated. He tells Judge Britt about a witness who was targeted on social media with one of Curliss's articles. He recounts the story of another witness, a white neighbor who had agreed to testify about the odor before the man's daughter, who works for Smithfield, called him—in Mike Kaeske's presence—and reamed him about it. After the daughter hung up, the man told Kaeske that one of Smithfield's lawyers had called his daughter twenty-five times since the plaintiffs put his name on their witness list. Under this pressure, the man folded. He told Kaeske he couldn't testify, not when his daughter and his grandson worked for Smithfield.

Kaeske is also worried about the jurors. The judge instructed them not to read the news or discuss the trial outside the courthouse, but all of them have smartphones and computers and social media accounts. Even if they aren't searching for information about the case, they could stumble across it. Or, worse, they could receive a targeted Facebook ad from the Pork Council or NC Farm Families. Kaeske reminds the judge that Farm Families was created by Smithfield and the Pork Council and that it continues to receive funding from both.

After laying all of this out, Kaeske asks Judge Britt to take action, to protect the witnesses and jurors from outside influence. He requests that the judge sequester the jury for the next trial on the calendar—*Artis*. He also asks that the judge use his authority to tone down the industry's rhetoric. He doesn't use the term "gag order" because it is freighted with baggage. Most courts refuse to ban parties from speaking to the press and the public out of concern for the First Amendment. But these circumstances are unprecedented. Neither Mona nor Mike has seen anything like this in their decades of legal practice.

As it turns out, neither has Judge Britt.

The judge takes the matter under advisement and directs his law clerks to investigate his options. Little does any of them know that in only a few short days, Mike Kaeske's worst fears will be realized.

The trial itself will be imperiled.

CHAPTER 29

INTO THE WHIRLWIND

Men in rage strike those that wish them best.
—*William Shakespeare*

**Raleigh
and Eastern
North Carolina
June 13–21, 2018**
Two weeks into the *McGowan* trial, the maelstrom reaches the jury. Word of it comes to Judge Britt through a bailiff before the morning session on Wednesday, June 13. According to an informant on the jury, some of the jurors have been conducting outside research about the case and reporting the results in whispers to their friends in the jury room. The topics of discussion include Mike Kaeske's Texas roots, the *McKiver* verdict, and the new Right to Farm bill, S711. The judge calls the lawyers into a conference in chambers. He is visibly disturbed.

"I've seen a few instances of this over the thirty-eight years I've been here," he tells them, "but not many, and this is by far the most serious that I've ever confronted."

His words echo in the silence and strike Mona Wallace and Mike Kaeske in the gut. On rare occasions, this kind of juror misconduct can be grounds for a mistrial.

To nail down the particulars, Judge Britt proposes a private inquiry. He will interview the informant first, with only the court reporter present. Then, he will invite one lawyer from each side to listen in as he interviews the remaining jurors. Any implicated jurors he will leave to the end. Both Kaeske and Mark Anderson signal their agreement, but

Mona makes an additional request: that the judge ask about any exposure the juror may have had to trial-related publicity outside the jury room. She tells the judge that Smithfield ads have been playing all over the radio, along with ads addressing the Right to Farm legislation. Also, the rhetoric coming out of Smithfield's surrogate, NC Farm Families, is continuing to filter back to her witnesses down east.

After the lawyers slip out, Judge Britt summons the informant into chambers. It is no small thing for a federal judge to request a private audience with a juror in the middle of a trial. The man trips over his own words. But eventually he gets his story out.

He says that sometime last week, one of the other male jurors started talking about Mike Kaeske, saying he knew where his firm was from, that he had investigated it on the Internet. The same male juror informed his colleagues that the legislature was considering a law that would ensure that there will be no more court cases like this in the future. The informant also alleges that two other jurors, both of them female, have violated the judge's media ban, and some people are starting to whisper that it is getting more and more difficult to remain impartial.

The judge thanks him for his candor, tells him it is critical to the integrity of the judicial process, and then sends him back to the jury room with the request that he not discuss their conversation with anyone.

With the informant gone, Judge Britt projects a rough transcript of their conversation on a television monitor in chambers and brings the attorneys up to speed. At that point, everyone other than Mike Kaeske and Mark Anderson decamps to the attorney rooms to wait.

The judge conducts his next interviews in numerical order. Since his instructions to the jury about not consulting the media have been unambiguous, it is hardly surprising that most of the jurors deny knowing much of anything. Their nervousness is palpable on the surface of their words. A few of them divulge sporadic details they've acquired through the grapevine, such as that Kaeske is from Texas, that the legislature is doing something that might impact the cases, and that the jury in *McKiver* returned a verdict for the plaintiffs. Others confess, almost sheepishly, that they have watched Netflix and YouTube on their phones and researched pedestrian things like dogs and jokes.

If the octogenarian judge is displeased by this, he doesn't say it. The days of asking juries not to turn on the nightly news, peruse the morning paper, or have pillow-talk conversations about the case with their spouses are long gone. The best any judge can hope for is that the jurors will abstain from actively seeking outside information.

As with any investigation of alleged wrongdoing, Judge Britt uncovers inconsistencies in the polyphonic narrative. But the jury room is a black box. None of the jurors admits to speaking to anyone about outside information.

After concluding the interviews, Judge Britt takes a brief recess, almost certainly to consult his law books about the mistrial motion Mark Anderson is already crafting in his head. The lawyers, meanwhile, rejoin their colleagues in the conference rooms down the hall.

When Kaeske walks through the door, he is ashen-faced but composed. There are moments in every trial where the risk of disaster is laid bare. But this trial has been surreal from the beginning, a bona fide shitshow. He meant the welcome mat outside his apartment as an inside joke. This morning, it feels more like a prophecy: death threats from down east; another Smithfield-led gambit to commandeer the state legislature; a whirlwind of rabble-rousing and propagandizing from the Pork Council and Farm Families on social media; and now allegations of juror misconduct. In the quiet of his mind, he's thinking, *What the fuck?*

In spite of the hijinks, he and the team have put on a compelling case. As in *McKiver,* Steve Wing delivered his posthumous testimony like an oracle. Shane Rogers mesmerized the jury with the marvel of Pig2Bac and the mystery of the odiferous glasses. The neighbors from Hallsville Road told their stories with courage and dignity. The Murphy men, Don Butler, John Sargent, and Kraig Westerbeek, gave the jury a thousand and one reasons to distrust Smithfield. A handyman who did some work for Barbara Gibbs told a colorful story about how the hog odor blowing off of Joey Carter's farm was so revolting that he had to leave Gibbs's property and drive downtown to eat his baloney sandwich.

Then there was Joey Carter. His cross-exam was every trial lawyer's dream. Instead of letting Mark Anderson turn Smithfield's poster boy into a martyr before the jury, Kaeske preempted him, calling the former police chief as an adverse witness. It was a masterstroke. Anderson didn't know what hit him, and neither did the lawman. Carter never got comfortable on the stand. He couldn't figure out how to play the victim, and his righteous grower schtick soon lost its shine. It was a glorious coup.

But all of that would be erased if Judge Britt declares a mistrial.

Across the room, Mona is worried about her clients. Lendora Farland was a rock star on the stand. She didn't just speak her own truth. She gave voice to her father, Linnill, her mother, Georgia, and to the entire community. Georgia was so moved by the experience that she made a quilt for Mona. It's all pastels and polka dots, with a dash of bolder colors and patterns thrown in. The Farlands have been the moral rudder of this case, and Lendora its soul. When she spoke about the hog waste, everyone in the courtroom listened.

The others held their own, too. Barbara Gibbs, a taciturn woman, came alive on the stand. It was as if an angel whispered in her ear, "Now is your chance to speak." The wallop she gave Smithfield surprised everyone. And Elvis and Vonnie, while nervous and shy, persevered and said their piece. How tragic it would be to tell them that it was all for nothing, that thanks to a few nosy jurors, they have to do it all over again.

Around Mike and Mona, the plaintiffs' team is trying hard not to unravel. Daniel and Mark, Whitney and Sophie, Linda Wike and Sam Egilman are all staring at the table or looking out the window. How many hundreds of hours have they devoted to this trial? And now they are two weeks in and so close to wrapping up their case in chief. Their last witness—Tom Butler—is scheduled to take the stand tomorrow. They feel the sting of sorrow and the cold sliver of fury at the possibility that all of their efforts could be upended.

Amid the gravity of their musings, they hear the sound of muffled laughter coming from the conference room on the other side of the wall. The voices of Smithfield's lawyers are indistinct, but their revelry is not. All the cackling and whooping and hollering is so raucous that it's as if the victory is already theirs. In a moment of gallows humor, Mark Doby half expects to hear the pop of a champagne cork.

When Judge Britt calls the lawyers back to his chambers, Mona goes along with Kaeske. The argument is heated, a knife fight. Mark Anderson contends the jury is tainted, the prejudice to Smithfield irreversible. Sure, the informant claimed that all the *ultra vires* chatter hasn't undermined his impartiality, but it's obvious that some jurors weren't being candid with the judge. The defense team draws Judge Britt's attention to a corpus of recent articles published by environmental groups describing the litigation in explicitly racial terms—a line of argument the judge ruled out of bounds in the courtroom. One article in particular, written by Lisa Sorg of NC Policy Watch, pointed out that the gallery was split down the middle between Black neighbors and white farmers and industry allies. If the jurors have been poking around on the Internet, it's possible their views have been contaminated by these not-so-subtle hints of racial bias.

There's an irony here, lurking just beneath the surface. While Mike Kaeske has steered clear of race in his presentation to the jury—even though the demographic split spotlighted by Lisa Sorg is real, as is the evidence of racial discrimination in the siting of hog operations—it is Smithfield's lawyers who played the race card and lost.

It happened during jury selection. The defense team used two of its three peremptory challenges to cull Black people from the panel, much as they had used three of their six peremptories in *McKiver*. This time, Kaeske took Lisa's advice and raised a *Batson* challenge, arguing that the strikes were racially motivated, and the judge actually *granted* the motion with respect to one of the jurors. It was an astonishing ruling, and exceedingly rare. Mark Anderson complained about it loudly, arguing that the judge had tilted the playing field against Smithfield. The judge seated the challenged juror anyway. In his frustration, Anderson tried one more tactic. He argued that the judge should scrap the entire venire and call a new group of prospective jurors. Judge Britt refused. Now, the defense lawyer is reviving the argument under a different guise. Send the jury home, he's saying. Justice demands a clean slate.

The judge listens carefully, then lets Mike Kaeske speak. Kaeske goes out of his way to remain calm. The stakes are momentous. An adverse ruling will not only derail the trial calendar, massively inconvenience the plaintiffs and witnesses, and add enormous expense, but it will hand the industry a public relations victory that it can leverage to attack the entire trial process.

Instead of focusing on individual jurors, Kaeske defends the jury as a whole. Given what is actually *in the record,* he says, the panel has not suffered an irremediable taint. Whatever the jurors have seen and heard and read, it's been on the surface of things. If they've been swayed at all, it isn't clear in what direction. And all of them have pledged their impartiality. To reboot the trial so late in the game would prejudice everyone. Better to let the proceedings continue and the jury deliver a verdict. At that point, the judge can take a poll to ensure that all the jurors are in agreement and none have been unduly influenced.

Judge Britt ponders this over lunch, then calls the attorneys back into his chambers. After hearing from both sides again, he asks Kaeske a piercing question: "Do you think that the court can have any confidence at all in what the jurors said?"

It's an impossible question to answer.

The judge takes the burden upon himself. He leaves the plaintiffs' team to sweat for another twenty minutes before issuing his decision. "Guys and gals," he says with twangy gravitas, "every decision I make lately seems to be of critical importance, but on full reflection and full consideration of everything, I'm going to deny the motion for a mistrial. I'm basing it primarily on the fact that each individual juror, after questioning from me, said that whatever went on back in the jury room, they felt they could be fair and impartial."

Mike Kaeske and Mona Wallace exhale their relief.

The judge asks Mark Anderson if he would like to challenge any particular juror. The defense lawyer refuses. "We're left with a group of people who have shown a lack of candor with the court," Anderson says. "I understand your ruling, but the whole panel is tainted and there is no way to intelligently cure that by trying to remove one or the other based on what we think they didn't tell you."

Kaeske asks for a few minutes to collect himself before diving back into his examination of Gregg Schmidt. The judge gives him ten, then takes the bench and summons the jury. The trial resumes as if the informant never said a word. But the doubts raised by his complaint can't be dispelled by a judicial pronouncement. Those suspicions linger like a miasma in the courtroom. Fortunately, the transcripts of the juror interviews will not be published until days later, but the winds of rage are already whirling in Murphysville.

Soon, the vortex will build into a hurricane.

Two days after Judge Britt denies Smithfield's mistrial motion, Jimmy Dixon, the loose-lipped populist from down east, publishes an opinion piece in his district's paper of record, the *Duplin Times*. It is a cavalcade of accusatory cant, at once nonsensical, apocalyptic, defamatory, and racist. A wise assistant would have taken away his pen.

He alleges that "Mona Lisa Wallace and her agents" recruited the plaintiffs to sue Smithfield—a demonstrably false claim. He disparages Judge Britt for having "an overt bias" against "our family livestock farmers." He paints a picture of economic predation, where "greedy white lawyers willing to prey on the race of our long-time black neighbors" promised "large sums of money" and prompted the neighbors to exaggerate their claims. He accuses Mike Kaeske and Lisa Blue of charging "big money flying here every week on their $30 million jets," when their commercial airline receipts prove otherwise. And he makes an absurd statement about Mona's financial arrangement with her clients, alleging that "most of these lawyers get as high as several thousand dollars per hour plus all the other millions of dollars of expenses before they take their 40%." With even a modest token of due diligence, Dixon would have learned that no lawyer on Earth charges several thousand dollars an hour—except, perhaps, to the mob—and that no plaintiffs' lawyer charges an hourly rate *in addition* to a contingency fee.

The Republican demagogue commits yet another faux pas when he breaks out his calculator. In Jimmy Dixon's telling, if Smithfield were to settle the litigation for the amount of the *McKiver* verdict, as reduced by the statutory cap, and Mona and Mike were to dole out that $3 million to the ten plaintiffs in that case only, "those 10 plaintiffs might get $10,000–$40,000, or maybe nothing at all." In a shockingly blinkered flourish, he writes: "I'll bet those good black folks would feel a lot different than when they heard the $50 million award in court!"

Leaving aside Dixon's bigotry and incomprehensible math, the hypothetical itself is ridiculous. Mass action settlements are not negotiated on the basis of the first bellwether case. They are negotiated on the totality of outstanding claims, after a sufficient sample of trials. At that point, and that point only, the lawyers recover their expenses, take their cut, and deliver the remainder to their clients. Under no circumstances would Mona and Mike pay out a global settlement of more than five hundred claims to ten plaintiffs alone. That would be malpractice.

But facts and figures are beside the point to the legislator from Duplin County. He sees fire burning in the hills. He's afraid that "Smithfield Foods will leave North Carolina and the tax bases of many eastern counties will be decimated." In Jimmy Dixon's vision of hog country Armageddon, he even harbors a concern for "Mr. and Mrs. Urbanite." In his closing, he writes: "We farmers can still produce enough food for ourselves, but the world will be a hungry place if these temporary nuisance claims prevail."

In the same edition of the *Duplin Times,* both Smithfield and NC Farm Families run full-color advertisements countering the lawsuits. Smithfield's messaging is glossier, less direct. It features a smiling farmer in a company hat standing in front of a cornfield. Emblazoned across the top is the slogan "We Make Good Food and Good Neighbors." Beside the farmer's face is this caption: "Smithfield Foods is one of the ten largest employers in North Carolina, providing over 10,000 jobs and supporting thousands of family farmers in the state." The ad concludes with the tagline: "Because we don't just make good food. We make 'Good Food. Responsibly.'"

Smithfield's surrogate, Farm Families, by contrast, shows no such restraint. In a shameless riff on the Holocaust poem by German pastor Martin Niemöller, Farm Families declares: "First, they came for Billy Kinlaw. In a Raleigh courtroom, the Texas lawyers dazzled a jury, twisting the facts about hog farming in North Carolina. The Kinlaw family's hog barns stand empty. And the lawyers got what they wanted—big money. Now, the Texas lawyers are coming after Joey Carter's farm. Carter, a hog farmer, volunteer firefighter, and police officer who wore the blue. That's not the end. There are more trials, against more farms, coming. The trials, with lawyers chasing money, could change Duplin County. Our economy could suffer a hard blow. Grocery stores and restaurants and all types of businesses will suffer. And the schools, too, as the tax base shrinks. They came first for Billy Kinlaw. Now, they've come for Joey Carter and they're a threat for us all."

Over the course of the next week, as Smithfield's lawyers parade their witnesses before the jury, NC Farm Families billboards and yard signs pop up all over hog country, especially in Duplin County, where the agricultural community, already polarized by the lawsuits, has gone tribal around the Joey Carter trial. STAND FOR HOG FARMERS, some of the signs read. NO FARMS = NO FOOD. Others are harsher. One billboard screams KEEPEM MAKIN BACON. Then below it on a blood-red banner: SHUT UP OR MOVE.

The plaintiffs greet this furor with wariness and weary resignation. For those who have made their home in Duplin for decades, some for generations, this campaign of intimidation compounds their sense of alienation. The drama unfolding in Judge Britt's courtroom is light-years distant from their streets, their neighborhoods, their porches and backyards. They have nowhere to retreat to, no other stores to shop in, no other restaurants to patronize. They have to live surrounded by the constant reminder of what many in the community think of them.

For the grandchildren and great-grandchildren of people once enslaved, this is not a novel experience. The demons of white supremacy have never been fully exorcised from the coastal plain. But before the neighbors took Smithfield to court, they had peace. They had to abide the pollution, the hog shit falling like rain on their houses, befouling the air and infecting the water. Yet their white neighbors were mostly kind to them, so long as they didn't complain. Now they get stares when they are out in public. They are vilified on social media. Their lawyers are being defamed in print. The man elected to represent them in the legislature has openly accused them of lying. And they have no idea how the story is going to end.

The first verdict was a triumph, but how many more indignities will they have to endure before the Murphy men agree to clean up the land, as Governor Hunt envisioned almost twenty years ago? This land is not the province of the white farmers alone. The property rights of Billy Kinlaw and Joey Carter are no more valid than those of Woodell McGowan and Elsie Herring. Yet white claims to the soil have always been prioritized over Black claims. The law has never truly admitted the equality of those who are equal in the eyes of God. This must change. The neighbors don't want to put a single farmer out of business. They want to live in harmony with everyone. They just want the spray to cease, the midnight truck runs to stop, the stink and the flies and the buzzards to go away. They agree that Duplin County is heaven on earth.

But if that is true, shouldn't its largest corporation treat it that way?

CHAPTER 30

TOTAL WAR

Hatred isn't something you're born with. It gets taught.
—*Mississippi Burning*

As the *McGowan* trial winds to a close, the tension in the courtroom reaches a boil, and the lawyers again come to blows. This time, the skirmish is between Mona Wallace and an attorney hired by Smithfield to represent Joey Carter. At issue is the concealment of documents.

For weeks, Mona has been laboring to obtain records from the Duplin County Soil & Water office relating to the early days of Carter's hog operation. All state-held records should have been produced during discovery, but a few of the oldest documents slipped through the cracks, or so the growers' lawyer wants Judge Britt to believe. In Mona's mind, the excuse is hogwash. She is certain that both the Soil & Water people and the growers' counsel have stonewalled her on production because they know what the old documents contain—a piece of evidence that would damage Joey Carter's credibility and Smithfield's case.

Now, at last, she has proof. Two nights ago, the growers' attorney finally coughed up the last of the missing documents. They are damning.

From the beginning of the trial, Smithfield has held up Joey Carter as a paragon of the grower community, a family man, and a public servant. When he was on the stand, Carter painted his own self-portrait using the same gilded strokes. The former police chief claimed that he could not understand the neighbors' allegations about his hog farm.

"I had no indication there was an odor issue," he told the jury.

Kaeske, acting surprised, replied, "I need to write that down. I never had—say what you said again. Never had any indication that there was an odor issue?"

"Right," Joey reiterated. "I've never had a complaint from anybody."

The old Soil & Water documents prove the opposite.

In March of 1985, when the state and federal regulators were helping Joey lay out his first lagoon and barns, a Soil & Water official wrote the following note: "Had three calls (Perry Williams, Linnill Farland, Laurie Jackson) from neighbors complaining about the lagoon being so close to their property. It will be about 850' from Mr. Farland's home, and there are 11 houses within about 1500'. Mr. Jackson said he and his brother plan to put a residential development on their field, adjacent to the lagoon. Discussed the problems that might be caused by neighbors in future with Joey, but he is determined to proceed."

Two months later, the same official made another handwritten note: "Joey said he has heard that his neighbors plan to sue him for damaging their property values."

Had these documents been properly disclosed, Mike Kaeske would have wielded them like a battle-axe and used them to punish Joey Carter on cross-examination. He would have been able to establish, beyond dispute, that one of Smithfield's primary defenses—that the neighbors never complained—was a bald-faced lie. But the records didn't come to light in discovery. They stayed buried until two nights ago.

When Smithfield rests its case, Judge Britt takes the matter up out of the presence of the jury. Mona lays out the story for him: the letters and emails she sent requesting the missing records; the visits her team made to the Soil & Water office (where Joey Carter's son now works); the people who told her that no more documents existed; then the eleventh-hour surprise—news that the growers' attorney had just waltzed into the Soil & Water office and left with the documents. At that point, Mona demanded that the Soil & Water people furnish her copies as well. She sent Maryclaire Farrington to collect them, but the Soil & Water people dragged their feet. They said the copies wouldn't be available until July 13, after the trial's conclusion.

By now, Mona's suspicions were piqued. She demanded that the growers' attorney turn them over. The lawyer rebuffed her at first. The documents were public, he said. They had been sitting in the Soil & Water filing cabinet since 1985, and Mona could have obtained them by a simple public records request. Mona explained that she had already jumped through every hoop required by the law, yet Soil & Water continued to dither. Only then, when Mona found herself in a bureaucratic box canyon and Joey Carter was off the stand, did the attorney disclose the records. In fact, he made it look like he was doing Mona a favor.

Judge Britt is decidedly unimpressed. Indeed, he is disturbed. But he can't change the past. What he can do is upbraid the growers' attorney. He tells the lawyer that while he may have complied with the letter of the law, he didn't comply with its spirit. Indeed, he accuses the man of bad faith. He also lays into the Soil & Water people.

"What's going on down in the Soil & Water Conservation office in Duplin County smells to high heaven," he says. "I can smell it here stronger than I smell the hog odor that's the subject of this lawsuit."

Unfortunately, as a federal judge, he has no authority to reprimand local officials. He promises to investigate the matter, but no one on the plaintiffs' side of the aisle expects anything to come of that.

As for the regulator's notes, the best the judge can offer the plaintiffs is the chance to admit them into evidence. Mike Kaeske isn't allowed to read the notes out loud to the jury because he isn't a witness. But the jury will have access to them in deliberations. And, maybe, a few of the jurors will take the time to read them and discern their meaning.

The neighbors complained. Joey Carter knew it and didn't care.

＊

On Monday, June 25, while Mike Kaeske and Mark Anderson are in the well of Judge Britt's courtroom delivering their closing arguments, the hog barons and their allies take to the streets to give vent to their rage. Buses descend on Raleigh from all points down east, ferrying hun-

dreds of hog farmers and their families to the Bicentennial Plaza, a wide
pedestrian mall connecting the Capitol building to the General Assembly. In the sultry heat of afternoon, a bevy of political heavyweights strut
across the stage and stir up the crowd.

Jimmy Dixon is there, with his consigliere from the state senate,
Brent Jackson. The Duplin representative kicks off the rally with a hoary
quote from Thomas Jefferson: "'Let the farmer forevermore be honored
in his calling, for they who labor the earth are the chosen people of
God.'" Raising his fist to the sunbaked sky, Dixon cries out, "Let us all
who are here today and believe this shout and cheer for joy!"

After a beat, the crowd erupts.

The lieutenant governor, Dan Forest, speaks. A Republican with a
Democrat for a boss, he wants nothing more than to boot Roy Cooper
from the governor's mansion. Lately, he's been cuddling up to the rural
white vote down east. It's not his native demographic. He's a big city
architect from Charlotte. He shows up at the rally looking like a venture
capitalist who just stepped out of a pitch meeting. He doesn't even take
off his blue iridium sunglasses when he assumes the podium. But he has
a silver tongue and a penchant for populism. After an ode to the American farmer, he takes a swipe at the industry's favorite bogeyman. "We
don't need big-time lawyers from California, New York, and other places
coming here and telling us how to raise our animals and grow our crops
in this state. We can do that just fine for ourselves."

After Forest comes Steve Troxler, the state commissioner of agriculture, his helmet of snow-white hair shimmering in the sun. He pushes
the laudatory rhetoric to the stops. "I hope the people of this nation and
this state will wake up and *revere* you," he says. "*Not* challenge you, *not*
take you to court, but *revere* you."

As the speechifying continues, a few blocks away, up on New Bern
Avenue, Mike Kaeske is offering the twelve jurors in Judge Britt's courtroom a contrary take on this moment in history.

"This is *not* normal agriculture," he argues. "Sticking five thousand
hogs in buildings a thousand feet from people's houses, that's not normal. It's different. Okay, you want to do it differently? Do it differently.
That's fine. We're not opposed to you doing it differently. But your property rights stop where our property rights start."

He pleads with the jurors to trust their instincts. "Common sense tells you that seven million gallons of feces and urine stored in an open-air pit a thousand feet from someone's house is going to stink. There aren't many different ways you can say it stinks."

He asks the jury to take a peek behind the curtain, to spot the fallacy in Smithfield's fear-mongering. "They want to talk about how it would be devastating to the community if Smithfield left. Who wants Smithfield to leave? Nobody wants Smithfield to leave. Maybe Smithfield wants you to believe that they would leave so that you would render a different verdict. But we can have hog operations, and we can have people at the same time."

Eventually, Kaeske makes his final pitch. "The way it gets fixed is through this process. That's why we're here. And how we do it—how you do it—is you speak in dollars and cents, because that's what corporations understand. It's the way they make their decisions. You saw the document from Mr. Westerbeek that said, 'We can't cost-justify based on odor alone.' You're now part of that process. You're now part of the process of telling Smithfield the cost they have to justify. Because if they have to justify the cost of lawsuits instead of fixing the problem, well, they'll go fix the problem. That's how lawsuits like this one are used to cause change and to compensate people that have been wronged."

When at last the judge dismisses the jury, Kaeske walks down the aisle and out of the courtroom with Mona and Lisa and Sophie and the rest of his team. He offers handshakes and hugs to the plaintiffs, sees the smiles on their faces, the tears in their eyes, and feels the residual glow of accomplishment, of finishing strong. He knows about the rally underway at Bicentennial Plaza, the massing of the hog kingdom and its allies. He knows that all of those farmers think that he and Mona are the Devil's handmaidens. The chatter on the Internet has been blistering. He's tuned most of it out, stayed focused on the trial. But he hasn't been able to suppress all of it. Mona has been getting calls from clients worried about the messages they are seeing on yard signs and billboards across the county. They are worried. They are intimidated. They are afraid. And there isn't a damn thing that he or Mona can do about it.

This trial is going to end in the courthouse, but the judgment won't remain there, especially if the verdict comes back in their favor. Like a river swollen by a storm surge, it will spill out into the community.

✳

On the second day of the jury's deliberations, Judge Britt takes matters into his own hands. He enters a gag order banning the lawyers, the parties, their agents, and any witnesses from talking to the media about the lawsuits, except for informational purposes. Out of concern for free speech, however, he makes no attempt to silence the war drums of NC Farm Families, the Pork Council, or Smithfield's allies in the statehouse. Unbound by the judge's fetters, they go right on fueling the wind shear of existential fear down east. By the time the jury reaches its verdict two days later, all of hog country is breathless, jittery, on edge.

As in *McKiver,* the jurors decide that Murphy-Brown has violated the Good Neighbor rule. They assign a modest value to compensate for the harm—$65,000 for Elvis and $65,000 for Vonnie. On the question of punitives, however, they wield a mace. They award the couple $12.5 million each—two and a half times what their predecessor jury awarded Joyce McKiver and her neighbors.

The response down east is hysterical. Shortly after the verdict, NC Farm Families posts a summary on Facebook with the tagline: "VERDICT: Hog farms are a nuisance." The post is unusually subdued and scrubbed of editorializing, but the 1,400 comments from the group's followers are not. Emotions run hot, and epithets are cast like stones.

The justice system is a "joke." The verdict is a "disgrace," "outrageous," "insane," a "gross miscarriage of justice." The jurors are castigated as "idiots" and accused of being "manipulated and deceived." The plaintiffs are denounced as "dumb bafoons [*sic*]," "heartless," "lazy" and "free-loaders." Many people opine that the neighbors should become vegetarians. Some say the plaintiffs should relocate: "This really ticks me off! If you don't like the country smell of Duplin County, MOVE, because we don't need you!" A few people go biblical: "I have to keep reminding myself that Jesus wants us to love one another. But how do you love someone who is destroying people's livelihood all bc of greed."

In the wake of the verdict, Joey Carter's son posts a Facebook lament. His family is heartbroken, he writes. His father built the hog farm "with his own hands." The trial process was a "living hell no farm family should have to endure." In court, "very little of our story could be told." The plaintiffs' lawyers "will answer to GOD for the devastation and division they are causing in our community and great state of NC." He appeals to the Fourth Circuit to deliver justice and thanks the community for standing by them. "In the coming days," he writes, "we know it will be hard and our communities will be full of anger, hate, and a desire for revenge." He exhorts everyone to rest in Providence. "Please remember we are all children of GOD and believers in his word and for that we will all be blessed."

When Jimmy Dixon reads this post, however, he doesn't light a votive candle and adopt a prayerful repose. In the wee hours of the morning, he logs on to Facebook and uncorks on Wallace & Graham, Judge Earl Britt, and Elsie Herring, whom he saw speak at the General Assembly about S711. He throws his fists low and lets the hatred fly.

"Well, Mr. Graham and Mona Lisa, how do you feel when you look at this family you have destroyed? How do you feel knowing you enabled the Texas lawyers to rape this family? Does it feel any different than when you raped the Kinlaw family? Probably not because you are getting ready to economically rape all the other families you have sued. Who trained the lady who lied to two different Committees in the General Assembly when she said, 'My mother's house is eight feet from a sprayfield, and my mother was a prisoner in her own house.'"

Dixon's invective turns libelous. He accuses Mona and Bill of working with a fictitious "deep-pocket financier" and "pimping" the plaintiffs to "scare Smithfield into settling." He alleges that Mona and Bill "unethically recruited" the plaintiffs to sign on to their "evil design"—even though Smithfield's own lawyer, Mark Anderson, admitted the opposite at the state court hearing way back in 2013. Dixon accuses Mike Kaeske, whom he calls "that buzzard from Texas," of "improper conduct in recruiting clients," when Mike didn't enter the case until 2015.

Dixon's conclusion borders on self-parody. "Do you brag to your neighbors about the horrific damage you are inflicting on these good folks?" he asks. "Probably not. You probably want to lay low and avoid any sunlight which usually disinfects all kinds of slim [sic]."

Not content with lashing out on social media, the Duplin legislator submits his screed to the *Goldsboro News-Argus,* a local paper, which publishes it under the headline "Greedy Lawyers Force Farmers to Pin

Hopes on Public Opinion." Just as Don Butler did years ago on the stage at the Sampson County Expo Center, Jimmy Dixon summons the kingdom to fight.

"We, the people," he writes, "must continue to rally and demand justice for the property rights of our hard-working family farmers who are in compliance with the laws and regulations that govern how they run their farms, and we must do it in the court of public opinion because we are damn sure not getting justice in Judge Earl Britt's courtroom."

The hog kingdom responds with total war.

Less than forty-eight hours after the verdict, the wife of one of the hog farmers involved in the suit fires up her own Facebook page and launches a brazen attack against the plaintiffs.

"OK y'all," she writes. "Here's the LIST (below) of all 471 NAMES to SHAME!!!!! Ya know, those who jumped onboard the 'MONEY' train!! PLEASE SHARE." After a shot at the lawyers, she goes on: "Made me so darn MAD as I typed out this list and seen SO MANY 'Familiar Names'!! Ugh . . . Check your 'Friend List' y'all . . . just say'n!!!!"

The comments are scorching. "Every single one of these names needs to be posted in every grocery store around eastern nc!!!!" a woman blares. "They should be forbidden to buy any kind of meat!!" Another says: "I think all these people on the list should be made to grow everything they eat. Banned completely from ever entering a grocery store or any store that sells pork or that's grown by any farmer period!!!!" One person suggests publishing the plaintiffs' names on a billboard along I-40. "Since these jerks don't like farmers," opines a woman, "they need to learn to forage like our ancestors thousands of years ago did." "Simply disgusting!!!" someone else screams. "Hope they choke on any pork, chicken, turkey or beef!!" "I'm ASHAMED to know these ppl & even more so because almost EVERYONE on this damn list eats meat!" offers another. "Where the hell do they think it comes from?"

For the plaintiffs, being outed like this, being publicly condemned by people they know, is a terrifying experience. While none of them has suffered violence, all of them have felt the pressure wave of intimidation. Denigrated on signs, called out at rallies, and now vilified on social media, they feel exposed. They know what this post will unleash. And they are right to fear harassment. In the grip of such dark energy, the mob will soon find ways to channel its rage into reprisals. One plaintiff will nearly get run off the road by a hog farmer. Another will see her new ice cream parlor targeted with a boycott.

And it isn't just the Black plaintiffs who are afraid. Randy Davis, one of the few white plaintiffs in the case, feels the concern acutely. He's seen how ruthless the hog barons can be in the way they have treated his neighbor, Don Webb. The old ARSI activist has received more threats than he can count. And Randy has his own experience to rely on, too. It seems like just yesterday that he caught a strange man lurking outside his house taking photographs, while his family was getting ready for church. When Randy confronted the man, the man sped off and disappeared. But not before Randy saw the pump-action shotgun in the passenger seat. Randy called the police and filed a report. A detective tracked down the car. It was a rental. The driver, as it turned out, was an investigator working for Smithfield's defense team.

The fallout from the *McGowan* verdict soon reaches beyond hog country's borders. In Salisbury, the phones at Wallace & Graham ring off the hook with threatening calls. Enraged hog farmers carpet-bomb the firm's Internet ratings with one-star reviews. The digital smear campaign is so comprehensive that people even trash Mona and Bill on Yelp.

In all their years of practicing law, in all their contretemps with corporate interests, neither Mona nor Bill has ever experienced anything like this. They shut down the firm's website and Facebook page. They give thought to engaging the media and telling their side of the story, and they talk through their options with Mike Kaeske and Lisa Blue. In the end, however, they decide against it. While another law firm might hire a public relations team and mount a strategic defense, Mona and Bill would rather keep their campaign of persuasion in the courtroom.

The only hearts and minds they care to win are in the jury box.

As for Jimmy Dixon, they agree to ignore him. He's a belligerent blowhard. They could sue him for defamation, but what would that accomplish? Better to let him bray at the moon. The power he wields is not in his pen; it's in the levers of the General Assembly. If they contend with him anywhere, they will contend with him there.

Ironically, they feel a measure of sympathy for the frightened growers. They are little more than pistons in Smithfield's everlasting gobstopper machine, the toil far outstripping the reward. But the industry's propagandists have spun their illusions well. People like Joey Carter will never believe that neither Mona Wallace nor Bill Graham, neither Mike Kaeske nor Lisa Blue, wants to hurt them. They will never admit that this lawsuit is about justice and dignity for the plaintiffs. That it's about forcing Smithfield to clean up the state.

The threats, on the other hand, the plaintiffs' team takes seriously. Most of them are surely harmless. But with the atmosphere so charged, with so many people fearing that their incomes and way of life are on the chopping block, all it would take is one sociopath with hog farming ties to grab his AR-15, drive up to Salisbury, and storm the law offices of Wallace & Graham like Adam Lanza.

On July 3, 2018, Mona and Bill hire a private security team to stand guard outside the firm.

The *Artis* trial is scheduled to begin in one week.

CHAPTER 31

THE HOG KING AND THE SAINT

The best revenge is not to be like your enemy.
—*Marcus Aurelius*

**Raleigh
and Eastern
North Carolina
Early July 2018**
While the hurricane of calumny rages on
unabated and hundreds of growers congregate
for yet another rally, this time at Joey Carter's
farm, Mona and Mike and the trial team hun-
ker down and prepare for *Artis*. They know
the sterling quality of the evidence they have
to offer—the stories that Joyce Messick and Jimmy Jacobs will tell, and
the horror show inside Dean Hilton's Greenwood operations. They also
know something Smithfield doesn't. They have a novel witness waiting
in the wings, a man of unimpeachable integrity whose tale should capti-
vate the jury. This case could break things open in the litigation. Yet, as
the last two months have proven, anything can happen.

Shortly before they return to the courtroom, Mona takes a trip to
Pender County with Linda Wike. The two women have spent a lot of
time on the road together these past few years. Linda is fearless behind
the wheel and imperturbable on long stretches of tarmac. It's a gift she
received from her late father, who showed her the wide world from inside
his tractor-trailer. They work while they drive, reviewing documents,
strategizing about witnesses, batting ideas off of Mike and John on the
phone, and playing three-dimensional mock chess with Smithfield's
case. Their synergy is familiar, their comments recombinant. If John is

Mona's right hand, Linda is her left. After thirteen years of collaboration, she can often read Mona's mind.

They stop in to see their clients on Piney Woods Road. They sit with
them in their living rooms and inquire about their families. Then, after
a time, they talk about the case, what it will be like for the plaintiffs to
take the stand and talk to the jury. This is the part of her job that Linda
loves most—face time with the clients. She respects these people. She
admires their kindness and grace, their long-suffering courage, the way
they have fought this fight without bitterness. Along the way, they have
come to trust her implicitly. They call her all the time. "Miss Linda,"
they say, "can you tell us what's going on?" She always picks up the
phone, always carves out time for them.

She and Mona walk the clients through the pageantry of testifying.
It won't be as painful as the depositions, Mona explains. No more baited
hooks and fishing expeditions, no more spurious probes about personal
matters. Mike Kaeske will guide them through their stories, and then
Jim Neale—the McGuireWoods attorney assigned to handle the *Artis*
trial—will ask them a few questions. There should be few surprises. And
Neale is a gentleman attorney, as was Mark Anderson. Their sole task as
witnesses is to tell the truth.

Mona and Linda break for lunch in the early afternoon. There's a
gas station down the road that serves the best burgers around, so say
the reviewers on Google. The squat brick building is part convenience
store, part grill. They place their order at the counter and pay with cash
instead of the firm's credit card. It is a lesson they learned a while back,
when they tried to book a hotel stay in person and heard from the desk
clerk that no rooms were available, despite a half-empty parking lot and
a range of options on the Internet. Everyone in hog country has heard
of Wallace & Graham, and many people are openly hostile to them. But
only the Murphy men and their associates know them on sight.

They slip into a booth, one of just a handful in this greasy spoon,
and listen to the sizzle of the grill while they wait on their food. They
try not to draw attention to themselves, but there is no way to remain
inconspicuous. They look like city people. They glance at the other
patrons, all men, hoping no one identifies them. Down here, they feel
the bull's-eye on their backs.

Before long, a white pickup truck pulls into the lot, and three men clamber out. They enter the restaurant and stroll up to the counter, a swagger in their step. They are company men, their logo-embossed polo shirts and ball caps like a uniform. Mona is in the restroom, but Linda sees them right away. Two of them are strangers to her. The other man, however, she recognizes instantly. She has never seen him in person. But his face is seared in her memory.

It is Wendell Murphy.

When Mona slips into the booth again, Linda gestures toward the old hog king, and Mona's eyes turn saucer-round. They watch Murphy in fascination, see the way the other men attend to him, the deference they pay. At the age of eighty, Murphy still carries himself like a lord. He and his underlings take the booth beside Mona and Linda and launch into a discussion of the hog market. The ladies find it surreal to listen to them, to think that this old man with a face like weathered parchment and hair as white as an egret is the one who started it all.

Mona catches his eye. In her curiosity, she can't help it. He doesn't seem surprised to see her, nor does he seem to care. He stares back implacably, then resumes his conversation. Mona feels no animosity toward him. She feels only the weight of the wrong. By his ingenuity and industriousness, he made a billion dollars raising hogs. He created thousands of jobs and helped feed the world. But when it became obvious that his business was befouling the land and making life intolerable for so many of his fellow citizens, he made up excuses, denied reality, and planted his feet firmly in the way of progress.

If Elsie Herring and Daphne McKoy, Linnill Farland and Joyce Messick are to rise, then the walls that Wendell Murphy built around his kingdom must fall.

Less than a week later, in the august precincts of the federal courthouse in Raleigh, Mike Kaeske rises to deliver his opening for the third time. The twelve people in the jury box watch him inquisitively. He greets them with a smile. All of the tingling nerves and wracking anxiety that trailed him into the courthouse are behind him now, jettisoned in the attorney room during five minutes of meditation with Lisa and Sophie.

Mindfulness is one of Lisa's many talents. But she's never deployed her expertise in a trial setting before. She led a meditation session for the first time in the *McGowan* case to help Mike tune out the howling of the mob. Now, it has become a trial day ritual, and Kaeske has come to rely on it, perhaps even to crave it. It restores his balance, reminds him of who he is and what he can do. It's a portal into the desert—a way out of the stress monster's labyrinth and back into himself.

He begins, as he always does, with the Good Neighbor rule. He makes eye contact with the jurors as the words roll off his tongue. He feels good about these people, as do Lisa and Mona and the rest of the team. There are ten women and two men, four college students, three educators, and one former platoon sergeant in the U.S. Marines. A jury that skews female and young is a jury that will listen carefully and be attuned to the emotion of their cause.

Over the next two hours, Kaeske tells his story. He introduces the jurors to Wendell Murphy, and constructs a time-lapse panorama of eastern North Carolina as it metamorphosed from a vast patchwork of small farms into the iron-fisted oligarchy controlled by the Five Families, and, after that, into the empire of Murphy-Brown.

With the backdrop painted and the adversary named, he fills in the foreground. He describes the land around Piney Woods Road. He tells them about the neighbors, almost all of whom are kin—Jimmy Jacobs and his sisters, Edna and Gertie; Jimmy Carr and Phyllis Wright; Ben and Diane Artis; Lucy Sidberry, whose ancestors acquired her parcel of sandy soil in the nineteenth century; and Joyce and Willie Messick, whose lives have been a sorrow song of loss and sacrifice.

He tells them about Joyce's hospice patients and Willie's love of horses, about the garden that Jimmy Jacobs tends like Beatrix Potter, and about the church that all of them attend a mile down the road. In 1987, Quarter M Farms, a company owned by Pete Murphy, Wendell's brother, built a hog farm behind the church. The congregation raised an outcry. They understood what 1,800 hogs would mean to their worship services, their weddings and funerals and summer potlucks on the lawn. The church was their gathering place, where they came together to lift holy hands, to meet friends and draw strength in suffering. The thought of Murphy's hogs squealing in captivity only a short distance away felt like an invasion. But Pete Murphy didn't listen. He brought the hogs anyway. Then his brother, Wendell, came and did the same.

In the mid-nineties, the first hog king elbowed his way into the neighborhood, building the facilities now known as Greenwood 1 and 2. The twin farms, with their 7,500 hogs, were a nightmare almost from the beginning. They racked up state violations by the fistful and spilled tens of thousands of gallons of wastewater into nearby rivers and wetlands. Like houses with a bloody history, the farms traded hands numerous times before finding their way into the portfolio of a young real estate entrepreneur, Dean Hilton, who bought them with a handful of his buddies. An aspiring porcine tycoon, Hilton has a stake in nearly twenty hog farms, with 100,000 hogs to his credit. He also owns a real estate agency, a mobile home park, a shopping center, a gym, and sixty or seventy rental properties. He has precious little time to worry about the Greenwood operations, and the neglect shows. Sick hogs have been left to die, dead hogs have been left to rot, and waste has built up until the cesspools overflow.

Kaeske puts a Smithfield audit report up on the big screen for the jury to see. "Hog bones present on ledge," he reads. "Hog bone in pen 34." He faces them again. "These are operations that are supposed to be growing hogs. Why are there bones?"

He leads them through more of Smithfield's records, accentuating the word "bones" until it seems to hang in the air like a feather in the wind. Bones. Bones. Why are there bones?

It's an arrow he's convinced that Smithfield cannot outrun.

Smithfield's defense team, however, has no interest in reprising Achilles. Its trial counsel for *Artis*, Jim Neale, is a former Army Ranger and light infantry platoon leader with the mind of a warfighter and the broad-shouldered, muscular build of a tugboat. When he rises to address the jury, he tries to knock Kaeske down with a single blow.

"It was one hour, ten minutes, and fifty-one seconds before Mr. Kaeske got to the issue that you're here to decide. That was when, in his opening statement, he first introduced you to his clients and their properties. One hour, ten minutes, and fifty-one seconds of other stuff."

If Kaeske painted a panorama, Neale limns a still life. "Lagoons and sprayfields, the industry, and waste management systems are not on trial," he intones. The issue before them is more limited, namely whether Murphy-Brown created a nuisance for six people on five different pieces of property during a seven-year period between 2011 and 2018.

It's simple, he tells them. The rest—"a generation's worth of bad news and history"—is just a distraction.

Yet for all Neale's insistence on microscopy, on limiting the aperture of the case to the lives of the plaintiffs, he can't avoid the temptation of a metanarrative. He tells a countervailing story about family farms and Easter ham and bacon, of free enterprise existing in harmony with the community on Piney Woods Road. Indeed, far from a wasteland, the plaintiffs' neighborhood is a lovely place. He emphasizes this in pointillist detail, talking about Willie Messick's horses and Jimmy Jacobs's collard greens. More than anything, the former Army Ranger wants the jury to hear that life on the plaintiffs' land is a good one, an enviable one, and that Murphy-Brown hasn't done one bit of damage to it.

It's a strong presentation, perhaps even better than Mark Anderson's. But Jim Neale faces a Herculean task. In order to sustain the Walden Pond narrative, he has to keep the jury's eyes from lingering long on two things that Mike Kaeske plans to spotlight: Smithfield's leading role in the hog wars over the past twenty-five years, and Dean Hilton's graveyard of bones.

The order of proof in *Artis* takes roughly the same shape as in *McKiver* and *McGowan*. After trying two cases to verdict, the people on Mike and Mona's side of the gallery know the testimony and evidence well enough to take the stand themselves. But to the twelve people sitting in the jury box, the production is brand-new, like a film on opening night. They are drawn in by the mesmeric cadence of Steve Wing's words, the undimmed light of conviction in his soulful eyes.

Jim Neale is smart enough to see this, and pugnacious enough not to let Wing go unscathed. His countermeasures, however, are peculiar. He uses Shane Rogers as a foil for a sideways snipe at the departed professor. His quibble is with semantics.

"You said you have reviewed Dr. Wing's testimony?" Neale asks.

"Part," Shane admits.

"You know he's an epidemiologist?"

"Yes, I do."

Here, the Army Ranger gets etymological. "Do you recall Mr.

Kaeske asking whether the word 'epidemiology' comes from the word 'epidemic'?"

"I don't remember that question in particular."

"You're not aware of an epidemic around Greenwood 1, are you?"

The question is silly, but Shane answers it gamely. "I'm not."

"You're not aware of an epidemic around Greenwood 2?"

"No."

"Or the Jennings Humphrey Farm?"

"An epidemic?"

"Yes, sir."

"If you mean like an epidemic disease outbreak—"

"That's what an epidemic is, isn't it, sir?"

At this point, Shane tries to offer a course correction. "It can be a disease outbreak. It depends on how you are defining 'disease,' I suppose. If you mean 'is there an epidemic?' in the sense that people around these operations are complaining of suffering of some sort, then, I mean, that's why we're here. If you mean by 'epidemic' that there's some kind of disease, like say an outbreak of salmonella, for instance, then, no, I'm not aware of that."

But Neale doesn't want to grant the distinction. "Let's stick with the outbreak of disease for a moment, if we can. You're not aware of an epidemic concerning an outbreak of disease at any hog farm on Piney Woods Road?"

"No," Shane says.

"For that matter, any hog farm anywhere in eastern North Carolina?"

"That I'm not sure of."

"Okay," Neale says, as if he's scored some kind of point. Then he takes an opening swipe at Shane personally. "Let's stick with what we're scientifically sure about, okay?"

Although Shane's face is a mask, inside he rolls his eyes. "Okay."

Most of the defense lawyer's cross is nitpicky. But Neale does get a few shots off. With eighty-eight plaintiffs in the discovery pool cases and a limited window of time to conduct his site studies, Shane only collected Pig2Bac and VOC samples from certain properties, those he felt were representative of the whole. In *Artis,* he collected samples at the homes of Jimmy Jacobs, Jimmy Carr, and Ben Artis, but not the others. Also, while a growing body of literature exists about Pig2Bac, no government agency has adopted it as a surrogate for hog odor. Nor has Shane or anyone else published a peer-reviewed study about its useful-ness as an odor indicator. It is cutting edge. And, yes, Shane had non-scientists (Mike Kaeske, John Hughes, and a young web designer named Carson Shank) helping him take swabs and send them to the lab. But these queries, whatever their legitimacy, are swallowed in the cloud of mind-numbing questions that Neale asks about chains of custody, cycle thresholds, and field blanks.

By the time Kaeske calls Joyce Messick to the stand on the fifth day of the trial, the jury has heard two distinguished men of letters explain in the vernacular of chemistry and public health what is self-evident from common sense—that confining thousands of hogs in enclosed barns, storing their waste in cesspools, and spraying it into the air near human habitations is not a solid plan if one has concern for the health and happiness of the neighbors.

Joyce Messick gives this axiom a face.

She is an exquisitely gentle woman with pillow-soft eyes and a smile that seems to creep up on her before flashing brightly. She endears herself to the jury within a handful of questions.

Kaeske shows her a picture of her home and asks, "What is the fur-thest you have ever lived from that spot in your entire life?"

"I'm not good with feet, but my parents' house was next door."

"Have you literally lived your entire life on this very same piece of dirt?"

"Yes," answers Joyce. In the globalized world of 2018, this admission sounds like something from the forgotten past. Here is a woman who has truly embraced her roots.

Kaeske develops the point further. "What is that like, every day going in the same driveway for fifty something—I won't say the exact number—years?"

"That's my castle," Joyce says proudly. "That's my home." The prop-erty came to her as an inheritance from her parents, who got it from her paternal grandmother. She isn't sure if the land goes back further in her family line, but her brother, Willie, might know. "That's where we was raised. That's all I know. I've never lived outside of my home."

Her eyes come alive in a different way when she talks about her hospice work, but there is a weariness behind them, a pain at once borrowed and shared. "The thing about working with the dying," she says, "I get to help them pass away peaceful, make them comfortable. I listen to their secrets, hold their hand and make them comfortable." She stays with all of her patients until they die. That means a lot to her, to be there until the end. Before hospice, she worked with Alzheimer's patients. She's been caring for sick people her entire adult life. After her son died in a motorcycle accident, she raised her granddaughter to adulthood. Her mother has dementia, and, though she lives down the road, Joyce cares for her needs too. She's also raising her nephew, who has sickle cell anemia. When Joyce gets home from her hospice work, she makes meals for her mother, her nephew, and Willie. It's the same every day.

"Every day?" Kaeske asks.

"Every day."

Fifteen minutes in and Joyce Messick has rendered herself untouchable. And she hasn't even started talking about her church.

Joyce has been at New Hope Missionary Baptist her entire life. She tells the jury about the homecoming celebrations the congregation used to have, the way the old women spread out all the food on the table in the yard, back when the air was clear. Her face darkens at the memory of Pete Murphy's hog farm. "It was terrible," she says about the effect of the odor. "It was stressful, and it was embarrassing." She remembers one event in particular—the funeral of Lucy Sidberry's mother. "When we have funerals, we use the dining room. After the burial, you come back and eat. Well, the people left. The smell was terrible."

These days, it's like that at her home, too. The stink of Murphy-Brown's hogs infuses the dew on her lawn. She smells it early in the morning. It gets into her uniform, and she takes it with her to work. When it rains, it's worse. And when the wind blows, it's inescapable. She doesn't put her windows up anymore, even in the spring when her house needs cleaning.

Eventually, Kaeske asks her why she agreed to join the lawsuit. Her plainspoken reply lays waste to years of Smithfield propaganda. "What they need to do is clean it up. I don't want the hogs gone. I love pork chop. I love bacon. But I don't love the odor."

Jim Neale's associate handles the cross-examination. Wisely, he keeps his distance, asks her nothing substantive, just a point of clarification, then takes his seat again.

There's a quiet in the courtroom when Joyce Messick steps down from the stand. Many eyes follow her as she walks down the aisle. They know where she's headed. She begged the jury to understand. She's needed back on Piney Woods Road, in the only home she has ever known. Her family is waiting for her there. When she disappears through the doors, it's as if a presence has departed, an outsized soul who has suffered more in five decades than most people would in three lifetimes, yet who has not been broken by it, who wakes up every day, often with the stench of hog shit in the air, and goes about loving the ones she's with. The afterglow left behind by Joyce Messick will persist throughout the trial. It is why Mike Kaeske called her as his first witness from the community.

In this cynical world, halos are rare. It's not often one gets to meet a living saint.

CHAPTER 32

WORLD ON FIRE

The path to paradise begins in hell.
—*Dante Alighieri*

Raleigh,
North Carolina
July 18–23, 2018

With the hog barons hemorrhaging sympathy, the plaintiffs' team offers them no quarter, no mercy. If the *McGowan* case was a trial by ordeal, *Artis* will be a trial by fire.

After Joyce Messick departs, Mike Kaeske calls Wesley Sewell to the witness stand. Sewell is a diamond dredged up by Mark Doby. He is a giant of a man, with florid pink skin, a neck thicker than his head, and a torso the size of a tractor tire. Yet he smiles readily and his eyes sparkle unexpectedly, as if they are accustomed to laugh. His voice, too, doesn't match his appearance. It has the pitch of a tenor and an unabashed twang.

He lives with his wife on Piney Woods Road, a hundred yards west of Joyce and Willie. A native of Pender County, he spent a lot of years down on the coast before returning home to care for his ailing mother and father-in-law. He's a retired police officer, a retired assistant fire chief, a former water rescue chief, a rescue diver, a dive master, a firearms instructor, and a first responder. In short, he's the guy you want with you in a gunfight or a disaster zone. He's also been on *Oprah*. A woman he once arrested for drunk driving submitted his name to the show as her guardian angel, someone who changed her life. Oprah brought him on and let him share the story with the world. Sewell is a truth teller. If it needs to be said, he'll say it. And if he says it, he means it. All of this is evident from the first word he speaks.

Wesley Sewell is bothered by the hog odor. He bought his house after seeing it online and making a couple of visits. He had no idea how close it was to a hog farm. He didn't realize that until the weather turned. It was a foggy day with a steady wind out of the east. The odor was so pungent that he jumped in his car and traced it to the source. That's when he saw Dean Hilton's barns rising over the fields. He can't sell the house because he's still looking after his mother and father-in-law. But his wife wants to move as soon as they can.

Mike Kaeske asks him to rate the odor on the spectrum of smells.

"Well," Sewell says, "I put it probably at number three, as some of the worst things I've smelled. I've had the misfortune of having to go to a plane crash that caught on fire, and I had to remove burnt bodies. And I've had to go in to a house, a trailer, and remove a person that had been dead for about a week on the toilet. Those smelled worse than the hog place smells."

"Other than that, do you put hog odor at number three?"

"Yes, sir," Sewell says.

He tells the jury the odor was once so bad that his wife got sick after walking outside. It's hard for him, too, because he loves the outdoors. He's an amateur horticulturalist. His backyard looks like a plant nursery. He keeps a bottle of OdoBan around to spray if the odor gets offensive. He also has a massive fly problem. He wears out fly swatters on a regular basis. He's never understood where the flies come from. He used to buy collard greens from Jimmy Jacobs. "They are the best collards around," he says. But then he and his wife saw the hog farm spraying waste on the fields near Jimmy's house, and he stopped buying them.

Kaeske asks him if he has any other complaints about the hog farm, and Sewell says he does. A while back a young attorney from McGuire-Woods stopped by his house to chat. He complained to the defense lawyer about water coming in through the back part of the property right after some really heavy rains. "It smelled just like the hog farm," Sewell recounts, looking at the jury. "And I said something about the possibility that the lagoon overflowed. And he got all irate and threw his hands up and everything. 'Don't say that!' And all this—"

Jim Neale is on his feet. "Objection to the hearsay, Your Honor."

"Sustained," says Judge Britt. "You can't tell what he said."

Kaeske presses the point, arguing that a statement by a defense attorney is admissible. The judge disagrees, but he allows Sewell to repeat the words he said to the young lawyer.

Sewell complies: "I gave him the color of what it looked like back there, and told him I knew what hog waste smelled like."

"When he came," Kaeske says, "did he ever give you any way to lodge further complaints?"

"No, sir. He did not."

"Did he ever send anyone else out to your house to either test the water in your backyard or ask you whether you have any further complaints?"

"No, sir. He did not."

"Did anyone from Smithfield in the last however many years it's been, did anyone ever come back to follow up with you about your complaints?"

"No, sir."

"And in that time since you've complained, have you noticed that it's gotten any better or any different?"

"It's the same, depending upon the weather, pretty much."

Kaeske asks if he's ever made a complaint to anyone other than the defense lawyer.

"No, sir," Sewell says. "I didn't know who to complain to. I know better than to call the sheriff's department. I wouldn't want to get laughed at for saying I can smell hog waste. They'd be like, 'What can we do about it?' So, no, sir, I never knew who to call, and still don't know."

Before Kaeske hands the man over to Jim Neale, he draws out one more feature of Sewell's character. Not only is he a first responder and a guardian angel with a green thumb, Wesley Sewell is an amateur baker. He bakes pound cakes at Christmas and delivers them to all the neighbors, including Joyce and Willie Messick and Jimmy Jacobs.

If Joyce Messick is Mother Teresa, the former police officer is a cross between Rambo and Santa Claus. His testimony is yet another lit match in a long string of them. By now, the smoke is rising high over the heads of the Murphy men. The air is crisping, and the sky is adance with the flickering glow.

The kingdom is burning.

✳

If Don Butler could rescue Smithfield from the flames, he surely would. But he can't. In one of the plaintiffs' team's more recent forays into the state's records, they discovered a secret buried in Butler's past, something so explosive that, if brought to light in the right way, it could shred every last stitch of the man's credibility with the jury.

Kaeske waits to deploy it until the hog barons' Cicero once again twists himself into a pretzel to avoid admitting the obvious—that hog odor is a nuisance. Butler's stance is an artful dodge: "If a farm is properly designed, located, and managed, it's very unlikely that it would be a problem for neighbors." Over and over again, Kaeske asks Butler about documents that came from Smithfield's files, complaints that neighbors had raised with the Murphy men, with local authorities, and with the media. And, over and over again, Butler defends the indefensible. He even denies that the smell readily attaches to people's clothes.

With the PR man turning on a spit, Kaeske merrily stokes the coals. He takes Butler's description of a "well-managed farm" and confronts him about Dean Hilton's graveyard of bones. He shows Butler the pictures from inside the Greenwood barns, all those hogs slathered in shit. Once again, Butler attempts to circumvent common sense. He isn't sure the black stuff smeared on the animals is feces. "It could be feed," he speculates. But even if it's feces, he can't make a judgment about whether the hog farm is well-managed.

Kaeske then drops the "b" word. "Do you ever have bones inside your hog operations?"

Butler says he doesn't.

"Do you know where you would get bones inside a hog operation?"

"The only way I can think of is if an animal died in there and the appropriate practices were not followed. That could result in bones. But in my twenty-seven years, I've never seen it."

"That would be bad management, correct?"

"That would be bad management."

Kaeske shows Butler a letter that Smithfield sent to Dean Hilton in 2016 requesting that he take concrete steps to clean up his Greenwood operations. "It says: 'During my visit to the farm, we had to euthanize several animals that should have already been euthanized—nineteen total.' Have you ever had a problem at your operation where nineteen animals that were supposed to have been euthanized haven't already been euthanized?"

"No," Butler says.

"That's an animal welfare issue, not euthanizing—putting out of their misery—animals that are supposed to be?"

Jim Neale lodges a fruitless objection, and Butler is forced to concede the point.

Kaeske circles back to Smithfield's letter to Dean Hilton: "It says here: 'During my visit to the farm, large numbers of rotten hogs and bones were left in the barns.' Did you ever have rotten hogs and bones in your barns?"

Neale objects again, and this time Judge Britt agrees. Butler's own farm is irrelevant to the present case. Kaeske, however, elicits the admission he is looking for: rotten hogs and bones are unacceptable. Under the rules of evidence, Kaeske isn't allowed to push Butler further, to force him to admit that Dean Hilton's mismanagement created a nuisance. That's not a fact. It's a legal conclusion. But the jurors are awake. There is no way they miss the point.

With Butler starting to broil, Kaeske offers the jury another history lesson—the uproar over the hog farms that once threatened the Pinehurst golf club, and the drive for a statewide ban on new lagoons and sprayfields. Butler admits what he can't deny—that, at the time of the moratorium, he believed that the state would soon phase out lagoons and sprayfields. But he qualifies the admission. "I believed then, and I believe now, that a properly designed, constructed, and managed lagoon and sprayfield system is a very good system. No system is perfect, but I know from experience, and lots of other people would agree with me, that when it's done right, these are very good systems."

It is here that Kaeske deploys his bombshell. "You say you know from experience. I guess that's in part your experience of running your own hog operation?"

"That and observation of hundreds of others."

"And your own hog operation," Kaeske says, making sure the jury is with him, "your own hog operation was the subject of complaints by *your own uncle* for the odor, correct?"

Butler's face turns a soft shade of purple. He had to know the question was coming. Kaeske raised it in each of the previous trials—the record he found buried in the state's archive. But in neither case did the query land quite like this, after such a thorough drubbing.

"I became aware that my late uncle complained about my farm to somebody," he allows cagily. "He never came to me to complain about it. He's now passed away." Butler takes a breath. "But I think it would be important for context here that my uncle was a nutcase. He hated my father, and I believe that was the basis for his complaint. It had nothing to do with the farm."

Kaeske, feeling the rush, lowers Butler's spit toward the flames. "So, I think this is important for context," he says, overtly mimicking the PR man. "When I first brought this to your attention, you didn't say anything about your uncle being a nutcase, did you?"

Butler squirms: "Well, I was trying to be polite, but—"

"No," Kaeske retorts. "The first time I asked you about it, you said honestly that you didn't know anything about the complaint, right?"

"That was an honest answer," Butler affirms.

"But in all the time since the first time I asked you until today, you never went and looked at the actual complaint to find—"

Butler tries to interrupt him. "I haven't—"

"Excuse me, sir," Kaeske says, then finishes his thought: "—to find out whether it was investigated by the state or not?"

"I can't react to a complaint that I know nothing about."

"I'm sorry, sir," Kaeske rejoins, relishing Butler's discomfort. "My question must not have been very good. It's now been some four months since I made you aware of the complaint that's right there in your file kept with the state for your farm, correct?"

"Yes," Butler concedes.

"You can go look at your own file for your own farm, right?"

Apparently, Butler has had enough of Kaeske's grilling. To escape the heat, he speaks his mind bluntly, pugnaciously. "I could if I wanted to. My uncle is dead. Problem solved."

It's a glorious moment for Mike Kaeske and the trial team, one that will make its way into the hog farm lore and inspire unceasing laughter in the years to come—the moment when the man who was Boss Hog's public face for three decades eviscerated himself on the stand. Now, whenever anyone at the Kaeske Law Firm or Wallace & Graham mentions Don Butler by name, the refrain comes back:

He's dead. Problem solved.

By the time Dean Hilton slides into the witness chair on the ninth day of trial, the earth beneath him—and Murphy-Brown—has been scorched. His only task is to avoid lighting any more matches. It should be simple. He's just the farmer, after all. He's not the multibillion-dollar corporation. Why shouldn't the jury sympathize with him? Okay, maybe his Greenwood operations are horrid to look at. But he can clean them up. He's a handsome young man with a beautiful family. He's a churchgoer, a successful entrepreneur. All he has to do is be humble, noncombative, mature enough to weather the criticism and promise to improve. Then he can go back to his life, back to his wife and kids, and forget all about this unfortunate spectacle.

But Mike Kaeske has no intention of letting him.

Dean Hilton is not just another contract grower; he's an aspiring hog baron, a miniature Smithfield, and he has presided over a boneyard, leaving his animals to die and cannibalize each other. His facilities are a putrefying disgrace, yet he's too busy to tend to them. He's the picture of entitled privilege. His indifference is without excuse.

The first part of Kaeske's examination is all about Smithfield—its procedures, its control over the hogs and feed, medicine and transport, even the height of the grass in the sprayfields. After that, he makes surgical inquiries about the Greenwood facilities—how often Hilton visits them, who his managers are, who is around during state inspections, anodyne stuff. For a while, Kaeske doesn't offer a hint of what is coming. Then, as if flipping a switch, he makes it personal.

He asks Hilton what he knows about his hog operations—about filling out spray reports, about spray schedules and lagoon sludge, about the volume of waste generated by the hogs. It turns out that a man with an ownership stake in twenty hog operations knows very little about an awful lot. He has people who keep track of all that, he says. But problems can arise when one is an absentee owner. During discovery, it came out that the Greenwood facilities had two sets of spray records, and they didn't add up. Hilton's farm manager was falsifying documents.

This touches a nerve. The young hog baron is clearly squeamish about the incident. He tries to hide behind the experts, to say that he turned the documents over to the people at Soil & Water and his attorneys and disclosed it to the court. But he's never actually gone back and investigated the incident himself. That's Kaeske's point. Why didn't the owner of the hog farm, after discovering evidence of fraud, take the time to figure out what happened?

Hilton's response comes out like a skipping record. "I turned it over to Soil & Water. I turned it over to the experts. I notified the courts. I notified you. To this day, nothing has ever come back that says there was any kind of violation."

It's a transparent dodge, a blatant attempt to manufacture deniability. But Kaeske will never get Hilton to admit that. What he can do is play the fraudster's video deposition to the jury. Hilton's former manager is utterly incredible. He divulges nothing about the scheme. All he does is plead the Fifth. But his guilty silence offers the jury a lesson almost as useful as the truth—yet another reason to distrust Dean Hilton, the owner of the boneyard.

Switching topics, Kaeske returns to the subject of Hilton's ignorance. The young hog baron doesn't know the name of the feed used at his Greenwood farms, or the ingredients in the feed. He doesn't know which antibiotics are used, or how much. He doesn't know the breed of the hogs in his barns, or their mortality rate, or about antibiotic-resistant bacteria. He knows next to nothing about the chemicals emitted by his lagoon, or whether hog farms have an effect on the environment. He's never read anything in the media or the scientific literature about the effects of hog operations on the community. But he does know that hog odor is not pleasant—at least some of the time.

When Kaeske interrogates Hilton about the control that Smithfield exerts over his farm, the young hog baron gets touchy again. He doesn't like the insinuation that he's Smithfield's underling.

"It's my farm," he says. "We make the decisions. It's my waste. We put it out. We try to be good neighbors. I don't want to be a bad neighbor. We've done the best to make efforts to improve that facility and do things correctly. And I think we've done that."

"Sir," Kaeske says, "I'm asking you a question about your contract. Your contract says that you've got to do things the way that Smithfield wants them done, right?"

The grower retorts: "My contract with Smithfield is no different than it would be with Prestage Farms or any other integrator. It's my farm. It's my responsibility. It's my waste."

At this point, Dean Hilton does something fascinating. He appeals to Judge Britt. "I don't know how else to answer the question, Your Honor."

"You might try just answering the question that's asked of you," replies the old judge.

After a few more fruitless thrusts and parries, Judge Britt delivers Hilton a stinging rebuke. "Several times I've had to try to encourage you to answer the questions that are asked of you. The way this thing works is this lawyer"—he points at Kaeske—"has the opportunity to ask you questions now. You must answer the questions he asks and nothing more. This lawyer"—he points at Jim Neale—"is going to have an opportunity to cross-examine you, and if he wants to bring something out that he thinks should be brought out, he can do that. But you must answer the question, and you don't dictate the way it goes. You answer the question he asks you."

"Yes, sir, Your Honor," says Hilton. "But—"

Judge Britt peers over his glasses. "But what?"

Everyone in the courtroom is still. No one has ever seen a witness contend with a judge.

"I'm just trying to answer the best I can."

"No, you're not doing it the way you're supposed to."

Dean Hilton isn't chastened. "I'm just trying to tell the truth."

By now, Judge Britt has run out of patience. "Young man, you either answer the questions that are asked of you, or I'm going to cite you for contempt of court."

"Your Honor," says Jim Neale, stepping in to avert a total meltdown, "the witness replied. Part of that is correct. And the admonition is heard loud and clear. He's attempting to answer the question, Your Honor. Understood."

The judge, however, is piqued. "Well, in the Court's observation, he's attempting to do his very best to evade the questions."

Even Neale seems taken aback. Gingerly, as if walking across glass, the defense lawyer asks Judge Britt to move on. The jurors, however, are riveted. They have just watched a jurist as mild-mannered as any who has ever sat on the bench threaten a witness with jail time.

When Jim Neale gets his turn, he labors to rehabilitate Hilton, showing him pictures of his wife and children and asking if they have to wear respirators to visit his hog barns or burn their clothes when they come home. The answers, of course, are no. Neale gives the grower latitude to talk about the pride he takes in growing hogs and contributing to the economy. He asks Hilton if anybody has ever told him they have a problem with odor from his farm.

"I've never been made aware or had a complaint filed," replies the young man.

Sitting at counsel table, Mike Kaeske knows this isn't true, and he has the documents to prove it. He takes it up on redirect. "Now, you said that you're very proud of the fact that in two and a half years you've had no violations and no complaints. Is that right?"

"I have not had any violation or complaints from my neighbors. No, sir," Hilton replies.

"Okay." Kaeske picks up a sheet of paper. "Why don't you know about this complaint that was made to the North Carolina Department of Environmental Quality, Division of Air Quality, in 2016?"

At first, Hilton tries to claim ignorance. "There was a call in there, but I don't think they ever found that there was any issue."

Kaeske doesn't budge. "Why don't you know about this complaint?"

"I wasn't made aware of it," Hilton concedes.

"Nobody made you aware of it, is that right?"

"That's correct."

"Do you know a gentleman by the name of Wesley Sewell?"

"No, sir. I do not."

"Did anybody from Smithfield ever tell you that a man by the name of Wesley Sewell who lives on Piney Woods Road was complaining about your hog operation?"

"No, sir."

Kaeske asks Hilton about another neighbor who voiced complaints about his hog farm, a man who lives across the street from Sewell. Hilton repeats his denial. Kaeske throws the name of a third complainant at him, then a fourth, each time eliciting the same stolid response.

With the young hog baron once again sporting an ostrich costume, Kaeske places Hilton's ignorance in a wider frame: "Smithfield never told you to go talk to your neighbors to find out how people are getting along with Smithfield's hogs, have they?"

Jim Neale lodges an objection, but Mike Kaeske doesn't care. He doesn't need an answer. The question was mostly rhetorical. It has never been Smithfield's practice to respond to community concerns with a flashlight. The company has always preferred a hatchet.

At last, Kaeske confronts Hilton about the bones. He's been biding his time, waiting for this moment, imagining the look on the man's face when he has to explain the skeletal remains. It's going to be *delicious*.

"Tell the members of the jury how many times in 2017 did Smithfield tell you that you had a problem with hog bones or carcasses or hides inside the Greenwood operations?"

The young hog baron plays dumb. "I don't remember any."

"You don't remember any?" Kaeske asks.

"No, sir."

Kaeske holds up the Smithfield letter he showed Don Butler. "Well, this one is in evidence, and it's from February of 2017. So that's pretty much a year later, right?"

Hilton is hemmed in. "Yes, sir."

Kaeske shows him the page. "And it says right here, 'carcasses, bones, hides not removed within 24 hours from the barn,' right?"

"That's what it says."

Kaeske's disbelief transmutes to incredulity. "And you don't know that that's one of *five times* in 2017 that on a site audit, the folks came in and said that there was—"

The young hog baron interrupts him testily. "No, sir. I do not."

"When did you all fire Dale Meyer?" Meyer is the manager who falsified spray records.

"I don't remember that exact date."

"Was it before or after this problem?"

"Before," Hilton concedes.

"So, this is already the new guy and he's still having problems with bones and hides and carcasses. Is that right?"

Dean Hilton is caught. He has nowhere to run. Yet, like Adam in the Garden, he passes the buck. "You know, you would have to ask Mr. Miller that."

"You don't know the answer?"

"I do not know the answer."

"Sir, you're involved in some twenty different hog operations, yeah?"

"Yes, sir."

"How many tens of thousands of Smithfield's hogs do you grow?"

"Hundred."

"One hundred thousand Smithfield hogs?"

Hilton nods, as if his mouth has suddenly stopped working.

Kaeske has a final question. It is a riddle with no solution. Either way, Hilton is damned. "And you run every one of those hog operations for Smithfield the same way that you run these, right?"

Hilton looks indignant, but his credibility is beyond repair. With two words, he concedes the field. "No, sir."

When Judge Britt excuses the young hog baron, he doesn't just exit the courtroom. He stomps out like a man scorned. His performance is so appalling, so unremittingly dreadful, that Mike and Lisa, Mona and Daniel and Linda will recall it in meticulous detail long after the trial is over. They will also remember the sympathy they feel for the other Hilton in the room: Dean's wife. She's sitting on Smithfield's side of the gallery, her eyes haunted and her face tear-stained.

She looks like she's been traumatized.

CHAPTER 33

THE FURIES

It is not light that we need, but fire;
it is not the gentle shower, but thunder. We need the storm,
the whirlwind, and the earthquake.
—*Frederick Douglass*

For all of Jim Neale's lawyerly tenacity and zeal, the former Army Ranger cannot stop the march of flames. Like Mark Anderson before him, his task in the courtroom is not merely challenging. It is damn near impossible. To defend Smithfield, Neale has to put lipstick on Dean Hilton's shit-stained pigs. He has to contend that acres of feces and urine left rotting in the open air doesn't stink enough to bother anyone. Not even the great Clarence Darrow could pull off such a feat. One by one, his witnesses go up in smoke. And those that don't—the neighbors that testify that the smell from the Greenwood facilities isn't frequent and doesn't really upset them—are devoured anyway, lost in the rubble of Smithfield's remorselessness and guilt.

There's Dr. Terry Coffey, Murphy-Brown's chief science and technology officer. He tries to bury the reality with science-speak, but crumbles when Mike Kaeske shows him pictures of gestation crates—cages Smithfield once used to contain its pregnant sows. The crates were so miserably cramped that the sows only had room to stand up and lie down, not to turn around. For some time, Smithfield contended that these cages were state of the art. But after much outcry, the company agreed to convert them to more humane group housing. It has already removed the cages from its company-owned farms, and it has offered incentives to its growers to upgrade to group housing, with a goal of full conversion by 2022. The question Coffey's testimony leaves in the mind of the jury: If Smithfield can transform its sow farms to eliminate the medieval cages, what is preventing it from dispensing, at last, with its lagoons and sprayfields?

Then there's Robert White Johnson, a retired lawyer who lives in Wilmington but owns land near the Greenwood facilities and hunts the forests down toward Route 53. He's a kindly gentleman, but his testimony seems overeager, as if his tale about smelling hog odor only once a year isn't the whole truth. On cross, Kaeske asks him about the insurance defense work he did for the Farm Bureau when he was practicing law. It turns out that Mr. Johnson is good friends with the Farm Bureau's president. Mike also asks him about a conversation he had with Mark Doby in which he admitted smelling hog odor about 10 percent of the time when he's out on his property. Eventually, Johnson concedes that he is not really clear how often he detects it. When Kaeske asks him how he would feel if he had to deal with hog spray blowing onto his land, and swarms of flies, and stink from dead trucks, and noise from delivery trucks, Johnson drops his guard. Yes, that would interfere with his enjoyment of the land, he says.

After Johnson, Neale calls Dr. Pam Dalton, Smithfield's odor expert. With her Nasal Ranger study banned from the courtroom, she is like an illusionist whose secrets have been disclosed to the audience. All her tricks are fool's gold. But after Jennifer Clancy's Chernobyl reenactment in *McKiver,* Smithfield has no other expert who can counter Shane Rogers. So, dutifully, Neale puts Dalton on the stand.

It does not go well for either of them.

On cross, Kaeske addresses her opinion that the human sense of smell is suggestible, that people often detect what they are expecting to detect—or told they should detect—and that those who have a smell suggested to them can become hypervigilant. It's a legitimate point, as far as it goes. But pushed too far, it becomes laughable.

With a touch of snark, Kaeske offers Dalton a hypothetical: "If I tell the members of the jury that it smells like chocolate chip cookies in here, and I say it long enough and loud enough, eventually, we're going to think it smells like chocolate chip cookies. Is that your deal?"

"People are going to start looking for the smell of chocolate chip cookies," she says. "And there are other odors, a perfume someone is wearing or something. They might start to think, well, that does smell a little bit like chocolate. It happens."

"So if we were to tell the members of the jury, I'm going to take you someplace and you're going to smell the best chocolate chip cookies ever. They've been baking chocolate chip cookies all day long, and those chocolate chip cookies are so good that every time I smell them my mouth waters. And then we walk the jurors into a Porta Potty sitting at a rock concert for three days, they're going to smell chocolate chip cookies, right?"

"No," Dalton concedes.

Kaeske asks her about the inspections she made of Greenwood 1 and 2 in June of 2016. He inquires what the hogs looked like in Greenwood 1. She says they looked mature, close to slaughter weight. He asks her the same about Greenwood 2, and she replies in kind.

"Now, expectations, you said, can affect people's sense of smell," Kaeske says. "Can expectations affect people's sense of sight as well?"

"We are much more confident about what we see than what we smell," Dalton replies.

"Okay," says Kaeske, almost gleefully. "The reason I ask is because on June 6th and June 7th, there weren't any hogs at Greenwood 2. Did you know that?"

Dalton is suddenly flustered. "No, I didn't. I mean, did I know that I was—"

"Standing right there and seeing fully grown hogs?" Kaeske finishes for her.

"No. It was a long time ago, and I must have been mistaken."

Kaeske goes on to elicit from her the reason her memory is faulty—that she didn't take any *notes* during her Greenwood inspections. Yet she was charging Smithfield $450 an hour.

Also, if she means to insinuate that the plaintiffs are biased in smelling hog odor, shouldn't she admit the bias in her research? While she's conducted many independent odor studies in her career, all of her swine-related work has been funded by Smithfield in connection to nuisance litigation—first in Missouri and now in North Carolina.

With Dalton twisting in the wind, Kaeske turns her into a weapon against Smithfield. He shows her the inventory records from Greenwood. In the month and a half preceding her two inspections, all six of Dean Hilton's barns stood empty. No hogs were present to defecate and urinate. No new waste was flushed into the lagoons. And when Smithfield *did* make a delivery to Greenwood 1 just before Dalton arrived, it didn't fill the barns to capacity. Instead, it placed 2,469 animals in barns capable of accommodating 3,800—a 35 percent reduction. So when Dalton assured the jury that she inspected the Greenwood facilities under normal operating conditions, that wasn't remotely accurate. She might not have been *aware* that Smithfield was choreographing her experience by depopulating and repopulating barns. But a marionette doesn't need to know that her puppeteer exists to be under the sway of the string.

In the wake of Dalton's demise, Jim Neale puts a medical doctor on the stand. Dr. Keith Ramsey is an infectious disease specialist who works with patients across the coastal plain. Ramsey offers a discordant—though not contradictory—opinion to Steve Wing's when he says that he has seen no evidence of increased respiratory illness or other maladies in patients living near hog farms. Ramsey admits that he is not an epidemiologist. He is speaking anecdotally, as a physician. He has never conducted a focused survey of his hog-farm-proximate patients, let alone published a peer-reviewed study on the subject.

What Ramsey *has* published is a study about the prevalence of MRSA (a bacterium found in hog waste) in the noses of patients admitted to hospitals in eastern North Carolina. According to the study, Duplin County residents did not show a higher MRSA prevalence than their counterparts outside the county. In analyzing the data set, Ramsey collaborated with Steve Wing and his team at UNC. They sampled roughly 100 MRSA-positive patients and 100 MRSA-negative patients, and they didn't find a linear correlation between the density of hogs in the area and MRSA in patients' noses. Their findings conflicted with other studies that *did* find a linear correlation, but they accorded with Ramsey's experience treating patients from down east.

On this basis, Ramsey offers a medical opinion to the jury: There are no human health effects caused by living close to hog farms.

Unfortunately for the good doctor, he is in the wrong courtroom. This isn't a lawsuit about the health effects of hog farms. This is a *nuisance* lawsuit. When it's Kaeske's turn to cross-examine the witness, he trains a spotlight on this point.

Dr. Ramsey is not an expert in all the ways that matter. He's not an expert on hog odor. He can't opine about whether that odor causes people to get angry or annoyed or embarrassed. He has no knowledge about whether frequent exposure to hog odor diminishes a neighbor's quality of life. Neither, frankly, is he an expert on those very *health effects of hog farms* that he doesn't believe exist, though he has shouldered his way into quasi-expert status with ad hoc commentary about his patients. In his deposition, he admitted that he couldn't name a single author in the world's scientific literature that has published findings on the subject, except for Steve Wing. All of this Ramsey concedes.

"Okay," Kaeske says. "Now, you know that nobody in this case is claiming that they've got MRSA or any other infection or any other disease that's caused by hog operations, correct?"

Ramsey nearly trips over himself affirming that. He doesn't seem to realize the question it raises in the mind of the objective observer: *Then why are you here?*

Since Kaeske can't ask that question directly without appearing intemperate, he does the next best thing. He dusts off all the public health literature that Ramsey has never read and throws study after study at the man until his illiteracy in the area is undeniable.

At this point, having established the doctor's near-total ignorance concerning the issues in the case, Kaeske cracks the spine on the MRSA study. It turns out the data set was highly constricted in size and geography. Out of some 500,000 people who were tested for MRSA in the hospital, only 240 patients made it into the survey. Also, the UNC team calculated the proximity of those 240 patients to hog farms using zip code data. They had no way to determine how many feet (or miles) people actually lived from the nearest CAFO. Even with those limitations, the survey showed that patients with MRSA were 4.76 times more likely to come from a zip code with a medium density of swine and 1.5 times more likely to report smelling hog odor at their homes. While patients who lived in zip codes with the *highest* density of swine didn't show that same correlation as the patients in the medium-density regions, the UNC team concluded that there *was* a direct link between MRSA and hog farms, just not a perfectly linear one.

Yet Dr. Ramsey made no mention of any of this in answering Jim Neale's questions. He sat in the witness chair and proceeded to diminish a study he participated in, a study that he reviewed before it was published, a study to which he affixed his own signature. All of that doesn't matter, apparently, because he doesn't agree with the study now.

Not when Smithfield is paying him $400 an hour to cast shade on Steve Wing.

If the Murphy men have a last line of defense in *Artis,* it is Christine Lawson, the state's hog farm inspector general at the Department of Environmental Quality, or DEQ. Her people administer the Swine General Permit, the regulatory regime governing all hog operations within the borders of North Carolina. They handle compliance with the growers, inspect the farms, and enforce the law. They don't address odor complaints. That is the province of the Division of Air Quality. But apart from that, Lawson is basically North Carolina's hog czar.

She is also the linchpin in Smithfield's argument that the industry is heavily regulated. If the Murphy men can prove that their growers are meeting every standard set by the legislature, how can the plaintiffs legitimately contend that Smithfield's actions have been wanton and willful and thus worthy of punitive damages?

In his direct exam, Jim Neale presents Lawson as an eminence in the field, a woman who understands better than anyone the burdens the law has placed on Murphy-Brown. Her degrees—bachelor's and master's—are in biological and agricultural engineering, and she completed all the coursework for a PhD. She has extensive experience with lagoons and sprayfields. After she joined the regulatory agency in 2006, she oversaw the tail end of research under the Smithfield Agreement. And in the nearly fifteen years since then, she has developed a widely recognized expertise in animal feeding operations in the state.

Lawson leads the jury through the legal requirements imposed by the Swine General Permit. Much of it is record-keeping: surveys of lagoon sludge, crop yield records, calibrations of waste application equipment, rainfall and irrigation records, analysis of lagoon waste and soils, and so on. There are substantive requirements, too, notably the prohibition on spraying when the land is saturated from rain and the "zero discharge" requirement—that no farm directly discharge waste from its facilities into the surface waters around it. She details the license that operators must obtain, the tests they must pass, and the requirement of continuing education—all reasons that grower-entrepreneurs like Dean Hilton often hire managers to handle the day-to-day operations.

She offers the jury a primer on the evolution of hog farm regulation in North Carolina: the 1995 setback requirement for residences, churches, and schools; the 1996 general statute establishing permits and inspections; the 1997 moratorium on new lagoons and sprayfields; the odor rules in 2000; and the five-year stages of the Swine General Permit. When it comes to lagoons and sprayfields, Christine Lawson is an apologist. She talks about nutrient levels and biological activity and the color of "healthy" wastewater with an almost sentimental affection.

Next, she gives the jury an overview of DEQ's approach to enforcement, which she calls "extensive and robust." If a notice of deficiency is not sufficient to correct a problem, her agency will seek civil penalties, and, if necessary, a court injunction. Jim Neale shows her a notice of violation issued to Gary Pridgen, the prior owner of Greenwood, for a wastewater discharge in 2011. DEQ takes discharges very seriously, Lawson says. While the farm owner is responsible under the law, the integrator (e.g., Murphy-Brown) often plays a role in enforcing compliance. DEQ always keeps the Murphy men in the loop about violations involving their growers.

Finally, Lawson explains the inspection process—the records review and the site visit. There is an investigative quality to a proper inspection. If the records don't add up, the inspector will interview the grower. But DEQ doesn't patrol the land and skies. Legal compliance is a collaborative process between her agency and the industry. Many of the regulations require the grower to self-report violations, such as when wastewater is discharged or the lagoon gets too full. The growers are expected to be honest. Lawson leaves the corollary unspoken: If the growers are dishonest, the entire system breaks down.

"Are you proud of the North Carolina regulations that govern the industry, ma'am?" Jim Neale asks, and Lawson answers in the affirmative. "Do you and your division do everything you can to enforce them uniformly and fairly?"

"Absolutely," replies the regulator. "This is my program. I take ownership in my job. I have personal integrity and this is what I do."

Before he concludes his exam, Neale hands her a bit of rhetorical polish to apply to his client. "You're in charge of ensuring or mitigating environmental risks imposed by hog farming in North Carolina, correct?" When she agrees, he asks, "Do you consider Smithfield to be a resource for you in helping you to accomplish that objective?"

Christine Lawson is more than happy to oblige. "As it relates to their company-owned and operated farms as well as their contract farms, yes."

To Mike Kaeske, who takes over the examination from Neale, this is balderdash, a textbook example of the far too cozy—and sometimes incestuous—relationship that regulators often cultivate with their rich corporate charges. It's a bureaucratic variant of the old saw about the fox guarding the henhouse. With soft-handed agencies like DEQ, it's more like the henhouse is tended by an old hound that is too sluggish and unsteady to prevent the fox's shenanigans. But before Kaeske gets to exposing Lawson's complicity, he needs to puncture her inflated ego.

"The permit that we're talking about is a water permit, right?" he asks.

"It's issued by the Department of Water Resources, yes, sir," replies Lawson.

"What it's meant to do is protect the water, right?"

"That's the primary purpose, yes."

Kaeske smiles inside. "You know this case is about odor?"

"I know that that's a large part of this case, yes, sir."

"Odor travels through the air?"

"Yes, sir, I'm aware."

"Okay," says Kaeske. "There is no air permit that applies to any swine facility in the State of North Carolina, correct?"

"There is no specific air quality permit that I'm aware of."

"So we're clear: The permit you were brought here by Smithfield to talk about today is a permit that applies to prevent discharges to the groundwater from animal waste, correct?"

Lawson admits this.

"Thank you, ma'am," says Kaeske. "As far as air permits are concerned, there are industries in the State of North Carolina that are obligated to have air permits, correct?"

If Lawson sees the blow coming, she can do nothing to stop it. "That's correct."

"The swine industry is not one of them?"

"No, sir."

"So, as much bacteria as the swine industry wants to put into the air, they're allowed to do it by the permit that you have, correct?"

"The permit we have does not address air quality issues," Lawson admits.

Kaeske absorbs the regulator's feeble energy and harnesses it to his advantage. He asks her a series of rapid-fire questions designed to elicit an eye-popping fact: The state's ten million market hogs annually excrete tens of billions of pounds of waste, all of which get flushed into the state's 3,300 lagoons at the state's 2,100 permitted hog farms, and all of which Lawson's agency is in charge of regulating. Of those 2,100 hog farms, some 700 to 800 are handled by only three inspectors in Fayetteville and another 800 are overseen by three inspectors in Wilmington.

"Makes for a busy year, yeah?" Kaeske inquires.

"Yes, sir," Lawson concedes.

But it gets worse. Her department's budget has suffered from the pruning axe wielded by the state legislature. Between 2011 and 2018, DEQ's share of appropriations fell from $205 million to $77 million. Some programs have been shifted to other agencies. Others have been cut entirely. One of the latter was the rapid response team that investigated fish kills in the Neuse River basin. Another was the well-drilling team, tasked with monitoring wells and assessing the quality of groundwater. Also, the Division of Soil & Water Conservation—the folks responsible for conducting hog farm inspections—is now under the aegis of Steve Troxler, the ag commissioner.

"That man," Kaeske says, "he's a straight-up elected official, right?"

"He is an elected official."

"So those folks report to an elected official, and that elected official gets almost all of his campaign contributions from the agricultural industry, right?"

"I don't know where his campaign contributions come from, but they do report to the commissioner of agriculture."

"And the commissioner of agriculture is a guy who promotes agriculture, correct?"

"That's part of his job," Lawson agrees.

Having established that her department is understaffed, underfunded, and subject to a biased command structure, Kaeske asks her about the honor system. "What are all the ways that folks can cheat with respect to their permit and you might never know about it?"

Jim Neale lodges an objection, but Judge Britt overrules it.

"All the ways someone can cheat?" Lawson asks.

"Yeah."

"Well, I'll come up with as many as I can. Although I'm not inclined to cheat, I'll do the best I can based on what I've seen. Falsification of records. That's number one."

Kaeske gets her to specify the many different records that can be falsified. There are quite a few of them. Hog growers can cheat on their lagoon samples, for instance, or their spraying records. In fact, Dean Hilton's former farm manager falsified records at Greenwood, yet DEQ's inspectors didn't uncover the malfeasance. The plaintiffs' team discovered it two years ago in the course of the litigation. All of this Lawson admits. After the Greenwood fraud came to light, she referred it to the State Bureau of Investigation, or SBI, because it was a criminal matter.

"Did you also say, 'And we need to take some enforcement action'?" Kaeske inquires.

Caught, Lawson stammers out a response. "I don't believe I . . . I don't think so."

Kaeske just stares at her. "Okay."

Suddenly, Christine Lawson is desperate to explain herself. "I think it would have been . . . the standard protocol would be that the regional office would investigate that. So it wouldn't come . . . it wouldn't come directly from my office. I was also told that I was not allowed to speak of it because it was provided by the court, and we were told not to talk about that at the time. So in early 2017, I was told not to talk about it because it was sealed by the court . . . We were told it was confidential information."

Kaeske gives her a disbelieving look. "You think Judge Britt issued some sort of order that prevents you from regulating someone?"

"No, sir," Lawson backpedals. "That is not what I'm saying."

"Well, I just want to make sure that I got it right," says Kaeske. "You're here to talk about how stringent these regulations are."

"Yes, sir."

"And I guess it is the case that these regulations are so stringent that someone can be referred to the State Bureau of Investigation for criminal activity, but no enforcement action be taken in two years against anybody with respect to the records violations."

The regulator has nowhere to run. "I suppose it's possible."

"Okay. Have you looked at the records?"

"Personally, no."

Kaeske feigns astonishment. "You haven't even seen them?"

"No, sir. I have not."

He hands her the document and points out where Hilton's former manager crossed out numbers and replaced them with fraudulent ones.

"This is the first time I've seen this," Lawson says.

"Okay. Well, how often do you think stuff like this happens?"

"I don't think it's common," replies Lawson.

"Is there a way for you to know?"

"The way that we know is we continue to do our compliance inspections."

Kaeske is tempted to laugh. "So here's what we've got. What we've got is the regulations that you're responsible for, and a known situation where somebody has violated those regulations by falsifying spray records. I guess what you're telling us is that the woman who is in charge of writing the permit and is at the top of the pyramid in terms of the regulations hasn't taken an opportunity to look at it to see how she might be able to prevent it in the future. Is that fair?"

Lawson replies with a Don Butler–style dodge. "I'm telling you that I have not looked at those specific records."

"Well, if you wanted to learn something about how this might happen in order to be able to prevent it in the future, the records are available, and you could look at them, correct?"

"That's correct."

Lawson is burnt toast. Everyone in the courtroom can see it. Kaeske could end his exam here, but he's enjoying himself too much. Besides, Christine Lawson is too insignificant a target to satisfy him. It's the entire flimsy, rotting state regulatory superstructure that he has in his sights. That superstructure is the final barrier that McGuireWoods has erected around the Murphy men. And Lawson is the guard at the gate.

So Kaeske presses in. He interrogates her about sludge records at Greenwood, revealing the glaring irregularities that her inspectors apparently missed. He shows her a photo depicting hardened lagoon sludge rising above the surface of the wastewater. The crust of feces was so thick that someone was walking on it as if it were a mud flat. The boot prints prove the point. Lawson doesn't really know what to say, so she sputters for a while before admitting that there should always be liquid on top of solids in a healthy, functioning lagoon.

The trial lawyer then shows her a picture of the shit-stained hogs inside Dean Hilton's barns. "Now, can you tell the members of the jury, do the conditions of these hogs in these pens, does this violate any of your regulations?"

"No," Lawson replies.

"Okay. Having barns that are that filthy, that doesn't violate any regulations, true?"

Neale raises an objection, but Judge Britt overrules him.

"Our regulations don't speak to the conditions inside the barns," Lawson confesses.

"You know the barns create odor that can get to the neighbors, right?"

"I know they can," says the regulator.

Kaeske shows Lawson another photograph. "Do you see here how all that manure is caked on those walls?"

"I do."

"No regulations that's violating, right?"

"Not that I'm aware of."

Kaeske next sets his sights on the inspection system. If the regula-

tions are threadbare with respect to animal treatment and CAFO clean-
liness, so is the system of enforcement. As Lawson tells it, a typical site
inspection— "compliance review"—takes two to four hours. Yet Kaeske
shows her a raft of inspection reports from Greenwood where the inspector spent only forty-five minutes at the farm, scribbled a few notes on the
form, and left. Sometimes, no one from the farm was even present when
the inspector completed the review.

"Now," Kaeske says, "the fact of the matter is that given the number
of inspections, the number of facilities to be inspected, the number of
inspectors that there are to do the inspections, and given the fact that
the keeping of the records is the honor system, it's tough to be thorough
with these inspections, isn't it?"

Lawson's discomfort is plain. "We're as thorough as we can possibly
be in what we do."

Kaeske asks her how many of the state's three thousand lagoons
holding all those billions of gallons of hog waste are leaking. She quib-
bles with him about semantics, says "leaking" isn't the right term. But
her techno-speak about lagoon design doesn't obscure Kaeske's point.
Most of the lagoons are over twenty years old. Lagoon liners can fail.
And if there is a crack or a hole in the lining, hog waste can leak into the
groundwater. But lagoon integrity is yet another issue about which her
"stringent regulations" are silent. Her inspectors don't drill holes to test
the liners and ensure that they are holding up. Her pronouncement that
properly designed lagoons don't leak is—after two decades without any
testing—an exercise in wishful thinking.

He asks her about hog farms that spray into the woods and into
creeks and waterways. Does DEQ use aerial surveillance to ensure that
the spray is staying within the permitted fields? Lawson says her department has deployed aerial surveillance on occasion, but her resources are
so tight these days, she rarely has the budget for it. The truth is—though
Kaeske doesn't raise it before the jury—the only outfit conducting rou-
tine aerial surveillance is Rick Dove's "Neuse River Air Force," the ragtag
crew of private pilots flying small planes out of New Bern and Chapel
Hill. Without their intelligence, DEQ would be clueless about the vast
majority of regulatory violations. But the regulators' ignorance isn't the
worst of it. Even when Lawson's people have evidence of a violation, they
are impotent to stop it.

Kaeske asks Lawson about an incident she witnessed from the air in 2011, where a grower was spraying into the woods. "From the air you could tell it was a violation?"

"When the spray was going into the woods, yes."

"And then you got on the ground and got to the site, and you could still tell that it was a violation, right?"

"Right."

"And with all of your power as the regulator, you couldn't stop the violation, right?"

"That's right."

After a brief pivot, Kaeske goes on: "And you had to get Kraig Westerbeek on the phone, and he had to give you permission to stop the violation that you, as the number one regulator of hog operations, were witnessing personally with your own eyes, right?"

Lawson admits it. When she couldn't reach the owner of the farm, she called Westerbeek, and he authorized her to turn the pump off. She had no power to intervene on her own to protect the environment despite being the head of the state's Department of Environmental Quality.

This concession—the last Kaeske elicits before Christine Lawson steps down—is the most excruciating she is forced to make. She is a proud woman, and she takes pride in her work. But like so many regulators in this era of mass deregulation and naked hostility from legislators like Jimmy Dixon, she doesn't have the backing of her employer, the state. Like the old hound guarding the chicken coop, she isn't swift or strong enough to defend the hens. The best she can do is bark at the fox, take a few swipes, and then retreat to the shadows to lick her wounds.

After four days of testimony, Jim Neale rests his case. Unlike Mark Anderson, he elects not to put Kraig Westerbeek on the stand. He leaves the jury with the testimony of a trio of neighbors, all of whom come off as strikingly anticlimactic. There is no way for Neale to repair the damage that Mike Kaeske has done to Smithfield's fortifications, no way to overcome the blaze that Steve Wing and Shane Rogers set with history and science, that Joyce Messick fanned with her compassion and pain, and that Don Butler and Dean Hilton fueled with their pathetic excuses and transparent bad faith.

There is nothing that the Murphy men can do now but wait. The same, however, is true of the plaintiffs.

The scepter of judgment is in the hands of the jury.

If the jurors cast their lots for Murphy-Brown—either with a hung jury, a defense verdict, or a small-dollar award—the hog barons might decide to try these cases for years longer, hoping to bleed Mona Wallace and Mike Kaeske dry. But if the jury comes back with a resounding verdict for the plaintiffs, there is a chance that Don Butler's vow might not hold. There's a chance the kingdom might bargain for peace.

After the lawyers deliver their closings, Judge Britt thanks the jury for their attentiveness and dispatches them to begin their deliberations. When the last juror disappears through the door just before 2:00 p.m. on August 2, a preternatural stillness descends on the courtroom, as if everyone has taken a collective breath. But the Murphy men don't intend to abide that silence. No, by God, they will speak. They have summoned the brightest stars in the Big Ag firmament to a roundtable at the State Fairgrounds. When the sun rises tomorrow, they will hold council. They will pontificate. They will pillory the judicial process.

And under their breath they will pray.

PART FIVE

THE RECKONING

No pain, no palm;
No thorns, no throne;
No gall, no glory;
No cross, no crown.
—*William Penn*

CHAPTER 34

RING THE BELLS

I do not care how dark the night;
I believe in the coming of the morning.
—*Dr. Joseph C. Price,*
Founder of Livingstone College,
Salisbury, North Carolina

**Raleigh,
North Carolina
August 3, 2018**

The rain falls like thunder on the plaza outside the Jim Martin Building, the huge storm-borne drops streaming from the sky in gouts. There are people milling everywhere outside the doors, hundreds and hundreds of them without shelter, all angling for the dwindling number of chairs in the auditorium and a live view of the dignitaries.

Among them is a willowy young woman twenty-two years old, with a charmer's smile, a spray of blonde hair, and a place at the front of the line. Her name is Karleigh Wike. At six-foot-four, she is even taller than her mother, Linda. After graduating from the University of Richmond this past May, she has spent a good deal of her post-collegiate summer assisting with the hog farm trials. She couldn't have designed a more ideal segue into the next season of her life—law school. Working alongside Mona and Mike, witnessing their debates in the war room, shadowing her mother and tending to the needs of the plaintiffs, she is light-years ahead of most budding 1Ls. She has witnessed high-stakes litigation from the inside, and she has come to love the thrill.

Her assignment this morning is the most unorthodox of her internship: to be the eyes and ears of the trial team at the National Ag Roundtable at the State Fairgrounds, a few miles west of the courthouse and down the road from the Wendell H. Murphy Football Center at NC State. Mona suggested the excursion, and Karleigh gamely agreed.

Heart thudding in her chest, she slips half-soaked into the auditorium and finds an empty chair at the rear. She recognizes a handful of faces in the swirling crowd of industry people, but she keeps her head down and hopes they won't notice her. She's dressed in street clothes, not a business suit, and she's wearing eyeglasses to disguise her features. A gifted confabulator, she strikes up a conversation with the man seated next to her. It turns out he is Joey Carter's pastor. The former police chief is sitting up front in the VIP section, as is Dean Hilton.

The dais is arranged in the shape of a U, with place cards for at least twenty. The politicians and Big Ag honchos arrive in a noisy horde, glad-handing for a minute or two before settling into their seats. Nearly all of them are white men well into the back nine of life: Mike Conaway, the Republican congressman from Texas and chairman of the House Agriculture Committee; Thom Tillis, the junior U.S. senator from North Carolina; Zippy Duvall, president of the American Farm Bureau Federation; Lieutenant Governor Dan Forest; Steve Troxler, the state ag commissioner; officials from Georgia, Texas, Delaware, and South Carolina; Dr. Kelly Zering from NC State; Dr. Howard Hill, a past president of the National Pork Producers Council; a platoon of representatives from the North Carolina statehouse, including Brent Jackson and Jimmy Dixon; and delegates from a host of industry groups. The only exception to this all-male recapitulation of bingo night at the Elks Lodge is a woman, Barb Glenn, from the National Association of State Departments of Agriculture. But she is just as pale and aging as the rest. The audience, too, is lily white. When Karleigh glances around the room, she sees only two or three people of color in the entire assembly.

The event's emcee is Congressman David Rouzer from North Carolina's Seventh Congressional District. He gavels in the meeting with a rousing call to arms: "There's one primary reason all of us are here. We have a crisis brewing in eastern North Carolina. That is a threat not only to North Carolina agriculture, but a threat to agriculture nationwide."

The other heavyweights soon add their drums to the beat. "I would describe what's going on as a blight," Steve Troxler declares, his face florid with disgust. "If we don't do something about this right now, there's not a farm in the country that is going to be safe."

Thom Tillis takes the council into the realm of fantasy, conjuring the joy of throwing the "trial lawyers" out of North Carolina. Not to be outdone, one of the state legislators likens the plaintiffs' lawyers to bank robbers, accusing them of trolling for dollars.

Eventually, Jimmy Dixon raises a finger. "I've been in some very special meetings with the highest levels of Smithfield Foods. And Smithfield Foods says that they will not settle. Thank God that Smithfield Foods has got the backbone to stand up to these lawsuits and not settle, which is what these plaintiff attorneys want."

Tucked away at the back of the room, Karleigh Wike bristles at these accusations. She has grown up around Mona Lisa Wallace. She knows the goodness in Mona's soul. She knows how hard Mona's team has fought for the neighbors, how many nights and weekends her mother has given up to bring these cases to trial. Although Karleigh doesn't know Mike and Lisa as well, she understands their motivation. The law is their livelihood. These cases need to pay for themselves. But that isn't what inspires them. They see in their clients' eyes what these politicos and powerbrokers are missing—the pain, the exhaustion, the years of travail. They hear the plaintiffs' cry for relief. And they want to deliver it.

These men, by contrast, have erased the plaintiffs from the picture. When they fret over the future of agribusiness, when they bemoan the treatment of Smithfield Foods, they aren't looking at Joyce Messick, the hospice nurse, or Jimmy Jacobs, the gardener. They aren't hearing the stories of Linnill and Georgia Farland and Woodell McGowan. They aren't looking at the little house on Beulah Herring Lane where Elsie Herring's mother lived her entire life. The neighbors are not a danger to anyone, except those standing in the way of change.

The rural way of life that these farmers so prize, it's *the plaintiffs'* way of life, too.

Across town at the federal courthouse, five floors beneath Judge Britt's courtroom, Maryclaire Farrington is playing cards with the *Artis* plaintiffs in the break room. She's a rising senior at Carolina now, and, like Karleigh, she has her eyes on law school. As she did during hog summer two years ago, she has been interning at Wallace & Graham since classes let out. Her role in the second and third trials has been more interpersonal than technical. She has been the chief liaison between the neighbors and the trial team. She has stayed with the neighbors at the Holiday Inn and sat beside them during the dead time between trial sessions, playing spades, telling jokes, and listening to them talk. She has fielded their questions when the proceedings have confused them, and when she hasn't known the answers, she has tracked them down. She has seen the joy on the plaintiffs' faces after they have testified—the resonant satisfaction of having told their truth, of knowing that the jury heard it. She has basked in the glow of their friendship and returned it in full measure. She loves the plaintiffs like her own family.

With the jury out, the *Artis* plaintiffs are on edge this morning, but they are trying not to show it. After the *McKiver* and *McGowan* trials, in which the jurors deliberated for days, no one on the trial team is expecting a verdict today. Nor, apparently, are the lawyers from McGuire-Woods. With the rally going on at the State Fairgrounds, the courthouse is mostly empty. When Linda Wike strides into the break room shortly after nine, the plaintiffs pay little attention to her. They have no reason to see her as a herald. But a herald she is.

"The jury's back," she says briskly. "We've gotta go."

"What?" exclaims Joyce Messick. "That's too quick!"

But Linda has no time to explain. "We've gotta go," she urges.

With the judge and the lawyers waiting, Maryclaire and the plaintiffs drop their cards and race toward the elevators. The ancient conveyor system takes its time escorting them to the seventh floor. Eventually, however, the doors slide open and they stream into the courtroom, fanning out into the gallery. Jimmy Jacobs sits beside Willie Messick; Jimmy's sisters, Gertie and Edna, take seats in front of them; and Joyce Messick and Lisa Blue claim the bench in front of the sisters. Maryclaire and the other clients take seats behind Jimmy, squeezing in beside Haven, Daniel, and Linda. The speed of the jury's decision leaves some of the team stranded—not just Karleigh at the roundtable but also Sam Egilman and Sophie Flynn at the apartments.

Mona Wallace is with Mike Kaeske at the plaintiffs' table. She watches as the ten women and two men make their way into the jury box. She maintains a pleasant expression, greeting them with her eyes and hoping for the best, but inside she is a tangled bundle of nerves. If her decades of trial experience have taught her anything, it's that plaintiffs' verdicts take time to negotiate. Rapid verdicts almost always go to the defendant. Perhaps this one is an exception. The optimist in her wants to believe that. But odds are their winning streak is over.

Beside Mona, Mike Kaeske is wearing a brave face. In truth, however, he is an anxious wreck. He can't fathom it. At the close of the evidence, he felt certain that the jury was his. Yet a minute ago, he had to grit his teeth and listen to Lisa Blue, always the good sport, congratulate Jim Neale on his probable victory. It was the classy thing to do. In a different case, Kaeske wouldn't begrudge him the win. But not here.

This case should be *theirs*.

The jury foreman is the former Marine. He has been attentive throughout the trial, jotting notes on his pad and studying witnesses like an armchair psychologist. Now, holding the verdict form, he watches them impassively, betraying nothing.

"Mr. Baker," says Judge Britt from the bench, "has the jury arrived at its verdict?"

"Yes, Your Honor, we have."

"You may hand the envelope to the clerk."

There is a soft rustle on the plaintiffs' side of the gallery as fingers black and white reach out and find each other, as shaking hands offer a squeeze. It's been this way on each of the three verdict days since April, the clients and their advocates united in body and spirit, as if to say "Whatever happens here, nothing can divide us. We are in this together."

In contrast to Mona and Mike, Joyce Messick is feeling encouraged. She has watched the jurors closely whenever she has been in the courtroom, and right now she is seeing something fascinating. They are not staring straight ahead, as they would be if they had decided for Smithfield. Their heads are tilted ever so slightly, and their eyes are glancing at her—no, not at *her,* but at all of them. It's as if the jurors are telling them, "We've got you. You have nothing to worry about."

After taking the envelope from the clerk, Judge Britt breaks the seal and begins to read. "Mr. Baker, as the foreperson of the jury, you have reported that the jury has arrived at the following verdict. With regard to issue number one, did the defendant substantially and unreasonably interfere with the plaintiffs' use and enjoyment of his or her property?"

For every plaintiff, the jury says, "Yes."

In the face of this unequivocal affirmation, Mona and Mike start to breathe again. Just as quickly, their minds shift to the question of value, how to monetize the harm. Yesterday, in his closing, Kaeske made a change to his script. He gave the jurors a number. He couldn't tell them about the statutory cap—that punitives and compensatory damages are linked—but he could give them a bull's-eye. He asked for $2 to $4 million per plaintiff, tying it to the cost of preventing future harm. On the matter of punitives, however, he left the question wide open. He reminded them of Smithfield's multibillion-dollar profits and asked them to deliver their verdict in the only language that the company would understand—the language of "Smithfield dollars."

"In response to issue number two," Judge Britt continues, "what amount of damages, if any, is the plaintiff entitled to recover from the defendant? You have answered, with regard to James Jacobs, $5 million."

Someone lets out a gasp. Mona blinks, as does Mike, while behind them in the gallery hands squeeze tighter still.

"With regard to plaintiff Jimmy Carr, you have answered $5 million. With regard to plaintiff Lucy Sidberry, you have answered $4 million. With regard to Joyce Messick, you have answered $3 million. And with regard to plaintiff Edna Allison, you have answered $3,500,000."

By the conclusion of the compensatories, the verdict is already over $20 million. That's $20 million that the statutory cap will not reduce, $20 million that will stand unmolested unless the judge finds some unlikely defect in the verdict. And that figure will increase to more than $23 million when Judge Britt realizes his mistake. Inadvertently, he skipped over Willie Messick's name. The jury awarded Willie $3 million, too, just like his sister, Joyce.

"In response to issue number three," the old jurist intones, "is the defendant liable to the plaintiff for punitive damages? You have answered with regard to James Jacobs, yes. Jimmy Carr, yes. Lucy Sidberry, yes. Joyce Messick, yes. Willie Messick, yes."

When the judge takes a breath, preparing himself to read the numbers, the neighbors witness something astonishing. The jurors are no longer just glancing at them; many are now meeting their eyes. A heavyset white woman in the back row smiles at Jimmy Jacobs. Two benches in front of Jimmy, Lisa is squeezing Joyce Messick's hand so hard that it's starting to hurt. But Joyce doesn't care. Her heart at this moment is as buoyant as the clouds on that resplendent day long ago when she rode her brother's horse, Bugshot, across land not yet despoiled by Wendell Murphy's hogs.

"And in response to issue four," says Judge Britt, "what amount of punitive damages, if any, does the jury in its discretion award to the plaintiff? You have answered: James Jacobs, $75 million. Jimmy Carr, $75 million. Lucy Sidberry, $75 million. Joyce Messick, $75 million. Willie Messick, $75 million. Edna Allison, $75 million."

The judge turns to the foreman. "Mr. Baker, I ask you, is that the verdict of the jury?"

"Yes, it is, Your Honor," replies the former Marine.

The final tally is $473.5 million. Just shy of half a billion dollars.

It is quite possibly the largest verdict in North Carolina history.

To ensure the jury is in agreement, the judge polls them individually. As the jurors raise their hands, one by one, affirming the integrity of the judgment, eyes moisten in the plaintiffs' gallery and fingers just as hastily wipe them away. Everyone is crying in unison, young and old, Black and white, the plaintiffs, the lawyers, the interns, Mona—who has always been a crier—and Mike, whose tears are a rarer thing. The surfeit of emotion is met with grins from the jurors, some of whom look like they want to leap over the bar and embrace everyone in sight.

As soon as the judge concludes the trial, the celebration begins. There are no words for a time such as this. People reach for each other and draw close, murmuring things no one will remember, as tears spill down cheeks and collect on chins and dampen the fibers of clothing.

Mike finds Haven and Lisa in the crowd, giving them an ineffable look that says "We did it!" And: "Holy shit!" This is the biggest verdict of his career. But it means so much more to him than that. Lives will be changed because of this. Futures will be rewritten.

A few feet away, Mona seeks out the plaintiffs, passing out hugs and felicitations. Her fondness for these people is boundless, as is her gratitude. They have been brave and steadfast, and indefatigably kind. They have waited so long and trusted so much. They deserve this victory more than any clients she has represented. Although the war isn't over and Smithfield has yet to concede, the verdict is a profound mercy.

Afterward, she shares a tender moment with her family, with Daniel, with Maryclaire, who is like a third child to her, and with Linda. There are so many other people Mona wishes could have been here to see this. Her husband, Lee, who has been her rock for forty years. Whitney, who has given her whole heart to this case, and Lane, who has contributed to this victory in her own way. John, her Steve Wozniak, a man whose brilliance knows no limits and whose poet's heart is always true. Mark Doby, whose gift for making friends supercharged so many of Mike's cross-examinations. Rick Dove, who has been fighting this battle forever. Tom Butler, whose testimony at the close of every case confirmed the truth of all that came before him. Steve Wing, one of the most compassionate human beings she has ever known. And Elsie Herring, the plaintiffs' Sojourner Truth, their fiercest warrior and truest ioneer.

Unbeknownst to Mona, many of these people are already in the loop, thanks to Mark Doby, who is playing the office clarion, dispersing the bonny news.

When the revelry spills out of the courtroom and into the lobby, Maryclaire breaks free of the group and rides the elevator down to the courthouse entrance. There, at the security gate, she greets Sophie and Sam, who are just arriving at the courthouse. She throws her wispy arms wide and embraces them with triumphal delight. She has never felt anything like this before, this sense of accomplishment, of fulfillment, of justice. None of them has.

Three trials. Three plaintiffs' verdicts. Over half a billion dollars.

Seven floors above them, an old man with silver hair combed back over his ears, the frame of a lumberjack, and the eyes of a clairvoyant is staring at Mona Wallace. It is Don Webb, the former hog farmer and ARSI activist. In his late seventies now, Don is unsteady on his feet. He has been unwell for some time, his heart on the cusp of failing him. But he has been a regular presence at these trials, as much as his health has allowed. He slow-walks toward Mona and spreads his arms. Mona melts into them and hugs him back with all her strength.

"I'm sick," Don says in his plainspoken way. "I'm not going to live much longer. You made me happy. Thank you."

＊

A few miles away at the State Fairgrounds, Karleigh Wike is staring at her phone, struggling to contain her emotions. She has been getting texts from her mother since the jury came back. She has shielded the screen from the people beside her, but her smile is irrepressible. The bells are ringing in Judge Britt's courtroom. The numbers defy her every expectation. She watches Jimmy Dixon as he blathers on, bashing the people she loves and bewailing the judicial system. She can't wait to see his reaction to the verdict.

The events at the courthouse don't stay secret for long. After the Duplin representative lapses into silence, Thom Tillis, the state's junior senator, lets out a sputter. "I believe while this hearing was going on, we've had an award of $75 million against the defendants," he says, with an air of incomprehension. Karleigh, who knows the actual figure, can't understand why he's off by so much. Perhaps, he read the message wrong. Regardless, $75 million is no mean sum. It's the *McKiver* and *McGowan* awards added together. And it sets Tillis off.

"Literally, while this meeting's going on another blow has been struck," he declares, "which is exactly why we can't leave this meeting and go back individually. We need to get to every commissioner of agriculture. We need to get to every speaker and senate leader in states that care about this issue. And we need to figure out how we continue to have this dialogue week after week after week until we pin them down. We need to prove to the people on the other side of this issue that we're bigger than them, that this is important, and we're going to stop them."

The atmosphere is suffocating, and Karleigh wishes she could escape. But she has a job to finish. She endures the rest of the bloviating and then trails the media into a press conference. With the cameras rolling and the rain pouring down, Steve Troxler paints the verdict as a skyfall event. "These nuisance lawsuits are just as harmful to agriculture as any disease that we could have in any of our industries nationwide," he says. "We need to raise public awareness. This is about your food supply."

Other denizens of Big Ag are equally grave. On the plaza outside, an industry man on the outskirts of the milling multitude is cradling his head in his hands as he talks on the phone. A friend of Mike Kaeske's who came to the trial for the closings happens to be there in the crowd. He sees the man's head droop, imagines the volcanic rage spewing through the phone line, and captures the scene with his camera. He sends the image through the data stream at light speed, and Kaeske, who wears his iPhone like an appendage, sees it instantly. In the months to come, this image will take on a kind of totemic significance for the hog farm team. It is a symbol of the old order creaking, cracking, convulsing, and crumbling down.

Before the *Artis* verdict, the hog barons acted like the princes of Troy, as if their walls would always hold. But no city is eternal, no reign without its end.

There is always a reckoning.

CHAPTER 35

DEUS EX MACHINA

The only question remaining, I think, is whether the
economic rights of the agribusiness corporation are more important
and will take priority over the basic human rights of people.
—*Professor John Ikerd, University of Missouri*

**Richmond,
Virginia
January 30, 2020**

The restaurant is called Shagbark. It's a farm-
to-table place on the West End of Richmond,
a late modernist fusion of reclaimed wood, exposed brick, plate glass, and globe lanterns,
with touches of rustic chic—antler chandeliers
hanging from the ceiling and heartwood pri-
vacy dividers mounted on iron rollers. Although most patrons sit in the
main dining area, there is a space in the back for larger parties. It is there
that Mona's team gathers on a wintry evening just after the Year of the
Pig—2019—gives way to the Year of the Rat—2020.

Mike and Haven claim one end of the cloth-draped table, and Mona
and Whitney join them on either side. John Hughes and Linda Wike
pair up, as they have for a decade at the office, with Linda's daughter, Karleigh—now in her first year at Campbell Law School—sitting
beneath the tall windows, and Daniel Wallace and Mark Doby rounding out the other end. Lisa Blue slips in beside Whitney, and Tom Butler,
tonight's guest of honor, squeezes in beside her.

The mood among the team is cheerful and unhurried. After years
of sharing the same trench, they can almost finish each other's thoughts.
Like any family, their relationships are complex. They have had their
squabbles and disagreements. But they have always found a way to band

together again, to exchange penance and absolution and move on with-out bitterness. Some of them would describe their affection as love, oth-ers as respect. But whatever its strain, it is evident in their interactions, their easy smiles and familiar banter, their inside jokes and storytelling. Tonight, however, something darker lurks just beneath the surface. It is the shadow of a question none of them can answer.

How will this story end?

After the high-water mark of the *Artis* verdict, no one anticipated that the following year and a half would be such an arduous slog. The $473 million award—reduced to $94 million by the statutory cap—accomplished what Mona and Mike had hoped: It forced the Murphy men to change. That autumn, Smithfield made sweeping improvements to its production practices, installing refrigerated dead boxes, replacing high-powered spray guns with subsurface injection and low-pressure irri-gation, and limiting its trucking schedule to daylight hours. Smithfield also announced the planned conversion of 90 percent of its lagoons into covered biogas digesters. The company's publicists spun these changes as an outgrowth of a broader sustainability initiative designed to cut green-house emissions across its supply chain, not a concession to the cudgel of $550 million in jury verdicts. But the targeted nature of the improve-ments, the tens of millions of dollars required to deploy them, and the timing of the announcement suggest otherwise.

The *Artis* verdict also snapped Don Butler's heraldic vow like a wish-bone and brought the hog barons to the bargaining table. At the joint request of the parties, Judge Britt modified the trial schedule to allow the lawyers to pursue settlement talks. Although the negotiations took place behind a veil of secrecy—lawyers are duty bound not to discuss such things—it is easy enough to imagine their general shape. Smith-field's lingua franca has always been cash, and three angry jury verdicts written in the same tongue amounted to an industry-wide riot act. With the horror of the *Artis* award lingering in the minds of the hog barons, the probability was high that the kingdom would make the necessary concessions and end the hemorrhaging.

But the Fates, in their caprice, turned against the plaintiffs. The Fourth Circuit Court of Appeals intervened.

In the last week of September, a three-judge panel in Richmond, Virginia, heard arguments on the gag order imposed by Judge Britt, limiting out-of-court statements by the parties and their lawyers. The panel could not have been more favorable to Smithfield. It included two luminaries of the conservative legal movement, J. Harvie Wilkinson and G. Steven Agee. At the hearing, Wilkinson lit his thinning hair on fire in protest of what he saw as an indefensible abridgment of free speech. His diatribe from the bench was not the same as a decision. But the signal it sent to the hog barons was as bright as a beacon of fire. The appellate court was singularly displeased with the Honorable William Earl Britt. How this turn of events played into the negotiations is anyone's guess, but at some point, the parties' attempt to resolve the cases broke down, and they found themselves back in the courtroom.

There were two more trials that fall and winter: the *Gillis* trial just before Christmas, and a second trial in the *McGowan* case in early 2019. After the *Artis* thunderbolt, the Murphy men benched McGuireWoods—as if the verdicts were somehow the fault of their attorneys, not the consequence of their own malfeasance—and brought in a new defense lawyer from none other than Dallas, Texas, Mike Kaeske's hometown. Neither Mona nor Mike had any idea how this Texas lawyer had managed to hitch his wagon to the hog farm gravy train. But they knew him from past asbestos cases. Indeed, some years ago, Kaeske had delivered the man a $9 million thumping at trial. The plaintiffs' team also knew something else. The Texas lawyer had an intriguing history with nuisance lawsuits—as a *plaintiff.* He had spearheaded a noise nuisance suit against a motocross track near a rural property he owns, and he had succeeded in shutting the operation down.

When the defense lawyer showed up in Raleigh, he made it his mission to bring Kaeske's "shitshow" philosophy of trial practice to life. He was fortunate. He didn't have to contend with Judge Britt. The elder jurist had taken a health-related break from the bench and appointed David Faber, a federal judge from West Virginia, to preside in his place.

From the beginning, it was apparent that Faber saw the cases through a different lens. His rulings had the effect of tilting the scales in Smithfield's direction, especially on the question of punitive damages. The new judge relegated all mention of the hog barons' willful indifference to the plaintiffs' suffering to a second phase of the trial. He barred Kaeske from talking about Smithfield's executive compensation or Chinese ownership. And he allowed Smithfield's lawyers to distinguish between the behavior of the Murphy men *before* the Smith-field merger in 2000 and their behavior *after* Joe Luter took the reins of Wendell Murphy's empire. Then, after all the evidence on punitives was in, Judge Faber ruled it insufficient, taking the matter out of the jury's hands. In spite of these headwinds, Kaeske didn't allow his nemesis from Texas to rankle him. Instead, he focused his energies on the only people in the courtroom whose approval he needed to win: the jurors.

In the end, they handed him the verdict.

Unlike the *Artis* jury, however, the award they delivered was small, just over $100,000. Faber's ruling on punitives limited them to annoy-ance and discomfort damages, and the plaintiffs on the slate—by Smith-field's design—were those farthest away from the company-owned Sholar Farm. Had the jury been evaluating the claims of Mary Tatum, Annjea-nette Gillis, or Allen Johnson, people who have lived for decades beside the five hog barns, two lagoons, and Olympic-stadium-sized sprayfields, they might have made a different calculation.

The Murphy men had something else going for them in *Gillis,* some-thing that no doubt influenced the jury award. For the first time, their pleas of good corporate citizenship didn't ring hollow. The improvements Smithfield had made to the Sholar Farm gave Gregg Schmidt and Kraig Westerbeek something to crow about on the stand, and crow about it they did. Schmidt told the jury about the refrigerated dead box that Smithfield had installed over the summer. He talked about the revised trucking schedule that eliminated night visits and the expanded feed bins that reduced the frequency of feed truck runs. Westerbeek gave the jury a tutorial about the low-odor AerWay spraying system that Smith-field put in place "to try to be responsive to neighbors." He droned on about the money the company had spent testing covered lagoons and biogas digesters, and he described the digesters currently installed on a hog operation owned by Murphy Family Ventures, Wendell and Dell Murphy's family shop.

Along with turning the Murphy men into champions of environ-mental sustainability, the changes at the Sholar Farm gave their new defense team a strategic advantage. Unlike Mark Anderson and Jim Neale, who were forced to contend that the plaintiffs' nuisance claims were manufactured or overblown, the lawyer from Dallas had the grounds to argue that, whatever inconvenience the odor might cause, Smithfield was working hard to address it.

Nevertheless, even with Judge Faber's favorable rulings and a plaintiff group engineered by the defense team, even with mitigation testimony about refrigerated dead boxes, daytime-only truck runs, low-odor spraying, and covered lagoons, Smithfield couldn't win.

With the score now four to zero in favor of the plaintiffs, Smithfield threw not only the contents of the kitchen sink but also the sink itself into the second Joey Carter trial. Fortunately, by the time the proceedings commenced, Judge Britt was back on the bench, as vigorous and quick-witted as ever. Also, the second *McGowan* trial featured the neighbors who had suffered the most from Carter's hog operation: Linnill Farland, the barber, and his quilting wife, Georgia. And this time, Mike Kaeske had the missing Soil & Water file in hand *before* he put the former police chief on the stand. As it turned out, Joey Carter was not as disastrous a witness as Dean Hilton. But he could not escape the fact that he knew before he brought in his first hogs that the neighbors didn't want them there. He knew, yet he didn't give a damn.

As in *McGowan 1,* the jury held it against him.

But the verdict did not come easily. Among the jurors, there was a defector, someone who had bought the Texas lawyer's pitch and decided to hold the rest hostage.

While most state courts permit up to three jurors in a civil case to disagree with the others without blowing up a trial, the federal system requires unanimous consent. The rule of unanimity offers the defense an advantage. To prevail, a plaintiff must win over every juror, while the defense can hang the jury by convincing only one person to dissent.

The jury in the second *McGowan* trial deliberated for three days. For the lawyers camped out at the courthouse, the hours passed like an iceberg adrift. In the vacuum of unknowing, Mona held fast to optimism, while Mike wrestled with doubt. No one wanted to talk about what was happening. But everyone understood the dynamics taking place in the jury room: the arguing and cajoling by the majority, the pleas for the holdout to cave. There were moments when the lawyers genuinely thought the jury would hang, that Mike's nemesis from Texas would collect his scalp and the hog barons would get their victory lap. But the neighbors down in the break room—all of them Black but one—never lost faith. They spent the long days in a posture of song and prayer, with bubbly Lendora Farland wearing the pastoral shawl for her community.

At last, the jury returned its verdict. It was clearly a negotiated compromise, a far cry from the ringing affirmation of *Artis*. But to the Farlands and the Carters, the Carltons and the Davises and Barbara Gibbs, it was cause for rejoicing. The total award, including compensatory and punitive damages, was $420,000. The hog barons no doubt danced a sprightly jig behind closed doors. But in the courtroom, a loss by a lesser margin is still a loss. After five consecutive plaintiffs' verdicts, the media gave the Murphy men a proper thrashing. And the McGowan neighbors left Raleigh with the pride of having struck another blow to the crown. How many more the hog kingdom could endure was anyone's guess.

Signs soon emerged that this one might be the last.

Smithfield filed a motion requesting that Judge Britt stay all future trials until the Fourth Circuit decided its appeal of the first verdict. The company also signaled its interest in resuming mediated negotiations. In response, John Hughes wrote that the stay should be conditioned upon a global resolution of all cases; otherwise, the trials should proceed. No word about the substance of these settlement negotiations leaked to the press, but in early June, after a status conference that the court sealed off from the public, Judge Britt entered an order freezing the entire litigation until the Fourth Circuit ruled on Smithfield's appeal.

The Fourth Circuit scheduled argument for January 31, 2020.

✳

In the American legal system, the last refuge of the damned is almost always the court of appeals. It is in these quiet corridors and exalted courtrooms bedecked with marble, brass, and polished wood that some of the brightest lawyers in the United States spar over the minutest points of civil procedure and the meaning of the Bill of Rights.

Since the appellate courts handle upwards of 50,000 cases a year, most parties adhere to the precept of parsimony in drafting their petitions. They focus on their strongest objections, the two or three issues that, if the trial judge had decided differently, might have changed the outcome at trial. The Murphy men, however, took a dragnet approach. They raised *seven* points of appeal, any of which, if granted, could scuttle the *McKiver* verdict and require a new trial.

The opening line of their appellate brief boomed like a cannon shot: "This suit is the tip of a spear aimed at North Carolina's agricultural economy." They attacked the punitive damages awards, contending that Judge Britt should have barred them like Judge Faber did in *Gillis*. They complained that Britt committed a reversible error when he allowed Mike Kaeske to tell the jury about the profits and executive compensation at Smithfield's Chinese parent, WH Group. They challenged Britt's dual rulings on expert witnesses—his decision to permit Shane Rogers to testify about Pig2Bac while prohibiting Pamela Dalton from testifying about her Nasal Ranger study. They contended—with unselfconscious irony—that Mona Wallace and John Hughes were wrong when they decided *not* to sue the growers in the federal suits. The growers, said Smithfield's lawyers, are necessary parties because the jury verdicts have consequences under their grower contracts. A farm found to be a legal nuisance could lose all of its hogs.

This argument entailed a fascinating admission. The industry's long-standing use of its "family farmers" as a human shield was no longer clandestine. It was visible for all to see. Also, the argument was a sleight-of-hand. What Murphy-Brown elected to do with the contracts of Billy Kinlaw, Joey Carter, and Dean Hilton after the verdicts landed was the decision of Murphy-Brown, no one else.

Yet this "necessary party" argument was hardly the most brazen in Smithfield's petition. On the basis of what might be the most abstruse technicality in North Carolina law, the hog kingdom's lawyers contended that HB467 (the 2017 Right to Farm Act bill ginned up to limit the damages available in nuisance suits) should have applied to the pending suits. To grant this argument, the appellate court would have to ignore the fact that the state House *removed* the retroactivity language from the bill when it passed Amendment One by two votes. The judges would also have to ignore the statements made by Jimmy Dixon and Brent Jackson on the floor of the General Assembly, clarifying that HB467 would only apply to *future* cases.

But the hog barons are nothing if not shameless. It's been their stock in trade since way back in 1999 when Wendell Murphy alleged without evidence—and then quietly backed away from the claim—that the lagoon breach at his own Vestal Farms operation, a spill that dumped 1.5 million gallons of hog waste into nearby wetlands, resulted from sabotage by environmental extremists.

Why not argue that HB467 means the opposite of what it says?

The plaintiffs struck back, and hard. "This suit is not the tip of any spear, and North Carolina's economy will be just fine," they argued in their response brief. "This is a private nuisance action where both sides presented their evidence to a jury, and the jury reached a verdict after weighing that evidence. The judicial process did exactly what it was supposed to do."

Their allies, too, brought their firepower to bear. Amicus briefs poured in from nonprofit organizations, activist groups, scientists, professors, and public interest law firms across the country. These "friends of the court" took the portrait of the hog wars offered by the plaintiffs in their brief and expanded it out into a Hudson River School panorama. The Waterkeeper Alliance described the hog barons' history of environmental abuse and the state's anemic—and often complicit—system of regulation. A consortium of public health experts and epidemiologists laid out the scientific consensus about the health risks of hog CAFOs and summarized the scorched-earth tactics employed by the industry to suppress research, intimidate and discredit scientists, subvert academic leadership, and abolish funding sources. And legal impact groups like Public Justice, the American Association for Justice, and Food & Water Watch decried the absurdity of Murphy-Brown's position on HB467 and the notion that the growers should have been sued.

Alongside this macro-level context, a pair of grassroots amici from down east—NCEJN and REACH—recounted the intimate story behind the conflict, the tale of the neighbors as they organized, collaborated on public health research, mounted publicity campaigns, and petitioned their representatives for justice, and as, time and again, the Murphy men prevailed.

Like they did during the trial phase, Mona and Mike prepared indefatigably for the appeal. Instead of arguing the case themselves, they hired an appellate specialist, Tillman Breckenridge, to captain the effort. They subjected him to hog farm boot camp, working his intellect from every angle. Kaeske even brought him out to his Park City mountaintop to moot the hearing. A veteran of many skirmishes in the higher courts, Tillman is every inch the equal of the man Smithfield retained to upend the verdict—the former solicitor general of Virginia, Stuart Raphael. In keeping with the racial fault line that has run between the neighbors and the industry for thirty years, Breckenridge is Black and Raphael is white.

Now, after months of anticipation, the day of the appeal is almost here. As the hog farm team tucks into its duck confit, Scottish salmon, and filet mignon at Shagbark, the law clerks at the court of appeals are making their last preparations. *Joyce McKiver v. Murphy-Brown* will be one of the first cases on the morning docket. Everything the neighbors and their lawyers have achieved over seven years is hanging in the balance. In their own way, each of the people at the table is wondering the same thing: Will this evening be remembered as a death watch or the twilight before the dawn? Three judges hold the scales. But contrary to popular myth, justice is never blind. It is gloriously—and often ignominiously—human.

This is the source of the chill in the room at Shagbark. The same conservative lions who scrapped the gag order like a piece of rotten meat, Harvie Wilkinson and Steven Agee, are on the panel tomorrow.

The assignment isn't a coincidence, or the consequence of some nefarious conspiracy. The appellate courts value continuity. Still, the plaintiffs' lawyers had hoped for a fresh bench. They have come so far together. They have humbled the hog barons, brought a hegemonic corporation to heel, and sparked what may well become a second industrial revolution in hog production. Whatever the Fourth Circuit decides, in these ways at least their five hundred clients and the people of North Carolina have already won.

Yet a cleaner supply chain is not the same as restitution. Elsie Herring will never get back the years she watched her mother and brother suffer from Major Murray's spray. Linnill Farland, now in the twilight of his life and battling cancer, will never use his barber shop again. His wife, Georgia, will never outlive the indignity of finding hog feces on her clothesline or watching Lendora's friends find other places to play. Daphne McKoy's children will never know the innocence of a hog-free childhood. Violet Branch will never recover the use of her poisoned wells. The stories among the plaintiffs are legion, and all are intensely personal. The remedy for their suffering cannot be limited to the future. It must address the past.

The hog kingdom must pay what is owed.

Yet on this evening, with their hearing before Wilkinson and Agee looming, it is hard for even the most inveterate optimists on Mona's team to shake the sense that the die is cast, that the verdicts are doomed, not by the power of Smithfield's arguments or by the weight of natural justice, but by an arbitrary flip of the coin.

Mike Kaeske captures this mordant sentiment midway through the meal. He's holding forth with his usual devil-may-care jocularity, when, suddenly, he leans in, eyes bright and sad.

"Sixty unanimous jurors found in our favor," he says, "and two judges could take it away."

CHAPTER 36

HIGHER LAW

So often in life, things that you regard as an impediment
turn out to be great good fortune.
—*Ruth Bader Ginsburg*

Richmond,
Virginia
January 31, 2020

There is a hush that attends the day of judgment, like the early morning quiet of a church-
yard, or the stillness of a monument caped with
stars. In generations past, there was a priestly
aspect to America's legal system, the belief that
human laws had their origin in divine law, and
that judges were men of the cloth, arbiters of truth, dispensers of justice, purveyors of peace. Even today, when gods and angels have been
relegated to courthouse friezes, the gavel still inspires a vestigial reverence in its supplicants. The law is the liturgy of modern America, one of
the last bastions of civic religion. Not every lawyer feels the hush when
they walk through the doors of a courthouse, but many do—the sense
that the pageantry has a higher purpose, that even if all the trappings
of bygone devotion are stripped away and replaced with a purely secular
creed, there is one article of faith still worth clinging to: the pursuit of
equal justice under law.

Mona Wallace is such a lawyer, as are Mike Kaeske and John
Hughes, Lisa Blue and all the rest. They feel it when they enter the
Lewis F. Powell Jr. Courthouse just shy of eight in the morning on the
last day of January 2020. They feel it as they muster in the lobby outside

the law library, as friends gather around them, exchanging smiles and hugs. There is Rick Dove, with his grizzled bearish face and laconic grin; Larry Baldwin, Rick's consigliere, who ditched his field clothes for a suit; Tom Butler, with his gentle drawl and messianic blue eyes; and Elsie Herring, the solitary plaintiff who made the trip from down east, looking regal in a brown-and-white dress with floral accents, her neck graced with a silver scarf. They feel it as they move together toward the antique elevator and stairwells, as they make the climb to the third floor.

The Blue Courtroom is just down the hall.

The vaulted chamber is an encomium to walnut. The tables for the attorneys and clerks, the seating in the gallery, the judges' bench, and the ornate paneling and molding on the walls, all are fashioned out of dark wood polished to a gleam. The double doors through which Mona and the team pass are plated with brass and swaddled in crimson leather. The space is illumined by four painted candelabra and blessed with natural light from tall windows that overlook the grounds of the state capitol. The only thing blue in the courtroom is the carpet, but the color anchors the space, imbuing it with soft light, like water in a harbor scene.

Mona claims the first bench on the right side of the gallery, making space for Whitney and Elsie Herring. Mark Doby and Daniel Wallace slide in beside Whitney, and Rick Dove occupies the bookend space by the aisle. Larry Baldwin sits behind Rick, with Mike Kaeske and Haven and Lisa Blue spreading out across the second row, and Linda, John, Karleigh, and Tom Butler taking the row behind them.

As the minutes pass, people crowd in around them until the gallery is full. Smithfield's side of the chamber is populated by familiar faces, among them Don Butler, Joey Carter, and Andy Curliss from the Pork Council. The atmosphere is charged, crackling with hidden feeling.

The courtroom deputy and the law clerks arrange the bench for the judges, placing name cards and binders before the high-backed chairs— all crimson leather like the courtroom doors. The seniormost judge, Harvie Wilkinson, is accorded the place of honor at the center, with Judge Agee on his right hand, and Judge Stephanie Thacker, an Obama appointee, on his left.

In an undertone, Mike Kaeske says, "I feel like one of those hogs waiting to go into the slaughterhouse."

When the judges appear, the courtroom deputy cries, "All rise!" As one, the assembly climbs to its feet and looks on as the trio of black-robed jurists ascend the creaky steps and settle into their seats.

After thirty-six years on the court of appeals—seven as chief judge—Harvie Wilkinson is a man at home on the bench. He is in his sunset years at seventy-five, his narrow head mostly bald, his bespectacled face craggy with wrinkles, but his smile still carries a hint of his departed youth. He greets the lawyers and the audience, and then calls the first case—a civil rights appeal, which occupies the next half hour. The circuit judges are whip-smart and engaged, peppering the lawyers with questions. The lawyers, in turn, do the required dance, offering their ablest replies. And then, just like that, the case is over, and the lawyers are shuttling toward the doors, making way for Stuart Raphael and Tillman Breckenridge to claim the counsel tables.

Raphael takes the podium first. He has the build of an Irish terrier, short and wiry, with an everyman face that would disappear in any lineup. But what he lacks in presence, he makes up for in wit. He speaks with the clipped cadence of the Beltway, and his words come out as if under a head of steam. Like all appellate attorneys, he is acutely conscious of the time. He knows that before long the light on the timer will turn amber, then red. He comes out of the gate like a greyhound. With Wilkinson and Agee before him, he sounds almost giddy.

In litigation parlance, a "hot bench" is an active judge. This bench is sizzling from the start. The circuit judges recognize the enormity of the stakes. Instead of waiting for Raphael to chart a course, Judge Agee steers it for him, inquiring why the plaintiffs should have sued the growers too. Raphael holds up Billy Kinlaw's contract, arguing that the jury's finding of nuisance caused Murphy-Brown to shut down the farm.

Judge Wilkinson, however, interjects a note of skepticism. "The point is made," he says in a reedy voice, "that whatever happened to Kinlaw was the result of the independent decision on the part of Murphy-Brown to stop dealing with Kinlaw."

This is precisely what Mike Kaeske explained to the jurors in every trial. The growers' fate did not belong to them. If they held Smithfield liable and Smithfield chose to shut down the farm, that choice—and its consequences for the farmer—would be on Smithfield alone.

But Raphael refuses to concede. He insists that the verdict left Billy Kinlaw in breach of his contract. There is truth in this. If a grower violates the law, he is technically in default, and the contract gives Smith-field the authority to terminate the relationship. But having authority is not the same as exercising it. Nothing in a grower's contract *requires* Smithfield to depopulate a hog farm after a nuisance verdict. Enforcement is a matter of discretion.

There's another dimension to the issue too, Wilkinson suggests. If the court were to adopt Raphael's position, it would not only overturn the jury verdict; it would strip the federal courts of jurisdiction. Unlike the company, Murphy-Brown, which is a resident of Virginia, the growers are citizens of North Carolina, like the plaintiffs. Requiring the growers to be named in the case would destroy the parties' diversity, the only basis for federal court involvement. And the Fourth Circuit has been reluctant to rescind jury verdicts when jurisdiction is on the line.

The former state solicitor general makes an effort to recover, spouting off case citations, but the old circuit judge has lost interest. He wants Raphael to talk about punitive damages.

So the attorney pivots and conjures an image of Billy Kinlaw, hallowed farmer and man of the soil. He says, in effect, "Tell me what this old farmer did, in following his contract, that was wanton and willful and indifferent to the rights of his neighbors." It would be a powerful point, if it weren't a naked bait-and-switch. Billy Kinlaw wasn't a defendant in the case.

Again, Wilkinson is dubious. "There was a lot of evidence before the jury about waste and the treatment of waste," he intones, "particularly about the fact that the waste was stored in open-air pits for a good long time, and the fact that you allowed the conditions to persist when some kind of cover to the open-air pits would have significantly mitigated it."

Back in the gallery, the plaintiffs' lawyers are glancing at each other, barely suppressing their surprise. They aren't sure what this is yet. They need to see how it plays out. But they are beginning to wonder if the tectonic plates are shifting beneath them.

On the defensive, Stuart Raphael commits a faux pas. He interrupts the circuit judge. If Wilkinson is miffed, he doesn't show it. But neither does he concede the right-of-way.

"In other words," the judge goes on, "there were all kinds of conditions. They weren't hidden conditions. They were open and obvious conditions, and yet they were allowed to persist over a good many years."

Raphael rejoins that the plaintiffs never complained. But Wilkinson is unconvinced. "The question I have is whether you can assert control in the contract to your advantage, and then, all of a sudden, back away from the control when it comes to a verdict and say, 'Oh, well, we had nothing to do with it'? I'm just wondering whether you're wearing two masks."

For the first time, Raphael's voice takes on a hint of strain. He directs the court to the Smithfield Agreement and the determination by NC State that none of the alternative waste disposal technologies were economically feasible. "Murphy-Brown was *entitled* to rely on that finding by the designee and on the attorney general agreement." "So the question is, 'What happened at Kinlaw that would warrant punitive damages?' They don't have an answer to that."

Rhetorically, it's an effective riposte, and the Smithfield Agreement is so deep in the weeds of the appellate record that none of the judges makes a comment about it.

At the urging of Steven Agee, Raphael moves on to the expert question. He inveighs against Judge Britt's decision to allow Shane Rogers to testify uninhibited while constraining Pamela Dalton. As soon as Raphael takes a breath, Judge Wilkinson sows another seed of doubt. The trial wasn't short, he says. It lasted four weeks. The standard of review is abuse of discretion—a very high bar. It is not for the appellate court to second-guess Judge Britt. The only question is whether Judge Britt rendered substantial justice.

Here, Judge Thacker adds her voice to the mix. While Smithfield didn't get to call Pam Dalton, it *did* have an expert to counter Shane Rogers. It had Jennifer Clancy. That's right, Judge Wilkinson affirms. Smithfield had Clancy.

By now, Stuart Raphael must realize that he is foundering, for his voice takes on a rapid-fire quality. He raises the 2017 Right to Farm Act.

"But the Right to Farm Act doesn't apply here," Wilkinson replies, leveling yet another broadside. "You would agree with that, wouldn't you? This is a pending case!"

Raphael shakes his head vehemently. "That's the entire issue. If it's clarifying, it does apply. If it's not, it doesn't."

This "clarifying" concept is a freak of North Carolina law. A bill that makes substantive changes to the law—that affects people's existing rights—can only apply to future lawsuits; else, it would violate the Constitution. But a bill that only "clarifies" the legal landscape, that merely adds color and definition but doesn't deprive people of rights, can apply to pending cases. On appeal, Smithfield is arguing that when the General Assembly limited the kinds of damages that neighbors can claim in farm nuisance suits, it didn't alter the law. It just made it clearer.

"But doesn't the text of the statute matter?" Wilkinson inquires.

"Of course, the text—" says Raphael, but Wilkinson talks over him.

"It says it does not apply to pending cases."

Raphael attempts a dodge. He points out that the pertinent language is at the end of the bill, and that the North Carolina Supreme Court, in a case called *Ray*, dismissed such footer language as standard boilerplate—a throwaway line. What's more important, says Raphael, is the *title* of the bill, and the title of HB467 says it is clarifying.

Wilkinson's bewilderment is plain. "So if the text of the amendment says it applies to causes of action arising on or after its effective date, that would seem to exclude pending cases."

Raphael replies as if exasperated: "It would if you hadn't read *Ray*."

From the vantage point of the gallery, the appellate lawyer is reeling like a fighter who has taken one too many blows to the head. He is also out of time. But the judges don't care about the red light on the podium. It isn't Raphael's fault; it's theirs. Wilkinson tosses out the timer. Then he sits back in his chair, and his eyes take on a peculiar glow.

"I'll speak in a general manner about what troubles me," he says. "When you look at the complaint and you look at the trial, the hog farming here certainly provides many jobs in eastern North Carolina. I understand that, and it's very important to the economy of the eastern part of the state. That's surely true, and not only that, it's important to our national food supply."

When Wilkinson takes a breath, everyone in the courtroom is silent, waiting for the blade to fall. And then it does. In the hands of the old judge, it falls like lightning.

"But it's harmful to the people who live nearby. You look at the *amicus* briefs. You look at the complaint. It's got to be environmentally harmful to the waterways. It's seeping into the water. Nobody wants another Flint, Michigan, tragedy down the road. This can't be good to children's respiratory systems. You're talking about wheezing and

headaches and things like that. The inhumanity to the animals, and the
mortality rate among the hogs. I suppose they're just animals, and some
people think they're ugly and they can treat them any way they want.
But . . ."

Wilkinson sighs. "You know, I just kept reading this case and I'm
thinking to myself, 'If this were my property, I would be outraged by
some of these conditions that were allowed to persist.' And I think, 'You
know, our less fortunate fellow citizens, they have property rights, too.
And many of the homes surrounding an operation of this sort don't go
for a high price. But the people that live in them, they have a right to
good health. They have a right to their enjoyment of their property.' I
thought, 'If these were McMansions surrounding these hog operations,
if these were the houses of the affluent, if these people were more politically powerful, wouldn't those conditions have been cleared up sooner,
rather than later?'"

No one on the plaintiffs' side of the gallery can see Stuart Raphael's
face, but everyone can imagine his stricken look. Mona glances at Elsie
Herring, moisture shining in her eyes. Behind her, Lisa is struggling to
hold herself together. John Hughes takes Linda Wike's hand and gives
Tom Butler's knee a squeeze. Even Mike Kaeske is blinking away tears.
None of them could have predicted this. None of them can believe what
they are witnessing.

When the old judge falls silent, the panel turns to address the
remaining issues and then calls Tillman Breckenridge to the podium.
But for Elsie and Mona, Mike and Lisa, and everyone around them, the
rest of the hearing is an afterthought. Their ears are ringing in wonder-
ment. The judge they most feared is the one who most understood them,
who looked past the cloud of legal distractions, and focused on the mol-
ten core of truth beneath their claims—the dignity of Elsie Herring, sitting on her mother's porch and looking out over her grandfather's land.
Elsie's wealth doesn't matter, nor does the value of her land. She has a
right to clean air and water, just like any other human being. She has the
right to breathe free beneath God's eternal sky.

And anyone who takes away that right is wrong.

As soon as the hearing concludes, Smithfield's lawyers and support-
ers empty out of the courthouse like finches scared from a bush. Later
on, the plaintiffs' team will see Don Butler and Andy Curliss walking

along the streets of Richmond looking shell-shocked, like men who just stumbled out of a foxhole. What the hog barons believed would be their last refuge turned into an abattoir. Even Harvie Wilkinson couldn't find an ounce of sympathy for them.

In the now vacant courtroom, Mona and Mike and the rest of their team trade instinctive hugs and handshakes with Elsie and Rick Dove, Larry Baldwin and Tom Butler. They feel as if the prospect of justice has suddenly come close.

Rick Dove puts his delight into words: "He got it. He saw that the people of North Carolina are suffering."

CHAPTER 37

WAITING FOR DAYLIGHT

They always say time changes things,
but you actually have to change them yourself.
—*Andy Warhol*

**Louisiana and
North Carolina
February–November
2020**

As the judges of the Fourth Circuit deliberate over the appeal, accolades start to pour in to the office of Wallace & Graham. In late February, the Southern Trial Lawyers Association honors Mona Lisa Wallace with the Tommy Malone Great American Eagle Award. The award, one of the most prestigious in the southern bar, gestures at something more empyrean than success in the courtroom. It is about the soul of a lawyer, about dignity, integrity, and bravery. In keeping with its namesake, Tommy Malone, a New South trailblazer who fought for society's castaways and championed civil rights, its recipients are defenders of the downtrodden, friends of the oppressed. Since the award was established fourteen years ago, all the honorees have been men.

Mona makes history as the first woman.

The ceremony is held in New Orleans, at the Ritz-Carlton on the fringes of the French Quarter. It's a Thursday just before Mardi Gras, and the ballroom is full of chatter and good cheer, the men wearing black tie and the women bedecked in regalia suited to the locale, some of the dresses fancy enough for a Royal Street ball. No masks are in sight, but there are beads and long necklaces festooned with eagles and fashioned after the American flag.

Mona is not alone at the head table. Her daughter, Whitney, is there with her, as are Monica and Buster Farrington, Maryclaire's parents, and two other friends from Salisbury. Together, they watch as the 2019 honoree, Chuck Monnett, strides to the podium. He is from North Carolina, too, a personal injury attorney from Charlotte, and he is a friend of Mona's, though that is not saying much—so many people are friends of Mona Wallace.

Monnett breaks the ice with a play on words. "I'm terrified," he says, surveying the audience, his mustachioed grin barely concealed. "I'm afraid that I lack the skills to tell you just how special Mona Lisa Wallace is, and how much she deserves this award."

His tribute to her is effulgent. Mona is a pathbreaker, he says, a woman who shattered the glass ceiling of small-town law in the South. Monnett traces the arc of Mona's star from her early days handling divorce work to the break she made with domestic practice to take up on behalf of the injured, the sick, and the abused.

"Few lawyers have done more good for more people than Mona Lisa Wallace," remarks Monnett. "In terms of the sheer number of dollars recovered, in terms of the sheer number of clients whose lives have been changed for the good, there is no lawyer more successful in North Carolina than this fine lady right here."

Monnett regales the crowd with colorful stories from Mona's trophy wall—the stuffed heads of modern-day robber barons she has brought home from the courtroom. He talks about her campaign against Duke Energy years before, about the payday lenders and car dealership scammers and steel magnates who bilked their employees out of retirement benefits that she has chastened and forced to change.

"What do you do after you've had all that success?" Monnett asks. "Well, you decide that you're going to take on the largest pork producer in the world."

Ripples of laughter radiate through the crowd.

"For years, she fought them. Five cases went to trial. Five plaintiffs' verdicts. The largest verdict ever returned in North Carolina."

Monnett shares a quote from Harvie Wilkinson's soliloquy at the Fourth Circuit, the old jurist's musings on the power imbalances in hog country, and the audience erupts in applause.

But Monnett isn't quite finished. He reprises Mona's public interest work, the years she has poured into Public Justice. He talks about her family and her philanthropy in Salisbury, the way she and Lee have invested in the public schools, the cancer center they endowed. There is so much more Monnett could say, so many points he missed in the service of brevity. He summons Mona to the stage and surrenders the podium, draping one of the beaded eagle necklaces over her head.

Mona is a longtime veteran of the stump, and she knows so many people in the room, but still she is nervous, humbled. She shares a quote about Tommy Malone's passion for civil rights, the way he framed the fight to which he devoted his life. It wasn't just a racial issue to him. It was a power struggle, a struggle for the powerless against the powerful.

"I think that's why I keep taking these cases," she says. "The Smithfield case almost killed me. It's been seven years. We tried five federal trials back-to-back in 2018 and 2019, and I was away from my family for two years—my children, my grandchildren. All of us who do these cases know what a sacrifice it is, and so do our family members." She offers a précis of the story. It is not exactly fodder for the dinner table, and the clatter of silverware fades away. The raw truth of it can't be euphemized. Mona's voice takes on a trace of her own revulsion, as if to say, "Can you believe this? Can you believe what these people lived with?"

She wraps up swiftly yet gracefully, sharing the praise. "None of us can do what we do without each other," she says. She talks about her lawyers, the effort they pour into her cases, and the support she has received. Then she waves and steps away from the podium.

Before she can return to her seat, however, Chuck Monnett lifts the award itself off the display table and places it in her hands. It is a soaring eagle sculpted out of bronze, beak curled and talons out, eyes locked on its prey. The symbolism could not be more apt. If Mona has a totem, it is a mother eagle—fierce and protective, noble and deadly, a friend you want, an enemy you don't. It is also the antitype of Boss Hog's own bronze sculpture—the wild boar, crafty and fearsome, resting on its haunches outside the Mad Boar Restaurant in Wallace. In Judge Britt's courtroom, the marauder of the forest met the queen of the skies.

As in the state of nature, the sky always wins.

✳

With the hog farm trials suspended for the time being, the turning earth seems to slow on its axis, returning a measure of normalcy to the lives of the plaintiffs and their lawyers. For Elsie Herring and Lendora Farland, Woodell McGowan and Joyce Messick, that means going back to work and spending more time with family, volunteering in their neighborhoods and endeavoring, to the best of their ability, not to dwell on the Damoclean sword hanging over their legal claims. The outcome has never been in their hands. It's in the hands of God.

The fracture lines in their community—blown into chasms by the jury verdicts—are still visible in the looks they receive in public and the whispers traded behind their backs. They will forever be marked by the stand they have taken. But this is the world they have known since they were children. And it is still a world that knows them. With the passage of time, the hog country faithful put away their yard signs, dial down the apocalyptic chatter on Facebook, and leave the neighbors alone. This peace, while perhaps artificial, feels like a mercy.

Many of the plaintiffs, especially those whose cases have been tried, stay in touch with Mona and Mike and the rest of the legal team while they await the Fourth Circuit's ruling. They are friends now, not just clients. When they pick up the phone or send a text, it isn't solely to ask for an update about the case. Sometimes they just want to say hello, to share something that happened to them, to maintain the connection they have built over so many years now.

For Mona, the return to normalcy means more time at the firm. At this stage in her career, one could forgive her for easing off the accelerator, taking up painting or yoga, and spending weeks at her beach house—or, better yet, leaving her law practice in the capable hands of Bill and John and Whitney, and embarking on an adventure with Lee. After all, she's sixty-six years old, and Lee is a decade older. But work is what she loves most, after her family. It's in her brain chemistry, the watermark of her personality. Even when she's at the beach, sky bright and waves rolling in, she can't settle down. For the people who love her, it's a source of constant humor. Without a malefactor in her sights, she doesn't know what to do with herself. The only time she seems at ease and undistracted is when she's with her grandkids. They get her full attention.

Linda Wike likes to joke that Mona will work until she dies: "I think I'm going to find her in this place one day years down the road. I can't see her ever leaving this place. Which means I will never leave this place." It's an oath Linda swore early in their collaboration, that she won't quit until Mona quits. Given Mona's stamina and corporate America's penchant for malfeasance, that day is likely many horizons away. Until then, in rain, snow, and sunshine, Mona will show up at the firm at nine in the morning, having worked in one way or another since the moment her head rose from the pillow, and she will labor until six or seven at night, her intensity never wavering, her smile always within reach. With a track record like hers, there is no shortage of cases for her to choose from.

She sues Bank of America, alleging that the nation's fourth-largest mortgage lender has been creating unwanted, yet lucrative, escrow accounts on mortgages where the borrower agreed to pay property taxes and insurance directly. In addition, after the worst outbreak of COVID-19 in North Carolina turns a Salisbury nursing home into a morgue, she takes the grieving families under wing and sues the company behind the facility—as well as its New York–based private equity owners—for gross negligence. It's a pro bono case at this stage, no money in it for the firm. But this is Mona's hometown. She can't allow such a wrong to stand unchallenged. As with the Smithfield cases, she wants to force the corporate retirement industry to change.

And it isn't just Mona on the hunt. Bill Graham is on the front lines of the mesothelioma wars, suing the manufacturers of asbestos products for lung damage and wrongful death. Not long ago, he landed a $32 million verdict on behalf of the widow of a tire-plant worker—the largest single-plaintiff verdict in the state.

The wheel of litigation at Wallace & Graham is like the wheel of time. Justice doesn't sleep. So neither do Mona and Bill.

Mike Kaeske, by contrast, takes the interlude as an excuse to get outside. He has spent the last five years—in his book, a complete life cycle—on the hog farm cases, and he is ready to trade in his suits for hiking boots. He grabs a few of his buddies, including Shane Rogers, and leads a trek across the highlands of Wyoming's Wind River Range.

After meandering through snow-capped peaks and glacier-fed lakes, they deploy their pack rafts on the waters of the Green River and follow the jade-tinted snake out of the wilderness. On the trail and around the campfire, Mike allows himself to unwind. He is a humorist and raconteur, swapping jokes and telling stories under the spangled cape of stars. But he never quite relinquishes his edge.

Not long after the trip, Kaeske ventures out again, this time with a new crew, exploring the ruins of Navajo villages and camping on the rim of Cedar Mesa in Utah, within sight of the great rock spires of the Valley of the Gods. He also takes Haven to Cabo, her happy place, and goes heli-skiing in Alaska. He is in no rush to reenter the arena, to take on a new client. His heart is still with the hog cases. He's still using pig emojis in his text messages, still talking with Mona and Daniel on the phone all the time. Until the Fourth Circuit delivers its ruling, he will find other ways to amuse himself, to push his tachometer to the red line.

With spring comes the Covid quarantine and an eerie kind of quiet. The weeks trickle into months like rivulets into a stream. Streets everywhere are empty and storefronts dark. At last, summer blossoms with the spark of surprise, and states across the country experiment with reopening. Cars flood the streets and people start to eat out again. Restive crowds flock to beaches and parks, and protesters march for racial justice.

The Fourth Circuit, however, remains silent.

The delay starts to drag, to weigh down the lawyers when they permit themselves to think about it. The court should have ruled by May or June. But June flies by in a haste, and then the dog days of July, and still the announcement doesn't come. Mona wakes up to the same thought each morning: *Surely it will be today.* But then today, too, passes without word from Richmond.

Something else arrives in its place—an award from Public Justice, one of America's premier public interest legal organizations. The hog farm team wins Trial Lawyer of the Year. It's the third occasion in as many years that Mona has made the short list. In 2018, she shared the top honor with her payday lending suits. Last year in San Diego, she and the others on the hog farm team came in second place. This year, however, the award is theirs alone. The ceremony is held remotely, over Zoom, with Erin Brockovich, the environmental activist, hosting the event from Los Angeles. Erin is yet another friend of Mona's. They share a kindred spirit.

Mona accepts the honor graciously, on behalf of the team. They are there with her at the firm—Bill Graham and John Hughes, Whitney and Daniel, Mark Doby and Linda Wike. Only Mike Kaeske and Lisa Blue can't be there in person. They are watching the livestream. Mona's speech is not scripted. She speaks off the cuff about her team, praises the plaintiffs for their bravery, and offers a tribute to Mike for his courtroom brilliance. Given the constraints of Zoom, the coronation takes place in silence, shorn of applause. But the audience's reaction is not difficult to imagine. Mona is a beloved figure at Public Justice, and the Smithfield litigation has been a modern-day War of the Roses.

Yet, still, the question remains unanswered: How will this story end? All five hundred of Mona's clients, all of her employees at the firm, all of the lawyers and staff around Mike and Lisa out west, are suspended in the inkwell of unknowing. They are waiting for daylight.

And then it comes. On the Thursday before Thanksgiving, the Fourth Circuit rules.

Shortly after nine o'clock, the electronic notice from the court lands in the inboxes of Mona and John Hughes, but neither of them sees it. They are in the big conference room, taking a Zoom deposition in the nursing home Covid case. Tillman Breckenridge is the first to catch the news. He shoots Mike Kaeske a text message, saying the opinion has dropped. But the sun has yet to rise over Park City. Kaeske is still asleep. It's only the biggest moment of the year for all of them, and one of the most important appellate rulings of their careers. Yet it floats in the digital ether until, at last, Kaeske wakes up and checks his phone.

He sends a text to Daniel Wallace, Mark Doby, and John Hughes, along with a screenshot of Tillman's message from two hours ago. *"Who has read the opinion?"*

Daniel and Mark reply in unison: *"Oh fuck, send it to us."*

To which Kaeske responds: *"I don't have it. 144 pages."*

At this point, alerted by the now incessant vibration of his phone, John Hughes wrests his focus from the carnage unfolding on the Zoom screen—Mona is in the process of skewering the COO of the elder-care management company for its dereliction of duty—and comprehends the situation in a glance. He gathers his laptop and relocates to the corner of the room to skim the opinion. Soon, he thinks better of it and decamps to his office, where he huddles with Daniel and Mark to pore over the court's words. Even with the amplifying effect of an adrenaline-fueled mind-meld, the three of them don't appreciate it right away. It takes time for their eyes to adjust to the brilliance of the light, for their ears to recognize the sing-song peal of the bells.

While Steven Agee issued an impassioned dissent, fulfilling every trope of the right-leaning, pro-business jurist, Harvie Wilkinson and Stephanie Thacker agreed with the neighbors on almost every point. And where they quibbled with Judge Britt—in their view, he shouldn't have allowed the jury to consider the profits of WH Group and the salaries of the hog giant's executives in calculating its verdict—they refused to order a new trial. Their remedy was modest: a hearing at which the trial court would recalibrate the punitive damages award without reference to corporate profits and salaries. Practically, such an undertaking could easily produce an identical outcome. To comply with the Fourth Circuit's order, Judge Britt could simply reimpose the amount of punitive damages permitted by the statutory cap—three times the compensatory award—and the plaintiffs would not lose a dime.

John Hughes and his young associates bring Mike Kaeske into the loop by phone and dispel his doomsday anxieties. After that, John scribbles a few words on a notepad and races back to the conference room to inform Mona. She's at a pivotal juncture in the nursing home deposition, and she waves him away, barely glancing at the pad. But the message is enough to give her pause.

"HOG OPINION IN."

She blinks, processing the implications at light speed. As if reading her mind, John delivers her a thumbs up. Mona nods, relief cascading through her body. She takes a breath, then sets her elation aside and returns to the Zoom screen. Her duty is to her clients.

It is thirty minutes before Mona wraps up the inquisition and glides into the lunch room, a star-bright twinkle in her eyes. Daniel and Mark are there, along with John Hughes, Whitney, and Linda Wike. When they see her in the doorway, all of them start talking at once. Everyone has a comment, a quote, an impression to share. The volume builds until they are almost yelling. Later on, none of them will recall the particulars. But they will remember the ecstasy, the Technicolor beauty of their communal release.

They will remember the sound of victory.

CHAPTER 38

FINAL JUDGMENT

> Truth never damages a cause that is just.
> —*Mahatma Gandhi*

It is late afternoon before the surge of frenetic energy at Wallace & Graham gives way to a more studious calm. As the hog farm team explores the majority opinion, they witness the glory of Smithfield's demise. To their surprise, the author of the court's ruling is Stephanie Thacker, not Harvie Wilkinson, despite Wilkinson's seniority on the panel. The old circuit judge elected instead to pen a concurring opinion. In light of Wilkinson's commanding posture at oral argument, his deference to Thacker is a mystery. For the moment, though, they set aside their curiosity and focus on Thacker's words.

The former Justice Department attorney approaches her task methodically. Her prose is workmanlike, unadorned. Yet she grants the hog kingdom no quarter, demolishing its arguments one by one and turning Smithfield's fortress of arrogance into a wasteland of rubble.

On the question of punitive damages, Thacker squeezes a drop of passion into her prose. There can be little doubt, she writes, that Smithfield knew its hog farms were a nuisance. The evidence of Smithfield's conscious disregard of the plaintiffs' rights is "abundant." Moreover, the hog barons' protestations of innocence are belied by their long-standing behavior. Smithfield "knew about likely harms, denied their existence, and fought for them not to come to light." According to Thacker, "this evidence is sufficient to support punitive damages." In a less formal context, the judge might have crowned her conclusion with an exclamation point. But in black-letter law, a period is as terminal as a bullet.

The jury's verdict stands.

*

In the madcap race to the end of the workday, Mona doesn't find a moment to peruse Judge Wilkinson's concurring opinion until the evening. She is at home with Lee, the house quiet and the sky dark, when she sits down to read. Ordinarily, she digests legal decisions with machine-like efficiency. But this one is special. She's been waiting ten months for the court to rule. This is a moment to be savored.

By the second paragraph, J. Harvie has unhinged her jaw and pinned it to the floor. His concurrence is a rhetorical diamond mine, replete with quotable gems. He writes as if inspired. But even his style is not as striking as the substance of his judgment. In issuing a tandem opinion with Judge Thacker, Wilkinson doesn't merely applaud the reasoning of his junior colleague. The old circuit judge—for decades one of the brightest stars in the conservative legal firmament—reads Smithfield the riot act. His anger at the hog giant is unsubtle. His desire isn't to confirm the fairness of the trial. That was Judge Thacker's job, and she handled it ably. His eye is on the jury's verdict, and his point is far more profound.

The verdict was "essentially a just one."

"It is past time," he writes, "to acknowledge the full harms that the unreformed practices of hog farming are inflicting." He is not blithe about the importance of the hog industry to the economy of eastern North Carolina. He admits it readily. He concedes, moreover, the critical role that Smithfield plays in preserving the nation's food supply. He calls the pig "an indispensable animal." But this precisely is the fount of his fury. If pigs are indispensable creatures, then no man or corporation should subject them to the "outrageous conditions" that the plaintiffs documented in Billy Kinlaw's hog sheds.

"How did it come to this?" Wilkinson muses. "What was missing from Kinlaw Farms—and from Murphy-Brown—was the recognition that treating animals better will benefit humans. What was neglected is that animal welfare and human welfare, far from advancing at cross-purposes, are actually integrally connected." With a few strokes of his pen, the old judge indicts the entire system of industrial hog production, blaming concentrated animal confinement and its attendant lagoons and sprayfields for "serious ecological risks that, when imprudently managed, bred horrible outcomes for pigs and humans alike."

Wilkinson's logic in linking the suffering of neighbors and hogs is remarkable both for its moral clarity and for its total absence from the trial record. The cruelty of hog confinement was not lost on Mona and Mike. They were sickened by what they saw inside the barns. They recognized that animal suffering is as much a hidden cost on Smithfield's balance sheet as the neighbors' travail. Yet they avoided mentioning it out of concern that they would prejudice the jury, giving Smithfield a ready argument on appeal.

From the outset of this case, Smithfield's lawyers have contended: "This case isn't about animal rights. It isn't about environmental justice. It isn't about asthma or high blood pressure or any other health condition allegedly suffered by the neighbors. It's about odor, nothing more." Not so, contends J. Harvie. A neighborhood is like an ecosystem. Everything is connected—the air, the soil, the water, the well-being of animals, and the health of human beings. Not even the most precise legal tweezers can prize apart the interrelated effects of industrial hog production. Only a holistic analysis will do.

The old circuit judge is only too happy to supply it.

After addressing the plight of the hogs, he turns his attention to the health of Smithfield's employees. He points out that nearly half of all CAFO workers who labor inside confinement sheds suffer from respiratory conditions of various kinds. The distress of the workers is a link in the causal chain between the misery of the hogs and the anguish of the neighbors. But the neighbors may not be the last link in the chain. The environmental hazards created by CAFOs don't magically disappear at the boundary of a neighborhood. The toxic air from hog sheds has been shown to impact the lungs of schoolchildren up to three miles away.

And the air is only one strand in the woven knot of nuisance. Smithfield's CAFOs breed flies and insects, both vectors for viral disease. The antibiotic regimen the company administers to its hogs give rise to antibiotic-resistant bacteria, a danger to animals and humans alike. Also,

Smithfield's dead boxes attract buzzards, another vector for pathogenic transit. With a porcine mortality rate of up to 10 percent, the chance of a disease outbreak is significant. But even apart from the risk of disease, the insects and carrion birds are obnoxious to the neighbors.

In Judge Wilkinson's view, the same kind of "interlocking dysfunctions" are present in Smithfield's waste-management system. It isn't just the drift of spray onto the neighbors' homes. The hog lagoons are not hermetically sealed. Many of them "leach waste material into both surface water and groundwater." Such leakage "can produce toxic algae blooms inimical to local wildlife" and seep into the wells whose water the neighbors use to drink and bathe. Then there is the issue of flooding. Heavy rainfall causes the lagoons to overflow and spreads waste material into the waterways, infecting the entire watershed. "Needless to say," Wilkinson writes, "deterioration in the local water quality is a grievous blow to both animal and human welfare."

This is yet another point that the hog farm team chose not to highlight at trial. But Harvie Wilkinson, surveying the case from his exalted perch, has no fear of being reversed. That is the beauty of a concurring opinion. It is not binding law. In a concurrence, a judge is liberated to hold forth without constraint, to opine about the character of justice and proclaim larger truths. Perhaps this is the reason Wilkinson yielded the privilege of speaking for the majority to Judge Thacker. He wanted to write like a pope speaking ex cathedra.

However one looks at it, says the old circuit judge, Smithfield's production model is fraught with "wreckage." Having charted the dimensions of the wrong, he has a question for the hog giant's executives—and the world: Why has this deplorable situation not been corrected in all these years? His answer is just as scathing: "These nuisance conditions were unlikely to have persisted for long—or even to have arisen at all—had the neighbors of Kinlaw Farms been wealthier or more politically powerful." This is precisely the point he made from the bench back in January. In committing it to the page, however, he hones the tip until it is scalpel sharp.

It is well-established—almost to the point of judicial notice—that environmental harms are visited disproportionately upon the dispossessed—here on minority populations and poor communities. But whether a home borders a golf course or a dirt road, it is a castle for those who reside in it. It is where children play and grow, friends sit and visit, and a life is built. Many plaintiffs in this suit have tended their hearths for generations—one family for almost 100 years. They are exactly whom the venerable tort of nuisance ought to protect.

The old judge takes a spiritual cue from Steve Wing, Don Webb, and Tom Butler and pronounces his judgment with Mosaic thunder. "Murphy-Brown's interference with their quiet enjoyment of their properties was unreasonable. It was willful, and it was wanton. The record fully supports the jury's finding that punitive damages were warranted."

Smithfield's sin, in Wilkinson's view, is not merely a violation of the law. It is a breach in the natural order of things, a human-inspired tear in the fabric of trust that binds the universe together. A wrong so pervasive demands a remedy equally inclusive. To restore the balance, Smithfield must do more than address the odor concerns of the neighbors. It must respect the rights of the entire community, human and animal, together with the earth itself.

In the annals of jurisprudence, Wilkinson's concurrence is one for the ages. And it brings Mona Wallace to tears. She reads it through twice, treasuring the enormity of the old circuit judge's gift. His words are like an epitaph to her struggle over the past seven and a half years, and to the plaintiffs' struggle across three decades.

She wipes the moistness from her eyes and calls Susan Webb, Don's wife, to pass along the joyous news. She wishes she could speak to Don himself, but his heart gave out in the fall of 2018, shortly after the *Artis* verdict. His memorial service brought out a throng, and the eulogies were rhapsodic and colorful, a fitting tribute to a country boy turned environmental pioneer, who saw the world as a pulpit and forced even the deaf to listen as he talked the truth.

After sharing a touching moment with Susan, Mona calls Elsie Herring. Though they are separated by two hundred miles, their conversation feels like an embrace. In a way they are soul sisters, their affection for each other as deep as if the bond were forged by blood, not circumstance. As delighted as Elsie is by the Fourth Circuit's decision, she is not surprised by it. Like her mother before her, she held fast to faith during the long months of silence. She remembered Judge Wilkinson's words at the hearing in January, the way he spoke with empathy about her community. She trusted that the court would deliver.

Over the next few days, Elsie's home phone and mobile ring off the hook. She takes the calls without hesitation, telling her story to every reporter who inquires, and her words splash across the Internet under headlines such as "Court Barbecues Smithfield's Claims, Giving Neighbors of Hog Farms Optimism," and "In Damning Opinion, Federal Appeals Court Rules Against Murphy-Brown." The environmental community, too, hails the ruling as a pivotal victory—and an opportunity to campaign yet again for reform.

In the aftermath of the ruling, Mona too spends much of her time on the telephone, celebrating with her clients and fielding calls from around the country. As soon as the Associated Press reports on the decision, the story hits the national wires. It is a seismic development in the world of Big Ag. Smithfield's allies were hoping for a wholesale reversal, a rebuke of the "urban jurors" who took a sledgehammer to their industry and Judge Britt who enabled their reproof.

The Fourth Circuit's decision leaves them sputtering.

The implications are colossal and widespread. With the hog barons on the mat, the lords of poultry could be next, and the magnates of beef after them. The trial bar is having daydreams about a phalanx of new lawsuits, and Public Justice, which is spearheading a legal campaign to reform America's food system, sees the ruling as an invitation to press harder for institutional reform.

The opportunities for engagement are plentiful, and the environment target rich. Over the last decade, state legislatures across the country have borrowed from Jimmy Dixon's playbook and erected a fortress of walls and moats around the largest agribusiness corporations. Under the banner of "Right to Farm," they have redefined the tort of nuisance, insulating farm operations from neighbor and citizen complaints, and passed "ag-gag" laws from Alabama to Montana that criminalize the activities of whistleblowers and undercover activists who are seeking to expose abusive conditions at animal CAFOs.

Energized by the Fourth Circuit's ruling, Public Justice and other legal impact organizations ratchet up their assault on the industry's fortifications and make significant advances in the courts. The Tenth Circuit Court of Appeals strikes down Kansas's "ag-gag" law on First Amendment grounds, and the Eighth Circuit clears the way for a similar challenge to an "ag-gag" law in Arkansas.

Meanwhile in Washington, D.C., a move is afoot to reimagine the entire enterprise of animal agriculture and curtail the monopolistic power of Goliath companies like Smithfield, Tyson, and JBS. Building on the foundation of the Packers & Stockyards Act, which reined in the aspirations of the robber barons to dominate America's meatpacking industry a century ago, Senator Cory Booker and Representative Ro Khanna introduce the Farm System Reform Act in Congress.

If enacted, the law would set a moratorium on the construction of new large animal CAFOs (e.g., a finishing farm with 2,500 hogs; a ranch with 1,000 cattle, or a chicken farm with a liquid manure handling system and 30,000 laying hens) and require the closure of all existing CAFOs of the same size by 2040, while funding buyouts and debt forgiveness for farmers and ranchers to facilitate the transition. The law would also eliminate many of the exploitative and anti-competitive practices of the agribusiness giants, leveling the playing field with their contract growers, and it would nationalize the legal standard set by the North Carolina litigation—that corporate integrators like Smithfield are responsible for all of the waste, pollution, and adverse health effects associated with their operations, even those under contract. Put simply, the Farm System Reform Act would take the spirit of Harvie Wilkinson's magnum opus and make it the law of the land.

To the people down east, however, the old judge's stirring words are more than sufficient for the moment.

The light emanating from the Fourth Circuit spreads like sunbeams across the coastal plain, brightening hearts just in time for a pandemic Thanksgiving. In a year beset by hardship and steeped in sorrow, with bread lines stretching for miles across America and COVID-19 infections reaching stratospheric heights, this victory feels like a warm wind of grace, like a divine whisper that the world is not yet lost, that justice is still possible for those who persevere, who stand on the side of the right.

Such is the perspective of the neighbors at least.

For Smithfield, the ruling is a devastating blow. In typical fashion, the company refuses to admit what is self-evident to everyone else. Its public relations team launches a preemptive strike in an attempt to stanch the bleeding. Shortly after the decision lands, Smithfield releases a surprise press statement signed by Keira Lombardo, now the company's chief administrative officer after an in-house shakeup that included the resignation of CEO Ken Sullivan. Lombardo turns the ruling on its head, quoting Judge Agee's dissent as if he wrote for the majority. She then regurgitates the same warmed-over pablum that the hog barons have served up for more than a generation—that no one understands the industry, that all the negative media and lawsuits and jury verdicts are biased and unfair, that Smithfield cares about farmers, and that it is committed to feeding the world.

In the aftermath of the Fourth Circuit's decision, however, this alternative vision of reality has the forlorn look of a field gone to seed. There is no other side of the story anymore. The truth has been tested in five trials and upheld by the court of appeals.

This is what justice looks like. Period.

The press release, however, is not just propagandistic. It contains a nugget of news: "We have resolved these cases through a settlement that will take into account the divided decision of the court. Information about the terms of the settlement will not be disclosed."

The meaning of these two sentences could not be more explosive. There will be no more trials, no more juries, no more appeals. The nuisance litigation is finally over.

What is the settlement worth? What blood price did Smithfield pay to stop the carnage? There is a chance that the details of the hog barons' surrender will eventually leak. Enterprising reporters will surely probe around the edges of secrecy, listening for any scrap of intelligence that might allow the public to see. But the lawyers on both sides are formidable, and the parties have no doubt signed nondisclosure agreements. The seal will probably hold.

Yet this much is evident: The plaintiffs will be compensated.

Reparations will be paid.

EPILOGUE
A Land of Pines

This small field seems bigger than the sky.
—*Thylias Moss, "Sweet Enough Ocean, Cotton"*

River Road
Wallace,
North Carolina
After the Verdicts

The land is quiet, recumbent, as I turn in to Beulah Herring Lane. The little pink house is set back from the road, a bright patch of color beneath the tall summer sky. Its centennial is closing in. Yet it stands undaunted, as proud as the day it was built. Midnight, Elsie's black Labrador, greets me in the driveway. He's a handsome animal, but intimidating. I can see why Elsie favors him. She shoos him away and invites me onto the porch. The living area is still a work zone, she says with regret, still under repair after the flooding from Hurricane Florence.

She takes a seat on one of the rocking chairs and I do the same. I have heard so much about her, seen clips of her in newsreels and documentaries, read about her in magazine articles and in the pages of books. But this is the first time I have met her. Her manner is unhurried, her voice relaxed yet firm. She wears the world lightly, her words uncalloused. Her tone is warm and approachable. She is happy to talk.

I start with an apology. She has told her story so many times before. It must be wearisome to tell it again. She shakes her head, her smile subtle but untroubled. She doesn't mind at all. Her story isn't over. Others have caught glimpses of it. But no one has captured the full sweep.

We rock lazily, nothing but time on our hands, as the breeze washes over us, whisking away the worst of the heat. The air is fresh today; the hog farmer hasn't been spraying. As the minutes pass, she tells me about her family, about her mother, Beulah, and her brother, Jesse; her daddy, Abram, and her Uncle Perl; her grandfather Immanuel and Miss Emily Teachey, the white woman who raised him. She tells me the story of the land, the eighty acres Immanuel acquired before the nineteenth century turned and Miss Emily passed on. She tells me how those eighty acres have been whittled down to thirty-five, according to the Duplin land records office. But that is a mistake, another wrong she needs to correct. She would love nothing more than to reassemble the broken pieces of her grandfather's estate before she dies.

She loves this land more than the world itself.

I ask her about the hog farm. It is invisible now, separated from her home by a thick buffer of trees. The industry planted them before her mother passed away. When the trees grew to their mature height, they blocked the pitter-patter of hog rain, but they didn't stop the odor. The sprayfield is still there, just beyond the buffer. Over the years, the hog farmer has adapted his irrigation techniques, retiring the big gun in favor of sprinklers and locating them as far away from her property line as possible. But these efforts have been only palliative, not a cure. The problem is the proximity of the hog factory to her home. The solution, as Tom Butler told all five juries, is to cover the lagoons and treat the waste as the hogs excrete it. Only then will the air be cleansed.

Elsie tells me about her activism, about Rick Dove and Don Webb, ARSI and REACH, about the hope they cultivated over so many years that a lawsuit might bring about change. Her eyes dance as she talks about Mona Wallace and Mike Kaeske. She knows how hard they have fought for her and the other neighbors. She loves them for it, and every member of their team. She is so proud of what they have accomplished, of the concessions they have elicited from Smithfield. But the battle against the hog barons isn't over, not for Elsie Herring. She wants the industry to honor the spirit of the Smithfield Agreement, to dispense with the lagoons and sprayfields once and for all. She wants final justice for the land. The end of the litigation is not the resolution of Elsie's story. She is not going to rest until that justice is served.

We talk about other things, too, as the afternoon melts away and the sky softens in anticipation of evening. I ask her if she ever gets lonely, living by herself. Sometimes she feels the void, she says, but her mother and brother are always close. Their memory keeps her company, as does Midnight, and her family and friends. She tells me that she visits the graves of Beulah and Jesse as often as she can. "I go on Mama's birthday," she says. "I go on Jesse's birthday. I go on Mother's Day. I go on Christmas. I take flowers. If I can get the flowers that I prefer, I always love to take my mother roses. I like to take my brother white flowers."

I ask her what will happen to her land when she passes, since she has no children. She says she thinks about it all the time. "I'm watching the young ladies and young men," she explains, "watching to see who shows responsibility, who shows a real understanding of what is important in life." She wants to leave the land in worthy hands.

But her heart is still young. She has a lot of living left to do before God calls her on. And living means working, volunteering, supporting her community. Elsie never stops. Her life is a testament to her mother, Beulah Stallings Herring.

It is Beulah's legacy that Elsie wishes to honor.

Hallsville Road, Beulaville, North Carolina

The heat is blistering, the humidity a wet blanket draped over the land, when I pull into Woodell McGowan's drive. His porch is spare, smaller than Elsie's, and spotlighted by the sun. He invites me into his living room and takes a seat across from me. He is a man of few words. That's the way God made him. But he's not as taciturn as he was when Daniel Wallace first met him back in 2014. I have heard the stories from many people now, the way Woodell has come to life again, the way he has embraced the neighborhood in a new way, taking on the role of community elder and keeping the Hall family spirit alive. But I want to hear the story from him.

It takes a while to get him talking, but eventually he picks up steam. He tells me what this place was like when he was a boy, the hundred acres that his mother owned with his aunt and uncle. He tells me of his peregrinations in the forest beyond the old homeplace, the camp he built in the meadow with the tent that shaded him from the sun, the way he swam in Limestone Creek and stalked every inch of ground until he could walk it blindfolded. As in his youth, he is alone again now, his wife having passed on. But he has found a remedy for loneliness.

He has taken up caring for his neighbors.

The change came over him in the most unusual way. Before the fifth trial, Mike and Lisa brought in a consultant trained in the techniques of psychodrama to help prepare the neighbors for the pressure cooker of the trial. For two days, the plaintiffs sat in a room inside one of the local churches with Mike and Lisa, Mona and Sophie, saying nothing at all about the lawsuit or Joey Carter's hogs. They talked about their families, their community, the way it was back in the old days, and the way it became after the hog farms sprouted up and the odor came.

They stepped into each other's shoes in role-playing exercises. They surprised each other with spontaneous displays of emotion. People who had once been close but had drifted away bonded again. In the midst of all this, Woodell had an epiphany. He saw the way he had let his friends down. "I'm sorry I haven't been around," he said. "I am going to make a commitment to all of you that I'm going to be a better neighbor." Since that day, he has been living out that promise, paying people visits and calling them on the phone.

It helps that Smithfield's hogs are gone, that Joey Carter's six barns haven't seen another animal since September 2018. The company depopulated the Greenwood facilities and the Sholar farm, too, after the verdicts, like it did Billy Kinlaw's farm. Woodell tells me what a relief it is not to worry about the odor, to go outside and breathe fresh air.

The forge of the trial aided the neighborhood bonding process, allowed the relational glue to set. I ask him what it was like to wait three days for the verdict. He smiles slightly, his face crinkling. The garrulousness of his response takes me by surprise.

"It was hard on all of us. But I'm the type of person that when I believe something, I just believe it. Every day, I would tell them, 'You know that you told the truth. You know you didn't get up there and lie. That's what matters. The truth will come out. The truth will win.'"

I tell him I met with Lendora, that I sat with her on her parents' porch and walked the length of the property by her side. I listened to her story of the past, of Linnill, the barber, and Georgia, the quilter, and the petition Lendora helped her father draft when Joey Carter showed up with his construction plans. Linnill is sick now, battling cancer. But Lendora is hoping he will improve enough that she can bring him home. When that happens, she is going to throw a party for the community in her parents' yard, the way they used to do before the hog waste drove them inside. She can do it now that the hogs are gone, now that the sprayfields are fallow and the air is clean again. I mention this to Woodell and he smiles with delight.

"That would be nice," he says. "All of us would go."

Woodell opens up about the verdict itself, what it means to the community. He tells me he's been poor his whole life. All of his neighbors have. They have gotten by like everyone else, but it hasn't been easy. When he thinks about the money the jury awarded, he feels satisfaction. But he didn't file suit to cash in. Neither did anyone else. He talked about it with his neighbors, and all were in agreement. "Money can't buy you clean air," he tells me. "Money can't buy not having to smell all the hog trucks in and out. Money can't buy that." The verdict was a sign that the jury believed them. That's what means the most to Woodell now.

That the jury believed.

Piney Woods Road, Willard, North Carolina

I drive down from Beulaville to Pender County on back roads, windows cracked to let in the scent of the sky. Around every country bend, the land reveals a fresh face, a novel interplay of light and shadow. Yet every scene is a variation on a common theme—fields of sandy soil, row crops in divergent stages of growth, tangled thickets of pine forest, ramparts of longleaf pine and crenellations of loblolly, and beneath them streambeds scoring the land like the forked lines on a weathered hand. In the solitude of these open spaces, beneath the gaze of the sun, time seems to lose its texture. Suddenly, the past feels close, almost close enough to touch. And I begin to understand.

Years ago, I would have used a different palette of words to describe this place. I would have called it blighted, forgotten, a blank page between the rolling hills of the Carolina Piedmont and the glittering beaches of the coast. I would have missed the truth because I would not have had eyes to see it. What makes a land beautiful isn't just the grace of its form, the bloom of its colors, or the fecundity of its ecological life.

That kind of beauty lives only on the surface of things. Beneath it, there is a deeper appeal, a pearl inside the shell.

Every place is lovely if it is loved.

It is this love that I see in the countenance of Joyce Messick when she welcomes me into her home. Everyone told me I needed to meet her. It isn't long before I realize why. Like Elsie and Woodell, she is a witness to history and a keeper of her family's light.

We sit at the table in her dining room, the television on in the background, her nephew and mother nearby. I ask her about the past, and she tells me about her parents, her daddy whose land this once was, and her grandmother who owned it before him. She tells me that there's a Messick Road nearby, somewhere up in the woods. That's where her daddy's family is from.

She is a soft-spoken woman. She takes time with her answers. But she is free with them, trusting. She tells me about her two brothers— James, whom she called "Red," and Willie, both of whom served in the army before coming home to Pender County. Her eyes grow moist when she mentions Red. He's gone now, but she loved him deeply. And he loved her back. He taught her so many things—how to swim and fish, how to throw daggers and ride horses. "I was always wanting to do whatever he did," she tells me. "I was outside with them all the time."

I ask her about her work, her hospice clients, the caretaking she does at home. I sense the weariness beneath her words. At first, her smiles are fleeting things, like rays of sunshine grappling with a thick curtain of cloud. But her voice is resonant, her memories felt.

She tells me about her neighbors, so many of whom are kin. She tells me what the land was like when she was a girl, back when Red and Willie rode their horses for miles through the woods—the train trestles where they used to camp, the Sand Hole where they swam, the gardens her mother tended in the backyard. We talk for a while about the hog farms that Paul Stanley built with support from Pete and Wendell Murphy, two of which Dean Hilton now owns. She is candid about the stink, about the toll it has taken on her life, her church, her home.

We talk about the case, about the experience of testifying, and the world-altering moment when the *Artis* jury returned its verdict. She brightens at the recollection. She calls out to her brother, Willie, who is outside on the porch, and he joins her at the table. They tell the story in stereo, the narrative pouring out of them as if it happened yesterday. They talk about the jurors with affection. Their happiness is uncomplicated. It is as if the burden of the years has slipped from their shoulders, as if the only truth that matters now is the mercy of that day.

And then they tell me about the aftermath, the depopulation of the barns. "After about a couple of months, we started to get some fresh air," Joyce says. "You can't imagine."

She's right. I can't imagine it, not completely. But I do my best to try.

When the time comes, I thank her for the stories and bid her and Willie goodbye. I pull out onto Piney Woods Road, the crowns of the loblollies and longleaf pines glistening in the last light of day, and stare down the bone-straight stretch of road toward the now-defunct hog farms. I roll my windows down all the way, smell the loamy fragrance of pine, and marvel at the blessedness of clean air. It is a gift I have taken for granted my entire life.

I marvel also at the irony. The one outcome that Joyce and Willie never asked for—the shuttering of the Greenwood farms—is what they have received. They never wished to end the industry, only to transform it, to redeem it from its excesses. They harbor no ill will toward the Murphy men. Their desire today is the same as it was in the beginning—to restore the sanctity of their ancestral land and to pass it along to generations yet to come.

As I drive away down the long line of pines, out toward the interstate and the wider world, I ponder the work that remains to be done, the stories yet to be told. The redemption of the land is not complete. Hog country may have had its reckoning and the industry may have vowed to change its ways. But most of the plaintiffs are not like Joyce and Willie. Most have yet to see the change, to fill their lungs with liberated air, to stand upon emancipated ground. The dollar is still the lodestar of Smithfield Foods, and the legislature is still its domain. Neighbors like Elsie understand this, as do folks like Tom Butler and Rick Dove, and the lawyers at Wallace & Graham. They won't relent until every commitment the industry made is realized, every promise fulfilled. Only then will the seeds of hope that the neighbors planted in the soil so long ago spread their leaves upward toward the sun.

Acknowledgments

This story would not exist without the kindness and patience of so many extraordinary people, who invited me into their homes and lives, who answered my questions, and who showed me the truth they have known so I could see it with my own eyes. A full accounting of my gratitude would go on far too long. So I will be concise.

To the neighbor-plaintiffs in eastern North Carolina (particularly Elsie Herring, Woodell McGowan, Joyce and Willie Messick, and Lendora Farland), to the lawyers who fought for them so valiantly in the courts (especially Mona Lisa Wallace and Mike Kaeske), to the legislators, former legislators, and political aides who worked tirelessly to resist the industry's attempts to scuttle the litigation (in particular Billy Richardson and Leigh Lawrence), to the activists who have been agitating for change for a generation (especially Rick Dove), and to the hog farmers courageous enough to speak to me (in particular Tom Butler), thank you for welcoming me into your world and bringing this tale to life.

To Susan Webb and Betsy Wing, thanks for helping me understand Don and Steve. They were giants of conscience. Their legacy will long endure. To Cindy Watson, thank you for taking a trip down memory lane and conjuring for me the hog wars of the nineties. And to all the others who shared your expertise and experience, please accept my sincerest gratitude.

Closer to home, I wish to thank my author friends: John Hart for introducing me to this story and being the first to exhort me to take it on; Aran Shetterly for coaching me on the finer points of narrative nonfiction; John Grisham for reading an early draft of the book, helping me find a home for it, and offering to pen the foreword; and Inman Majors for standing behind me at a critical inflection point in my story. The writing life can be a lonely one. All of you make it easier—and bring out the shine.

As always, my wife, Marcy, and my children, Samuel and Kalia, were an unfailing encouragement. I could not do what I do without your steadfast love and patience, and your faith in the meaning of the work. You call forth the best in me. A life without you would be shadows and dust.

To my agent, Danny Baror, thanks for joining me in this new chapter of my writing journey. We have walked a lot of miles together over the years. Thank you for continuing to believe in me as an author and as a human being. I'm honored by your unflagging support and friendship.

To Suzanne Herz, Maria Goldverg, Reagan Arthur, and the rest of my publishing team at Knopf Doubleday, thank you for embracing the story with such passion and for bringing me into the Penguin Random House family. Much like raising a child, it takes a village to bring a book into the world. Thank you for your countless efforts on my behalf. Our collaboration has been a joy. I hope it lasts for many years to come.

Finally, I wish to offer a word of thanks to all those who encouraged me to try my hand at writing nonfiction, despite my stubborn insistence that I was a novelist and that my craft wasn't journalism but storytelling. There were a number of important voices, but two stand out: Brian Lipson and Dan Raines. You saw the potential for a book like *Wastelands* long before I did. How grateful I am that you pressed the point.

For the record, you were right.

Notes

The following notes detail the documentary source material upon which I based key factual claims in the book. They are numbered according to the pages on which the claims appear. All claims not referenced in these notes are drawn from in-person conversations or from my own knowledge of the subject matter, or are so widely reported that I regard them as indisputable.

PROLOGUE

2   The event, dubbed the National Ag Roundtable: N.C. Farm Bureau livestream of National Ag Roundtable, August 3, 2018; "Massive Hog Trial Verdict as Elected Leaders Rally for Farmers," WRAL.com, August 3, 2018.

3   "We have a crisis brewing in eastern North Carolina," says one: Congressman David Rouzer, N.C. Farm Bureau livestream of National Ag Roundtable, August 3, 2018.

3   "I would describe what's going on as a blight," declares: N.C. Commissioner of Agriculture Steve Troxler, ibid.

3   The most august of the dignitaries: U.S. Senator Thom Tillis, ibid.

3   One of the state legislators compares: State Representative Ken Goodman, ibid.

3   pork industry's fairest friend: State Representative Jimmy Dixon, ibid.

4   defamed as pimps and rapists: Jimmy Dixon, post on his personal Facebook page, June 30, 2018.

4   disinformation campaigns: See notes on chapters 28–30: Numerous Facebook posts, blog posts, and advertisements by N.C. Farm Families and N.C. Pork Council throughout duration of trials.

4   political power-brokering: Transcript of N.C. House Floor Debate, Bill 467, April 10, 2017.

2. THE CHAMPION

22   The Taylor case has been eating: First Amended Complaint, *Victoria Taylor v. McGill Environmental Systems of N.C., Inc.,* Case No. 7:13-CV-270-D, Doc. 66, EDNC.

23   The cause of death: Findings of coroner and OSHA, ibid. at ¶ 1.

23   other workers had been severely injured: OSHA 300 injury log, ibid. at ¶ 35–36. Statements of Tim Artis, Ricky Robinson, and Norman Johnson, ibid. at ¶ 45–49. Generally, ibid. at ¶ 52–61.

23   Mona has evidence: Ibid. at ¶ 14, 32–35, 38, 46, 52–53, 58–62, 71–73.

24   agreed to compensate: Duke Energy Corporation, Form 10-K for the year ended Dec. 31, 2002, footnote (a); "Workers Get Payoffs in Asbestos Lawsuits," *News & Observer* (Raleigh, NC), January 7, 2004.

26   A Georgia boy from Savannah: https://web.archive.org/web/20200221120212/ www.middletonfirm.com/richard-h-middleton-jr/; Barry Estabrook, *Pig Tales* (New York: W. W. Norton, 2015), p. 140.

27   In four counties alone: USDA's National Agricultural Statistics Service, "North Carolina Agricultural Statistics," 2017–2018, p. 42.

27   All those hogs generate: "New Studies Show That Lagoons Are Leaking: Groundwater, Rivers Affected by Waste," *News & Observer* (Raleigh, NC), February 19, 1995 (part of Pulitzer Prize–winning "Boss Hog" series).

27   close to two thousand across the state: Testimony of Gregg Schmidt, Transcript of Jury Trial, Day 9, *Joyce McKiver v. Murphy-Brown, LLC,* April 13, 2018, p. 90.

27   Back in the eighties and nineties: *News & Observer* "Boss Hog" series generally.

27   Between lagoon spills and flooding: Ibid.; JoAnn Burkholder, et al., "Impacts to a Coastal River and Estuary from Rupture of a Large Swine Waste Holding Lagoon," *Journal of Environmental Quality,* Nov.–Dec. 1997; "Boss Hog: The Dark Side of America's Top Pork Producer," *Rolling Stone,* December 14, 2006; "North Carolina's Hog Waste Problem Has a Long History. Why Wasn't It Solved in Time for Hurricane Florence?" *Pacific Standard,* September 16, 2018; "I saw Florence sending millions of gallons of animal poop flooding across North Carolina," *The Washington Post,* September 22, 2018.

27   environmental groups have taken: "Waterkeeper Lawsuits Target Pork Industry," www.nationalhogfarmer.com, May 15, 2001; "River Advocates Allege Clean Water Act Violations by N.C. Hog Operation," Southern Environmental Law Center press release, February 9, 2010.

27   Middleton and his trial partner: Estabrook, *Pig Tales,* p. 142; "Whose Side Is the Farm Bureau On?," Food and Environmental Reporting Network, July 17, 2012.

28   Premium Standard Farms, to settle: "Big Pig's $39 Million Settlement Smells like a Bacony Victory," *St. Louis Post-Dispatch,* October 4, 2012.

3. DOWN EAST

30   There are nine million hogs: "North Carolina Agricultural Statistics," 2017–2018, p. 35.

30   there are nearly thirty-five hogs: Ibid., p. 42; U.S. Census Bureau, Duplin
      County, 2019.

31   In more than a dozen nuisance suits: "Big Pig's $39 Million Settlement,"
      St. Louis Post-Dispatch, October 4, 2012; Estabrook, *Pig Tales,* p. 142; "Missouri
      Jury Awards Residents $11 Million in Damages from Living Under Cloud of
      Stench Caused by Industrial Hog Farms," PR Newswire, March 5, 2010; Cor-
      don M. Smart, "The 'Right to Commit Nuisance' in North Carolina: A Histori-
      cal Analysis of the Right-to-Farm Act," *UNC Law Review,* 94 N.C. L. Rev. 2097
      (2016) at footnote 177 ("noting the success of the two lawyers in securing over
      $32 million in jury verdicts").

31   they also negotiated a consent decree: "Whose Side Is the Farm Bureau On?"
      Food and Environment Reporting Network, July 17, 2012.

36   the Mad Boar is a pet project: "Family-Owned Business: Murphy Family Ven-
      tures of Wallace," *Business NC,* October 1, 2019.

35   River Landing is the brainchild: "2006 Masters of the Pork Industry—Wendell
      & Dell Murphy," *National Hog Farmer,* May 15, 2006; Joint Findings of Fact,
      Murfam Farms, LLC v. United States, Case No. 1:06-CV-245-EJD, Doc. 123,
      Court of Federal Claims, p. 7.

37   Dr. Susan Schiffman, a professor: "Powerhouse of Senses, Smell, at Last Gets Its
      Due," *New York Times,* February 14, 1995.

38   One of her studies: Susan Schiffman, et al., "The effect of environmental odors
      emanating from commercial swine operations on the mood of nearby residents,"
      Brain Research Bulletin, Volume 37, Issue 4, 1995.

38   a state-sponsored odor task force: "N.C. Mega-Hog Farm Runs Afoul of Neigh-
      bors," *Washington Post,* December 22, 1996; "Options for Managing Odor,"
      Report from North Carolina Swine Odor Task Force, March 1, 1995.

38   a new odor-related study: Minutes of the North Carolina Pork Council and
      Farmers for Fairness Steering Committee Meeting, January 17, 1997, admitted
      as part of Plaintiffs' Exhibit 58 at the Trial of *McKiver v. Murphy-Brown, LLC*
      (recounting comment from Lois Britt of Murphy Family Farms saying that
      "Dr. Susan Schiffman's direction for her odor study should be reviewed to deter-
      mine if recommendations had been required" and "[i]f so, then Dr. Schiffman
      should make recommendations for controlling odor.").

38   a reliable industry ally: "NC State Honors Linda and Wendell Murphy with the
      2014 Menscer Cup," NC State University, November 20, 2014; NC Pork Coun-
      cil Funded Research, www.ncpork.org.

38   Dell Murphy's wife: UNC Board of Governors web profile of Wendy Floyd
      Murphy, www.uncbog.com/bog/murphy-wendy/.

38   Lois Britt, the former: Organization of the University, the University of North
      Carolina Board of Governors, Lois Britt, Secretary, term expiring in 2001,
      https://www.ecu.edu/cs-acad/aa/customcf/grcat/grcat0001/S1.html.

4. FORTUNATE SONS

40   Wendell Murphy was the first: "Wendell H. Murphy: Hard Work & Inspiration," part of the three-part interview/documentary series *Biographical Conversations,* UNC-TV, 2011.

40   Murphy was born: Ibid.

41   "I thought my skull": Ibid.

41   The banks offered to loan him: Ibid.

41   He dickered with the bankers: Ibid.

41   It enabled him to invest: Ibid.

42   Luter made his entrance: Lynn Waltz, *Hog Wild* (Iowa City: University of Iowa Press, 2018), p. 11.

42   As in Murphy's family: "The Ham Man," *Virginia Living,* September 25, 2009.

42   Since revolutionary times: *Hog Wild,* p. 11.

42   "It was tough, hard work": "The Ham Man," *Virginia Living.*

42   He returned to Smithfield: Ibid.

42   Despite being callow, arrogant, and untested: Ibid.

43   he received a buyout query: Ibid.

43   Before long, they would drive: "Master of the Quick Turnaround, Joseph W. Luter III Brings Home the Bacon for Smithfield Foods," *Richmond Times-Dispatch,* September 1, 1987.

43   It was a cholera epidemic: "Wendell H. Murphy: Hard Work & Inspiration," interview with UNC-TV.

43   The poultry industry: Ibid.; Christopher Leonard, *The Meat Racket* (New York: Simon & Schuster, 2014), p. 56.

43   Ever the optimist: "Wendell H. Murphy: Hard Work & Inspiration," interview with UNC-TV.

44   The tobacco market was in the midst: "Money Talks: The Smell of Money," *News & Observer* (Raleigh, NC), February 24, 1995 (part of the Pulitzer Prize–winning "Boss Hog" series).

44   Before long, he had so many takers: Ibid.

44   The CAFOs he deployed: Ibid.

44   The average hog produces: "New Studies Show That Lagoons Are Leaking," *News & Observer* (two to four times the fecal matter); "Boss Hog," *Rolling Stone* (three times); "Massive Hog Feedlot Proposed in Fillmore County," *Fillmore County Journal,* May 28, 2018 (ten times the fecal matter, according to Dr. Mark Sobsey at UNC).

44   Murphy wanted to minimize: "New Studies Show That Lagoons Are Leaking," *News & Observer* ("Wendell Murphy said his company now spends the extra money to put clay liners in lagoons." Before that, they were just giant open-air pits, the oldest and cheapest form of waste containment in the history of mankind).

45   no one stopped to inquire: See generally the testimony of the neighbor-plaintiffs in all five federal trials.

45   newly minted rich kid Joe Luter: "The Ham Man," *Virginia Living.*

45   Accused of falsifying earnings reports: "Master of the Quick Turnaround," *Richmond Times-Dispatch.*

45   "They lost money in December": Ibid.

45   By the end of the decade: Ibid.

46   He acquired packing plants: Ibid.

46   Luter took the packing world: Ibid.; "Boss Hog," *Rolling Stone.*

46   he developed a taste: "Master of the Quick Turnaround," *Richmond Times-Dispatch.*

46   buying a yacht and a posh apartment: "Boss Hog," *Rolling Stone;* "Hog King Luter Flips, Gets Married, Keeps Moving," *The Observer,* January 29, 2001.

46   While Murphy was multiplying: "Murphy's Law: For Murphy, Good Government Means Good Business," *News & Observer,* February 22, 1995 (part of Pulitzer Prize–winning "Boss Hog" series).

46   Luter was ramping up: "Master of the Quick Turnaround," *Richmond Times-Dispatch;* "Straight Talk from Smithfield's Joe Luter," *National Hog Farmer,* May 1, 2000; "Boss Hog," *Rolling Stone.*

46   Luter needed Murphy's hogs: "Straight Talk," *National Hog Farmer.*

46   Murphy needed Luter to buy: "Wendell H. Murphy: Toward Merger," interview with UNC-TV.

46   Wendell Murphy had an epiphany: Trial transcript, *Murfam Farms v. U.S.,* testimony of Wendell H. Murphy, p. 1281; "2006 Masters of the Pork Industry," *National Hog Farmer;* "Wendell H. Murphy: Toward Merger," interview with UNC-TV.

46   In 1989, Murphy went: Trial transcript, *Murfam Farms v. U.S.,* pp. 1282–83; "2006 Masters of the Pork Industry," *National Hog Farmer;* "Wendell H. Murphy: Toward Merger," interview with UNC-TV.

46   Luter, who already had: Trial transcript, *Murfam Farms v. U.S.,* testimony of Wendell Murphy, pp. 1281–82; "2006 Masters of the Pork Industry," *National Hog Farmer;* "Straight Talk," *National Hog Farmer; Hog Wild,* pp. 25–26.

46   But Murphy balked when his financial advisors: Trial transcript, *Murfam Farms v. U.S.,* testimony of Wendell Murphy, p. 1282.

47   Instead, in 1991, he took a seat: Defendant's Proposed Additional Findings, *Murfam Farms v. U.S.,* p. 5 (citing trial testimony of Wendell Murphy).

47   By late 1997, Murphy was the unqualified champion: "The Ray Kroc of Pigsties," *Forbes,* October 12, 1997.

47   As for Luter, in 1991: *Hog Wild,* pp. 9, 25.

47   "By 1994, taxpayers were spending": *The Meat Racket,* p. 165.

48   Enacted in 1996, the Freedom to Farm Act: Ibid.

48   Freedom to Farm was an unqualified failure: Ibid.

48   Murphy and his fellow producers: "Wendell H. Murphy: Toward Merger," interview with UNC-TV.

48   Wendell Murphy started hemorrhaging cash: Ibid.; "2006 Masters of the Pork Industry," *National Hog Farmer.*

49   "It was bad": "Wendell H. Murphy: Toward Merger," interview with UNC-TV.

49   In 1999, Joe Luter bought: Defendant's Proposed Additional Findings, *Murfam Farms v. U.S.,* p. 10 (citing trial testimony of Wendell Murphy, Harry Murphy, and Joyce Murphy).

49   Given the popularity: "Wendell H. Murphy: Toward Merger," interview with UNC-TV.

49   He also bought out Carroll's Foods: Ibid.

49   "We are proud to report": "Straight Talk," *National Hog Farmer.*

49   For the next seven years: *Hog Wild,* pp. 162–63.

49   a short walk: "The Ham Man," *Virginia Living.*

49   Luter fought a decade-long war: See generally *Hog Wild.*

49   Murphy won himself a seat: "Murphy's Law," *News & Observer.*

5. DARK ARTS

53   the odor-affected zone: Dr. Steve Wing, et al., "Integrating Epidemiology, Education, and Organizing for Environmental Justice: Community Health Effects of Industrial Hog Operations," *American Journal of Public Health* 98, no. 8 (August 2008).

54   A fruit-and-vegetable farmer: "NC State Senator Pushed for Law, Then Sought Money It Provided," *News & Observer,* December 20, 2016.

54   He has worn enough board hats: "Brent Jackson's Biography," Vote Smart website, https://justfacts.votesmart.org/candidate/biography/117775/brent-jackson.

54   Like Jackson, he is a farmer: Transcript of House Judiciary III Committee Hearing, North Carolina General Assembly, March 29, 2017, p. 2; Floor Debate on HB467, North Carolina House of Representatives, April 10, 2017 ("My children and my grandchildren have walked gleefully with me through my hog houses, and through my turkey houses . . .").

54   in the mold of Jesse Helms: "The New Crop—Rep. Jimmy Dixon," NC Policy Watch, January 28, 2011. (In the interview, Dixon cited Helms as one of his "biggest political influences" alongside Ronald Reagan and Harry Truman.)

54   Jackson takes up the hog farmers' banner: "The Fight for the Right to Farm in North Carolina," *NC Pork Report,* the official magazine of the North Carolina Pork Council, Fall 2018, p. 22.

54   In fact, it is the specter of Middleton's: Ibid.

55   the first Right to Farm laws: "The Fight for the Right to Farm," *NC Pork Report,* Fall 2018.

55   In 1994, the North Carolina Court of Appeals: *Durham v. Britt,* 117 N.C. App. 250, 451 S.E.2d. 1 (1994).

55   the folks living near: Steve Wing and Jill Johnston, "Industrial Hog Operations in North Carolina Disproportionately Impact African-Americans, Hispanics and American Indians," UNC Chapel Hill, *UNC-Report,* August 29, 2014; "The World Eats Cheap Bacon at the Expense of North Carolina's Rural Poor," *Quartz,* July 14, 2015.

55   It was the Pork Council: "The fight for the Right to Farm," *NC Pork Report,* Fall 2018.

56   Jackson's bill gets ambushed: Ibid.

56   While the bill: House Bill 614, North Carolina General Assembly, Session 2013, https://www.ncleg.gov/Sessions/2013/Bills/House/PDF/H614v1.pdf.

56   the worst parts of the bill: Legislative History of House Bill 614, North Carolina General Assembly, https://www.ncleg.gov/BillLookup/2013/H614 (May 7, 2013 bill substitute striking the "rebuttable presumption" clause).

56   they seek to narrow: Ibid. (June 11, 2013 bill substitute proposed by Senate Committee on Agriculture, Environment, and Natural Resources).

56   Middleton and Speer included the growers: See, e.g., "Missouri Jury Awards $1.95 Million in Hog Lawsuit," *Wichita (KS) Eagle,* May 9, 2011 ("Iowa-based Synergy, which owned the hogs, and Kenoma, the local company that raised them, are liable for damages . . ."); "Neighbors Sue Hog Farm over Odors," *Columbia (MO) Daily Tribune,* December 3, 2008 ("The residents are seeking actual and punitive damages from the two companies operating the CAFO . . . as well as the hog farmers themselves.").

57   twelve days after the Right to Farm bill: Legislative History of House Bill 614, North Carolina General Assembly (H614 signed into law by governor on July 18, 2013).

57   the *Sampson Independent* runs a story: "Area Pork Producers Stand Behind Their Practices," *Sampson (NC) Independent,* August 4, 2013.

57   the hog industry holds its first summit: "Sampson County Friends of Agriculture," *Sampson Weekly,* August 23–29, 2013, pp. 1, 4.

57   Jimmy Dixon is there, wearing: Ibid., p. 1 (photograph).

57   Brent Jackson is with him: Ibid. (photograph).

58   Other state politicos: Ibid., p. 1 (photograph), p. 4.

58   "I don't need to remind you": Ibid., p. 4.

58   When Butler takes the stage: Ibid., p. 4.

59   "This is an attack": Ibid., p. 4.

59   another company has offered: "China's Shuanghui in $4.7B deal for Smithfield," *USA Today,* May 29, 2013.

6. THE BUTCHER

60   Ultimately valued at $7.1 billion: "Pork Firm Smithfield Sold to China's Shuanghui for $7.1 Billion," *Los Angeles Times,* May 29, 2013. (The $7.1 billion figure includes debt, whereas the $4.7 billion figure does not.)

60   largest acquisition of an American company: "Smithfield: How Sausage Was Made," *Wall Street Journal,* June 5, 2013.

60   It has been in the works: Ibid.

60   "We ought to do something together": Ibid.

60   China holds a strategic pork reserve: "How China Purchased a Prime Cut of America's Pork Industry," *Reveal News,* January 24, 2015.

60   And Shuanghui is the keeper: Ibid.

61   he resists the overtures: "How Sausage Was Made," *Wall Street Journal.* (Shuanghui looked into Smithfield's financials in 2009, then in February 2013, after the

Chinese government's 2011 Five-Year Plan went into effect, pursued Smithfield aggressively.)

61   Luter's favorite phrase: "Straight Talk," *National Hog Farmer.*

61   Born in 1940, Wan: "Cashing In on Pork Chops: Chinese Supplier to Become Billionaire on Share Sale," *Sydney Morning Herald,* July 31, 2014; Profile of Wan Long, Forbes.com, https://www.forbes.com/profile/wan-long/#28519ab93679; First Amended Complaint, *Anderson v. Murphy-Brown, LLC,* Case No. 7:14-CV-183-BR, EDNC, Doc. 32, Exh. 12, Declaration of Limei Dai, p. 1 (translation of Chinese language website description of Wan Long, http://www .shuanghui.net/html/category/about/lhrjs); "Smithfield Deal's Architect, China's Wan Long, Came from Humble Roots," *Wall Street Journal,* July 10, 2013.

61   At the age of nineteen: Ibid.; "How China Purchased a Prime Cut," *Reveal News.*

61   After soldiering for a number of years: "Smithfield Deal's Architect," *Wall Street Journal.*

61   in 1984, they offered him the helm: Ibid.; Declaration of Limei Dai, p. 2.

61   exporting its products: "Smithfield Deal's Architect," *Wall Street Journal.*

61   He was the first meatpacker: "How China Purchased a Prime Cut," *Reveal News.*

62   he engineered a buyout: "Smithfield Deal's Architect," *Wall Street Journal.*

62   those provincial elites elected him: Testimony of Usha C. V. Haley, U.S. Senate Committee on Agriculture, Nutrition, and Forestry, July 10, 2013, p. 10. ("For the past 15 years, he has been a member of China's National People's Congress.")

62   In its twelfth Five-Year Plan: Testimony of Usha Haley, p. 7.

62   encouraged the purchase of farmland: "How China Purchased a Prime Cut," *Reveal News.*

62   buying spree, increasing China's stake: Ibid.

62   encouraged investments in biotechnology: Testimony of Usha Haley, pp. 7–8.

62   When the call comes in: "How China Purchased a Prime Cut," *Reveal News.*

62   He is enjoying a posh retirement: "The Ham Man," *Virginia Living.*

62   His longtime CFO and protégé: "How China Purchased a Prime Cut," *Reveal News;* "Accomplished," *Meat + Poultry,* March 15, 2016, https://www .meatpoultry.com/articles/19162-accomplished.

62   Pope cut his teeth: "Accomplished," *Meat + Poultry.*

63   Pope has been obsessed: "How China Purchased a Prime Cut," *Reveal News.*

63   it has only 7 percent: Testimony of Daniel M. Slane, U.S. Senate Committee on Agriculture, Nutrition, and Forestry, July 10, 2013, p. 3; see also Testimony of Usha Haley, p. 16 (8 percent).

63   hog producer's heaven: Testimony of Usha Haley, p. 17; testimony of Daniel Slane, p. 4.

63   Its share price: "How China Purchased a Prime Cut," *Reveal News.*

63   Smithfield's stock into the single digits: Historical Price Data for NYSE:SFD, Smithfield Foods, Inc., Yahoo Finance.

63   a global outbreak of "swine flu": "Accomplished," *Meat + Poultry;* "The Lesson of Swine Flu," *The Atlantic,* June 15, 2009, https://www.theatlantic.com/health/ archive/2009/06/the-lesson-of-swine-flu/19246/.

63   though later testing found no evidence: "Mexican Government Clears Smith-
        field," *National Hog Farmer,* May 11, 2009, https://www.nationalhogfarmer
        .com/health-diseases/news/0511-smithfield-not-H1N1-cause.

63   a spike in the price of feed: "Accomplished," *Meat + Poultry;* "Impacts of Etha-
        nol Policy on Corn Prices: A Review and Meta-Analysis of Recent Evidence,"
        National Center for Environmental Economics, August 2013, https://www
        .epa.gov/sites/default/files/2014-12/documents/impacts_of_ethanol_policy_on
        _corn_prices.pdf.

63   one of Smithfield's mouthiest investors: "How Sausage Was Made," *Wall Street
        Journal* (the activist investor was Continental Grain Co.); "Accomplished," *Meat
        + Poultry.*

63   Pope has been in talks: "How China Purchased a Prime Cut," *Reveal News.*

63   One of Shuanghui's investors: "Smithfield Deal's Architect," *Wall Street Jour-
        nal.* ("Winston Wen, the son of former premier, Wen Jiabao, invested after the
        buyout.")

63   the man who is about to replace him: Ibid. (The incoming premier was Li
        Keqiang.)

63   Larry Pope is totally unprepared: "How China Purchased a Prime Cut," *Reveal
        News.*

64   Wan has taken the U.S. company's market capitalization: Ibid.

64   Even Joe Luter reluctantly concedes: "How Sausage Was Made," *Wall Street
        Journal.*

64   The Shuanghui takeover bid: "Who's Behind the Chinese Takeover of the
        World's Biggest Pork Producer?" *PBS News Hour,* September 12, 2014, https://
        www.pbs.org/newshour/show/whos-behind-chinese-takeover-worlds-biggest
        -pork-producer.

64   In industry after industry: Testimony of Usha Haley, pp. 4–6.

64   it's obvious why Wan Long: Testimony of Daniel Slane, p. 4; testimony of Usha
        Haley, p. 17.

65   The cost of raising a hog: "Why Is China Treating North Carolina like the
        Developing World?" *Rolling Stone,* March 19, 2018.

65   It has invested in treatment facilities: "Embracing Sustainability in Our Busi-
        ness," WH Group, http://www.wh-group.com/en/sustainability/environment
        .php.

65   senators on Capitol Hill: Hearing before U.S. Senate Committee on Agriculture,
        Nutrition & Forestry, July 10, 2013 (video footage), https://www.agriculture
        .senate.gov/hearings/smithfield-and-beyond_examining-foreign-purchases-of
        -american-food-companies.

65   Larry Pope settles into the hot seat: Ibid.; "How China Purchased a Prime Cut,"
        Reveal News.

65   The answer, as reported by Reuters: "Smithfield CEO Could Make About $46.6
        mln from Shuanghui Deal," Reuters, June 19, 2013.

65   Senator Pat Roberts of Kansas: Video footage of U.S. Senate Hearing, July 10,
        2013.

66   The Chinese government is, indeed: "How China Purchased a Prime Cut," *Reveal News.*

66   The state-owned Bank of China: Ibid.; "Why Is China Treating North Carolina," *Rolling Stone.*

66   In Robert Wan's words: "How China Purchased a Prime Cut," *Reveal News.*

66   "the Chinese government has absolutely no ownership stake": Video footage of U.S. Senate hearing, July 10, 2013; testimony of C. Larry Pope, U.S. Senate hearing, July 10, 2013, p. 3.

67   The announcement lands on September 6: "U.S. Security Panel Clears a Chinese Takeover of Smithfield Foods," *New York Times,* September 6, 2013.

67   the historic deal closes: "Shuanghui International and Smithfield Foods Complete Strategic Combination, Creating a Leading Global Pork Enterprise," Joint Press Release, September 26, 2013, https://www.prnewswire.com/news-releases/ shuanghui-international-and-smithfield-foods-complete-strategic-combination -creating-a-leading-global-pork-enterprise-225395622.html.

7. ACTS OF WAR

68   In a filing with the Raleigh court: Defendants' Motion to Prohibit the Admission of the Middleton Law Firm, L.L.C. and the Speer Law Firm, P.A. to Appear *Pro Hac Vice, Alderman v. Smithfield Foods,* September 17, 2013.

68   There are affidavits attached: Ibid.

69   State Senator Brent Jackson publishes: Sen. Brent Jackson, N.C. Senate, "Farming Under Attack by Out-of-State Lawyers," *Sampson Independent,* September 24, 2013, included in Exh. 5 to Plaintiffs' Brief in Support of Motion for *Pro Hac Vice.*

70   Mona fires back her reply: Plaintiffs' Brief in Support of Motion for *Pro Hac Vice* Admission and in Opposition to "Defendants' Motion to Prohibit the Admission of the Middleton Law Firm, L.L.C. and the Speer Law Firm, P.A. to Appear *Pro Hac Vice," Alderman v. Smithfield Foods, Inc.,* October 7, 2013.

70   They spoke at a conference: Ibid., p. 8, and Exh. 6, Affidavit of Richard H. Middleton, Jr.

70   signed up their first clients in 2004: Ibid.

70   The scene that unfolds: Transcript of Proceedings in the General Court of Justice, Superior Court Division, held in Wake County, Raleigh, North Carolina, commencing during the October 15, 2013, Civil Session, before the Honorable Donald W. Stephens, Judge Presiding, *Alderman v. Smithfield Foods.*

71   Indeed, before long, *Super Lawyers*: "'Our Atticus Finch': How Morehead Scholar Wade Smith Ushered in a New Generation of Criminal Defense Attorneys," *Super Lawyers,* March 10, 2016.

71   "Eventually, I think": Transcript of October 15, 2013, Hearing, p. 2.

71   He knows her history: Ibid, p. 7.

71   She tells him it's about both: Ibid., pp. 6–9.

71   "I believe you, North Carolina lawyer": Ibid., p. 9.

71   Mona offers the judge: Ibid., pp. 10–11.

72   Like a prizefighter: Ibid., pp. 12–13.

72   He tells a story: Ibid., pp. 13–15.

72   And he talks at length: Ibid., pp. 13–17, 24–28.

72   He doesn't deny: Ibid., p. 27 (quoting from Affidavit of Richard Middleton about Middleton's involvement with environmental and citizen action groups since 2004).

72   But Middleton and Speer are different: Ibid., p. 28.

72   "I've heard everything you said": Ibid., p. 30.

72   The judge launches: Ibid., pp. 30–32.

73   "This is not about the lawyers": Ibid., pp. 34–35.

73   The judge summons Wade Smith: Ibid., p. 38.

73   "Your Honor, you are quite correct": Ibid., p. 39.

73   "Good morning, Ms. Branch": Ibid.

74   Smith spins his argument: Ibid., pp. 40–46.

74   "Nothing is going to be done": Ibid., p. 40.

74   it is Mona's character: Ibid., pp. 46, 50.

74   He knows Wade Smith: Transcript of Audio Recording of January 10, 2014, Hearing Before the Honorable Donald W. Stephens, in the Wake County Courthouse, Raleigh, North Carolina, *Alderman v. Smithfield Foods,* p. 3.

74   The judge retires to his chambers: Transcript of October 15, 2013, Hearing, p. 55.

8. THE FOUNTAINHEAD

80   he hired a local attorney: Letter from Richard L. Burrows to Ms. Elsie Herring, c/o Beulah Herring, 114 Beulah Herring Lane, Wallace, North Carolina 28466, Re: Major Murray vs. Elsie Herring, June 24, 1998.

81   So said one of his friends: Funeral of Don Webb, Stantonsburg United Methodist Church, October 31, 2018 (video footage).

82   "Don't bother about that smell": Ibid. (confirmed by Rick Dove).

83   Forrest started yelling: Recollections of Elsie Herring and Cindy Watson in multiple corroborating interviews. See also "The Reformer," *Triad City Beat,* July 13, 2017, which recounts in brief the story of the confrontation and the reporter's calls to the Murray residence: "A call to Murray, who is in his eighties and has since sold the farm, was answered by a woman who told a reporter he would not talk to her 'today, tomorrow, or the day after' and then hung up. In a subsequent call, the woman said Murray didn't remember Watson and didn't want to talk about interactions with Herring. She ended the call by saying 'You better not call here no more. We got something, we can take care of all this now—them, you, whatever. Now don't call here no more.'"

84   Forrest started seething again: Recollections of Elsie Herring and Cindy Watson in multiple corroborating interviews. I attempted to contact Forrest Murray for comment, but he did not respond to my query.

84   "I just figured you": Ibid., clarifying the story in "The Reformer," *Triad City Beat,* in which the reporter quoted Major ("Buddy") Murray as saying "Just remember, I am a damn Democrat, and you must be just a n***** lover."

85   "I don't understand what you're saying": Recollections of Cindy Watson and Elsie Herring in multiple corroborating interviews. (Butler and Carroll's eventually agreed to plant a tree buffer on the disputed land that lies between Beulah Herring's home and the sprayfield on the Murray side.)

9. THE FIVE FAMILIES

86   It was a modest setback requirement: "Swine Farm Siting Act," S.L. 1995-420 (SB1080), enacted by the North Carolina General Assembly on July 11, 1995.

87   North Carolina's paper of record: The series was titled "Boss Hog: The Power of Pork, North Carolina's Pork Revolution," *News & Observer,* February 19–28, 1995, winner of the 1996 Pulitzer Prize in Public Service.

88   In their telling, Murphy: "Murphy's Law," *News & Observer.*

88   dismissed the coverage as hogwash: "Wendell H. Murphy: Business & Politics," interview with UNC-TV.

88   "drive-by shooting": "Sampson County Friends of Agriculture," *Sampson Weekly,* August 23–29, 2013, p. 4.

88   In Robeson County: Memorandum from Don Butler to Sonny Faison of Carroll's Foods, September 24, 1996, admitted as Plaintiffs' Exhibit 46-1 at the trial of *Artis v. Murphy-Brown, LLC,* 7:14-CV-237-BR, EDNC.

88   In Bladen County, the board of health: Letter from Don Butler and Carroll's Foods, Inc. to Mr. Don Yousey, Director of the Bladen County Health Department, Re: Proposed ILO Ordinance, September 17, 1996, admitted as Plaintiffs' Exhibit 54 at the trial of *Artis v. Murphy Brown, LLC.*

88   Don Butler, a Bladen County native: Ibid.

88   Carroll's would air its grievances: Ibid.

89   Until, that is, the hog expansion imperiled: Conversations with Cindy Watson; "Hogs' Halt," *The Economist,* September 18, 1997.

89   Wendell Murphy was in the room: "Golfers Take on Pork Producers over Hog-Farm Rules," *News & Observer,* February 27, 1997.

89   The next day, Cindy opened *The News & Observer*: Ibid.

89   called for a moratorium of two years: Conversations with Cindy Watson; "Hogs' Halt," *The Economist.*

90   he signed the two-year moratorium into law: Ibid.

90   the Five Families of Pork set aside: Memorandum from Don Butler to Sonny Faison, Gregg Schmidt, and Bob McLeod, Re: Update on activities of Farmers for Fairness Oversight Committee, January 22, 1997, admitted as part of Plaintiffs' Exhibit 58 at the trial of *McKiver v. Murphy-Brown, LLC,* 7:14-CV-180-BR, EDNC (listing Lois Britt and Don Butler as members of the 1997 Farmers for Fairness Steering Committee, and detailing an "education day" the organization had arranged for political lobbyists whose job in "the upcoming legislative

session was to fight introduction or passage of any 'new regulations' on hog
farming.").

90   Jim Stocker of Murphy Family Farms said: Minutes of the North Carolina Pork
Council and Farmers for Fairness Steering Committee Meeting, January 17,
1997, admitted as part of Plaintiffs' Exhibit 58 at the trial of *McKiver v. Murphy-Brown, LLC* (Stocker quoted in the "FINAL COMMENTS").

90   The group then engaged: Public Opinion Survey Summary by John McLaughlin & Associates for North Carolina Farmers for Fairness, May 1997, admitted as
Plaintiffs' Exhibits 292 and 293 at the trial of *McKiver v. Murphy-Brown, LLC.*

90   The Farmers for Fairness rebranding: Ibid.

91   Phase two, which the group debuted: Memorandum from Carter Wrenn to Nick
Weaver, Lois Britt, and Lu-Ann Cole, March 4, 1998, attaching what "appears
to be a poll taken by Farmers for Fairness in Cindy Watson's district around
February 8th," admitted as part of Plaintiffs' Exhibit 294 at the trial of *McKiver
v. Murphy-Brown, LLC* (detailing an extensive conversation between a national
public opinion pollster and a citizen in Duplin County about hog farming and
Cindy Watson); constituent letter from Rep. Richard Morgan, dated April 28,
1998, about the Farmers for Fairness campaign against him, admitted as part of
Plaintiffs' Exhibit 294 at the trial of *McKiver v. Murphy-Brown, LLC.*

91   Farmers for Fairness spent millions: Farmers for Fairness opinion poll on Cindy
Watson; Richard Morgan letter; conversations with Cindy Watson (she pegged
the total campaign expenditures at $3 million).

91   Cindy Watson complained: "Watson Asks State Elections Board to Investigate
Farmers for Fairness," *Jacksonville (NC) Daily News,* January 29, 1998; conversations with Cindy Watson.

91   Richard Morgan castigated: Richard Morgan letter.

91   "Jim Hunt's your governor": Conversations with Cindy Watson.

91   She lost the primary: Ibid.

92   She raised the idea: Conversations with Elsie Herring and Rick Dove.

92   the lawyers agreed to speak: Ibid.; Plaintiff's Brief in Support of Motion for *Pro
Hac Vice,* Exh. 6, Affidavit of Richard Middleton ¶ 14.

93   That first appearance: Conversations with Elsie Herring and Rick Dove; Affidavit of Richard Middleton ¶ 15–16.

93   Charlie Speer drove out: Conversations with Elsie Herring.

94   Buddy Murray got too old: Ibid.; "The Reformer," *Triad City Beat.*

94   The call she was hoping for: Conversations with Elsie Herring.

10. TABULA RASA

96   "I normally sign these": The account of the hearing comes from the transcript of
the January 10, 2014, hearing, *Alderman v. Smithfield Foods,* pp. 3–12.

11. APPEALING TO CAESAR

101 When Judge Stephens enters his order: Order of Judge Donald W. Stephens
     Striking Prior Appointment of Pro Hac Vice Counsel, *Alderman v. Smithfield
     Foods*, January 13, 2014 ("Out-of-state lawyers Charles F. Speer, Peter Brit-
     ton Bieri, Richard H. Middleton, Jr., Stephen A. Sael and Scott Harrison are
     relieved of further representation of Plaintiffs in this case.").

101 In short order, they initiate: Request for Prelitigation Mediation of Farm Nui-
     sance Dispute, Case No. 14-R-36, Duplin County Superior Court, April 15,
     2014 (due to the peculiarities of state law, the first filing in the new suit was not
     a complaint but a request for prelitigation mediation).

101 the new filing includes plaintiffs: Hill Allen's Motion to Withdraw as to Certain
     Claimants (Listed Below) Only, *In re: Request for Prelitigation Mediation of Farm
     Nuisance Dispute*, Case No. 14-R-36, Duplin County Superior Court, May 5,
     2014.

103 Judge Parsons delivers his ruling: Order of Judge W. Douglas Parsons Deny-
     ing Pro Hac Vice Admission, *In re: Request for Prelitigation Mediation of Farm
     Nuisance Dispute*, May 21, 2014; "Law Firms Pursuing Hog Farm Fight Denied,"
     Civitas Media, May 9, 2014 ("Parsons ultimately denied the motion after hear-
     ing 90 minutes of arguments on both sides, stating he considered the arguments
     and all information, including affidavits, exhibits and transcripts from prior
     hearings.").

105 After the deal closed, the IRS alleged: See generally Complaint for Readjust-
     ment of Partnership Items Under Code Section 6226, *Murfam Farms v. U.S.*,
     Case No. 1:06-CV-245, Court of Federal Claims, March 28, 2006.

105 roughly $90 million: Testimony of Wendell Murphy, trial transcript of *Murfam
     Farms v. U.S.*, p. 1199 (Q. "Do you remember during the meeting or after the
     meeting that the E&Y quantified that the Murphy family was going to have
     approximately $90 million of capital gains from the excluded assets in the
     Smithfield transaction?" A. "I do not recall the number." Q. "Was it your under-
     standing that by entering into the COBRA transaction, that the $90 million
     of capital gains was going to be offset?" A. "My understanding is that our taxes
     would be reduced, sir.").

105 Murphy filed suit: Complaint, *Murfam Farms v. U.S.*

105 He had declined to pursue: Testimony of Wendell Murphy, trial transcript of
     Murfam Farms v. U.S., p. 1282.

106 Murphy-Brown was an LLC whose sole member: Corrected Opening Brief of
     Defendant-Appellant, *McKiver v. Murphy-Brown, LLC*, Case No 19-1019, United
     States Court of Appeals for the Fourth Circuit, February 27, 2019, Disclosure of
     Corporate Affiliations and Other Interests ("The sole member of Murphy-Brown
     LLC is John Morrell & Co., which is a wholly-owned subsidiary of Smithfield
     Foods, Inc. In turn, Smithfield Foods, Inc. is owned by United Global Foods
     (US), Inc., which is owned by Ipopema 127, which is owned by SFDS Malta
     Limited, which is owned by Rotary Vortex Limited, which is owned by WH
     Group Limited.").

106   the new corporate filings for Murphy-Brown: North Carolina Secretary of
      State Business Search, https://www.sosnc.gov/online_services/search/Business
      _Registration_Results.

12. A MAN FOR ALL SEASONS

112   His findings were as striking: Steve Wing, et al., "Environmental Injustice in
      North Carolina's Hog Industry," *Environmental Health Perspectives* 108, no. 3
      (March 2000).

112   Wing accepted an invitation: Steve Wing, "Social Responsibility and Research
      Ethics in Community-Driven Studies of Industrialized Hog Production," *Envi-
      ronmental Health Perspectives* 110, no. 5 (May 2002).

112   They issued a tentative rebuke: Ibid.

113   One of these boosters: Ibid.

113   Despite this backlash, Wing persisted: Ibid.

113   One of the industry's lobbyists confronted Wing: Ibid.

113   the state Department of Health published: Wing, "Social Responsibility"; Steve
      Wing and Susanne Wolf, "Intensive Livestock Operations, Health, and Quality
      of Life Among Eastern North Carolina Residents," *Environmental Health Per-
      spectives* 108, no. 3 (March 2000).

113   lawyers from the North Carolina Pork Council: Letter from Charles D. Case
      to Steve Wing and Susanne Wolf at UNC–Chapel Hill, Re: Public Records
      Request, May 7, 1999.

113   Wing could claim no exemption: Wing, "Social Responsibility."

114   he had made that promise: Ibid.

114   The university's attorney showed no concern: Ibid.

114   The response among UNC's mandarins varied: Ibid.

114   One official told him: Ibid.

114   the university's attorney allowed: Ibid.

114   Wing delivered a lecture: Ibid.

114   The pork producers showed up en masse: Ibid.

114   an assistant professor at another state university: Ibid.

114   survey that pegged the industry: Maria Mirabelli, Steve Wing, et al., "Asthma
      Symptoms Among Adolescents Attending Public Schools Located near Con-
      fined Swine Feeding Operations," *Environmental Health Perspectives* 118, no. 1
      (July 2006); Virginia Guidry, Amy Lowman, Devon Hall, Dolthula Baron, and
      Steve Wing, "Challenges and Benefits of Conducting Environmental Justice
      Research in a School Setting," *New Solutions* 24, no. 2 (August 1, 2014); Virginia
      Guidry, Christine Gray, Devon Hall, and Steve Wing, "Data Quality from a
      Longitudinal Study of Adolescent Health at Schools near Industrial Livestock
      Facilities," *Annals of Epidemiology* 25, no. 7 (March 17, 2015).

114   a study that documented: Steve Wing, et al., "Air Pollution and Odor in Com-
      munities near Industrial Swine Operations," *Environmental Health Perspectives*
      116, no. 10, June 2008.

114   established the long-term damage: Rachel Avery, Steve Wing, et al., "Odor from

Industrial Hog Farming Operations and Mucosal Immune Function in Neighbors," *Archives of Environmental Health* 59, no. 2 (February 2004); Steve Wing, et al., "Integrating Epidemiology, Education and Organizing for Environmental Justice: Community Health Effects of Industrial Hog Operations," *American Journal of Public Health* 98, no. 8 (August 2008); Steve Wing, et al., "Air Pollution from Industrial Swine Operations and Blood Pressure of Neighboring Residents," *Environmental Health Perspectives* 121, no. 1 (January 2013).

114   he updated his prior investigation: Steve Wing and Jill Johnston, "Industrial Hog Operations in North Carolina Disproportionately Impact African-Americans, Hispanics and American Indians," August 29, 2014.

117   When Smithfield opens: Defendant's Memorandum in Support of Motion to Dismiss, *In re: Swine Nuisance Litigation,* Master Case. No. 5:15-CV-13-BR, Doc. 14, March 25, 2015; Defendant's Memorandum in Support of Motion to Strike Objectionable Paragraphs and Exhibits in Plaintiffs' Amended Complaints, *In re: Swine Nuisance Litigation,* Doc. 16, March 25, 2015.

117   He dusts off the law books: Order on Defendant's Motion to Dismiss, *In re: Swine Nuisance Litigation,* Doc. 31, June 25, 2015; Order on Motion to Strike, *In re: Swine Nuisance Litigation,* Doc. 32, June 29, 2015.

117   two years from now: See notes on chapters 20–22.

118   knocks out a third draft: See, e.g., Plaintiffs' Second Amended Complaint, *Anderson v. Murphy-Brown, LLC,* Case No. 7:14-CV-183, Doc. 34, July 31, 2015.

13. THE CLOUD AND THE FLAME

120   He reads about the lagoon breach: "Hog Waste Spilled in Duplin County; Cause Unknown," *Duplin Times,* March 4, 1999.

120   He unearths photos: Various articles and photographs, *Duplin Times,* September 23 and September 30, 1999.

120   article about the investigation: "Warsaw School Will No Longer Group Whites," *Duplin Times,* August 5, 1993.

122   She was fourteen: Conversations with Lendora Farland; Plaintiffs' Second Amended Complaint, *McGowan v. Murphy-Brown, LLC,* Case No. 7:14-CV-182-BR, Doc. 34, ¶ 121–25, July 31, 2015; testimony of Lendora Farland, trial transcript of *McGowan v. Murphy-Brown* (First Trial), June 6, 2018, pp. 7–115; testimony of Lendora Farland, Linnill Farland, and Georgia Farland, trial transcript of *McGowan v. Murphy-Brown* (Second Trial), February 8, 2019, pp. 61–228, and February 11, 2019, pp. 9–31.

123   This opposition from the neighbors: Testimony of Joey Carter, trial transcript of *McGowan v. Murphy-Brown (McGowan I),* June 8, 2018, pp. 85–179; June 11, 2018, pp. 5–235; June 12, 2018, pp. 6–99.

123   Joey Carter's father: Ibid.

123   Hog farming was a side business: Ibid.

124   He had the power of arrest: Ibid.

14. HUNTING THE UNICORN

127   The grower brought a claim: Complaint in Adversary Proceeding, *In re: D&B Swine Farms, Inc., D&B Swine Farms, Inc. v. Murphy-Brown, L.L.C. and Smithfield Foods, Inc.,* Case No. 09-160, U.S. Bankruptcy Court for the Eastern District of North Carolina, Doc. 1, July 30, 2009.

127   It's the first grower agreement he has ever seen: Premium Standard Farms of North Carolina, Inc., Amended and Restated Nursery Contract Grower Agreement, September 4, 2001, attached as Exhibit 2 to Plaintiffs' Response in Opposition to Motion to Seal Document, *In re: Swine Nuisance Litigation,* Doc. 226-2, November 7, 2016.

128   he happens across an article: "What to Do About Pig Poop? North Carolina Fights a Rising Tide," *National Geographic,* October 30, 2014.

132   the company had entered into an accord: Agreement By and Between the Attorney General of North Carolina; Smithfield Foods, Inc.; Brown's of Carolina, Inc.; Carroll's Foods, Inc.; Murphy Farms, Inc.; Carroll's Foods of Virginia, Inc.; and Quarter M Farms, Inc., July 25, 2000 (hereafter "Smithfield Agreement"). https://projects.ncsu.edu/cals/waste_mgt/smithfield_projects/agreement.pdf.

132   The reports they published in 2004 and 2005: Development of Environmentally Superior Technologies: Phase 1 Report, July 26, 2004. https://projects .ncsu.edu/cals/waste_mgt/smithfield_projects/phase1report04/phase1report .htm; Development of Environmentally Superior Technologies: Phase 2 Report, July 25, 2005, https://projects.ncsu.edu/cals/waste_mgt/smithfield_projects/ phase2report05/phase2report.htm.

132   a report from 2006: Development of Environmentally Superior Technologies: Phase 3 Report, March 8, 2006. https://projects.ncsu.edu/cals/waste_mgt/ smithfield_projects/phase3report06/phase3report.htm.

132   the economic subcommittee took it a step further: Economics Subcommittee Report, Appendix D to Smithfield Agreement Phase 3 Report. https://projects .ncsu.edu/cals/waste_mgt/smithfield_projects/phase3report06/pdfs/Appendix %20D.pdf.

133   reporting a 25 percent reduction: Phase 1 Environmentally Superior Technologies Contingent Determinations, November 1, 2007. https://projects.ncsu.edu/cals/ waste_mgt/smithfield_projects/supersoils2ndgeneration/ss2ndgenerationreport .html.

15. OUTSIDE MAN

141   A pilot buddy of Rick's: "Looking Down," Bob Epting.

16. A VISION ON THE MOUNTAIN

148   Their first pick is *McKiver*: See Plaintiffs' Second Amended Complaint, *McKiver v. Murphy-Brown, LLC,* Case No. 7:14-CV-180, EDNC, Doc. 34. July 31, 2015.

149   the Farlands' claim is golden: See Plaintiffs' Second Amended Complaint, *McGowan v. Murphy-Brown, LLC,* Case No. 7:14-CV-182, EDNC, Doc. 34, July 31, 2015.

149   When they get to the *Anderson* case: See Plaintiffs' Second Amended Com-
       plaint, *Anderson v. Murphy-Brown, LLC,* Case No. 7:14-CV-183, EDNC, Doc.
       34, July 31, 2015.

151   they land on *Gillis*: See Plaintiffs' Third Amended Complaint, *Gillis v. Murphy-
       Brown, LLC,* Case No. 7:14-CV-185, EDNC, Doc. 42, July 31, 2015.

17. HOG SUMMER

158   The Mitchell Norris farm was a Murphy-allied facility: See, e.g., Odor Best
       Management Plan, Mitchell Norris Farms #1 and 2, prepared by Mitchell Nor-
       ris, farm owner, and Kraig Westerbeek, technical specialist, Murphy Farms,
       May 29, 2001.

158   the Norris farm was the subject: See, e.g., Assessments of Health Symptoms
       Reported to Be Associated with Odors from Animal Operations, North Caro-
       lina Department of Health and Human Services, Division of Epidemiology,
       May 12, 1999, submitted by Chris Priest, Julia Priest, and Karen Priest of Bladen
       County, against the Mitchell Norris Farm; note dated August 16, 1999, from
       Karen Priest to Mitchell Norris about odor log she has kept since January 1,
       1995; Complaint Investigation Report, North Carolina Division of Air Quality,
       Complainant: Alex Hair, Date: February 5, 2004; letter from Debra A. Foster to
       Governor Michael Easley about "the horrible stench of the hog farm very close
       by" and its effect on East Bladen High School, December 12, 2006.

158   his typical straight man schtick: Declaration of Alex Hair, May 2, 2017.

159   The parents, predictably, blew a gasket: Ibid.; letter from Debra Foster to
       Gov. Easley.

159   The state required Norris: Odor Best Management Plan; letter from NCDENR
       to Mitchell Norris, Subject: Air Permit No. 09497 R01, Mitchell Norris Hog
       Farms, March 28, 2005, and attached Air Permit.

159   He had to plant: Ibid.

159   he had to dispense with the big guns: Ibid.

159   the matter of the air permit: Letter from NCDENR to Mitchell Norris, Subject:
       Air Permit.

159   His integrator, Murphy-Brown: See, e.g., Odor Best Management Plan, May 29,
       2001.

161   The organization is a Smithfield plant: Defendant's Objections and Responses
       to Plaintiffs' Amended Request for Admissions on Preliminary Issues, filed
       in *Artis v. Murphy-Brown, LLC,* Doc. 229-3, August 9, 2018 (see Request for
       Admissions #78-83, 86, 87).

161   One document in particular sparkles: Email exchange involving Keira Lom-
       bardo, Ken Sullivan, Don Butler, and Gregg Schmidt, Subject: Approval for
       NCFF media campaign funding, December 21, 2015, admitted as Plaintiffs'
       Exhibit 794 at the trial of *McKiver v. Murphy-Brown, LLC.*

161   The first Farm Families ads start running: NC Farm Families posts video of
       "Struggle" on YouTube, January 22, 2016. (The YouTube link to "Struggle" has
       since been decommissioned, but the Facebook post is still visible.)

161 A second round runs in February: NCFF posts video of "Hog Farming Polluting Our Rivers? I Don't Think So" on YouTube, February 18, 2016, https://www.youtube.com/watch?v=gkGthET1cIU.

161 a third in April: NCFF posts video of "Cycle" on YouTube, April 18, 2016, https://www.youtube.com/watch?v=Hw6cksCdhvc.

163 It's a shot of Linnill Farland: Photo of Linnill Farland submitted as Plaintiffs' Exhibit 1612-45 at the trial of *McGowan v. Murphy-Brown, LLC.*

165 a hog truck trundles: Photos of hog truck at night by home of Jimmy Jacobs, submitted as Plaintiffs' Exhibits 1579-46 and 1579-47 at the trial of *Artis v. Murphy-Brown, LLC.*

166 Steve Wing's *de bene esse* deposition: Video Deposition of Dr. Steve Wing, August 24–25, 2016.

18. THE MURPHY MEN

168 John Sargent, the vice president: Compilation of clips from Video Deposition of John Sargent, September 27, 2016, used at the trial of *Artis v. Murphy-Brown, LLC.*

169 "We do not control the growers": Ibid.

170 The next Smithfield executive: Compilation of clips from video deposition of Kraig Westerbeek, November 21, 2016, used at the trial of *McKiver v. Murphy-Brown, LLC.*

170 The documents Kaeske shows him: Ibid.

171 Don Butler doesn't help: Transcript of video deposition of Don Butler, November 29, 2016, with lines 14–25 on p. 228 redacted.

171 After decades spent flogging: Ibid.

19. FATE AND TRANSPORT

175 an eclectic indie rock band: Bee Children, *Veranophonic* © 2014, and *Gather the Exiles* © 2018.

175 local fame as a "ghostbuster": "Is Your House Haunted? Or Just Dirty?" *Huffington Post,* April 5, 2015.

175 A hog farm with thousands of pigs: See generally Expert Report of Shane Rogers, January 20, 2017, filed in *Artis v. Murphy-Brown, LLC,* Doc. 88-17, June 4, 2018; testimony of Shane Rogers, trial transcript of *McKiver v. Murphy-Brown, LLC,* April 4, 2018, pp. 25–108, April 5, 2018, pp. 10–220, April 6, 2018, pp. 7–165.

176 The name of the signature marker: Expert Report of Shane Rogers, p. 23, et al.

176 fourteen of the tests come back positive: Ibid., p. 71.

177 It's in Mary Tatum's kitchen: Transcript of Video Deposition of Shane Rogers, February 21, 2017, p. 29.

178 By order of the court: Order Re: Site Inspections, *In re: NC Swine Farm Nuisance Litigation,* Case No. 5:15-CV-13-BR, EDNC, Doc. 214, October 19, 2016.

178 she's a microbiology consultant: Expert Rebuttal Report of Jennifer Clancy, filed in *McKiver v. Murphy-Brown, LLC,* Doc. 122-2, March 9, 2018, pp. 2–3.

179 Smithfield's lawyers hired her: Ibid., p. 4.

179   she will conduct no observable science: Testimony of Jennifer Clancy, trial
        transcript of *McKiver v. Murphy-Brown, LLC,* April 19, 2018, morning session,
        pp. 17–112, April 19, 2018, afternoon session, pp. 7–38.

179   The Greenwood 1 facility: See, e.g., photos and videos admitted as Plaintiffs'
        Exhibits 1323-46, 1323-51, 1480-6, 1480-16, 1490-103, 1490-117, 1490-135, 1490-
        136, 1490-161, 1490-194, 1490-204, 1490-293, 1490-296, 1490-425, 1490-458,
        1490-485, 1490-493, 1490-551, 1490-568, 1490-576, 1490-578, 1490-582, 1492-
        121, 1492-127, 1492-131, 1492-199, 1492-201, 1492-306, 1493-18, and 1580-151 in
        the trial of *Artis v. Murphy-Brown, LLC.*

179   Pigs are surprisingly intelligent creatures: Estabrook, *Pig Tales,* pp. 33–44.

180   Then there are the skeletons: Murphy-Brown, LLC, Site Visit Audit, Pridgen
        Farm 4, April 20, 2012, admitted as Plaintiffs' Exhibit 1728-1 in trial of *Artis
        v. Murphy-Brown, LLC;* Smithfield Site Visit Audit, Greenwood Finishing
        #2, February 27, 2017, admitted as Plaintiffs' Exhibit 1728-11 in trial of *Artis
        v. Murphy-Brown, LLC;* letter from Smithfield to Dean Hilton, Greenwood
        Finishing Farm, Re: Site #6334/6335, March 16, 2016, admitted as Plaintiffs'
        Exhibit 1616 in trial of *Artis v. Murphy-Brown, LLC.*

180   the freshly scrubbed appearance: See, e.g., video admitted as Plaintiffs' Exhibits
        1607-708, 1607-903, 1607-904, 1607-946, and 1607-951 at the trial of *McGowan
        v. Murphy-Brown, LLC (McGowan 1).*

180   he's convinced that Super Soils: Expert Report of Viney P. Aneja, *In re: NC
        Swine Farm Nuisance Litigation,* Case No. 5:15-CV-13-BR, EDNC, Doc. 393-
        31, May 16, 2017, pp. 20–21.

180   The third generation of Super Soils, renamed: Ibid.; Mike Williams, NCSU, Eval-
        uation of Generation 3 Treatment Technology for Swine Waste, August 19, 2013,
        https://projects.ncsu.edu/cals/waste_mgt/smithfield_projects/CWMTF-Report.pdf.

180   it was affordable: Expert Report of Viney P. Aneja, pp. 20–21.

181   As the hogs go about their business: See, e.g., photos and videos admitted as
        Plaintiffs' Exhibits 1607-42, 1607-87, 1607-295, and 1607-736 at the trial of
        McGowan v. Murphy-Brown, LLC (McGowan 1).

182   The readings jump from near zero: Expert Report of Shane Rogers, pp. 64–65.

183   The video footage he captures: See videos admitted as Plaintiffs' Exhibits 1494-
        543, 1494-544, and 1494-545 at the trial of *McGowan v. Murphy-Brown, LLC
        (McGowan 1).*

20. COMPANY TOWN

185   There are echoes of this: See generally *The Meat Racket.*

186   Its goal is singular and undisguised: "House Bill 467 Would Shield Industrial
        Hog Industry from Many Legal Claims," N.C. Policy Watch, March 29, 2017.

186   transgender bathroom bill: "North Carolina Bans Local Anti-Discrimination
        Policies," *New York Times,* March 23, 2016.

186   Jimmy Dixon introduces a bill: See House Bill 467, General Assembly of North
        Carolina, March 23, 2017, https://www.ncleg.gov/BillLookup/2017/h467.

187   He's taken $115,000: "State Representative Jimmy Dixon Collected $115,000

from Big Pork, Then Tried to Make the Industry's Legal Troubles Go Away," *IndyWeek,* April 5, 2017.

188   though later in the press: Op-ed by Rep. Jimmy Dixon, "Greedy Lawyers Force Farmers to Pin Hopes on Public Opinion," *Greensboro News-Argus,* on or about June 30, 2018. ("About a year ago, Bill Graham met with me and several of my Republican colleagues in the General Assembly to lobby us to not change our nuisance laws. At one point in the conversation, I told Mr. Graham how much damage he was going to inflict on small family farmers with these unwarranted nuisance claims. He then said, 'No, Rep. Dixon, you don't understand. It is not about the family farmers, it is about the wealthy Chinese owners, and they can afford to pay us.'")

188   the Duplin politician will fall: See, e.g., transcript of House Judiciary III Committee Hearing, North Carolina General Assembly, April 5, 2017, comments of Rep. Jimmy Dixon.

189   Way back in 1610: William Blackstone, *Commentaries on the Laws of England,* entry on "Nuisance"; *William Aldred's Case,* 77 Eng. Rep. 816; Jon Guze, "This Little Piggy Went to Court," John Locke Foundation, April 12, 2017, https://www.johnlocke.org/update/this-little-piggy-went-to-court/.

190   Stam works up a "Dear Colleague" letter: Letter from Paul ("Skip") Stam to Hon. Jonathan Jordan, et al., NC House of Representatives, Re: House Bill 467—Agriculture and Forestry Nuisance Remedies, March 31, 2017.

190   the Judiciary Committee takes it up: Minutes of House Judiciary III Committee Hearing, March 29, 2017; transcript of House Judiciary III Committee Hearing, March 29, 2017.

190   They come out in droves: Ibid.

191   leads with a quote from Abe Lincoln: Transcript of March 29, 2017, Judiciary Committee Hearing; "Jimmy Dixon Collected $115,000 from Big Pork," *IndyWeek.*

191   Dixon then pleads the bill's merits: Transcript of March 29, 2017, Judiciary Committee Hearing.

191   Mona's team agreed to waive: Stipulation as to Certain Claims and Evidence, *In re: NC Swine Farm Nuisance Litigation,* Doc. 250, December 2, 2016.

191   "I'm going to use": Transcript of March 29, 2017, Judiciary Committee Hearing, exchange between Rep. Dixon and Rep. Lehman.

192   "What is the fair market value": Ibid., Comments of Victoria Cunningham.

192   "The CAFO industry": Ibid., Comments of Larry Baldwin.

192   "My name is Elsie Herring": Ibid., Comments of Elsie Herring.

192   In another setting, he will suggest: House Floor Debate, Bill 467, NC General Assembly, April 10, 2017.

21. THE PEOPLE'S CIRCUS

194   They score another coup when Robert Orr: Letter from Robert F. Orr to Hon. Tamara Barringer, NC Senate, Re: SB460—Agriculture and Forestry Nuisance Remedies, April 3, 2017.

195   The John Locke Foundation: "This Little Piggy," John Locke Foundation.

195   The people come with knives out: Minutes of House Judiciary III Committee Hearing, NC General Assembly, April 5, 2017; transcript of April 5, 2017, Judiciary Committee Hearing.

195   he has done a little due diligence: Transcript of April 5, 2017, Judiciary Committee Hearing, exchange between Rep. Amos Quick and Rep. Jimmy Dixon.

195   Dixon, to his credit: Ibid.

196   Dixon isn't interested in talking: Ibid.

196   Quick tries a different tack: Ibid.

196   Jimmy Dixon takes refuge in denial: Ibid.

197   There's a man who works: Ibid., Comments of Hilton Monroe.

197   There's a military veteran: Ibid., Comments of Isaac Ward.

197   There's a hog farmer from Duplin: Ibid., Comments of Jeff Spetting.

197   "I'm a *former* hog farmer": Ibid., Comments of Don Webb.

197   the last speaker from the gallery: Ibid., Comments of Mark Dorosin, UNC Center for Civil Rights.

198   "All those in favor": Transcript of April 5, 2017 Judiciary Committee Hearing, comments of Rep. Jordan.

198   The full House takes up the bill: "Hog Waste Bill Speeds Through NC House," WRAL.com, April 6, 2017, and embedded video of proceedings on House floor, April 6, 2017.

198   That is what happens with HB467: Ibid.

22. AMENDMENT ONE

202   he decides he can't support it: Transcript of House Floor Debate, Bill 467, April 10, 2017, comments of John Blust; email from John Blust to Skip Stam, April 10, 2017, 11:27 a.m., Subject: Re: Stam re House Bill 467.

202   Pat McElraft, a blustery Republican: Email string between Rep. Pat McElraft, Rep. John Blust, and Rep. Lee Zachary, Subject: HB 467 and HB 470, April 9–10, 2017.

203   packing them into the visitors' mezzanine: Photos and video footage of floor debate and vote on HB467, Amendment One, April 10, 2017, WRAL.com, https://www.wral.com/news/state/nccapitol/video/16637012/.

203   The legislators rise for the prayer: Ibid.

207   "The clerk will lock the machine": Video footage of Floor Debate and Vote on HB467, Amendment One, April 10, 2017, WRAL.com, https://www.wral.com/news/state/nccapitol/video/16637012/.

207   Moore ignores this unwritten rule: House Roll Call Vote Transcript for Roll Call #198, 2017–2018 Session, HB467, https://www.ncleg.gov/Legislation/Votes/RollCallVoteTranscript/2017/H/198.

207   Only two members rise: Video footage of Floor Debate and Vote on HB467, Amendment One, April 10, 2017, WRAL.com, https://www.wral.com/news/state/nccapitol/video/16637012/.

207   It meets a similar reception: HB467, NC General Assembly, https://www.ncleg
       .gov/BillLookup/2017/h467.

23. FIRST WORDS

215   Judge Britt issues an omnibus order: Order on various motions, *In re: NC Swine
       Farm Nuisance Litigation,* Doc. 476, November 8, 2017.

215   the old judge hears arguments: Transcript of Motion Hearing, *In re: NC Swine
       Farm Nuisance Litigation,* Doc. 489, December 4, 2017.

24. CLOUD OF WITNESSES

220   he lays out the Good Neighbor rule: Trial transcript of *McKiver v. Murphy-
       Brown, LLC,* April 3, 2018, p. 6.

221   three of its six peremptory challenges: Redacted trial transcript of *McKiver v.
       Murphy-Brown, LLC,* April 2, 2018, pp. 119–22.

221   His opening is equal parts: See generally trial transcript of *McKiver v. Murphy-
       Brown, LLC,* April 3, 2018, pp. 6–68.

25. BLOODSPORT

230   Wing communicates to the jury: Video testimony of Dr. Steve Wing, trial tran-
       script of *McKiver v. Murphy-Brown, LLC,* April 4, 2018; video deposition of
       Dr. Steve Wing, August 24–25, 2016.

230   Then Shane Rogers takes the stand: See testimony of Shane Rogers, trial tran-
       script of *McKiver v. Murphy-Brown, LLC,* April 4, 2018, pp. 25–108; April 5,
       2018, pp. 10–220; April 6, 2018, pp. 7–165.

230   Shane shows the jury: See, e.g., photos and videos admitted as Plaintiffs' Exhib-
       its 1494-37, 1494-43, 1494-58, 1494-92, 1494-128, 1494-180, 1494-646, and 1494-
       719 at the trial of *McKiver v. Murphy-Brown, LLC.*

230   Mike Kaeske trots out: Trial transcript of *McKiver v. Murphy-Brown, LLC,*
       April 5, 2018, pp. 10–11.

230   christens the pig: Trial transcript of *McKiver v. Murphy-Brown, LLC,* April 6,
       2018, p. 7.

231   Daphne McKoy, the youngest: Testimony of Daphne McKoy, trial transcript
       of *McKiver v. Murphy-Brown, LLC,* April 6, 2018, pp. 165–224; April 9, 2018,
       pp. 6–49.

232   He calls Kraig Westerbeek and John Sargent: Video testimony of Kraig West-
       erbeek, trial transcript of *McKiver v. Murphy-Brown, LLC,* April 9, 2018, p. 84;
       video testimony of John Sargent, trial transcript of *McKiver v. Murphy-Brown,
       LLC,* April 11, 2018, pp. 152–53.

232   Butler is a smooth operator: Testimony of Don Butler, trial transcript of *McKiver
       v. Murphy-Brown, LLC,* April 10, 2018, pp. 33–168; April 11, 2018, pp. 3–152.

26. A TRAITOR TO HIS KIND

241   He calls Billy Kinlaw: Testimony of Billy Kinlaw, trial transcript of *McKiver v. Murphy-Brown, LLC,* April 12, 2018, pp. 130–215; April 13, 2018, pp. 11–41.

242   Kaeske summons his "boss," Gregg Schmidt: Testimony of Gregg Schmidt, trial transcript of *McKiver v. Murphy-Brown, LLC,* April 13, 2018, pp. 41–110.

245   he had hosted a group of EPA officials: Letter from EPA to William G. Ross, Jr., NC DEQ, Re: Letter of Concern, January 12, 2017, pp. 4–5.

245   The EPA was in the process: Ibid.

247   Mike Kaeske guides him through his story: Testimony of Tom Butler, trial transcript of *McKiver v. Murphy-Brown, LLC,* April 16, 2018, pp. 21–104.

27. SEE NO EVIL, SMELL NO EVIL

252   There's a horse trainer: Testimony of Ted Carson, trial transcript of *McKiver v. Murphy-Brown, LLC,* April 18, 2018, pp. 36–96.

252   There's a game warden: Testimony of Michael Nunnery, trial transcript of *McKiver v. Murphy-Brown, LLC,* April 18, 2018, pp. 96–152.

252   There's a couple: Testimony of Jacquelyne Creed-Enloe and Mark Enloe, trial transcript of *McKiver v. Murphy-Brown, LLC,* April 18, 2018, pp. 38–87.

252   And there's a chiropractor: Testimony of Dr. Danny Ellis, trial transcript of *McKiver v. Murphy-Brown, LLC,* April 20, 2018, pp. 62–122.

253   Whenever Ted Carson: Testimony of Ted Carson, Trial Transcript of *McKiver v. Murphy-Brown, LLC,* April 18, 2018, pp. 36–96.

253   The game warden, Nunnery: Testimony of Michael Nunnery, Trial Transcript of *McKiver v. Murphy-Brown, LLC,* April 18, 2018, pp. 96–152.

253   The couple, Gigi and Mark: Testimony of Jacquelyne Creed-Enloe and Mark Enloe, Trial Transcript of *McKiver v. Murphy-Brown, LLC,* April 18, 2018, pp. 38–87.

253   When Dr. Ellis takes the stand: Testimony of Dr. Danny Ellis, Trial Transcript of *McKiver v. Murphy-Brown, LLC,* April 20, 2018, pp. 62–122.

253   the story of another local landowner: Testimony of Dale Bollinger, Trial Transcript of *McKiver v. Murphy-Brown, LLC,* April 12, 2018, pp. 40–95.

254   Dr. Ellis, by contrast: Testimony of Dr. Danny Ellis, Trial Transcript of *McKiver v. Murphy-Brown, LLC,* April 20, 2018, pp. 62–122.

256   The first, Dr. Todd See: Testimony of Dr. Todd See, trial transcript of *McKiver v. Murphy-Brown, LLC,* April 17, 2018, pp. 6–193.

257   a veteran of the Missouri litigation: Order on plaintiffs' motion to exclude or limit the expert testimony of Pamela Dalton, Ph.D., *McKiver v. Murphy-Brown, LLC,* Doc. 234, April 19, 2018.

257   a sympathetic voice for the industry: Pamela Dalton, et al., "A Multi-Year Field Olfactometry Study near a Concentrated Animal Feeding Operation," *Journal of the Air & Waste Management Association* 61:12, 1398–408 (2011) (This article grew out of Dalton's expert work in the Missouri litigation on behalf of Premium Standard Farms.).

257   she conducted a study: Expert Report of Pamela Dalton, filed as Exhibit 1 to

Plaintiffs' Memorandum in Support of Its Motion in Limine for Exclusions of Opinions of Pamela Dalton, Ph.D., *McKiver v. Murphy-Brown, LLC,* Doc. 96, February 19, 2018.

257   Judge Britt, however, found fault with her methodology: Order on plaintiffs' motion to exclude or limit the expert testimony of Pamela Dalton, Ph.D., *McKiver v. Murphy-Brown, LLC,* Doc. 234, April 19, 2018.

257   Most of Clancy's testimony: Testimony of Jennifer Clancy, trial transcript of *McKiver v. Murphy-Brown, LLC,* April 19, 2018, Morning Session, pp. 17–112, April 19, 2018, Afternoon Session, pp. 7–38.

260   Smithfield's last witness: Testimony of Kraig Westerbeek, trial transcript of *McKiver v. Murphy-Brown, LLC,* April 20, 2018, pp. 122–205; April 23, 2018, pp. 8–96.

28. PITCHFORKS ON THE DOORSTEP OF JUSTICE

263   Mike Kaeske and Mark Anderson deliver: Trial transcript of *McKiver v. Murphy-Brown, LLC,* April 24, 2018.

263   Mike Kaeske kills it: Ibid., pp. 124–38.

264   The verdict lands just after two o'clock: Trial transcript of *McKiver v. Murphy-Brown, LLC,* April 26, 2018; verdict, *McKiver v. Murphy-Brown, LLC,* Doc. 267, April 26, 2018.

266   Fifty million is the headline that ran: "Jury Awards Hog Farm Neighbors $50 Million," *News & Observer,* April 26, 2018.

266   scathing four-page press release: Smithfield Foods Extended Statement Regarding McKiver v. Murphy-Brown Verdict, April 27, 2018, https://investors .smithfieldfoods.com/2018-04-27-Smithfield-Foods-Extended-Statement -Regarding-McKiver-v-Murphy-Brown-Verdict.

267   it castigates Judge Britt: Ibid.

267   The Pork Council rails: Statement by North Carolina Pork Council on verdict in *McKiver v. Murphy-Brown,* April 26, 2018, https://www.ncpork.org/statement -north-carolina-pork-council-verdict-mckiver-vs-murphy-brown/.

267   "How does this end?": "Questions About the Nuisance Lawsuit," NC Farm Families, May 1, 2018, https://www.ncfarmfamilies.com/farmkeepersblog/2018/ 05/01/questions-about-the-nuisance-lawsuit.

267   Indeed, no less a personage: "Perdue Calls Smithfield Decision 'Despicable,' Farm Bureau Agrees," *The Fence Post,* May 2, 2018, https://www.thefencepost .com/news/perdue-calls-smithfield-decision-despicable-farm-bureau-agrees/.

267   The bill—codified as S711: Senate Bill 711, North Carolina General Assembly, 2017–2018 Session, https://www.ncleg.gov/BillLookup/2017/s711; "NC Farm Act, Fattened with Protections for Hog Industry, Up for Senate Vote at Noon," N.C. Policy Watch, June 7, 2018; "After Court Loss, N.C. Pork Producer Turns to Legislature for a Win," N.C. Policy Watch, June 8, 2018.

268   a remarkable fourteen-minute rant: "Lawmaker Calls Out House Leadership, Colleagues During Farm Bill Debate," WRAL.com, June 14, 2018, with embedded video of floor comments by Rep. John Blust, https://www.wral

.com/lawmaker-calls-out-house-leadership-colleagues-during-farm-bill-debate/
17627825/.

269   Both chambers pass S711: Senate Bill 711, North Carolina General Assembly,
      2017–2018 Session, https://www.ncleg.gov/BillLookup/2017/s711; "House Over-
      rides Veto of N.C. Farm Act in a Blow to Individual Rights and Public Health,"
      Environmental Defense Fund, June 27, 2018, https://www.edf.org/media/house
      -overrides-veto-nc-farm-act-blow-individual-rights-and-public-health.

269   "existential threat": "Residents Raise a Stink over Pig Farms in North Carolina,"
      Wall Street Journal, May 30, 2018.

270   Smithfield announced a new $100 million: "Smithfield Foods to Invest $100M
      in NC Pork Plant," AP News, August 22, 2017.

270   a blog post that fuels the frenzy: "Eastern North Carolina is Under Attack," NC
      Pork Council, May 31, 2018, https://www.ncpork.org/eastern-north-carolina
      -attack/.

270   Curliss launches another broadside: "In Nuisance Trial, Fact Twisting About
      Who Got There First," NC Pork Council, June 1, 2018, https://www.ncpork
      .org/fact-twisting/.

271   Kaeske told the jury: Plaintiffs' Opening Statement, trial transcript of *McGowan
      v. Murphy-Brown, LLC (McGowan I),* May 30, 2018, pp. 31–91.

271   Richard Mole sends an email: Email from Richard Mole to Kaeske Law Firm,
      Subject: Farmer, June 1, 2018, 8:55 p.m., sent through "Contact Us" web form
      on kaeskelaw.com.

271   the Kaeske Law Firm receives a web message: Email from "American As Can
      Be" to Kaeske Law Firm, Subject: Pigs, June 2, 2018, 7:27 a.m., sent through
      "Contact Us" web form on kaeskelaw.com.

272   Kaeske shows the emails to Judge Britt: Trial transcript of *McGowan v. Murphy-
      Brown, LLC (McGowan I),* June 4, 2018, pp. 4–13.

29. INTO THE WHIRLWIND

274   Word of it comes to Judge Britt: Trial transcript of *McGowan v. Murphy-Brown,
      LLC (McGowan I),* June 13, 2018, pp. 4–57.

276   Judge Britt takes a brief recess: Ibid., p. 57.

276   Steve Wing delivered his posthumous testimony: Video testimony of Steve Wing,
      trial transcript of *McGowan v. Murphy-Brown, LLC (McGowan I),* May 31, 2018.

276   Shane Rogers mesmerized the jury: Testimony of Shane Rogers, trial transcript
      of *McGowan v. Murphy-Brown, LLC (McGowan I),* May 31, 2018, pp. 9–29;
      June 1, 2018, pp. 9–116; June 4, 2018, pp. 15–216; June 5, 2018, Morning Session,
      pp. 4–124; June 5, 2018, Afternoon Session, pp. 3–78.

276   The neighbors from Hallsville Road: See testimony of Lendora Farland, trial
      transcript of *McGowan v. Murphy-Brown, LLC (McGowan I),* June 6, 2018,
      pp. 7–115; testimony of Barbara Gibbs, ibid., pp. 115–54; testimony of Elvis
      Williams, trial transcript of *McGowan v. Murphy-Brown, LLC (McGowan I),*
      June 12, 2018, pp. 99–198; testimony of Vonnie Williams, trial transcript of
      McGowan v. Murphy-Brown, LLC (McGowan I), June 12, 2018, pp. 198–226.

276   The Murphy men, Don Butler: See testimony of Don Butler, trial transcript
      of *McGowan v. Murphy-Brown, LLC (McGowan 1)*, June 6, 2018, pp. 154–206;
      June 7, 2018, pp. 4–195; June 8, 2018, pp. 6–66; video testimony of John Sar-
      gent, trial transcript of *McGowan v. Murphy-Brown, LLC (McGowan 1)*, June 8,
      2018, p. 80; video testimony of Kraig Westerbeek, ibid., p. 81.

276   Then there was Joey Carter: Testimony of Joey Carter, trial transcript of
      McGowan v. Murphy-Brown, LLC (McGowan 1), June 8, 2018, pp. 85–177;
      June 11, 2018, pp. 5–235; June 12, 2018, pp. 6–99.

277   Lendora Farland was a rock star: Testimony of Lendora Farland, trial of
      McGowan 1.

277   Barbara Gibbs, a taciturn woman: Testimony of Barbara Gibbs, trial of
      McGowan 1.

277   And Elvis and Vonnie: Testimony of Elvis Williams and Vonnie Williams, trial
      of *McGowan 1*.

277   When Judge Britt calls the lawyers back: Trial transcript of *McGowan v. Murphy-
      Brown, LLC (McGowan 1)*, June 13, 2018, pp. 57–70.

278   Kaeske took Lisa's advice: Trial transcript of *McGowan v. Murphy-Brown, LLC
      (McGowan 1)*, May 29, 2018, pp. 108–16.

278   Mark Anderson complained: Ibid., p. 115.

278   He argued that the judge should scrap: Ibid.

279   Judge Britt ponders this over lunch: Trial transcript of *McGowan v. Murphy-
      Brown, LLC (McGowan 1)*, June 13, 2018, pp. 71–76.

279   publishes an opinion piece: Op-ed by Rep. Jimmy Dixon, "Right to Farm Laws
      Should Be Honored," *Duplin Times*, June 14, 2018.

281   Smithfield's messaging is glossier: *Duplin Times*, June 14, 2018, p. 6B.

281   "First, they came for Billy Kinlaw": Ibid., p. 7C.

30. TOTAL WAR

283   the lawyers again come to blows: Trial transcript of *McGowan v. Murphy-Brown,
      LLC (McGowan 1)*, June 22, 2018, pp. 77–103; trial transcript of *McGowan v.
      Murphy-Brown, LLC (McGowan 1)*, June 27, 2018, pp. 2–32.

285   the hog barons and their allies: "Group Rallies in Support of Agriculture in
      NC," WRAL.com, and embedded videos of event, https://www.wral.com/group
      -rallies-in-support-of-agriculture-in-nc/17654403/.

286   Mike Kaeske is offering the twelve jurors: Plaintiffs' Closing Argument, trial
      transcript of *McGowan v. Murphy-Brown, LLC (McGowan 1)*, June 25, 2018,
      pp. 9–60, 122–43.

288   Judge Britt takes matters into his own hands: Order in *McGowan v. Murphy-
      Brown, LLC*, Doc. 267, June 27, 2018.

288   As in *McKiver*, the jurors decide: Trial transcript of *McGowan v. Murphy-Brown,
      LLC (McGowan 1)*, June 29, 2018, pp. 2–8; verdict in *McGowan v. Murphy-
      Brown, LLC (McGowan 1)*, Doc. 279, June 29, 2018.

288   NC Farm Families posts a summary: Facebook post, NC Farm Families, June 29,
      2018, https://www.facebook.com/ncfarmfamilies/posts/the-verdict-is-in-in-the

-case-of-williams-v-murphy-brown-llc-and-the-joey-carter/211509601539 6591/.

288   Joey Carter's son posts: Facebook post by Matthew Carter, June 29, 2018, reposted by NC Pork Council, https://www.facebook.com/NCPork/posts/ we-are-indeed-all-heartbroken-and-praying-for-you-today-my-family-is-heart -broke/2175387205837228/.

289   He throws his fists low: Facebook post by Jimmy Dixon, June 30, 2018.

289   even though Smithfield's own lawyer: Transcript of October 15, 2013 hearing, *Alderman v. Smithfield Foods, Inc.*, Wake County Superior Court, p. 14 ("As Ms. Wallace said, we didn't hear anything about her law firm.").

289   Dixon accuses Mike Kaeske: Facebook post by Jimmy Dixon, June 30, 2018.

289   the Duplin legislator submits his screed: "Greedy Lawyers Force Farmers to Pin Hopes on Public Opinion," *Goldsboro News-Argus,* on or about June 30, 2018.

290   "OK y'all," she writes: Facebook post by Denise Stone-Byrd, July 1, 2018, followed by comments.

291   Randy Davis, one: Affidavit of Randy Davis, October 30, 2014.

31. THE HOG KING AND THE SAINT

295   he made a billion dollars raising hogs: "The Ray Kroc of Pigsties," *Forbes.*

296   He introduces the jurors: Opening Statement of Mike Kaeske, trial transcript of *Artis v. Murphy-Brown, LLC,* July 11, 2018, pp. 11–77.

297   "It was one hour, ten minutes": Opening Statement of Jim Neale, trial transcript of *Artis v. Murphy-Brown, LLC,* July 11, 2018, pp. 77–131.

298   the mesmeric cadence of Steve Wing's words: Video testimony of Dr. Steve Wing, trial transcript of *Artis v. Murphy-Brown, LLC,* July 11, 2018, p. 131; trial transcript of *Artis v. Murphy-Brown, LLC,* July 12, 2018, p. 6.

298   "You said you have reviewed": Testimony of Shane Rogers, trial transcript of *Artis v. Murphy-Brown, LLC,* July 16, 2018, pp. 16–17.

299   Most of the defense lawyer's cross: Ibid., pp. 17–94; testimony of Shane Rogers, trial transcript of *Artis v. Murphy-Brown, LLC,* July 17, 2018, pp. 4–130.

300   Joyce Messick gives this axiom: Testimony of Joyce Messick, trial transcript of *Artis v. Murphy-Brown, LLC,* July 17, 2018, pp. 195–216; July 18, 2018, pp. 6–14.

32. WORLD ON FIRE

303   Sewell is a diamond: Testimony of Wesley Sewell, trial transcript of *Artis v. Murphy-Brown, LLC,* July 18, 2018, pp. 14–59.

306   If Don Butler could rescue: Testimony of Don Butler, trial transcript of *Artis v. Murphy-Brown, LLC,* July 18, 2018, pp. 126–69; July 19, 2018, pp. 5–221, July 20, 2018, pp. 6–128.

309   By the time Dean Hilton: Testimony of Dean Hilton, trial transcript of *Artis v. Murphy-Brown, LLC,* July 23, 2018, pp. 90–248.

310   What he can do is play: Video Testimony of Dale Meyer, trial transcript of *Artis v. Murphy-Brown, LLC,* July 23, 2018, p. 248.

33. THE FURIES

315   There's Dr. Terry Coffey: Testimony of Dr. Terry Coffey, pp. 23–164.

316   Then there's Robert White Johnson: Testimony of Robert White Johnson, trial transcript of *Artis v. Murphy-Brown, LLC,* July 26, 2018, pp. 164–214.

316   Neale calls Dr. Pam Dalton: Testimony of Dr. Pam Dalton, trial transcript of *Artis v. Murphy-Brown, LLC,* July 27, 2018, pp. 12–162.

318   Jim Neale puts a medical doctor: Testimony of Dr. Keith Ramsey, trial transcript of *Artis v. Murphy-Brown, LLC,* July 31, 2018, pp. 5–107.

320   it is Christine Lawson: Testimony of Christine Lawson, trial transcript of *Artis v. Murphy-Brown, LLC,* July 30, 2018, pp. 6–166.

328   a trio of neighbors: Testimony of Robbie Cauley, trial transcript of *Artis v. Murphy-Brown, LLC,* July 31, 2018, pp. 107–43; testimony of Linda Dougherty, ibid., pp. 143–61; testimony of Hans Lonander, ibid., pp. 161–90.

329   After the lawyers deliver their closings: Closing Arguments, trial transcript of *Artis v. Murphy-Brown, LLC,* August 2, 2018, pp. 12–130.

34. RING THE BELLS

333   the National Ag Roundtable at the State Fairgrounds: NC Farm Bureau live stream of National Ag Roundtable; "Massive Hog Trial Verdict as Elected Leaders Rally for Farmers," WRAL.com, August 3, 2018.

337   "Mr. Baker," says Judge Britt: Trial transcript of *Artis v. Murphy-Brown, LLC,* August 3, 2018, pp. 6–8; verdict, *Artis v. Murphy-Brown, LLC,* Doc. 221, August 3, 2018.

341   A few miles away: NC Farm Bureau live stream of National Ag Roundtable; "Massive Hog Trial Verdict as Elected Leaders Rally for Farmers," WRAL.com, August 3, 2018.

35. DEUS EX MACHINA

344   Smithfield made sweeping improvements: "Smithfield Foods Announces Landmark Investment to Reduce Greenhouse Gas Emissions," *GlobeNewswire,* October 25, 2018 (discussing covering and converting existing hog lagoons to covered digesters, reducing truck traffic on its hog farms, and adopting low-trajectory application tools to apply recycled nutrients to farmland); testimony of Gregg Schmidt, trial transcript of *Gillis v. Murphy-Brown, LLC,* November 29, 2018, pp. 166–81 (refrigerated dead boxes, revised trucking schedules, expanded feed bins); testimony of Kraig Westerbeek, trial transcript of *Gillis v. Murphy-Brown, LLC,* Case No. 7:14-CV-185-BR, EDNC, December 3, 2018, pp. 235–41 (Aer-Way system, refrigerated dead boxes, revised trucking schedule, feed bins), pp. 243–59 (testing of lagoon covers and biogas digesters).

344   Judge Britt modified the trial schedule: Joint Motion for Continuance and Stay of Discovery, *In re: NC Swine Farm Nuisance Litigation,* Doc. 513, ¶ 6; Order on the Parties' Joint Motion for Continuance and Stay of Discovery, *In re: NC Swine Farm Nuisance Litigation,* Doc. 517, August 23, 2018.

344   a three-judge panel: Audio recording of oral argument on gag order appeal, *In re:*

Murphy-Brown, LLC, Case No. 18-1762, United States Court of Appeals for the Fourth Circuit, September 25, 2018, https://www.ca4.uscourts.gov/OAarchive/mp3/18-1762-20180925.mp3; Published Opinion Denying Motion to Dismiss Appeal and Granting Petition for Writ of Mandamus, Doc. 50, October 29, 2018.

345   the Murphy men benched McGuireWoods: Notice of Appearance of Robert Edwin Thackston on behalf of Murphy-Brown, LLC, *Gillis v. Murphy-Brown, LLC,* Doc. 162, September 21, 2018.

345   He had spearheaded: "Pure MX Park's Battle Update," Vital MX, February 2, 2011, https://www.vitalmx.com/forums/Moto=Related, 20/Pure-MX-Parks-battle-update, 1210135 ("Robert Thackston, a Dallas lawyer with a weekend home in Montalba, has filed a lawsuit in Anderson County demanding Pure MX be shut down"); "HPTY Represents over 20 Landowners in Pro Bono Nuisance Suit," Hawkins Parnell Thackston & Young, LLP, March, 2011 ("A team from Dallas including Robert Thackston . . . represented over 20 landowners in a nuisance suit to abate the noise from a motocross track in a serene country community. After a trial on a temporary injunction and intense public debate, the case resolved and the track closed.").

345   appointed David Faber: Amended Designation of a Senior United States Judge for Service in Another District Within the Circuit, *Gillis v. Murphy-Brown, LLC,* Doc. 154, August 6, 2018.

345   His rulings had the effect: See, e.g., Order Granting Defendant's Motion to Bifurcate the Issues of Compensatory and Punitive Damages, *Gillis v. Murphy-Brown, LLC,* Doc. 184, October 24, 2018; Memorandum Opinion on Order to Bifurcate, *Gillis v. Murphy-Brown, LLC,* Doc. 249; Judge Faber's decision to exclude evidence about executive compensation at Murphy-Brown LLC and profits at Smithfield's Chinese parent company, WH Group, in punitive damages phase, trial transcript of *Gillis v. Murphy-Brown, LLC,* December 12, 2018, pp. 22–28. Judge Faber's decision to exclude a raft of exhibits relating to the defendant's knowledge of the odor problem, ibid., December 13, 2018, pp. 4–23.

345   The new judge relegated: Order and Memorandum Opinion on bifurcation.

345   He barred Kaeske from talking: Trial transcript of *Gillis v. Murphy-Brown, LLC,* December 12, 2018, pp. 22–28.

345   And he allowed Smithfield's lawyers: Opening Statement of Jim Neale in Punitive Damages Phase, trial transcript of *Gillis v. Murphy-Brown, LLC,* December 12, 2018, p. 62 (overruling the objection made by Mike Kaeske that the law holds Smithfield responsible "all the way back" to the founding of the farm, not just since the 2000 merger).

346   the refrigerated dead box: Testimony of Gregg Schmidt, trial transcript of *Gillis v. Murphy-Brown, LLC,* November 29, 2018, pp. 166–76.

346   the revised trucking schedule: Ibid., pp. 176–78.

346   the expanded feed bins that reduced: Ibid., pp. 180–81.

346   a tutorial about the low-odor AerWay: Testimony of Kraig Westerbeek, trial transcript of *Gillis v. Murphy-Brown, LLC,* December 3, 2018, pp. 235–41.

346   the money the company had spent testing: Ibid., pp. 243–59.

346   the digesters currently installed: Ibid., pp. 253–54.

346   the lawyer from Dallas had the grounds: Closing argument by Robert Thackston, trial transcript of *Gillis v. Murphy-Brown, LLC,* December 6, 2018, pp. 66–69, 91–94.

347   the second McGowan trial featured the neighbors: See video testimony of Linnill Farland, trial transcript of *McGowan v. Murphy-Brown, LLC (McGowan 2),* February 8, 2019, p. 217; testimony of Georgia Mae Farland, Ibid., pp. 220–39; February 11, 2019, pp. 9–31.

347   Joey Carter was not as disastrous a witness: Testimony of Joey Carter, trial transcript of *McGowan v. Murphy-Brown, LLC (McGowan 2),* February 14, 2019, pp. 211–41; February 15, 2019, pp. 9–232; February 19, 2019, pp. 10–239; February 20, 2019, pp. 5–224.

347   he could not escape: Ibid., February 15, 2019, pp. 69–75.

348   The total award, including: Verdict, *McGowan v. Murphy-Brown, LLC (McGowan 2),* Doc. 582, March 8, 2019.

348   the media gave the Murphy men: "Jury Awards Plaintiffs $420,000 as Smithfield Loses Fifth Hog Nuisance Trial," N.C. Policy Watch, March 11, 2019; "Fifth North Carolina Nuisance Case Lands Another Blow to Pig Farmers," AgWeb, March 11, 2019.

348   Smithfield filed a motion: Motion to Stay Trials Pending Appeal, *In re: NC Swine Farm Nuisance Litigation,* Doc. 557, February 12, 2019 ("Staying the 2019 trial until the Fourth Circuit resolves these appeals will encourage settlement . . .").

348   the stay should be conditioned: Plaintiffs' Response to Defendant's Request to Stay Trials, *In re: NC Swine Farm Nuisance Litigation,* Doc. 567, April 24, 2019.

348   after a status conference: SEALED Telephonic status conference, *In re: NC Swine Farm Nuisance Litigation,* Doc. 569, May 31, 2019.

348   Judge Britt entered an order: Order Staying All Cases, *In re: NC Swine Farm Nuisance Litigation,* Doc. 570, June 3, 2019.

349   took a dragnet approach: Corrected Opening Brief of Defendant-Appellant, *McKiver v. Murphy-Brown, LLC,* Case No. 19-1019, Fourth Circuit Court of Appeals, February 27, 2019.

349   the state House *removed*: Amendment One to HB467 adopted on April 10, 2017, NC General Assembly, https://www.ncleg.gov/BillLookup/2017/h467.

349   the statements made by Jimmy Dixon and Brent Jackson: Comments of Jimmy Dixon, transcript of final House debate on HB467, April 27, 2017 ("In addition to maintaining absolutely zero retroactivity relative to causes of action filed . . . we articulated that very clearly so that there could be no misunderstanding . . . This act is effective when it becomes law and applies to causes of action commenced or brought on or after that date"); transcript of final Senate debate on HB467, April 26, 2017 ("This Bill does not pertain to anything dealing with pending lawsuits, and it becomes effective when it becomes law.").

350   the lagoon breach at his own Vestal Farms operation: "Hog Waste Spilled in Duplin County; Cause Unknown," *Duplin Times,* March 4, 1999 ("Murphy Farms officials wondered whether vandals could have played a role"); "Wen-

dell H. Murphy: Toward Merger," interview with UNC-TV (Q: "At the time, a Murphy Farms official speculated that environmentalists may have sabotaged the lagoon? Did you believe at that time that that could be true?" A: "At first we thought about the sabotage, but then we decided that it was a result of the individual who was operating that equipment and moving that water from one lagoon to the other, and it ran over.").

350   The plaintiffs struck back, and hard: Brief of Appellees, *McKiver v. Murphy-Brown, LLC,* Fourth Circuit Appeal, April 29, 2019.

350   The Waterkeeper Alliance described: Brief for *Amicus Curiae* Waterkeeper Alliance in Support of Appellees, *McKiver v. Murphy-Brown, LLC,* Fourth Circuit Appeal, May 3, 2019.

350   consortium of public health experts: Unopposed Brief of *Amicus Curiae* Dr. Lawrence B. Cahoon, Elizabeth Christenson, Dr. Brett Doherty, Mike Dolan Fliss, Dr. Jill Johnston, Bob Martin, Dr. Sarah Rhodes, Dr. Ana Maria Rule, Dr. Sacoby Wilson & Dr. Courtney Woods in Support of Plaintiffs-Appellees, *McKiver v. Murphy-Brown, LLC,* Fourth Circuit Appeal, May 6, 2019.

350   legal impact groups like Public Justice: Corrected Unopposed Brief for *Amicus Curiae* of Public Justice and Food & Water Watch in Support of Appellees, *McKiver v. Murphy-Brown, LLC,* Fourth Circuit Appeal, May 7, 2019; brief of American Association for Justice as *Amicus Curiae* in Support of Plaintiffs-Appellees and Affirmance, *McKiver v. Murphy-Brown, LLC,* Fourth Circuit Appeal, May 6, 2019.

352   a pair of grassroots amici from down east: *Amicus Curiae* Brief for the North Carolina Environmental Justice Network and the Rural Empowerment Association for Community Help in Support of Plaintiffs-Appellees and Affirmance, *McKiver v. Murphy-Brown, LLC,* Fourth Circuit Appeal, May 6, 2019.

36. HIGHER LAW

355   Raphael takes the podium first: Audio recording of hearing before Hon. J. Harvie Wilkinson, G. Steven Agee, and Stephanie D. Thacker on *McKiver v. Murphy-Brown, LLC,* Case No. 19-1019, Fourth Circuit Court of Appeals, January 31, 2020, https://www.ca4.uscourts.gov/OAarchive/mp3/19-1019-20200131.mp3.

37. WAITING FOR DAYLIGHT

361   The Southern Trial Lawyers Association honors Mona: Tommy Malone Great American Eagle Award Past Honorees, https://www.southerntriallawyers.com/tommy_malone_great_american_ea.php.

365   She sues Bank of America: Class Action Complaint, *Zahran v. Bank of America, N.A.,* Case No. 3:20-CV-427, U.S. District Court for Western District of North Carolina.

365   she takes the grieving families under wing: "Family Files Personal Injury Lawsuit Against Salisbury Nursing Home at Center of COVID-19 Outbreak," https://wallacegraham.com/wg-in-the-news/family-files-personal-injury-lawsuit-against-salisbury-nursing-home-at-center-of-covid-19-outbreak/.

365   he landed a $32 million verdict: "Wallace & Graham Wins $32.7 Million Meso-
       thelioma Verdict—the Largest of Its Kind in North Carolina History," https://
       www.usmesotheliomalaw.com/blog/2018/11/wallace-graham-wins-327-million
       -mesothelioma-verdict-the-largest-of-its-kind-in-north-carolina.

366   an award from Public Justice: Public Justice Trial Lawyer of the Year, https://
       www.publicjustice.net/trial-lawyer-year-award/.

367   the Fourth Circuit rules: *McKiver v. Murphy-Brown, LLC,* Case No. 19-1019,
       Fourth Circuit Court of Appeals, Published Opinion, November 19, 2020.

38. FINAL JUDGMENT

370   the author of the court's ruling: *McKiver v. Murphy-Brown, LLC,* Case No. 19-
       1019, Fourth Circuit Published Opinion, pp. 4–67.

371   Judge Wilkinson's concurring opinion: *McKiver v. Murphy-Brown, LLC,* Case
       No. 19-1019, Fourth Circuit Published Opinion, pp. 68–82.

375   under headlines such as: "Court Barbecues Smithfield's Claims, Giving Neigh-
       bors of Hog Farms Optimism," *IndyWeek,* December 9, 2020; "In Damning
       Opinion, Federal Appeals Court Rules Against Murphy-Brown," NC Policy
       Watch, November 19, 2020.

375   the Associated Press reports: "Court Upholds Hog Verdict; Smithfield
       Announces Settlement," Associated Press, November 19, 2020.

375   Public Justice, which is spearheading: Public Justice, Food Project, https://food
       .publicjustice.net.

375   passed "ag-gag" laws: "Summary of Anti-Whistleblower ('Ag-Gag') Legisla-
       tion," Animal Welfare Institute, https://awionline.org/content/anti-whistleblower
       -legislation.

376   The Tenth Circuit Court of Appeals: "'Ag-gag' Laws: An Update of Recent
       Legal Developments," The National Agricultural Law Center, https://national
       aglawcenter.org/ag-gag-laws-an-update-of-recent-legal-developments/.

376   the Eighth Circuit clears the way: "Public Justice and Allies Secure Win in
       Arkansas Ag-Gag Law," Public Justice, https://www.publicjustice.net/public
       -justice-and-allies-secure-win-in-arkansas-ag-gag-law/.

376   a move is afoot: "Booker Reintroduces Bill to Reform Farm System With
       Expanded Support from Farm, Labor, Environment, Public Health, Faith Based
       and Animal Welfare Groups," Press Release from Senator Cory Booker, https://
       www.booker.senate.gov/news/press/booker-reintroduces-bill-to-reform-farm
       -system-with-expanded-support-from-farm-labor-environment-public-health
       -faith-based-and-animal-welfare-groups.

377   Its public relations team launches: Smithfield Foods Statement Regarding
       Appellate Court Decision, November 19, 2020.

377   "We have resolved these cases": Ibid.; "Deal Ends Years of Legal Battles over
       Environmental Impact of Traditional Farming Methods," Wallace & Graham,
       https://wallacegraham.com/wg-in-the-news/smithfield-settles-lawsuits-over
       -noise-smell-of-hog-farms-in-north-carolina/.

Index

Page numbers followed by "n" indicate endnotes.

About the Author

CORBAN ADDISON is the internationally best-selling author of four novels, *A Walk Across the Sun, The Garden of Burning Sand, The Tears of Dark Water* (winner of the inaugural Wilbur Smith Adventure Writing Prize), and *A Harvest of Thorns,* all of which address some of today's most pressing human rights issues. *Wastelands* is his first work of nonfiction. An attorney, activist, and world traveler, he lives with his wife and children in Virginia.

A Note on the Type

This book was set in Adobe Garamond. Designed for the Adobe Corporation by Robert Slimbach, the fonts are based on types first cut by Claude Garamond (ca. 1480–1561). Garamond was a pupil of Geoffroy Tory and is believed to have followed the Venetian models, although he introduced a number of important differences, and it is to him that we owe the letter we now know as "old style." He gave to his letters a certain elegance and feeling of movement that won their creator an immediate reputation and the patronage of Francis I of France.

Typeset by Scribe, Philadelphia, Pennsylvania
Printed and bound by Sheridan Minnesota, a CJK Group Company,
   Brainerd, Minnesota
Designed by Maria Carella